# 50th Royal Tank Regiment:
## The Complete History

Stephen D Hamilton

The Lutterworth Press
CAMBRIDGE

> To the Officers, NCOs and Troopers
> of the 50th Royal Tank Regiment who 'Feared Naught'
> and subsequently gave their lives.
>
> As the sun beats down upon the Wadi Zigzaou,
> There's no mines, no bombs, no guns firing now.
> As for the glory, the killing, the dying, the pain,
> Only battered Valentines and scattered graves remain.

The Lutterworth Press
P.O. Box 60
Cambridge
CB1 2NT

British Library Cataloguing in Publication Data:
A catalogue record is available from the British Library.

ISBN 0 7188 2938 7

Copyright © Stephen D Hamilton 1996

The rights of Stephen D Hamilton to be identified as the
Author of this work have been asserted by him in accordance with the
Copyright Designs and Patents Act 1988.

All rights reserved. No part of this publication may be reproduced,
stored in a retrieval system or transmitted in any form or by any means,
electronic, mechanical, photocopying, recording or otherwise,
without the prior permission in writing of the Publisher.

Printed in Great Britain by Galliard (Printers) Ltd, Great Yarmouth

# Contents

| | |
|---|---|
| FOREWORD by Colonel V J Senior MC | vii |
| PREFACE | viii |
| INTRODUCTION by Brigadier H B C Watkins MBE | xi |

Chapter 1
'KING'S REGULATIONS' – Early days of the regiment ... 13

Chapter 2
INTO THE BLUE – First Alamein ... 26

Chapter 3
'NOW YOU CAN SEE WHAT TO FIRE AT, BLOODY GREAT JERRY TANKS' – Battle of Alam Halfa ... 44

Chapter 4
'O GOD OF BATTLES, STEEL MY SOLDIERS' HEARTS' – Battle of Alamein ... 58

Chapter 5
THROUGH THE TAGURA GATE – To Tripoli and beyond ... 77

Chapter 6
'JOHN HAS GONE' – Battle of Mareth ... 90

Chapter 7
BATTLE FOR THE GABES GAP – Wadi Akarit and Sfax ... 112

Chapter 8
'WE MUST ALL BE TANK MINDED' – The end in North Africa ... 127

Chapter 9
'BLOODY ROUGH' – The fight for Sicily ... 135

Chapter 10
'STUCK IN THE MIDDLE OF MABEL' – The Italian Campaign ... 163

Chapter 11
'THE THIN RED LINE OF BLACK HATS' – Action in Greece ... 204

Chapter 12
HOMEWARD BOUND – Victory and disbandment ... 236

| | |
|---|---|
| ANNEX A: Roll of Honour | 246 |
| ANNEX B: Honours and Awards | 261 |
| ANNEX C: Officers of 50 RTR | 266 |
| ANNEX D: Wounded in action | 272 |
| ANNEX E: Missing in action | 276 |
| ANNEX F: Those who served – nominal Role of 50 RTR | 279 |
| ANNEX H: C Squadron men's mess | 296 |
| BIBLIOGRAPHY | 300 |

# List of Illustrations

1. New and inexperienced recruits, Winash Farm, Bristol, late 1939. (Alban Gould)
2. A Squadron's 'Rodney' during a publicity tour of Bristol, September 1941. (author's collection)
3. Prior to embarkation, Lt G Halse, Capt J Bishop and Lt J Hobbs. (J Bishop)
4. Lt Col. John E Cairnes shortly after taking command of 50 RTR. (Mrs J Cairnes)
5. *SS Mooltan*. (author's collection)
6. B Squadron's Eight Troop shortly after arriving in North Africa. (F August)
7. 50 RTR Valentine being delivered to the front line, July 1942. (Tank Museum)
8. Major Walter Bazley and Padre John Hart. (Dr Ellis)
9. A Squadron's Fitters' lorry, August 1942. (A Abbess)
10. 5 Baker, one of only 3 Valentines to return from B Squadron's action at Munnassib, September 1942. (F August)
11. Major G Russell and his crew just prior to the battle of Alamein. (author's collection)
12. The whole of Regimental Headquarters just prior to the battle of Alamein. (Flaherty family)
13. Officers of RHQ, October 1942. (J Orbach)
14. Major Russell and the Adjutant Capt G Chapman en route to Tripoli, January 1943. (Dr Ellis)
15. Lt Ted Bond, first into the Wadi Zigzaou. (Mr D Heeley)
16. Cpl E Prett, badly wounded at the very beginning of the Mareth battle. (E Prett)
17. 'Ramillies', the A Squadron Valentine that blocked the crossing of the Wadi Zigazou, March 1943. (Tank Museum)
18. 'Hawkins', the remains of Col Cairnes' Valentine. (Tank Museum)
19. 'Hood', the remains of Major Maclaren's Valentine. (Tank Museum)
20. Another casualty of the Mareth battle . (Tank Museum)
21. RMO Capt Ellis, who played such a vital part in saving wounded tank members at Mareth. (Dr Ellis)
22. Tpr Watkin who drove the RMO throughout the Mareth battle. (Dr Ellis)
23. B Squadron Valentine towing an anti-tank gun across the anti-tank ditch at Wadi Akarit, April 1943. (IWM)
24. C Squadron (part of SPEARFORCE) leaving the Akarit position for the main road and Sfax, April 1943. (IWM)
25. Pat Clifford (left), author's grandfather, killed in action, April 1943. (author's collection)
26. Shermans of 50 RTR shortly before they left North Africa for Sicily. (IWM)

27. Lt Ingham of C Squadron's Eleven Troop, after 3 hours at sea, reveals the destination as Sicily. (IWM)
28. Capt Vic Senior (right) and Major Dickie Venn of C Squadron, Sicily 1943. (T Stanton)
29. Troopers Gill and Crowther, Recce Troop, both killed on the outskirts of Vizzini, July 1943. (Mrs D Buttle)
30. Padre John Hart conducting Church Parade, Ramacca, Sicily. (IWM)
31. 50 RTR open leaguer, Ramacca, Sicily. (IWM)
32. Signalman Schofield entertaining Messrs Furnival and Campbell, Ramacca. (IWM)
33. The only known photograph of the whole of 50 RTR on parade in Sicily, August 1943. (Dr Ellis)
34. Inspection by the Brigade Commander Sicily, August 1943. (Dr Ellis)
35. Col. G Russell receiving his well-earned DSO from General Montgomery. (Dr Ellis)
36. 50 RTR's echelon vehicles prior to landing in Italy. (IWM)
37. Typical conditions of the Sangro battle. (IWM)
38. One the German tanks knocked out by Lt Willson. (T Stanton)
39. C Squadron tea-party with members of the 8th Indian Division, Italy 1943. (T Wilson)
40. Members of C Squadron, Italy 1943. (T Wilson)
41. Cooking arrangements 50 RTR style, Italy 1943. (T Wilson)
42. Relaxing in Palestine, August 1944. (Flaherty family)
43. *HMS Aurora.* (author's collection)
44. C Squadron's Nine Troop providing the Guard at the British Embassy Athens, October 1944. (G Thomas)
45. All ranks party in Athens, October 1944. (Flaherty family)
46. Demonstration in Omonia Square Athens, December 1944. The tanks belong to 46 RTR. (IWM)
47. Officers of the regiment outside Manna Barracks, October 1944. (J Masters)
48. Jack Hedley, C Squadron's Medical Corporal. (J Hedley)
49. Sergeants of 50 RTR. (W Green)
50. Staghound armoured cars of 50 RTR. On the right is Tpr Thomas who was with the author's grandfather, when L/Cpl Clifford was killed. (G Thomas)
51. Officers and men of C Squadron. (G Thomas)
52. Greece, 1945.
53. B Squadron firing demonstration for the Greek General Staff, February 1946. (Tank Museum)
54. Members of the Sparta patrol March 1946. (author's collection)
55. Two of the regiment's casualties Phaleron War Cemetery 1945. (author's collection)

# List of Maps

1. 'Into the Blue'
   Site of the regiment's first two actions at Ruin Ridge (Miteirya) 22 and 27 July 1942.

2. El Alamein
   Dispositions of 51st Highland Division and movements of 50 RTR during the early stages of the battle, 23/24 October 1942.

3. Supercharge
   Final two attempts to break out into the open desert, 1/2 and 3/4 November 1942.

4. Mareth
   Battle of Mareth and squadron movements on 22 March 1943.

5. Wadi Akarit
   Site of battle fought 6 April 1943.

6. Advance to Enfidaville
   Advance from the Akarit position to Sfax and Enfidaville.

7. Path Through Sicily
   General plan of Sicily showing route taken by 50 RTR during the campaign, July and August 1943.

8. Sangro
   The regiment's attempts to cross the river, November 1943.

9. Battle of the Sangro and Moro Operations
   The routes followed by the Regiment in the above operations, November and December 1943.

10. Athens
    The Thin Red Line of Black Hats

# Foreword
## By Colonel V J Senior MC

This is a remarkable book since it was written by someone who never served in 50th Royal Tank Regiment. It is factual, comprehensive and detailed. For this I can vouch.

After research into the death of his grandfather, Lance-Corporal Paddy Clifford, who was killed in action with the regiment in North Africa, the author developed an astonishing love and respect for the regiment and for its members, both living and dead. The result is this book which I know entailed many months of intense research and labour, interviews and correspondence.

I joined 50 RTR as a newly-commissioned subaltern just before the Battle of Alamein and I left as regimental second-in-command three years later. For the regiment, this was a period of almost continuous contact with the enemy. Steve Hamilton relates its history with uncanny insight and perception, as I well know.

It is a fine tribute to a great regiment and I can commend it to prospective readers, especially military historians. I doubt whether there has ever been such a thorough and detailed record of any territorial regiment.

Colonel V J Senior MC
18 August 1993

# Preface

In October 1989, during a holiday to Tunisia, I visited my grandfather's grave in Sfax War Cemetery – the first member of the family to do so.

I had always known he had been killed during the war in North Africa, but that was all I knew. As a young boy I had asked the usual questions – did he kill anybody? How did he get killed? What did he do? – all to be dismissed as a young boy's curiosity. It was not until many years later I discovered none of the family knew the answers to these questions. They had been quite content with the story; three tanks went out on patrol and only one came back.

While walking from the cemetery, I made the decision to discover, if possible, what had happened to him. Returning home, I telephoned the local branch of the RTR Association and they put me in touch with the Secretary of 50 RTR Old Comrades Association, Don Ellery, whom it turned out, my grandfather had driven through the Alamein battle.

I then advertised for members of The Fiftieth to get in touch with me; those who did supplied more names. Gradually the picture was coming together. After a 400 mile round trip to Bovington to view any war diaries they held, I discovered that the date of my grandfather's death was missing.

The next step was a visit to the Public Record Office at Kew where, in the war diary for April 1943, there it was, an account of my grandfather's death. It was a very emotional moment for me. I can remember reading the entry over and over again.

Though the diary gave a very good account of the overall action, I wanted to know more. After about nine months of research, letter writing and visiting, I had discovered and written to five of the nine men of his Troop who were present at his death. I had also written to many others from 50 RTR and had gathered a wealth of information. One or two suggested I had enough information to write a history. It was while visiting a member of the regiment who lived locally that I finally decided to go ahead with the project.

Having already written to many men asking where they were in April 1943 and if they knew my grandfather, I started writing to them again, this time explaining precisely what I was doing and asking for their memories and recollections. The response took me by surprise; letters kept arriving, all in praise for what I was doing. It seemed I was getting the full support of the very men about whom I now intended to write a book.

With thanks to them all – this is their book.

Since I began my research into the history of 50 RTR, I have contacted a considerable number of people. I was well aware that one day I would have to sit down and acknowledge them in this section of the book, but in which order? Should it be by rank or should the person who gave the most assistance be first? My final decision was probably the best. I have dozens of files with all the letters and correspondence that I received during my research in the order that they were received, and so in that order, my thanks go out to them all.

Mr G Holmes, Assistant Librarian at the Tank Museum. Mrs Smith at the Ministry of Defence Record Office. Staff at the Imperial War Museum. Miss M Martin at the Museum of the Gordon Highlanders. Mr A R McKinnell at the Museum of the Black Watch. Margaret A Easey of the Army Chaplains' Department. Heinz Becker of the Afrika Korps Association. Staff at the National Army Museum. Peter Thwaites at the Royal Signals Museum. Mr Bill Green of Bristol for his help with citations and the 44 branches of the RTR Associations. Lieutenant-Colonel Bill Woodhouse for all his editing skills and advice, and the very talented Paul France of Ravensburg, Germany, who drew the maps and illustrations from information gathered from my many visits to the battlefields. Last but certainly not least, was Tracey, who was always there when I needed her help.

During my research I was also fortunate to meet a number of people. On the personal side, there was George Thomas, who was with my grandfather on the day he died. John Gibberd who kindly put me up for two days and went through my very first manuscript. Freddie August for his constant letter writing, excellent memory and moral support over the last six years. There were others, of course, but one stands out just that little more than the rest, Mrs June Cairnes.

The following persons all served with 50 RTR and all have given valuable assistance, for without them this book could never have been written. Sadly a number of them (*) have passed to the 'Green Fields Beyond' and never saw the finished article, but their words and their spirit can still be found within this text:

| Don Ellery | V J Senior | Jack Adams |
| R L Williams | D G Ward | Sidney Adams* |
| Harry Dorras | Freddie August | John Gibberd |
| Richard Worsfold | Brian Chidell | Michael Thompson |
| Joe Heppell | Gerry Keohane | E Cowell |
| Jack Hedley | W King | Douglas Stockall |

Harry Hayward
Cyril Epstein
F R Pimm
Tom Youldon
E Wrankmore
Norman Morris
E Manwaring-White
Jock Lowe
Robert Blundell
Alan Abbess
G E Wynn
G E Prett
Danny Lewis
Bill Blayne
Joe Hart

H J Squire
Percy Wadey
S L Ricketts
S J Midwinter*
John C Bishop*
J Greaves
Ivor Sambells
John Orbach
F Penny*
Michael Waddell
Tom M Wilson
Anthony R P Ellis
Lloyd Daw
Alban Gould

George Thomas
Alister Smith
Vic Brealey*
J Cockayne*
Tom Stanton
Tony Moreton
John Smale*
Reg Bryant
F Stevens
E Wills
Brandon Lush
Ken Bull
Joe Hart
John Masters

And a very special thank you to:

Mrs June Cairnes, Mrs J Hayward (née Russell), Mrs D Buttle (née Crowther), and the family of John Flaherty.

Brigadier H B C Watkins who knew how much this work meant to me – an officer and a gentleman who went 'above and beyond the call of duty' to help me in any way he could, and who perhaps epitomises the spirit of the Royal Tank Regiment.

The two Dedications at the front of the book are from the following sources: taken from a wreath laid at the El Alamein War Cemetery on the 50th anniversary of the battle by Mr K Bull; written in June 1943 by Capt Ted Bond after returning to the Mareth battlefield.

In July 1995 as a final act in preparing my work, I asked Brigadier John D Masters just how good were the 50th? (Reminding him at the same time, that Brigadier G W Richards had once said they were the 'best'.) He replied:

> It was blessed with quite different but really first class COs during the length of its active service. It had fine squadron leaders and the rest of us just did our bit in great comradeship.
>
> It never failed in any task it was given. I believe Brigadier Richards is right.

I believe they are both right and I sincerely hope that I have done the 50th Royal Tank Regiment justice within this book. 50 RTR was once described to me as 'a very small cog in a very big wheel'; that may well be true. But no matter how hard it was driven, it never once cracked under pressure. Whatever material that cog was made of, it was special, very special – and I hope you, as the reader, will find the answer.

Steve Hamilton
Ravensburg, July 1995

# Introduction
## By Brigadier H B C Watkins MBE

Half a century has passed since the events described in this book took the 50th Royal Tank Regiment from its home-spun beginnings in Bristol in 1939, as an offshoot of the 44th battalion (as it was then properly designated), through the hard-fought battles of the Western Desert and North Africa – from Alamein to Enfidaville, covering themselves with glory at Mareth as they went – and on to Sicily and Italy, finally ending their war on the streets of Athens suppressing the communist insurgency in Greece.

We now live in an era in which large scale, sophisticated wars tend to be short and sharp – though many civil wars seem interminable. There are relatively few men alive today who survived the long slog of the war in the Mediterranean theatre from 1939 to 1945 so that it is, perhaps, not always easy for today's readers to comprehend the full measure of the courage and fortitude demanded of the men of the Eighth Army in those days. This deeply researched and authentic account of the trials, tribulations and triumphs of a territorial regiment will leave them in no doubt.

Whilst former members of the 50th Royal Tank Regiment would probably dismiss any suggestion that they had a harder row to hoe than most Eighth Army regiments, Steve Hamilton's authentic story, based as it is upon the regimental war diary and the personal accounts of those who served, makes it very clear that the regiment did have a very tough war indeed and, from what he has written, it is plain that the consistency of their performance, their fortitude under the most trying climatic conditions and their ability to 'mend ship' after taking a hard knock in battle and plunge straight back into the fight, all represent a contribution to the Second World War of which not only the members of the 50th but of the Royal Tank Regiment as a whole may be justly proud.

If you have never fought in a tank battle, it is hard to appreciate what it was like to live day after day in the field in an undergunned tank like the Valentine, knowing full well that any encounter with the enemy's tanks would almost certainly end in British casualties – with squadron and troop commanders moving from tank to tank as their own were shot from under them. Yet there was no hesitation, no giving up – there was a job to be done, usually involving the support or protection of their comrades in the infantry, and the 50th did it, regardless of cost. Nor did life become much easier when the regiment switched to the larger and better armed Sherman, whose incendiary qualities when struck by armour piercing shot caused the Germans to christen it 'The Tommy Cooker'.

There was another, hidden, menace to be faced – the mine. Mines covered the battlefields in profusion. With only limited means of detecting and clearing them available, tank casualties due to mines were all too common. Only those who have lived in a mine-infested area know the cold feeling they bring to the pit of the stomach – a feeling that has a horribly erosive effect upon morale, as do incessant mortar and shell fire, let alone the concealed anti-tank gun.

Today's reader should think deeply about the sustained courage of the men whose deeds are described so vividly in this book. Think too, about the wonderful spirit of comradeship that pervaded the regimental 'family' – epitomised, perhaps, by the unfailing support given to the tank crews by Major Walter Bazley and his echelon, so that never once were the tanks left unreplenished despite the fact that replenishment was often perforce carried out under fire.

To have gone through all they did in their tanks and then to operate so successfully as infantry in Greece, was in itself a final tribute to the quality of the professionalism and courage which characterised that great territorial regiment, now, sadly, long disbanded and only a proud and glorious name in the annals of the Royal Tank Regiment.

# Chapter 1
# 'KING'S REGULATIONS'

## Early Days of the Regiment

In 1938 six infantry battalions of the Territorial Army were converted into tank battalions: one of these, the 6th Battalion the Gloucestershire Regiment, commanded by Lieutenant-Colonel E N Gardiner MC TD, became 44 Royal Tank Corps (RTC), which was stationed at St Michael's Hill, Bristol.

At this time, the Royal Tank Corps was used as the nucleus for the expanding Royal Armoured Corps, and as a corps within a corps was not permissible, the RTC became the Royal Tank Regiment (RTR), and the individual units dropped the battalion title and became regiments in their own right.

In April 1939, the Royal Tank Regiment doubled the strength of its territorial regiments. Six more were added to the original six and 44 RTR were joined at Bristol by 50 RTR. A nucleus of officers, NCOs and men from 44 RTR formed a basis for the new regiment, which was subsequently brought up to strength by recruiting and new intakes. Thus was born the 50th Royal Tank Regiment which was to last for only seven years. But when disbanded in 1946 it had a record second to none. This is the story of the 50th Royal Tank Regiment.

As in all territorial units, the men would gather at weekends and two evenings in the week. If they attended regularly they would be allowed to join the annual two-week camp, which was the highlight of the Territorial Army's year. It was no different in 1939, and on 19 August 50 RTR left Bristol for its first annual camp at Hedge End Camp (Perham Down) on Salisbury Plain. Two weeks of training and exercises under the supervision of the regular battalions, 5 and 8 RTR, followed. They were due to be back in Bristol on 2 September. However, events in Europe changed for the worse, and these part-time soldiers were about to become full-time soldiers.

At 1620 hours on 1 September 1939 the Fiftieth received orders to mobilize and were ordered to move from their camp at Perham Down to East Bristol colliery at Speedwell, under command of Lieutenant-Colonel H M Brown, the regiment's first commanding officer. This move was completed by midnight of the 2nd and on the following day war was declared on Germany and 50 RTR was moved to the old 44 RTR billet at the Coliseum, Park Row in Bristol. Early that evening five women from the Auxiliary Territorial Service reported for duty as cooks; the move and the task of adapting the Coliseum was completed the next day.

But on 5 September the regiment had to move again; it was thought that the Coliseum would be too vulnerable in an air raid. Billets were organised by the Adjutant, Captain A G F Mathers, in Brislington, a Bristol suburb. A and C squadrons were billeted in Brislington House and The Beeches respectively, both part of a lunatic asylum, while B Squadron was put in Winash Farm. Shortly after this move, Major R Hazledine took over as Adjutant and Colonel P G J Gueterbock CB DSO MC TD, became the regiment's Honorary Colonel. Major O F Curtoys, who had formed C Squadron in Yate and Chipping Sodbury became second-in-command.

Over the next few days the men dug slit trenches for air raid cover. During the rest of the month the men got their billets into shape and work details were issued; officers reconnoitred suitable training grounds; all ranks were issued with gas masks. Some administrative problems had to be sorted out, as when the regiment's meat ration did not appear – the ship carrying it had docked at the wrong port – and a local landowner complained that his rabbits were disappearing. More billets had to be found for future intakes. Then, on 24 October, 50 RTR received its first Vickers Medium Tank.

On 11 November 47 men were posted to the regiment, the first draft of other ranks. Though he was not actually in the first draft, the following account by Trooper John Gibberd of C Squadron gives the reader a good impression of what it must have been like for those young men:

A sergeant shouted across at me from outside the mess tent, 'Trooper Gibberd, don't you want any breakfast?' 'No', was my brief but honest reply. 'No what?' 'The idiot', I thought, 'Isn't it obvious what,' so I remained silent. 'NO WHAT?' 'No breakfast,' was my reply. Laughter. I wasn't trying to take the mickey, I was far too overawed by the strange new world I had been dumped in for that.

I remember when approaching one young 'one pipper' I gave a very enthusiastic salute, longest way up shortest way down, as per King's Regulations, but was he grateful? Not a bit! 'Trooper, why did you salute me with your left hand?' Couldn't he see I was carrying mess tins in my right hand? I didn't try to explain – no pleasing some people.

Our RSM, who had been in the army for centuries and whose head contained nothing but a copy of King's Regulations, told

Figure 1: New and inexperienced recruits, Winash Farm Bristol, late 1939 (Alban Gould)

the lads when he was drilling them that they looked like a lot of pansies going down Piccadilly. Well, many of those 'pansies' blossomed into pretty useful types, while our RSM didn't go abroad as he had a heart condition. We all knew he didn't have a heart.

This was in fact Regimental Sergeant-Major Smith, a regular soldier with over twenty years' service. He had at some time lost an eye, though it is said he could see more with that one eye than most men could with two. Discipline was his forte and he was held in awe by everyone, including the Colonel. Subalterns were his favourite target and guard mountings could, at times, be quite hilarious, but woe betide any trooper caught with a smile on his face. RSM Smith was not permitted to go abroad with 'his' regiment – 'a devastating blow to a man who had put his heart and soul into turning a "shower" into a fine regiment. All subsequent credits earned by 50 RTR must have stemmed from the training and discipline administered by RSM Smith.'

On the 15th, Colonel Brown held the regiment's first Order Group and the first task of the regiment was detailed. This was one common to most units in the United Kingdom at that time – the defence and protection of vulnerable points. For 50 RTR, these included the fuel storage depot at Chittening (Avonmouth) and Whitchurch airfield. In addition a 'flying column' was organised to protect any threatened area in the vicinity.

Cambrai Day was celebrated on 20 November with special meals, games and entertainment. That evening the following telegram was sent to Buckingham Palace

> Officers and Other ranks, Royal Tank Regiment assembled at Bristol, with humble duty send loyal greetings to their Colonel-in-Chief on the twenty second anniversary of the Cambrai battle.

Shortly afterwards came this response

> Please express to officers and other ranks, Royal Tank Regiment, assembled at Bristol on the twenty-second anniversary of Cambrai Day, my sincere thanks for the loyal greetings.
>
> GEORGE R.I. Colonel-in-Chief

A stand-to message was received before the night's entertainment had finished and all ranks returned to their billets; half an hour later the message was cancelled.

December passed quietly – a number of officers were posted in and some returned from courses; a draft of 30 recruits arrived. On the 7th, the regiment's first padre arrived, Captain C S G Godfrey Thomas. Later, on the 16th, a very successful Christmas party was held for 300 children at the 'Happy Warrior' canteen. The year ended with another officer and fourteen other ranks being posted to The Fiftieth from 40 and 46 RTR.

The early months of 1940 were also uneventful for the 50th, as they were at the front in France. The regiment was gradually becoming a more integrated and better trained unit. At this time there was plenty of opportunity for sport and rivalry with the 42nd and 44th RTR's which helped to foster a growing *esprit de corps*; a further draft of men and several new officers added to the unit's strength.

Squadron Sergeant Major John Cockayne of B Squadron remembers joining the Regiment:

> I joined The Fiftieth in 1940, the Regimental Sergeant-Major taking the parade came out, called the men on parade and called the roll, we found half of them were missing. He asked 'where the hell are they?' They were in the billets, and that's how it was, not a care in the world, no discipline, a shambles. But by the time it came to go into action, the RSM had turned the 50th into a grand regiment – the whole brigade was – they were a great lot; the spirit was good and they were confident.

In May, following the defeats in France, all officers were ordered to carry loaded revolvers. The regiment was moved to 'Glyndiffon Park', Llandwrog, North Wales where training and exercises could be carried out while three troops and a Bren carrier were made available to guard Pennhas aerodrome. Three days of trench digging were followed by a practice manning of the camp defences.

Most of July was spent on tactical training, track training, vehicle maintenance and beach patrols. Track training consisted of replacing and repairing broken links in the tank tracks. A weak track pin was fitted, allowing the track to be broken. The damaged link could then be replaced or removed – very much the same procedure as replacing or removing links from a bicycle chain. In the middle of the month the regiment moved to Llantrisant, near Caernarvon in South Wales, where during the following weeks exercises were held in conjunction with other units. Enemy air activity in the area occasionally necessitated taking cover in slit trenches, but there were no casualties.

After a year in which 50 RTR had been mobilized, trained and moved around the country, it was already showing signs of the quality which was to stand it in good stead in the bitter years to come. How many men at this stage could have envisaged what they were to experience when the final order for action eventually came? How high was their morale? After all, the British Expeditionary Force had been driven from France, the Battle of Britain was at its height and Hitler's bombers had constantly bombed London and other major cities, leaving an estimated 90,000 casualties in London alone.

In the first week of October there was a move to new winter quarters at Blundellsands. On the 19th, Headquarter Squadron was formed and then, on 21 October 1940, the regiment's first Mark 3 Infantry Tank (the Valentine) arrived. The tank reputedly got its name because the manufacturers had conceived it on St Valentine's Day, 1938. This is disputed by Vickers, however, the value of this excellent tank was indisputable.

Manufactured by Vickers-Armstrong Limited, the Valentine was primarily intended for supporting attacking infantry, but despite this the tank was generally used in a cruiser tank role, especially in the desert where it was to make its name. The basic layout owed something to the earlier A9 and A10 tanks but the Valentine was a far more flexible design which ran to eleven marks and mounted a variety of weapons, ranging from the two-pounder to the 75mm gun.

It had a crew of three – driver, gunner/radio operator and commander/loader (the regimental commander had a slightly modified version, which enabled three men to man the turret). Although reasonably well protected for its day, the Valentine was fitted with a two-pounder gun as main armament, plus a coaxial Besa 7.92mm machine gun; a Bren gun and Thompson sub-machine-gun were also carried.

For the next three years the Valentine was to become home and shelter for the men of 50 RTR. Men would become part of it and it part of them. Trooper Les Garland of the Regimental Echelon recalls:

After essential training in North Wales, about 300 of us were sent to Liverpool. Here we were sorted out for different squadrons and duties for tank training. When assembled and names called there were two Garlands, but only one entry. They had my initials – but the other Garland's number and, of course, in the army only numbers count, so I was left unplaced for about two weeks and then sent to A Squadron. By that time all tank positions had been filled and I was eventually given a lorry when they arrived.

On 1 November, 50 RTR and two other territorial tank regiments, 40 and 46 RTR, were formed into 23 Armoured Brigade, having previously formed part of 23 Army Tank Brigade, and 50 RTR then moved to Whitby, where regimental headquarters were set up in the Royal Hotel. The 9th and 10th of the month saw the Luftwaffe turning their attention on Whitby, but no damage or casualties were suffered by the regiment. Cambrai Day was celebrated in the usual style on the 22nd with inter-squadron football and hockey matches, followed by a dance at the Spa ballroom. The month ended with Lieutenant-Colonel Stuart Hayward taking command of the regiment.

December was a quiet month, starting with a brigade signals exercise and a four day boxing tournament held at the Spa ballroom. But the year did not end to the liking of the men, for on 31 December a regimental cross-country run was held for all ranks! There was heavy snow during the first weeks of 1941 and the regiment was busy with night marches, cross-country runs and arms inspections; then training with the new Valentines, followed by driving and maintenance tests.

The Valentine, with only two men in the turret, now presented its problems. The gunner/radio operator could not do both jobs at the same time. The commander had to direct the gunner onto the target, act as loader, control the driver, respond to instructions on the radio and at the same time fight his tank. If, in addition, he was troop leader, he also had to control the other two tanks in the troop and report to his squadron commander. It soon became apparent that an enormous amount of training would have to be carried out, before tank crews would be ready to fight their tanks.

In March the regiment moved again, this time to Swindon by Salisbury Plain. Here troop training went ahead and entraining and harbouring exercises were carried out at night. There were larger-scale exercises on Salisbury Plain with the involvement of the regiment's A and B Echelons. Gunnery practice was held at Chiseldon ranges and then the tanks moved to Castlemartin for ten days' battle practice and range firing. The day after they arrived back the regiment received orders for yet another move – to Bordon where they stayed for twelve days during which they threw grenades on the bombing range.

The 50th were then stationed at Crowborough in Sussex where they gave tank demonstrations. They were constantly moving around the

*Figure 2: A Squadron's 'Rodney' during a publicity tour of Bristol, September 1941. 'Rodney' had to drop out just short of Tripoli. (Author's collection)*

area exercising and taking part in mock battles. Trooper John Gibberd recalls one amusing event with a radio:

The press of a switch determined whether a tank commander spoke to his driver or was 'on the air' for everyone to hear. Our C squadron commander in England was a somewhat elderly gentleman. On one of our pretend battles in the Crowborough district we all heard the boss's voice say 'Nash, pass me up my sandwiches'; a little later and a little louder: 'NASH, PASS ME UP MY SANDWICHES'. This happened a third time before someone – not an officer – growled 'Get off the air you silly old . . .' We had a severe lecture on wireless discipline – the offender remained anonymous.

When not on training exercises there were plenty of opportunities for sport – the regiment entered a swimming gala and won the relay race. In October there was a concert in the NAAFI put on by the ENSA Minstrels (Entertainments National Service Association). Then on 2 December, orders were received to paint the tanks yellow, fit sand flaps and prepare to move overseas. The next day half the regiment were sent on embarkation leave for six days, the other half receiving their leave on the 10th. The usual Christmas celebrations were held and on 5 January all tank armament was inspected.

The regiment's departure for service overseas was postponed so that more embarkation leave was given in late March and it was not until May 1942 that the regiment finally left Crowborough to embark at

*Figure 3: The Soldierly figure of Lt-Col. John Elliot Cairnes, shortly after taking command of 50 RTR. (Mrs J Cairnes)*

Glasgow. In the meantime in April the man arrived who would finally lead the regiment into battle former second-in-command of the Derbyshire Yeomanry: the incomparable Lieutenant-Colonel J E Cairnes.

John Elliot Cairnes was born on Christmas Day 1904, at Killester, County Dublin. He was educated at Castle Park Preparatory School near Dublin, then at Rugby School from 1918 until 1922, when he went to Sandhurst. After passing out he joined the Royal Tank Corps. He was a brilliant sportsman, rugby initially being his main love. While at school he was in the First XV for three years and captained the Northern Public Schools when they played the Southern. He played rugby for the Army, but while at Sandhurst dislocated his shoulder while playing and took up hockey instead, being selected to play for both England and Ireland. He chose Ireland.

From 1929 to 1935 he served in India, mostly in Delhi and Lahore, with the 11th Armoured Car Company. While there he won the All-India Squash Championship and nearly died from an attack of typhoid. As a result he got six months, sick leave at home in Ireland. During his sick leave he married June Jameson in April 1932; she joined him in India. Although sport was his main hobby, he was a great reader of Kipling, Brooke, Buchan and Shakespeare. He was an excellent story teller and raconteur.

In 1929 while assistant Adjutant at Bovington, John Cairnes wrote and compiled *A Short History of the Royal Tank Corps* which, for a short time, became their official history.

He was a man who had the gift of leadership. He also had the wonderful gift for remembering a face – within three weeks of joining The Fiftieth he had learned every man's name, where they came from, and whether they were married. John and his wife had two daughters, the younger of whom was born at the time of Alamein. Although he knew of her birth, he never saw her.

At the same time a new second-in-command arrived, Major G E Russell, who would very soon form an excellent working relationship with Colonel Cairnes.

On 1 May, while still at Crowborough the regiment was inspected by His Majesty King George VI. The following morning the first train party left for Glasgow and overseas service; the remaining two train parties left on the 5th. Trooper John Gibberd remembers one amusing event the night before embarkation:

> On the night before we were to embark and, perhaps realising it was their last opportunity, some of the other ranks went out and got thoroughly drunk.
>
> The early morning parade was a little unsteady, to put it mildly. Johnny Orbach was the duty officer, possibly the only one who was sober, but that is pure speculation. He came prancing up and executed the necessary saluting and about-turning with great enthusiasm and precision.
>
> Then came a loud comment from the front rank – 'shit-hot that'. J.O. had great difficulty in suppressing a laugh and old Major Fanning, who looked half asleep and less than half sober, was obviously amused too.

On 6 May 1942, 23 Armoured Brigade consisting of 40 RTR (Lieutenant Colonel H V Dunbar) 46 RTR (Lieutenant Colonel T C A Clarke) and 50 RTR, joined 24 Armoured Brigade (41, 45 and 47 RTR) to form the 8th Armoured Division (commanded by Major General C W Norman until 23 August 1942, then by Major General C H Gairdner). The divisional badge was a black square containing a green circle and the letters 'GO' in the circle. For obvious reasons they were known as the 'GO Boys'. 23

*Figure 4: Prior to embarkation, (from right to left) Lt G Halse, Capt J Bishop and Lt J Hobbs. (J Bishop)*

Armoured Brigade, which at this time was under command of Brigadier Lawrence Misa, embarked on HMT *Mooltan*, while 8th Armoured Division headquarters sailed on the P&O liner *Strathnaver*.

Lieutenant Colonel John Cairnes wrote at the time:

We had a long tiring journey to get to our port and actually arrived an hour late, and after the rest of our party who had started seven hours behind us. I think our train must have lost its way in the night for we were up to time at our last halt.

We had a bad start from our station (Crowborough) as the authorities entraining us were so stupid. I got very angry and gave the local Railway Transport Officer a rocket and some advice which he ignored, so that Howard Dunbar and his lot had exactly the same nonsense later in the day. We started from Crowborough and stopped at Andover and Derby; we were thankful to reach our destination. No absentees, in fact we are a man over-strength but as Howard has one deserter we will hand over our extra man to him. Our chaps have greatly impressed the powers that be here, who think they are the best disciplined men they have ever seen in all their 30-odd years experience. Certainly the chaps have been magnificent, and I am really proud to be in command of them.

On 11 May the ship left the Clyde and moved out to sea, linking up with the convoy and escort ships of the Royal Navy. After eleven days at sea, land was sighted at about 0700 hours on the 22nd. The *Mooltan* harboured at Freetown, Sierra Leone, West Africa, for four days but the men were not allowed to leave the ship, mainly as a precaution against malaria and other fevers; though Captain Atkinson was allowed to visit his fiancée, who had been serving in Freetown as a nurse for the previous two years. On the 26th they left Freetown and five days later the island of St Helena was sighted at about 2200 hours on 31 May.

The ship arrived at Capetown on 6 June, after a month at sea. The men having had nothing to do other than guard and fatigue duties. A Squadron, however, were organised into naval 'watches' manning anti-aircraft guns. They were allowed to play 'Housey Housey', the only gambling game permitted in the Army, which survived the war as 'Bingo'. All the men wanted to do was to get off the ship – for a lot of

*Figure 5:* SS Mooltan, *which carried the personnel of 23 Armoured Brigade to North Africa May-July 1942. Built in 1923 for P&O, she became an armed merchant cruiser in 1939. Two years later she was given over to trooping. Returning to commercial service in 1948, she was broken up in 1954. (Author's collection)*

them this was their first sea voyage – so while at Capetown they took full advantage of the shore leave granted.

On 7 June the regiment was moved to the 'Retreat' rest camp at Polzmore, about 20 miles from the coast, where they spent the night under canvas in torrential rain. They returned to the *Mooltan* on 9 June, after a very welcome break from the ship and the sea. On the 11th they sailed from Capetown; on the afternoon of the 19th the south-east tip of Madagascar was sighted and on the 23rd the convoy slowed down and separated, the cargo ships destined for Madagascar veering to port and going on their way. The rest of the convoy then returned to full speed ahead.

On the 28 June, The Fiftieth gave a concert for officers, sisters and warrant officers in the dining hall, compered by Second-Lieutenant M Thompson, produced by Second-Lieutenant Orbach and performed by Majors Russell and Bazley, Lieutenants Jolley, Halse and Rushbrooke and Troopers Marquand, Attwooll, Fricker and Stacey. Trooper Cottrill and his band provided the music. The concert received a fantastic reception, and a further five performances were requested. The following morning Aden was sighted and the ship arrived in port at 0900 hours; again no shore leave was granted, although Brigadier Misa left the ship to fly direct to Cairo for orders. The convoy left Aden on 1 July at 0900 hours bearing west and then north, heading for Suez via the Red Sea.

The weather was now beginning to get very hot and the ship arrived at Port Tewfik on 5 July; orders to disembark immediately were issued, but due to some delay the men actually left the ship between 2200 hours and 2400 hours that night. They said goodbye to the *Mooltan*, and some no doubt were glad to see the back of her.

The voyage of the 8th Armoured Division was not without incident. The commander of 24 Armoured Brigade had flown to North Africa to prepare for the arrival of his brigade, which was known to be wanted urgently. *SS Scythia* carrying his headquarters and two of his regiments was delayed in Capetown for repairs. The American ship *USS Orizaba* carrying part of the Support Group was sent to Bombay by mistake. A third ship *SS Elysia*, sailing independently, was attacked by Japanese raiders on 5 June and sank on the 9th. Fate had played its hand: 23 Armoured Brigade had to take the place of the 24th.

Aboard the *Mooltan* on its arrival in North Africa was a man who deserves a special mention. He went on to fight his own kind of war and win a great deal of respect from the men of 50 RTR. The padre, Captain John Hart, was well known in the regiment and came into contact with all ranks at some stage of the war. He was born in 1903, gained a Bachelor of Arts degree at Cambridge in 1924, and in 1926, while at Bristol, became a deacon and then a priest in 1927. The following year he gained his Master of Arts degree, again at Cambridge. He was at the Church of St Paul's, Bedminster, from 1926-9; at Holy Trinity, Chesterfield from 1930-5 and at St Matthew's, Brighton from 1935. He served with the Royal Tank Regiment from 1941, and embarked with them for the Middle East in 1942 remaining with them until 1944. He received an MBE and was mentioned in depatches in 1945. After the war, he became rector of Hollington (1949-59) and Rendcomb (1959-67), rector of Colesbourne and priest in charge of St Andrews, Bexhill-on-Sea, Sussex from 1967 to 1972, when he retired, dying in 1979.

Travelling with Captain Hart was another padre, the Reverend Ned Mulligan, a Methodist minister. Though originally posted to 8th Armoured Division headquarters, he was about to begin the first of twenty four different posting within 23 Armoured Brigade. It was not long before every man in the brigade knew his face. He and Captain Hart would in the future ensure they would always be where they were needed most.

## Chapter 2
## INTO THE BLUE

### First Alamein

When 50 RTR went into action for the first time, they were joining a battle that had actually begun on 2 July and which was to go down in history as 'First Alamein'. Rommel had sent his forces down both sides of Miteiriya Ridge hoping to bypass the Alamein position. This successful manoeuvre was repeated again at Ruweisat Ridge, but was repulsed by the 1st and 2nd South African Brigades in the north, and by the 1st Light Armoured Division and 22 Armoured Brigade in the south. North of Miteiriya, the German 90th Light Division had run straight into the British 4th Armoured Brigade and stopped. Having been stopped well short of their objectives the Axis forces turned to every point of the compass, so that the German and Italian positions stretched from the sea in the north to the Qattara Depression in the south. The scene was now set for Auchinleck to counter-attack, an operation of which 50 RTR would now be a part.

The regiment left Suez by train at 0200 hours on 6 July, heading for El Qassassin, arriving at 1030 hours. From there, they were sent to the camp at Tel el Kebir. On arrival the men were issued with sun helmets, totally unsuitable for use in tanks, and which were soon 'LOST IN ACTION'.

News of an urgent move to the Western Desert was received and the regiment had to be prepared for action by 14 July; full preparations were now started. Squadron Sergeant Major Percy Lewis recalls:

> After landing at Port Tewfik, we were met with a sand storm, tents put up for us by an advance party were being blown apart, that's where we first tasted tea made with heavily chlorinated water and ate food with lots of sand in it. We were supposed to have had an acclimatising period to get used to the heat, sandstorms and dysentery, but due to the urgency we had to get the tanks battle-worthy and move up to the front line.

23 Armoured Brigade was now preparing for action. When the tanks finally arrived they were taken directly to No.4 Base Ordnance Workshop at Geneifa for refitting; due to ordnance errors many of them

*Figure 6: New arrivals in the desert. Eight Troop of B Squadron: (from rear row left to right) Tatchell, Beck, Paul, French, Adolph, Butcher, Gatskill, Greenham, Nicholas, Gaskell. Qassassin Camp, July 1942. (F August)*

had had vital components removed. The Fiftieth were informed that they were to be the reserve regiment and priority must go to 40 and 46 RTR in re-equipping. On 15 July a satisfactory brigade exercise was held. On the 17th an advance party from the regiment left for the concentration area at El Hammam. Early the following morning 23 Armoured Brigade moved up to El Hammam, and were ready for action. Trooper Robert Blundell recalls:

> The first crews collected their tanks and went out into the 'blue' a name given to the fighting zone. I was taken off 'spare crews' and given the job of driving the squadron jeep, which put you at the squadron leader's disposal – delivering messages – laying field telephone cables. I also did a lot of driving to and fro between Squadron Headquarters, Regimental Headquarters and the Brigade Headquarters, I liked the job.

At 0600 hours on 19 July, Colonel Cairnes reconnoitred the front line near the coast, by the Alexandria-Sollum road, about two miles west of El Alamein railway station. On 20 July the regiment moved forward to the concentration area at Hatiyet el Shammama, with the men travelling in trucks by day and the tanks moving on transporters by night. The regiment was then incorporated into a regimental group, under the command of Brigadier Richards of 1st Army Tank Brigade. One tank was lost on the same day when it fell into a concealed disused well, two men being injured.

Next day orders were received to move to a night concentration area at Hill 26, to support some Australian infantry (A Echelon remained north of the coast road and were attacked by Stukas, while B Echelon were some six miles to the east). This came as a great surprise to Colonel Cairnes, since for the last two years the regiment had been training as an independent armoured unit. At 2100 hours that night of 21 July the Valentine tanks of 50 RTR moved forward to a night harbour near the tank start line.

Meanwhile the remainder of 23 Armoured Brigade, 40 and 46 RTR, had been sent further south to attack Axis positions along the southern edge of Ruweisat Ridge the next day.

The organisation of an armoured regiment at this time consisted of a headquarter squadron and three tank squadrons. Each tank squadron had a headquarters of four tanks, and four troops, each of three tanks (A Squadron numbered Troops 1-4, B Squadron 5-8 and C Squadron 9-12). In addition, Regimental Headquarters consisted of four tanks – a total of 52 tanks. In each squadron at this time there would be a major in command, a captain as second-in-command, another captain, a squadron sergeant major, four troop leaders (usually lieutenants), four troop sergeants and four troop corporals. Regimental Headquarters would consist of the commanding officer, second-in-command, adjutant and navigating officer.

The regimental wheeled vehicles were organised into two Echelons. A Echelon would keep the tanks supplied with fuel, rations and

*Figure 7: 50 RTR Valentine being delivered to the front line, July 1942. (Tank Museum)*

ammunition, while B Echelon consisted of spare crews, regimental offices, stores, fitters etc.

As for communication between the tanks, most had the No 11 set which would work adequately over a regimental area and, by retuning, as a squadron set. Among the tanks of Regimental Headquarters one would be designated rear link and would act as a signal station between regiment and brigade.

Were they ready for battle? A few of the men had seen action before with the armoured car companies in India, or with the British Expeditionary Force in France in 1940, a few had already fought in the desert's early battles, but for the majority it was a new and frightening experience.

Battle is a harrowing business. In addition to the physical risks of death or injury, the soldier is subjected to the intense psychological pressures generated by exhaustion, privation, noise, worries about family and friends, and the sight of comrades being killed and wounded. It is less easy to quantify fighting spirit than material resources such as tanks and guns, but its presence can be identified readily. There are moments in battle when logic suggests that embarking upon a particular course of action – attacking against heavy odds, or defending an untenable position, is fruitless to the point of being suicidal. But fighting spirit, with all its complex chemistry of individual and collective needs, loyalties and pressures, can urge men to go forward or stand firm, even in the face of death. Field Marshal Earl Haig, the First World War commander, once said: 'Men are not brave by nature.' Fighting spirit enabling the soldier to meet the stress of battle has to be built up during training, and depends on comradeship, leadership and discipline. Field Marshal Montgomery believed that 'the morale of the soldier is the greatest single factor in war.'

50 RTR, like other armoured regiments, used its own names for each tank – the choice depending largely upon the commanding officer. Regimental Headquarters tanks began with the letter 'H' such as 'Hood' and 'Hawkins'. A Squadron used the letter 'R', such as 'Reliance', 'Respond' and 'Redoubtable', B Squadron the letter 'B', such as 'Broke' and 'Badger', and C Squadron, the letter 'C', such as 'Cotswold', 'Cheviot' and 'Chiltern'. In most cases the names had some kind of naval connection. It was also at this time that the brigade adopted its famous Liver Bird emblem, in honour of its senior regiment, 40 RTR.

On Wednesday 22 July, the regiment went into action for the first time in the area of Ruin Ridge (Ruin Ridge actually forms part of Miteiriya Ridge and was given the name by the Australians), south west of El Alamein railway station, in support of the 24th Infantry Brigade of the 9th Australian Infantry Division. Here a defensive position or 'box' had been established some months before to check the

Axis advance on Alexandria. This box was held entirely by South African and Australian troops.

The 1st Army Tank Brigade, including 50 RTR Regimental Group, was allotted the task of driving westward. However, control of the supporting units was retained by Brigadier Richards, leaving Colonel Cairnes to fight his own regiment. Colonel John Cairnes wrote at the time:

> Our battalion was then taken from the brigade and formed a Regimental Group in armoured brigade commanded by Richards (Rikky). My command became almost a brigade, I had a battery of Royal Horse Artillery, a battery of anti-tank guns, a troop of 60 sappers, a company of The Rifle Brigade, and a section of ambulances all suddenly put under my command.
>
> When the whole party leaguered just behind the front it covered a few square miles. I found it rather an alarming prospect to command such a big force. However Rikky was most helpful and the officers commanding each unit were an excellent lot.
>
> My own key people such as adjutant, second-in-command, quartermaster, echelon commanders, squadron leaders etc, had proved excellent and I really had few worries, though I didn't fancy much the role of infantry tanks allotted to us.

The attached units to which Colonel Cairnes referred were all part of 23 Armoured Brigade Group, which, apart from the three tank regiments consisted of: 5 Regiment Royal Horse Artillery, 73 Anti-Tank Regiment Royal Artillery, 37th Light Anti-Aircraft Battery Royal Artillery and 7th Battalion The Rifle Brigade.

It was hoped the Australian infantry would clear the enemy positions to the south of Ruin Ridge. Unfortunately, the concentration area given to 50 RTR the night before the battle was surrounded by a salt marsh, through which the approach to the area ran. In the darkness, a number of the tanks became bogged, due to bad picketing of the route by military police supplied from XXX Corps. As a result of this, five tanks including two smoke laying tanks, did not go into battle the next day. The regiment was held in readiness in its concentration area from dawn until late afternoon, awaiting orders to move, while artillery which was sited immediately in the rear, fired over the tanks almost continuously throughout the day.

At midday Colonel Cairnes reconnoitred the Qattara track running south west from the Alamein box, in case the regiment was to be used there in support of an Australian infantry brigade. At 1630 hours he was called to brigade headquarters and given the task of attacking Ruin Ridge (on the Qattara track) in support of the 2/28th Battalion of the 24th Australian Infantry Brigade, in the early evening – an entirely different type of manoeuvre from the exploitation westward previously planned, and one in which neither 50 RTR nor the Australians had had any previous experience or training.

Colonel Cairnes returned to his unit and had just enough time to give his orders to the squadron commanders and troop leaders, since the leading squadron was due at the start line at 1845 hours.

The plan was a set-piece infantry/tank attack in which A Squadron, preceded by Bren gun carriers, was to lead in staggered line on a frontage of 600 yards, stretching from 600 yards west of the Qattara track and advancing south-west, parallel to the track. The infantry accompanied by sappers were to ride on B Squadron tanks, following as a second wave. Following again were a line of infantry on foot, followed by the Regimental Headquarters tanks moving with the infantry battalion commander. C Squadron, commanded by Major Dickie Venn, whose task was covering fire for the dismounted infantry, was in reserve and the right flank was patrolled by scout cars. On reaching the objective, the infantry were to consolidate on the reverse slope – the slope facing away from the enemy. What actually happened was entirely different.

For the operation, 50 RTR were given the support of an Australian battery of 25-pounder guns. While Colonel Cairnes was giving out orders, the Australian gunners were given another fire task. It was a great shock to Colonel Cairnes to find that his battery of guns had been taken away. This left him with one battery of medium guns – which had no smoke shells – under the direction of Lieutenant Davis.

One of the chief difficulties of the whole operation was that 50 RTR had no time to get to know the Australians they were supporting nor to plan the close co-operation required for an attack of this type.

As the tanks and infantry waited on the start line, a report came in that a reconnaissance aircraft had seen over twenty gun positions, infantry digging in and hundreds of enemy vehicles all along the ridge. Grim news, but 50 RTR and the Australians were now committed.

The start line was the telegraph wire a mile south of the railway station. The leading squadron, commanded by Major Alan Styles, crossed this at 1845 hours, while the artillery put down a creeping barrage covering the south of Ruin Ridge. The whole regiment was forced to pass through four narrow gaps not more than 200 yards apart in the minefield, parallel to the telegraph wires and 1,000 yards south of it.

As the two forward squadrons approached the objective, Major Alan Hughes, commanding B Squadron, reported that most of the Australians had failed to get onto his tanks at the start line. In actual fact, the sappers had been ordered off the tanks by their own officers, they then watched in horror as 50 RTR headed for a known minefield.

Two miles from the objective, the regiment was subjected to intense artillery fire from the right flank, one scout car was knocked out and its commander, Sergeant Hewins, was killed; Colonel Cairnes immediately asked for smoke protection on this flank, but none was laid. Regimental Headquarters then came under shell fire from the right and anti-tank fire from the front. Colonel Cairnes was receiving little information from the leading tanks, other than that they were on the objective and under fire from anti-tank guns at very close range.

Fire, particularly from 50mm guns, was so fierce that A Squadron were driven east over the track by its intensity and suffered casualties on the minefield east of the Qattara track. They asked for infantry support, but wireless communications with Brigade Headquarters broke down due to evening atmospherics and enemy jamming. As soon as Regimental Headquarters got into the thick of the battle they became involved in a running fight just short of the objective and the navigating officer, Captain Atkinson, had his tank knocked out by enemy gunfire.

It was now necessary to attempt to lay a smoke screen on the right flank, by using the tanks' 2-inch and 3-inch smoke mortars. Visibility in the centre was now almost nil, since the tanks were attacking with the sun full in their faces and into the dust and smoke of the enemy defensive fire.

The infantry were so slow in moving up that C Squadron had to go forward in front of them to try and lead them on. This failed, as they had already been ordered to consolidate although still 1½ miles from their objective. The climax of the battle came with the whole regiment milling around on and just short of the objective, engaging anti-tank and machine gun positions and waiting for the infantry to consolidate. But the infantry were not coming and as darkness fell 50 RTR disengaged northwards in accordance with previous instructions. By midnight the Australians thought the objective had been achieved, the infantry were digging in and the tanks were back in their leaguer area. But Brigadier Richards, who was also armoured adviser to the Australians, sensed something was wrong and at 0130 hours drove forward to the infantry. He returned with the news that the 2/28th Battalion was more than a mile short of the objective.

Ruin Ridge gained its name from the remains of a Muslim tomb situated there. However, halfway between the start line and the objective lay another ridge with ruins, and it was this ridge that the infantry assumed to be the objective and following orders dug in there. They then tried to call the tanks back believing 50 RTR had gone too far. Percy Lewis recalls:

> It was a frightening experience, we were green- horns and officers tried to comply with the training book as taught but it didn't work out. I was a tank gunner in that first action. After we were knocked out the three of us abandoned the tank but unfortunately our driver, Frank Mitchell, was struck by shrapnel and suffered a

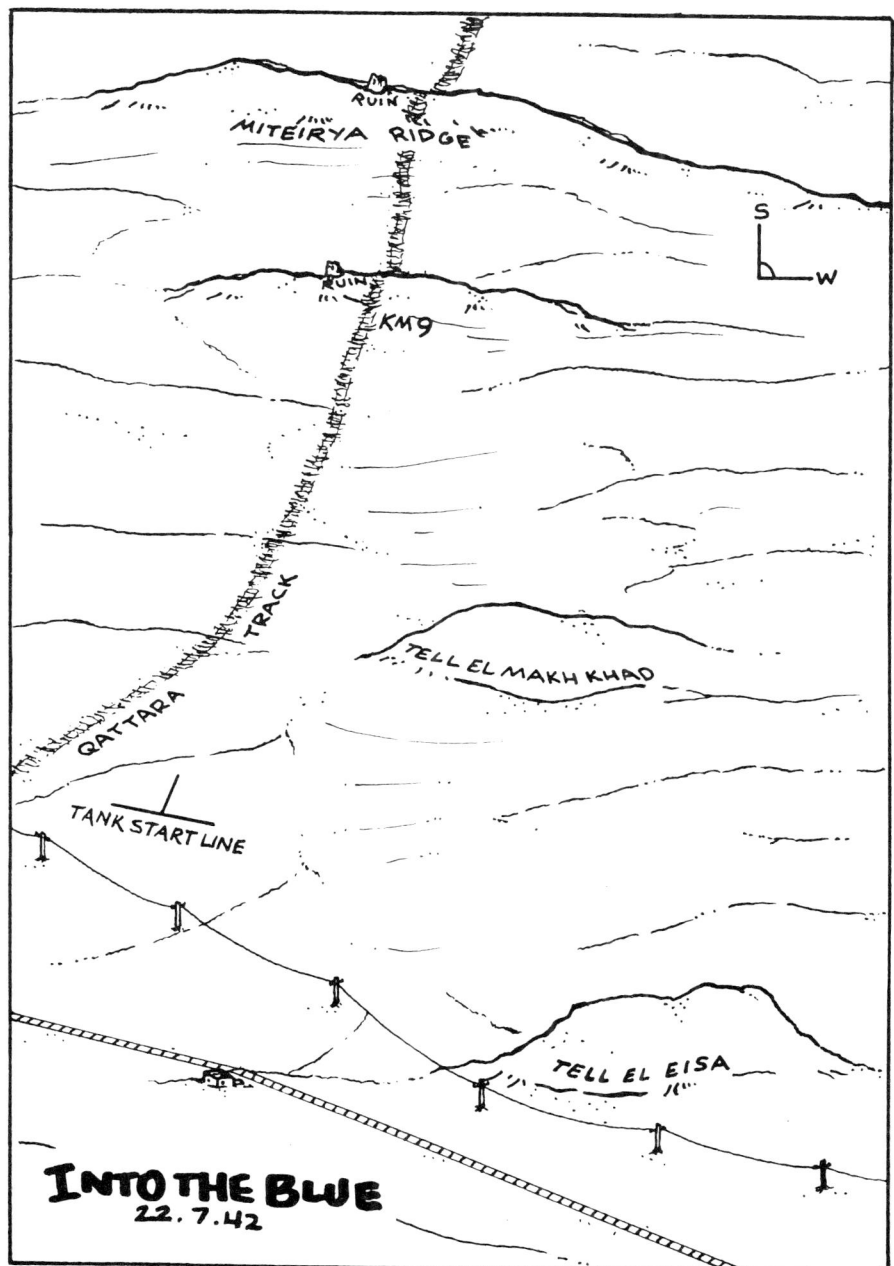

*Map 1: 'Into the Blue'. Site of the regiment's first two actions at Ruin Ridge (Miteirya) 22 and 27 July 1942.*

severe wound in the backside. The sergeant and I managed to stagger along supporting Frank but not knowing which way the British lines were, as it was quite dark now apart from exploding shell fire. It was every man for himself. We took short rests when out of immediate danger and it was almost two o'clock in the morning when we finally met a couple of our own tanks and crews. We rested until early dawn swapping tales of our experiences; later an Aussie troop carrier passed by and we managed to get them to take Frank to a field hospital, I never saw him again until after the war.

Twenty-four out of 47 tanks rallied inside the minefields just east of the Qattara track. At dawn the next morning, it was discovered that the Australian infantry were holding a line running west from the nine kilometre mark on the Qattara track and had never reached their objective.

One Australian unit did however achieve its allotted task. They had been ordered to attack and destroy Rommel's most reliable source of information in North Africa, the Panzerarmee's signals interception unit known as Nachr-Fern-Aufkl-Kp 621. This highly experienced unit had become expert at reading British radio traffic, which was then evaluated for Rommel.

Lieutenant L F (Bill) Williams, commanding a troop in B Squadron describes his part in the regiment's first action:

I remember the Australians riding on our tanks as we gaily sailed off into the blue. B Squadron moved off in a 'two up' formation, my troop being in the second wave. We were very quickly in the mire, and heavily shot at. The Australians soon dropped off. The squadrons were all mixed up in a minefield and there was complete chaos. In our experience everything went wrong. On the objective we sustained quite large casualties, and a few were taken prisoner. Then the light failed and we rallied back.

Quite frankly, by then I did not know where I was going and did not know north from south. I distinctly remember the Squadron Leader ordering us to rally on him and when I asked on the wireless where he was, he said he had his hand stuck up in the air and eventually I was able to identify his tank.

Brigadier Misa arrived in the leaguer area soon after the regiment had concentrated and congratulated Colonel Cairnes on the way in which The Fiftieth had carried out its tasks, and on the fighting spirit of all ranks after the battle, despite casualties, especially since very few had ever been under fire before. Particularly good work was done by the ambulance section and by the Regimental Medical Officer, Captain John Bishop, who was frequently operating in front of the infantry, despite Colonel Cairnes' insistence that he should not be so far forward. Captain

Bishop was quite surprised to get a 'ticking off' after the action, from his commanding officer. Personnel casualties in this first action amounted to two officers and five other ranks killed, one officer and six other ranks wounded, and 19 other ranks missing in action. Vehicle casualties were 23 tanks and one scout car belonging to the Reconnaissance Troop. Of these, ten tanks were recovered. Tanks were also recovered belonging to 8 RTR and 44 RTR, who had been operating in this area some time before 22 July.

Captain John Orbach recalls this first action:

I commanded the Reconnaissance Troop on the right of the regiment in the attack that was launched on 22 July 1942, past Tel el Eisa and the Alamein railway station.

We worked southwest in support of an Australian infantry battalion. The regiment took a lot of casualties and I lost Sergeant Hewins. We rallied after the attack was called off and chatted together over an evening meal while listening for the missing tanks to come in. Captain Hobbs of A Squadron was among those killed and Captain Cliff Walters of B Squadron was wounded.

Before the battle Colonel Cairnes had been very apprehensive about the forthcoming operation with the Australian infantry, due not only to the reputation they had already gained in the desert, but to the fact that this particular Australian unit had never worked with tanks before. This is how Colonel Cairnes saw his regiment go into action for the first time:

Our first party with them was unrehearsed and at short notice. We moved up and owing to some bloody policemen the whole battalion of tanks were directed on to a salt marsh which we knew we had to avoid and five tanks were bogged before I arrived on the scene to stop all movement.

No one got any sleep that night. We stood to all next day and then about 4pm I went to Australian brigade headquarters to receive orders to attack with an Australian battalion in a different direction to the one originally planned. I rushed back to my headquarters getting back about 5.45pm and as soon as I had given contrary orders we jumped into our machines and were off, crossing the start line at 6.45pm. As we moved off two batteries of guns which I had been given to support us were taken away, and I had no time to protest, all I had left was a battery of medium guns which had no smoke, the one thing I wanted.

Off we went through a minefield which our sappers had cleared gaps in, behind a big artillery concentration. The Aussies, some of which I tried to carry in on our tanks, sauntered along painfully slowly and we crawled along through a hail of shells and everything else the Bosche could fling at us. Our leading squadron to avoid the anti-tank guns swung over to the left and ran onto an uncharted minefield which accounted for about 14 of our tanks! The second squadron reached the objective and plastered up the Bosche, but were nearly two miles ahead of the Aussies who started digging in on a ridge which they seemed to think was the objective. Nothing I could do would make them change their minds and come on.

I had not meant to get the four tanks of my headquarters involved in the fighting, but when the Aussies stopped and I decided to go on we ran into the thick of it, and milled around like a circus, with tracer shells and bullets and all sorts of things flying around us, and our guns blazing at the gun flashes which was all we could see. Most of the Bosche shells were coming out of the evening sun and we couldn't see them.

Our little smoke mortars was all the smoke protection we could get. We fired those mortars as fast as we could shoot them and I reckon that's what saved us. Our very gallant medium gunners' forward observation officer who was travelling in a light truck, and was constantly running across to jump on my tank and ask for instructions, was fatally wounded from a direct hit on his vehicle and died on the back of one of our tanks as we came out. He was a great chap and died like a hero.

He wasn't wearing a tin hat and he sat on the outside of his truck waving his hand to all and sundry as shells burst all round. He did his utmost for us but there was little he could really give us. What we needed was smoke. It was a very fierce action indeed.

My navigating officer had one tank taken from under him but was in another in a couple of seconds. My crew were in good form and enjoyed things when we joined in the general dogfight. They didn't care much for waiting about watching the proceedings. My operator got a bit excited once when the Bren gun appeared to fall to pieces, but we soon had it working again.

Actually we were hit by anti-tank gun shells twice, one passing right through the hull under the floor and I didn't realise until afterwards we had been touched!

As it got dark I had to call off the tanks, and they all fell in behind me as we left the battlefield. It was quite dark as we passed through the Aussies who were digging in like fury, and then I met the commander of my Rifle Brigade company, a great chap called Major Steve Trappes-Lomax. I had never been so glad to see anyone. I asked him where the mines were and he told me they were all around me.

He then guided us back through a gap in the minefield and we leaguered in the open just beyond. Unfortunately, one tank coming in later with a wounded crew ran over a mine and up it went. As the mines were British, laid by Germans, they were appallingly efficient and made a horrible mess of some of the tanks.

Only 24 out of the 47 tanks came into leaguer that night. A lot of the crews came in later, but our losses appeared to be devilishly heavy.

Our losses shook me a bit at first. I thought the higher commanders might think we made a mess of things, but our divisional commander and all the brigade commanders, as well as all the other chaps in the brigade appear to have heard glossy accounts of our action. Even the Aussie General Morshead seemed satisfied.

Afterwards, a few things seemed quite comical: our medical officer in his ridiculous little jeep motoring along as if out for a pleasure drive and then leaving it to help some Aussie wounded right in the forefront of things; two Huns rushing back towards us with their hands up pursued by a tank; a blazing Hun truck going past me and finally coming to a halt, a blazing wreck; a Bosche officer in a shell hole with a mass of Red Cross chaps around him, probably an observation officer, but I let him go; a Bosche ammunition lorry going up in a glorious flash.

John Cockayne, Squadron Sergeant-Major in B Squadron remembers vividly 50 RTR's first action:

I had a Matilda, but this broke down the day before the action and I was given a Valentine from 24 Armoured Brigade about an hour before we went in. There was everything wrong with it; the wireless didn't work, and the Besa kept jamming after every short burst.

A Squadron led the way followed by us. We had some Australians riding on our tank – they didn't get off until two of them had been killed nearer the position. We hadn't gone a mile when we lost tanks on mines; we passed no end of A Squadron tanks that had gone up on mines.

As we got nearer the position I was wounded in the neck and arm by an air burst then, as we got onto the position, a Jerry jumped onto our tank and tried to bayonet me through the top of the open turret. As we struggled his bayonet went through my right hand. With my left hand I managed to reach the tommy gun in the turret; I think I gave him the full magazine.

Shortly afterwards our tank was knocked out by what must have been an anti-tank gun. We decided to close down and sit it out until it got dark, which must have been about 9.00pm.

We got out of the tank and followed our tank tracks back

towards our lines. We had gone about half a mile when we came across Dennis Greenham, who I think was wounded. We picked him up, got a further half mile when a Jerry halftrack picked us up.

They took us to the German/Italian Army Headquarters, about six of us in all. We were sitting on a small sandhill under guard pondering on what we thought was a flop, but we must have caused some damage, because behind us were about 150 to 200 bodies of their own blokes, laid in lines.

Meanwhile in the south along Ruweisat Ridge, the remainder of 23 Armoured Brigade had been almost annihilated in a grossly mismanaged attack along the southern edge of the ridge, in an almost exact replica of the Charge of the Light Brigade nearly 100 years before.

Both 40 and 46 RTR were committed to action that day: few desert attacks had less chance of success than this one. Nehring (of the Afrika Korps) on the morning of 22 July, after over-running the armour-bare New Zealanders and watching 23 Armoured Brigade press in tight formation along the southern edge of Ruweisat, strewing tanks on mines and dying in scores before the raging 88mm guns, might have repeated Wellington's words – 'They came on in the same old way and we stopped them in the same old way.'

Everywhere, including 50 RTR's attack against Ruin Ridge, 23 Armoured Brigade left a trail of wrecked machinery, losing well over 100 tanks and over 200 men in actions characterised by supreme gallantry. Rommel's fading hopes now rose accordingly, recognising this considerable defensive success as a stabilising factor to his slowly coalescing defence.

At 0430 hours on 23 July, 50 RTR broke leaguer and dispersed to a fresh area, and by noon they were back on Hill 26. Three days were then spent re-organising, awaiting replacements and recovery.

The operation of 22 July had been controlled by Lieutenant General W H E Gott's XIII Corps Headquarters and, like every military failure, a scapegoat had to be found. Brigadier Lawrence Misa, who had only followed orders, was relieved of his command and with the rank of colonel was given the task of handling replacements at Abbassia Barracks in Cairo. General Gott, however, was given command of the Eighth Army, but was killed before he could assume it. Brigadier Misa was not the only man to lose his job; the commanding officer of the Australians supporting 50 RTR, Lieutenant Colonel Cox, was also replaced.

Command of 23 Armoured Brigade was now given to Brigadier G W Richards of 1 Army Tank Brigade. Richards was a thinking soldier, staff trained and technically expert, who made an analytical study of every action. This excellent soldier would, in a short time, turn the 23rd into one of the best, if not the best, armoured brigade in North Africa.

The regiment's second action on 27 July had originally been planned to meet the possibilities of supporting the 2/28th or 2/43rd Australian infantry battalions in their renewed attacks on Ruin Ridge, or of exploiting their success in a drive westward. 50 RTR, less C Squadron, moved forward to await orders. At 1000 hours a new plan was put into instant operation. The 2/28th battalion had gained their original objective, the 2/43rd had not started and, although the 2/28th were on Ruin Ridge, they had not cleared a wide enough gap in the minefield and the enemy had succeeded in knocking out all their ammunition lorries as they tried to come forward. As a result the Australians were in serious trouble and in a position in which they might be forced to surrender through lack of ammunition. This appears to have been what happened, though one strongpoint did hold out until midday.

50 RTR's role was to relieve these forces, the first of which was known to have surrendered at 1010 hours. B Squadron advanced along the track to the gap in the minefield which was being enlarged. C Squadron advanced to give protection on their right. A Squadron was held in reserve.

The regiment was on the move within 20 minutes of the orders reaching them, once again with negligible infantry support. B Squadron were badly held up by the fact that the lanes through the minefields were not clearly marked and C Squadron, who had made very good progress as they had not encountered the minefield, came in for very heavy anti-tank and shell fire from the depression on their right.

Due to wireless failure and the artillery liaison officer being killed, artillery support never achieved maximum effect, and the leading tanks were doubly confused by the fact that when they reached their objective there was no infantry support and by the laying down of smoke by B Squadron themselves; this had the unlucky effect of silhouetting C Squadron, who had got well forward. Five enemy tanks were reported in the area and C Squadron claimed to have destroyed two. In view of the fact that it was impossible to assist the 2/28th, Colonel Cairnes rallied the squadrons behind Tel el Makh Khad, the feature west of the seven kilometre mark on the Qattara track, where the 2/43th were digging in. The regiment leaguered in this area for the night, having lost thirteen tanks of which four were recovered. Personnel casualties were five killed, inluding one officer, one other rank wounded, and one officer and fifteen other ranks missing in action.

To replace the casualties lost in The Fiftieth's first two actions, on 28 July Major Walter Bazley made the following request for reinforcements: Warrant officers (class II), 3; squadron sergeant-majors, 1; sergeants, 5; corporals, 8; and troopers, 26 – a total of 43 men.

On that day, the regiment leaguered well inside the Australian

*Figure 8: Major Walter Bazley and Padre John Hart. (Dr Ellis)*

minefield, but an enemy dive-bombing attack left 50 RTR with three casualties: Lieutenant Ian Brown who was badly wounded in the leg, and Corporal Lidgley and Trooper Milsom, all of A Squadron. Lidgley subsequently died of his wounds. On the 31st the regiment moved back across the railway to Hill 26.

The last few days of July 1942 are recounted here by Colonel Cairnes: We were shattered the next day to hear that the 40th and 46th had been given the most impossible and ridiculous task and had appallingly heavy casualties. Out of our 100 tanks only 10 were fit to fight after the battle. Howard Dunbar was fatally wounded and they had no less than 25 officer casualties. The 40th and 46th fought like tigers from all accounts but they were caught by anti-tank guns on a minefield which was supposed to have been cleared.

A couple of days later when I had most of my tanks again we had another battle, only two squadrons involved this time and I just kept in the background and watched the party.

They went to the rescue of an Australian battalion which was cut off, but we were sent in much too late at very short notice and it was a forlorn hope at the very least.

The squadrons fought well and did some damage but I lost 9 tanks and achieved nothing really, and a lot of the tanks which returned were badly shot about without smoke protection, which I insisted (in vain) on having this time.

We had no sooner rallied when we were dive bombed and machine-gunned by two Stukas, very unpleasant. I lay along my tank which I hadn't time to get into and watched the bullets kicking up the dust close to my behind, which seemed a bit unhealthy.

My ambulance was hit with bullets and one man was seriously injured. The light anti-aircraft section failed to hit the Stukas, but got two Messerschmitts later. The most difficult air attack to counter is the high flying attack by a fighter, who drops little bombs most of the time and you never hear them coming down. One such bomb caught three chaps standing by their tank the other day.

50 RTR had now seen action, thrown in at the deep end; both men and machines had stood up well to the task. But one cannot help wondering what would have happened if the higher command had had the same view as Alan Moorehead, correspondent for the *Daily Express*:

It was a brand new brigade of tanks from England. The crews had been trained and trained thoroughly but they were new to the desert. Only three weeks before they had come ashore at Suez with their Valentine tanks. One wondered if it was a good thing to send troops into action immediately they arrived in the desert.

The guns will shoot just the same, of course, but it was not quite like Salisbury Plain. It was not like manoeuvres. If petrol ran out it was not just a matter of running back two miles down the road and taking the first left where there is a filling station. Maybe the petrol supply vehicles did not arrive in the desert . . . . Maybe you had to take a compass bearing to find the nearest petrol dump, which is just a spot on the map. Maybe you were not too good at reading a compass and you missed the way. Maybe the dump had moved when you got to it. There was no workshop at hand if a track broke or a gun stuck. It was hot and the heat played tricks with the eyesight. Then again everything disappeared under dust and smoke once the action was joined, and the best eyesight in the world wasn't much good to you half the time.

However, on Thursday 13 August, things were about to change. General B L Montgomery took command of the Eighth Army, though it was not officially announced until six days later.

A tragic sequel to the July fighting occurred on 17 August to members of 23 Armoured Brigade who had been captured during those first actions. On that day, the Italian transport ship *Nino Bixio* (7137 tonnes) was being escorted by the destroyers *Da Recco* and *Saetta* along with the torpedo boats *Castore*, *Orione* and *Polluce*. While this small convoy was approaching Navarino Island, it was attacked by the British submarine *Turbulent* (herself sunk the following March) commanded by Commander Linton. The *Nino Bixio* was struck by torpedoes; aboard the ship were 2,000 Allied prisoners of war, of whom 336 perished, including some members of 23 Armoured Brigade and 50 RTR.

John Cockayne, who you will recall was captured during the regiment's first action, continues his story:

I wasn't on the one that was sunk, but I was up on deck; we were sailing almost side by side, no distance at all.

For the first day and a half to two days, we had no trouble sailing. During our travels up and down the desert, we had had no food, apart from the Italian biscuits, and very little to drink; they did give us some 'bully', but Italian 'bully' consisted of a piece of gristle in a can of water – the most revolting thing you ever set eyes on. We had been used to good food and the sight of this stuff, you just could not face it! Hunger had not really got to us, but by the time we got up to Benghazi I think everybody was suffering from dysentery.

So, the first thing on the boats was latrines; we had two rope ladders in the holds and they allowed three at a time to go up on deck. There was a gap in the railings of the ship and on the side of the ship there was a plank strapped on, and you went on, held the rail, slid along the plank and dropped it into the sea. As soon as you finished we used to get in the queue to go again.

When we were attacked, I was up on deck and by that time we were heading up the Adriatic very close to the heel of Italy, but we were going up the Greek coast. The other ship got hit by two torpedoes, one in the forward hold and one in the back, and she went over. We stayed with them for some time. All the Italians jumped overboard – they all had life belts, we picked a lot of them up. We swung round then and went into Brindisi, where we caught sight of the whole Italian fleet lined up in dock – 40 or 50 ships. We were landed at Brindisi and spent one night there before being sent down to Bari for two weeks. We had only been there about two days, when the survivors were brought over and joined us there. They were all in shorts and shirts – well, what was left of them, and were in a pretty rough state. When the ship had been torpedoed the sprinklers went off to add to the confusion and they were covered from head to foot in foam. There were a few hundred perished, but I only knew of two lads from our lot who died; Trooper Thompson and Sergeant Riley. I think most of the casualties were in the forward hold.

Dennis Shreeve, a Sergeant in A Squadron – he'd got a lot of minor wounds; his legs were peppered with small pieces of shrapnel from the ship. The two Greatbanks – they were with them, both out of B Squadron. We all stuck together then and were moved up to Campo 70. According to the survivors who joined us at Bari, the ship never sank – it was towed and grounded on the Greek coast, and the lads were brought from Greece to Bari in a Greek boat.

We stayed at Campo 70 until the Italian army capitulated; just before the capitulation, they took out all the troopers and lance corporals and shipped them off to Germany. On the day of the capitulation all the guards disappeared, so we went off into the countryside. We didn't go far because what we were after was information – the Italians did not know anything, only rumours. Had we known that our troops had just landed on the heel of Italy, as we were only a 100-150 miles away from them, we could have made our way to them.

Five days after the capitulation the Germans came in with a hell of a lot of troops and rounded us up. Any Italians caught harbouring us were shot, there were no two ways about that. We were then shipped off to Germany, calling at Thoren in Poland for a few days and then on to Stalag 5B, which was at Mulburg, midway between Leipzig and Berlin and we were there until the big air offensives started.

I was on the escape committee at Stalag 5B and we thought we had got a nice little outlet. We were getting two or three men out a week, but eventually after four or five weeks we looked out at the front gates and saw a party of prisoners – they were all the ones we thought we had shipped off to Switzerland. They had been picking them up as they arrived at the border. It was at this time the Germans started breaking us up. I was in a party that went to Stalag 347 – this was at the end of 1944 and there were only a few of the 50th's lads left with us – Ron Bull was one of the last I kept in touch with.

Two or three weeks before the British troops moved up that way they started marching us off in the direction of Lubeck. We were marching in columns and it was then I decided that I wasn't going any further. Me and a chap out of the artillery slipped the column and laid up. We came out of the woods one day to go to a well for some water, when a woman called us over and told us that the British were in the area, so we headed down the road and the first unit we came to was a tank unit.

## Chapter 3
## 'NOW YOU CAN SEE WHAT TO FIRE AT, BLOODY GREAT JERRY TANKS'

### Battle of Alam Halfa

The coming battle of Alam Halfa was to be Rommel's last attempt to break through to the Nile valley. It was also General Montgomery's first battle in the Western Desert. Both had reputations to protect. Rommel was anxious to gain another quick victory with his ever-dwindling resources, while Montgomery had to consolidate his convalescing army as a prelude to the campaign that was to follow. On the night of 30/31 August Rommel repeated the tactics which had served so well at Gazala – diversionary attacks in the north while the main army swung to the south to outflank the allies and cut their supply lines. But the presence of the British 7th Armoured Division forced him to pull up short of his intended targets. Lack of fuel and the stubborn resistance of the Eighth Army finally ended any hope Rommel had of reaching the Nile.

50 RTR would now be meeting the Afrika Korps. Everyone was full of stories about the famous Afrika Korps composed of 15th and 21st Panzer Divisions, who usually operated in conjunction with the almost equally well known 90th Light Division, which, equipped with a high proportion of anti-tank guns, acted as handmaiden to the two armoured divisions. These three were Rommel's special pride; he had trained them himself and often led them into battle. There was a feeling of complete mutual trust throughout this hard hitting group. They were probably the best German formations encountered by Allied forces during the war. What is more, they always fought cleanly.

On 1 August, a German spotter plane swooped very low and slowly over 50 RTR's position, Colonel Cairnes wrote:

> We let fly with everything we had got, even my pistol came into action. The funniest sight was Wally Bazley who commands my Headquarter Squadron, standing stark naked with a tommy gun firing into the blue, for without his glasses he was far too blind to see the plane. The plane was hit by something, but we didn't see it fall.

*Figure 9: One of the more well known photographs to come out of the desert A Squadron's Fitters' lorry (from left to right) Sgt Tuvey, Cpl G Robinson, Sgt W Youdel, L/Cpl A Abbess, Tpr L Daw, Tpr L Palmer, Sgt Vaughen, August 1942. (A Abbess)*

For the first week in August, 50 RTR were to remain under the command of the 9th Australian division; their role would be to counter-attack and support the Australians should their position be threatened. On the 7th, 50 RTR's leaguer area was attacked by Stukas, just as the A Echelon vehicles were arriving to replenish the tanks and their crews. Trooper Davis, driving the cook's truck, was killed by shrapnel. At 2030 hours on 8 August, 40 RTR took over from The Fiftieth, who were to travel by night to a new area at Alam el Dakar. The regiment also received its first nine bags of mail since leaving England. Six days of training and exercises followed before moving on again, this time to Alam el Baoshaza. Things seemed fairly quiet at this time, with the regiment again training and exercising with other units, then on 31 August at 0420 hours the order 'action stations' was received. The Germans had penetrated the forward positions on Ruweisat Ridge, and were attacking with tanks in the south. As the morning wore on, it became apparent that the main enemy thrust with armour was in the south. The Fiftieth was ordered to form up on the left of an Australian brigade. By this time the position on Ruweisat Ridge had been restored and an enemy raid on the Australian positions in the north had been repulsed.

On 31 August, Lieutenant-General Horrocks commanding XIII Corps had specifically asked for the support of 23 Armoured Brigade. He wrote:

By approximately 11am we had definitely identified the whole of the Afrika Korps and the 90th Light Division in the south, so the other attacks which had been made, notably against XXX Corps front, were only diversionary. I rang up Monty and asked for the 23rd Armoured Brigade, with its 149 Valentine tanks, to come under my orders as promised. He agreed, so Brigadier Richards started moving his brigade to the positions which he had reconnoitred during the exercises. By 1400 hours he was there, all along the north side of the hill running between Alam el Halfa and the position occupied by the New Zealand Division.

The Fiftieth occupied their battle positions by the El Aguri Tomb south-east of Dier el Himma, where they sat in commanding positions of their own choosing, to stop the enemy should he swing north or north-east from the south. To their right front were 40 RTR and on the left was part of 22 Armoured Brigade.

The Reconnaissance Troop, now commanded by Lieutenant Ted Jenkins (Lieutenant Orbach had been promoted to Intelligence Officer in place of Captain Rushbrooke), was sent forward to watch for the approach of the enemy. In the late afternoon The Fiftieth advanced to support the units of 22 Armoured Brigade engaging the German tanks, but owing to failing light and the Germans withdrawing, they did not make contact with the enemy. 50 RTR then withdrew to a position north-west of where they had leaguered the previous night. The situation was then that large forces of enemy armour were facing north and north-east, and had concentrated a few thousand yards to the south; 50 RTR were now preparing for a heavy attack on its positions at dawn on 1 September.

At first light on 1 September the regiment had occupied its battle positions with two squadrons forward and one in reserve. The Reconnaissance Troop, which was well forward, kept sending information about enemy movements to the south and south-west in the Taria and Daayis Depressions. As the day progressed, most of the German armour went well east of The Fiftieth and was fully engaged by 22 Armoured Brigade. By late afternoon the Germans had not been able to break through to the east, and several columns of tanks were seen forming up immediately to the south, evidently for an attack on 50 RTR, the success of which would give them a road to Alam Halfa, which had been established as Rommel's objective.

B Squadron was sent forward to the right, with orders to withdraw if attacked; the idea was to draw the enemy tanks into a pocket between 50 RTR and the remainder of the brigade, and eventually onto the six-pounder guns of 73 Anti-Tank Regiment Royal Artillery. A Squadron had one troop well forward on the left to watch for any enemy movement in that direction. The regiment was in a good commanding position and determined to hold their ground. Some enemy tanks moved towards the position but were driven off by 40 RTR. The Germans, had they tried to penetrate in this area, would have suffered heavy casualties, so instead of a full scale assault on the position, they tried to draw 50 RTR away and onto their own anti-tank guns.

On 2 September 50 RTR remained in their positions all day, with only a few patrols going out towards Tarfa and Daayis. On the 3rd, B Squadron, commanded by Major Alan Hughes, was sent to support the 28th (Maori) Infantry Battalion, commanded by Lieutenant-Colonel Fred Baker of the 5th New Zealand Infantry Brigade, in a night attack to close the gap through which the enemy armour in the south had come (Colonel Baker would in the ensuing action converse over the air in Maori, thus completely mystifying enemy listeners).

In the first part of the action, 6 New Zealand Brigade failed to make their objectives but 5 New Zealand Brigade's attack was successful; B Squadron advanced but mistook German lights for a Verey signal and as a result they overshot their area and came in contact with an infantry position of the 90th Light Division and a German tank and transport leaguer. For a few moments nothing happened, both sides being taken completely by surprise, then B Squadron opened fire at almost point-blank range. So quick were B Squadron to react, that only one German tank was able to reply and this was knocked out within a few minutes. However, the anti-tank guns began to hit back and B Squadron were ordered to withdraw. At this critical time, the squadron had radio problems and Major Hughes began to lose contact with his tanks. In turning about, however, they ran onto enemy mines and lost several tanks to these and enemy fire. One tank driven by Trooper Hamblin and commanded by Lieutenant Nixon hit a mine and broke a track; despite the obvious predicament, Hamblin repaired the track sufficiently to allow them to return to their leaguer. But for Lieutenant Nixon the night's work was not yet over; he took over his troop corporal's tank.

At first light it was decided to withdraw the New Zealand infantry, as most of them had not reached their objectives. B Squadron, with their six remaining tanks, advanced to a ridge to cover the withdrawal. This was done with complete success, but they lost three more tanks from artillery and anti-tank fire. Brigadier Richards stated that 'in spite of early casualties the tanks entirely fulfilled the roles assigned to them.' B Squadron had lost eight men killed, including Major Hughes, whom Colonel Cairnes regarded as his best squadron leader, seven wounded and twelve missing in action. Only three tanks managed to return to their leaguer after the action. Trooper Freddie August, a gunner/

operator in B Squadron's Five Troop recalls his introduction to battle in early September 1942:

> We had missed the two battles of 22 and 27 July – as spare crews we were left behind in B Echelon with other spare crews. Early in August though, we were whisked up to join the regiment, having picked up reconditioned tanks on the way, so we had two or three weeks to get acclimatised to desert conditions.
>
> B Squadron was detailed as duty squadron and to our dismay Five Troop was detailed as duty troop. This meant we would have to be on the air all the daylight hours, with the tank engines running, whilst the rest of the regiment closed down. As Valentine tanks had no separate charging plant, engines had to be kept running to keep the batteries charged. I was on the corporal's tank.
>
> We were lying behind this low ridge out of sight of the enemy in turret down positions, while Rommel's troops moved east down in the Depression.
>
> Our first call soon came from the CO, asking our troop officer to report on what he could see of the enemy's activity. He replied that he would have to move forward to do this. The CO seemed most annoyed and thought he would give our position away if he did this and forbade him to move.
>
> Our Recce Troop, in Dingo scout cars, were out forward passing back information. They then came on the air calling for assistance as they were being harried by some Italian armoured cars. The CO then came on the air and asked our troop officer if he had heard that and when he said, 'Yes, sir', the CO came out with, 'Then why the blazes aren't you doing something about it?' 'At once, sir!' he replied.
>
> To us, he said, 'Follow me, men!' and away he went, with us trailing behind. Just as we reached the crest of the ridge, another message came from our Recce Troop, saying 'Assistance no longer required, as South African friends have done the necessary.'
>
> It was a day or two later when we were told that our Squadron was to help man an attack by the New Zealanders in an effort to cut off the enemy's retreat back to his own lines. We were kept waiting for hours waiting for the 'off', all packed up in the tanks and it was dark, before the order was given to move off in two columns of tanks with soft vehicles in the centre – supplies and a machine-gun company were taken up to the Maori battalion whom we were to help during the attack.
>
> After the order to move off, we were soon passing through a gap in our own minefield which had been taped and marked with shaded blue lights. During this passage, our progress was lit up

by parachute flares being dropped from an aircraft and it came as no surprise when a bomb or bombs were dropped. Our only casualty was a truck which was set on fire. We managed to form up again after the initial scattering, though what became of the soft vehicles I've no idea.

After a mile or two, the squadron commander came on the air asking our navigating officer if he was sure of his direction and if he was on a compass course. The answer was rather surprising as he said he hadn't got a compass, but was 'marching on a star!'

Whilst we were breasting a ridge, a fierce fire fight was seen to our right front – quite spectacular, flashes and loud explosions, tracers flying about everywhere. I said to our tank commander, who had been silent (we had both been able to stand and look out of the turret since the start) that it looked like a Brock's benefit. As I got no reply, I said, 'You know, November 5th, Guy Fawkes?' Still no answer, so I concluded that his headset wasn't working.

Not long after this our leading tanks began reporting that they were running into an enemy leaguer and asked for orders. I was expecting an order to draw back and shoot them up (the enemy). With our tanks all milling around, the squadron commander thought the best thing would be to withdraw and ordered the tanks about and rally back to MABEL (MABEL was the code name for the gap in the minefield).

As our corporal still said nothing, I reached under the two-pounder and shook our driver's shoulder, removed his headset and told him the Major's orders. I told the driver to come round hard on his right stick, which he managed OK, scraping a truck and running over some bundles at the side of the truck on the way; I remember hoping there was nobody in those bundles.

When one of our tanks asked the OC to fire a Verey light, so that he could orientate himself, the OC refused, saying it would give his position away, but said, 'keep the moon on your right and head due north'; this was good enough for me and I passed it on to our driver.

We were quickly on our way and now seemed to be all on our own, when suddenly one of our tanks crossed in front of us heading straight for the full moon. I was startled to hear our corporal's voice ordering our driver to 'follow that tank!' Knowing this was quite wrong, I just had to countermand this and told our driver to continue as he was, which fortunately he did.

We were now on our own again and I was getting rather anxious; we then came upon a stationary truck with the driver standing alongside. I jumped down and asked if we could help and he said 'no'. I then asked him if he had seen any tanks or knew where MABEL was. He said 'No mate, all I know is that we are in the middle of a minefield'. Hastily retracing my footsteps I remounted and we gingerly continued on our way. About this time I heard the Major calling up his Squadron to report signals.

Again and again he called, but no-one responded, so the next time he called I reported 'Five Baker OK over'. Acknowledging my reply, the Major's relief was obvious. We were told to report when we arrived back at MABEL, which we did shortly after – recognisable by the still burning truck. I was told to park by his tank and 'Charlie Dog Baker Uncle' (Close Down and Brew Up).

Too tired to have a meal we kipped down in the tank as best as we could, closed the lid and enjoyed a few hours' shut-eye. Opening the flaps at first light, I counted seven, including ours – so we had lost eight tanks from when we started and not a shot fired.

After a hurried wash and shave and a bite to eat, a tank commanders' conference was called. When this finished our corporal came running back to our tank, seized his maps, binoculars and bale out bag and was about to leave, so I asked him what he was up to. He said that Mr Nixon's tank had to go back to the workshops for repair and he was to go with it.

I was relieved that we now had a new tank commander and I looked forward to resuming my proper role as gunner/operator. Our six tanks lost no time in setting out to cover the withdrawal of the Maori troops, under cover of a smoke screen laid down by our 25-pounder guns. I thought it best to remain in my seat now that I had an officer on board; the guns were all loaded and ready to fire and it seemed no time at all before we had arrived at the place where the artillery were just finishing a magnificent opaque smoke screen – no mistake this time, I thought.

We now began what was to me a very peculiar manoeuvre, all six Valentine tanks in line ahead. We proceeded to parade up and down in front of the smoke screen, several hundred yards long. With our guns pointing up the rear of the tank in front, I failed to see how we could be of any help to the New Zealanders, so I traversed my two-pounder to face the smoke screen, aware also that our side armour would not be much protection against an anti-tank shot. I was also aware at the end of the line as we turned about, our other five tanks passed in front of my sighting scope. I was then startled to hear my tank commander ordering me to keep the gun pointed at twelve o'clock (straight ahead) as he found it difficult to follow the Major! I declined to hear this and pretended to be deaf. Then I heard my first fire order of the war.

It was not what I expected; instead of an order as in our training

'Gunner, AP Action. Traverse (right or left) steady – on – hornet or ant (tank or anti-tank) range 500' – what I received was 'Now you can see what to fire at, bloody great Jerry tanks!' I yelled to him to get me on them, but he told me to join him looking out of the turret top! – As we had had it drummed into us at the training regiment that 'he who shooteth first liveth longest', I was flabbergasted and hurriedly popped up, leaving the gun where I had been sitting, shoulder in the gun crutch, finger on the trigger, eye to gun sight and left hand grasping the power traverse.

Outside I could now see through the now thinning smoke, half a dozen or so ominous looking shapes, tanks or anti-tank guns. I resumed my seat and tried to pick them out in the small field of view of the sighting telescope. At last I got onto one and loosed off a belated round. I am sure I scored a hit as I saw the tracer or the round itself sky upwards into the blue. I then waited for my tank commander to reload the two-pounder, his job in a three-man tank.

It was then I realised that he had no intention or most likely didn't know that, so I had the awkward task of reloading the gun from the gunner's side. While I was engaged in doing this I became aware of an altercation going on between our commander and our driver, who was refusing to take the tank back to where we had been, saying that it was 'bloody murder' and a 'killing ground'. To this the commander was threatening to shoot him for disobeying an order in the face of the enemy and our driver was telling him to 'drive the bloody thing yourself'.

Our tank commander must have seen my questioning look, as he then explained what had happened. Three of our tanks had been knocked out and our driver had against his orders, taken the tank out of range and was refusing to go back. I was asked for my opinion and said we would be a sitting duck if we went back, as this was open desert with no cover. So we called up the artillery and asked for more smoke, but the wind was now increasing and the smoke soon disappeared.

The Maoris were now drifting back through the disappearing smoke. Looking from our open turret the scene reminded us of an old World War One film, especially as Jerry were now using their deadly air burst shells, which would probably be fired from their 88mm anti-aircraft guns. Singly and in small groups, the Maoris passed our vehicles giving us the thumbs up sign as they did so. Among them we spied a black beret – a wounded 'tanky' was being supported by two stalwart New Zealanders. They handed him over to us and between us we managed to get him up on the tank and then made tracks for Doc Bishop's RAP tent,

*Figure 10: 5 Baker, one of only 3 Valentines to return from B Squadron's action at Munnassib, September 1942. (F August)*

handing him down into Doc's tender care. We received confirmation that the OC had been killed, along with his driver (I believe).

Shooed away from the Red Cross tent, we met our supporting artillery and their CO promptly gave us a convincing demonstration of the efficiency of their 25-pounders, when a sole Italian tank appeared over a distant crest. A short burst stopped it in its tracks and nobody got out.

We remained with the gunners until last light and then we received orders to return to the regimental leaguer, which was not a minute too soon, as our fuel tank was nearly empty.

Looking back, I am sure that our driver's refusal to return saved our lives. We then formed the nucleus, as eight troop, of a reconstituted B Squadron. We were told by our new squadron commander, Major Peter Carter, that the other blokes would look to us for guidance – talk about the blind leading the blind!

On 4 September, the enemy had begun to withdraw in earnest and on the 5th it was apparent the main striking force was being taken back behind the minefields, covered by the usual screen of anti-tank guns and a few tanks. The 23 Armoured Brigade advanced to take up battle positions on the next ridge south, and sent out strong patrols consisting of two troops of tanks, one six-pounder anti-tank gun and a section of sappers, who kept the enemy under observation and harried them as much as possible. It was during one of these patrols that Lieutenant J Halse was wounded in the neck when a shell burst in front of his tank. The following is a letter from 5 New Zealand Brigade to 50 RTR

concerning the action fought on 3/4 September 1942.
7 September 42

Dear Col Cairnes,
I would like to express, on behalf of my brigade, our admiration for the conduct of B Squadron which supported us in the action at MUNNASSIB on Sept 3/4th. We particularly admired the spirited manner in which the 6 remaining tanks came forward to meet the enemy tanks in the morning counter attack, their gallant action was largely responsible for averting a disaster to our 28th New Zealand (Maori) Bn.

We are all very sorry indeed that Major Hughes was killed, I hope that you will recommend him for a Mention in Despatches, if he had survived I certainly would have recommended a decoration. Will you please convey to B Squadron our thanks and admiration for their conduct and our good wishes for their fortune in the future.

                              Yours sincerely
                              C.O. 5th New Zealand Brigade.

On 6 September, the regiment returned to its old leaguer area near Alam el Baoshaza. Some anti-tank gunners occupying the eastern edge of the leaguer became very irate because they were surrounded by the regiment's tanks, which would provide an ideal target for the Luftwaffe.

The following day all tank crews were engaged on maintenance but orders were received to return to the battle positions as at 1 September. This turned out to be only a precautionary measure, due to a lot of enemy activity in the area. The regiment returned to its original leaguer before last light. Shortly after the actions on 3/4 September, 23 Armoured Brigade was joined by 8 RTR.

For the forthcoming operations, the brigade was to be deployed with 8 RTR supporting the 1st South African Division, 40 RTR supporting the 9th Australian Division, 50 RTR supporting the 51st Highland Division, while 46 RTR was to be held in brigade reserve. All were under command of XXX Corps.

A training order was received from Brigade Headquarters on the 9th, stating that The Fiftieth was to train with 51st Highland Division in an infantry support role. Four days' leave in Alexandria was allowed for five per cent of the regiment's strength on the 11th and a number of visits were arranged to the area now occupied by 22 Armoured Brigade to see knocked out German Mark III and IV tanks; Stukas were active in the area at the time and bombed the Greek position just east of The Fiftieth.

On 12 and 13 September, the Commanding Officer talked to all crews about the preparations for the big offensive which would soon be coming. The regiment then moved to a new area, taking over ground occupied by the Staffordshire Yeomanry. At the same time the regiment's quartermaster, Lieutenant D Robertson was posted to XXX Corps headquarters as a captain and was replaced by Lieutenant Bumpas, formerly regimental sergeant-major of the Queen's Bays.

Colonel Cairnes wrote on 13 September:

> We moved a bit today. It is a great sight seeing the battalion bowling along all around like one big fleet. The dust kicked up by each vehicle on hard stony ground is just enough to give the impression of a bow wave. A large force of tanks moving spread out like this at a good speed is always to me a thrilling sight.

They had now reached 'M' area, near the Qattara Depression. This piece of desert was very similar to their allocated objective. The men knew this area as 'In the wadis'. From the 14th until the end of the month, the regiment's time was spent training with men of the Highland Division and getting to know their opposite numbers. Some of the Scots even managed to drive the tanks for a while. The regiment also had its first experience of a mobile bath unit. During this training A Squadron set out one morning on a routine exercise. One tank however developed steering trouble, attempts to rectify the situation failed so the tank was ordered back to the regimental leaguer. With the brake adjustment gone the tank was continually steering to one side. Despite, the efforts of the driver to keep the tank on any sort of course, before long it had drifted well away from its intended direction. By late afternoon they were completely lost. By a stroke of luck they arrived at a well worn track along which the regiment's Echelon was passing, and with their help were guided back to the leaguer.

Each squadron commander also personally supervised and tested the accuracy of each of his gunners. Freddie August recalls:

> We were the first of B Squadron to shoot. The Major, standing on the back of the tank, called into the turret and told me to try and hit a 44 gallon oil drum, which he had set up as a target about 500 yards away. I was to call out the strike and what alteration I would make to secure a hit. I could use three rounds, a round was loaded and I waited for a fire order. 'What are you waiting for gunner ?' So I shouted 'Firing' and pulled the trigger. 'You stupid so and so' said the Major, 'You nearly knocked me off the tank'. 'Sorry sir,' I said.
>
> When the smoke and dust cleared, nothing could be seen. 'What have you done with my target?' said the Major. 'I think I've knocked it into the dead ground,' I replied. Being short-sighted, I had used the tank commander's binoculars to get spot-on accuracy, by aligning the telescopic gun sight with a squint up the gun barrel. 'Good shooting gunner,' said the Major, 'now I

will have to see about some more targets.'

George Morrice MM of the 1st battalion Gordon Highlanders remembers the 51st Highland Division's association with 50 RTR:

We arrived in Egypt in August 1942. We were involved in some stiff training, which sometimes involved co-operation with the tanks, and as I was a platoon sergeant, acting commander, I met a lot of chaps from 50 RTR.

There was one incident I remember very well. We had to get into slit trenches and let the tanks roll over the top. One of the sergeants I was talking to was not happy about this, neither was I. The ground was too soft. The other platoon commanders, who were officers, came over to see me. After discussion we went to the company commander, who called it off.

It appeared that the Australians had done this with some success, but the ground had been much harder – the idea being to place grenades under the tanks as they went over.

The members of 50 RTR gave us their utmost support right up until the campaign ended in May 1943, and we could always depend on their assistance when we landed in a tight spot.

Things were now building up for what was to become the turning point in the desert campaign, a major offensive was being set in motion and the second battle of Alamein was about to be fought.

Trooper Stanley Midwinter recalls events prior to the battle:

Just before the battle of Alamein, Harold Mattock, my partner, and I spent some time on forward recce – we used to go out just before dawn as far forward as we could, until we could see the enemy very closely. The OPs came out to us in their Honey tanks for information. The clouds of sand that they threw up brought us to the attention of the enemy who started to explore us with their guns. Fortunately they always used a box formation, and as long as you missed the first you were sitting pretty – you just dodged into the last shell hole each time until they left off.

On another occasion Mattock and I came upon a group of Italians and we thought it was our lot, but they dropped their weapons and put up their hands. We had the job of taking them to the cages at the rear. By the time we handed them over it was quite dark, so we decided to stay put for the night, but Mr Orbach turned up and he had other ideas and sent us back to the unit.

Percy Wadey of C Squadron remembers the time before Alamein:

About ten days before the battle of Alamein, my troop commander asked me if I would like to speak home to my family on the wireless, and told me to report to the wireless truck at 6.00pm with a written message of so many words. Having received no mail since leaving England I was unaware that my mother and brother had died.

50 RTR's part in the forthcoming offensive would be:
1. An advance on 51st Highland Division's front at the beginning of the operation on the night of 23/24 October 1942.
2. An advance with 152 Highland Infantry Brigade on 2nd New Zealand Division's front on the night of 1/2 November, with the aim of forcing a fresh bridgehead to let the main armour through.
3. An attack with 5 Indian Infantry Brigade on the night of 3/4 November, with the aim of widening the bulge made by the New Zealand Division's attack.

During the 22nd, Colonel Cairnes informed the recently promoted Captain Williams of B Squadron, that Major Venn, officer commanding C Squadron, had reported sick and that he would now be commanding C Squadron. As he was leaving, Colonel Cairnes promptly promoted Williams to Major with the words 'By the way, you had better get yourself a crown as well.' That evening the padre held a short service, attended by nearly all the officers and men of the regiment who sang 'Abide with me' and 'O God our help in ages past'. Following the service Colonel Cairnes held a final pre-battle conference for his squadron leaders.

The regiment spent the daylight hours of 23 October in a concentration area north of the railway line, a few hundred yards west of Alamein station. Although the tanks were not visible from the enemy's most forward observation posts on the ground, they had to avoid being spotted from the air. There was the minimum of movement in the concentration area and the tanks remained stationary under their sun shields. The covers proved to be extraordinarily good camouflage, and from a distance of a few hundred yards it was difficult to distinguish the tanks from lorries, even on the ground.

Trooper Les Garland of A Echelon recalls:

Before Alamein I was part of a team working fourteen hours a day (no extra pay) erecting tank hides at the forward positions. During the day we travelled back to base and collected a prefabricated sectional truck. This was made of a timber frame and canvas coloured to resemble a truck. As soon as it was dark we advanced to the forward position and at pre-arranged places erected the frames to resemble a lorry. Soon after midnight tanks would arrive and move into cover – a back canvas concealed the tank completely. The tank crews were ordered not to wear their black berets and all traces of tank tracks in the sand were obliterated to avoid detection by aerial photography. This continued for about a week until all The Fiftieth tanks were under cover.

The men were in good spirits all day, and much appreciated the meal of a good hot stew and 'duff' which the Echelon brought up in the early evening. They were supposed to be on hard rations, but no questions were asked as to how this meal was provided. Trooper Reg Bryant of the 8th Armoured Division Headquarters recalls:

In the days before the battle of Alamein, some of us were deployed in trucks and half-tracks and were sent out into the desert. Our job was to send out false wireless messages to try and confuse the enemy as to the area of attack. Also in the desert were dummy dumps of petrol, water and canvas tanks etc. We went around these sending out our dud messages. When the attack started on 23/24 October, 8th Armoured Division Headquarters was about five miles behind the line. The Fiftieth, as part of 23 Armoured Brigade, went forward with the Eighth Army.

Despite the enormous number of tanks which the Eighth Army had accumulated for the Alamein operations, 23 Armoured Brigade was the only armour at the disposal of XXX Corps, commanded by Lieutenant General Sir Oliver Leese.

On the 23rd Colonel Cairnes wrote:

We are going into battle tonight with the famous Highland Division and have great hopes of kicking Rommel and his pals right out of Africa. The Jocks are in great heart and we are carrying as many as we can on the outside of our machines. With any luck it should be brilliant moonlight, but the last couple of nights have been cloudy and we might have some rain.

Not a gun appears to be firing. It looks as if the Bosche have not suspected anything yet. I hope we get off to a good start, it will make things so much easier if we do.

We are proud to be in the centre in the van of the battle, I have just given my chaps a 'pep talk' and we are all in great heart out here.

# Chapter 4
# 'O GOD OF BATTLES, STEEL MY SOLDIERS' HEARTS'[1]

## Second Battle of Alamein

At Alamein in October the Eighth Army was facing an enemy position whose flanks could not be turned. The Mediterranean sea lay to the north and the great Qattara Depression to the south. This left Montgomery with only one choice, direct frontal assault. But this could and would not be carried out until the Eighth Army had overwhelming superiority. Time was on Montgomery's side: the Allies now controlled the supply lines, and troops and equipment could arrive at leisure, while the Afrika Korps, starved of equipment, would start the battle without Rommel. He was in Germany recuperating from a recent illness.

During the morning of 23 October Montgomery had this personal message read out to all ranks:

The battle which is now about to begin will be one of the decisive battles of history. It will be the turning point of the war, the Lord, mighty in battle, will give us the victory.

Major General Wimberley, commanding 51st Highland Division, visited 50 RTR in the afternoon. He drove up alone in his scout car to ask if there were any last-minute difficulties. In his headquarters at Burg el Arab, General Montgomery was preparing for the third British offensive in North Africa, operation LIGHTFOOT. In the light of experience gained at Alam Halfa, he had demanded new commanders for XXX Corps and 7th Armoured Division. For the former he got Lieutenant-General Oliver Leese and for the latter Major-General A F Harding.

One of Montgomery's early decisions was where to make the first attack. If he launched his assault in the northern sector, between Ruweisat Ridge and the sea, he believed there was a good chance of taking Rommel by surprise. Also the desert in the south would play the same part as the sea, in offering a complete obstacle to the Axis forces in the event of LIGHTFOOT succeeding, thus forcing Rommel to retreat in a westerly direction and out of Egypt.

The success of LIGHTFOOT required the organisation of an extra army corps, X Corps, in addition to XIII and XXX Corps, and the success

1. *Henry V*

of operation BERTRAM, which was intended to convince Axis headquarters that any attack would come in the south, consisted of siting dummy vehicles and tanks and even a pipeline in that area.

The details of LIGHTFOOT would be guarded so well that all low ranking officers and NCOs would not be informed of the date of attack until two days before.

Despite this enormous effort of organisation and planning, the Prime Minister had been pushing for an earlier timed assault, but on the insistence of General Sir Alan Brooke, Chief of the Imperial General Staff, Churchill was persuaded that the offensive should not commence until the October full moon on the 23rd.

The following table taken from the British Official History shows the strengths of the opposing forces on the Alamein front on 23 October 1942:

|  | German | Italian | British |
|---|---|---|---|
| Infantry Battalions | 71 | 40 | 85 |
| Field/Medium Guns | 460 | 260 | 908 |
| Anti-Tank Guns | 850 | 300 | 1,451 |
| Tanks | 496 |  | 1,029 |
| Armoured Cars | 192 |  | 435 |

The scene was now set for the largest offensive yet seen in the desert. Corporal John Smale recalls:

> We consisted mostly of young men – physically fit, keen, a strong sense of duty, training to work as a team, and the majority with a good sense of humour. It was this that held us together, as we had had very heavy casualties and were receiving replacements all the time. It was tough going but every time you met others, there was a lot of laughter and jokes.
>
> I remember in the desert when we were due to attack (generally around 2200 hours) the padre used to come up to the line and give us a short service. Ninety nine per cent were anxious to go to that service (who should go was generally decided by cutting cards) because of concern of what was going to happen during the next few hours.

As darkness fell the tank crews removed their camouflage, and at about 1930 hours the regiment moved off on the STAR track (one of six constructed for the armoured advance, running from 'Sydney Road' to the front line) to a position on the Qattara track, just by the railway crossing. Here they waited for the opening of the artillery barrage, which was to be the signal for the operation to begin. There was a full moon and visibility was very good except for a few drifting clouds. The lighting and policing of routes to the start line was good.

A Squadron, with one company from the 1st Battalion the Gordon

Highlanders aboard their tanks, had already moved independently to a position west of the Qattara track from which they were to move on 153 Brigade's front (on the axis of the 5/7th Battalion The Gordon Highlanders). B Squadron with one assault troop of the Reconnaissance Squadron (51st Highland Division) aboard, were leading the remainder of the regiment, followed by regimental headquarters, then C Squadron, with one company from the Argyll and Sutherland Highlanders aboard. C Squadron were to travel as far as the RED Line and then swing onto the axis of 7 Battalion Argyll and Sutherland Highlanders, preparatory to putting in a final attack on STIRLING. The Scottish infantry would be identifiable in the darkness by a white Saint Andrew's cross worn across their back-packs, a legacy of World War One. At this time the whole front was quiet.

At 2140 hours, on Friday 23 October 1942, the silence was split by the opening up of the artillery behind the tanks. They were firing a series of concentrations on known enemy gun positions before bringing down the barrage on the enemy forward defended localities (FDL) at 2200 hours. The sky was lit by the flash of the guns in a huge semi-circle. At about 2200 hours the tanks moved forward through their own minefields to a position just beyond the start line where they waited for the gaps to be made in any minefields encountered on the line of advance.

Writing in 1967, Field Marshal Montgomery described the opening barrage of the battle of Alamein:

The night of October 23rd was clear, with a brilliant moon. As zero hour approached we heard the bombers flying overhead to play their part in the conflict.

At exactly 9.40pm the artillery opened up with a terrific crash on the enemy gun positions and ammunition dumps, firing at a combined rate of over 1,000 rounds a minute; air bombing of the positions added to the noise, and to the destruction wrought. At 9.55pm the artillery ceased as suddenly as it had begun. Absolute silence followed – a breathless stillness. In the sky, above the 8th Army's hidden battle array two searchlight beams pointed long still fingers into the sky. Five minutes passed. What happened next is well described in Barton Maughan's brilliant book, *Australia in the War of 1939-45*:

'At 10.00pm the two beams swung inwards, intersected and stopped, forming a pointed arch dimly seen in the moonlit vault, like a remote symbol of crossed swords. At that instant the British guns opened a barrage of unimaginable intensity, eclipsing their first performance, and to the urgent drumming of the guns the infantrymen stepped out from their start lines in slow, measured paces at the even rate of 75 yards per minute.'

*Figure 11: Major G Russell and his crew just prior to the battle of Alamein (from left to right) Tpr Litten, Maj Russell, Tpr Furnival, Tpr Cooper. (Author's collection)*

The fight was on. Actually at 10.00pm I was in bed. There was nothing I could do at that time. The battle was now in the hands of my subordinate generals.

As the leading tanks of B Squadron reached the first minefield and the assault troops dismounted, they reported that gapping of the minefield was going extremely slowly and, should the tanks remain in this position they would begin to suffer heavy casualties. Colonel Cairnes then sent The Fiftieth's second-in-command, Major Geoff Russell, forward to evaluate the situation within the enemy minefields. Russell, accompanied by Corporal Lewis, very soon reported over the radio that the assault troops of the Reconnaissance Squadron had struck the first minefield, which was laid with anti-tank, anti-personnel and variable pressure mines. At this time the assault troops and the Royal Engineer gapping parties were under heavy fire from enemy artillery, mortars and machine guns.

Major Russell reported that Major Hutchinson, commanding the Reconnaissance Squadron, and his accompanying sapper officer (Lieutenant Jucker), had both been wounded. Jucker's second-in-command, a sergeant, had also been hit. Both the assault troops and the sappers were suffering casualties, and Major Russell was himself hit in the leg and thrown 20 feet by a shell burst which deafened him in one ear. Despite this, Russell began to supervise the remaining assault troops and engineers in gapping the minefield. Meanwhile, Corporal Lewis in their scout car kept Colonel Cairnes informed of the situation, which was now becoming critical. During the next few hours Lewis's scout car received two direct hits from artillery fire.

The Scorpion (a Matilda flail tank designed to blow up mines), which had been allotted to 50 RTR to help force the gaps, could not be found at this stage, and the Sappers had no automatic detectors in their equipment. The gap had to be forced by prodding with bayonets.

Major Russell deployed the Reconnaissance Squadron in a bridgehead on the far side of the minefield to cover the sappers, and then returned to continue supervising the gapping. In addition to anti-personnel mines, booby traps were encountered. One was set on an abandoned enemy anti-tank gun, one wheel of which had been lifted off and a trip wire attached to it, so that any attempt to put the wheel back onto the axle would touch off the explosive. This trap and others were neutralised by the sappers.

The minefield was about 150 yards deep and progress was very slow, due to the fire under which the sappers were working, casualties, and the absence of both the Scorpion and automatic detectors. The divisional commander was warned that progress was slow, so he ordered 50 RTR to get through at all costs. The regiment had priority over all other traffic and if necessary they were to use gaps on any other lanes that happened to be convenient. Colonel Cairnes ordered C Squadron to reconnoitre to the right and attempt to get through on the Argylls' lanes. This they did, and having disappeared into the night, later reported that they were making their way through, but with great difficulty.

As the tanks and infantry moved forward, one of the officers checking the guiding tapes through the minefield for the last time, turned to watch the barrage and the first advance:

> Through the din we made out other sounds – the whine of shells overhead, the clatter of machine-guns . . . and eventually the pipes. Then we saw a sight that will live forever in our memories – line upon line of steel-helmeted figures with rifles at the high port, bayonets catching the moonlight, and over all the wailing of the pipes . . . . As they passed they gave us the thumbs up sign, and we watched them plod on towards the enemy lines, which by this time were shrouded in smoke. Our final sight of them was just as they entered the smoke, with the enemy's defensive fire falling among them.

It was during this early part of the battle that Major Russell became aware of a group of Germans advancing towards him with their hands up. It was bright moonlight and he noticed one man with his hands in his pockets. Major Russell called out at once, 'If you don't put your hands up I will shoot.' The reply came back in a broad Scots accent,

*Figure 12: The whole of Regimental Headquarters just prior to the battle of Alamein. Col. Cairnes (front, centre), his driver John Flaherty sitting on the extreme right. The remainder of his crew Tpr Robins and L/Cpl Russell have crosses above them. (Flaherty Family)*

'Dinna' shoot I'm the escort.' He had no weapon of any sort and was slightly wounded.

It was not until about 0230 hours on the 24th, that Major Russell reported the gap in the first enemy minefield to be clear. In the meantime, the medical officer, Captain John Bishop, along with his driver, Trooper Midwinter, had been tending casualties in the minefield and evacuating them on twin stretchers fixed over the engine covers of his scout car. Time and time again, they drove into the minefields and artillery fire, a feat which won them both gallantry awards.

Captain Bishop had been a doctor in pre-war Birmingham where he worked at the city hospital. He joined the Territorial Army in July 1939 and sailed with The Fiftieth to North Africa. He recalls his short stay in the desert, thus:

> Shortly after arriving in the desert, the main medical problem was 'Gyppy tummy', which I think we all had at some stage. Jaundice was not really a problem for me as the incubation period was about three months.
>
> The action I recall the most was at Alamein; there were casualties of course, but not as many as we had expected. I probably treated more Highlanders than I did our own chaps. One big problem was getting the wounded out of knocked-out tanks as in the majority of cases, all we could do for the wounded was to apply a No 1 Field Dressing and give them a morphine injection, prior to loading them onto our scout car, which had

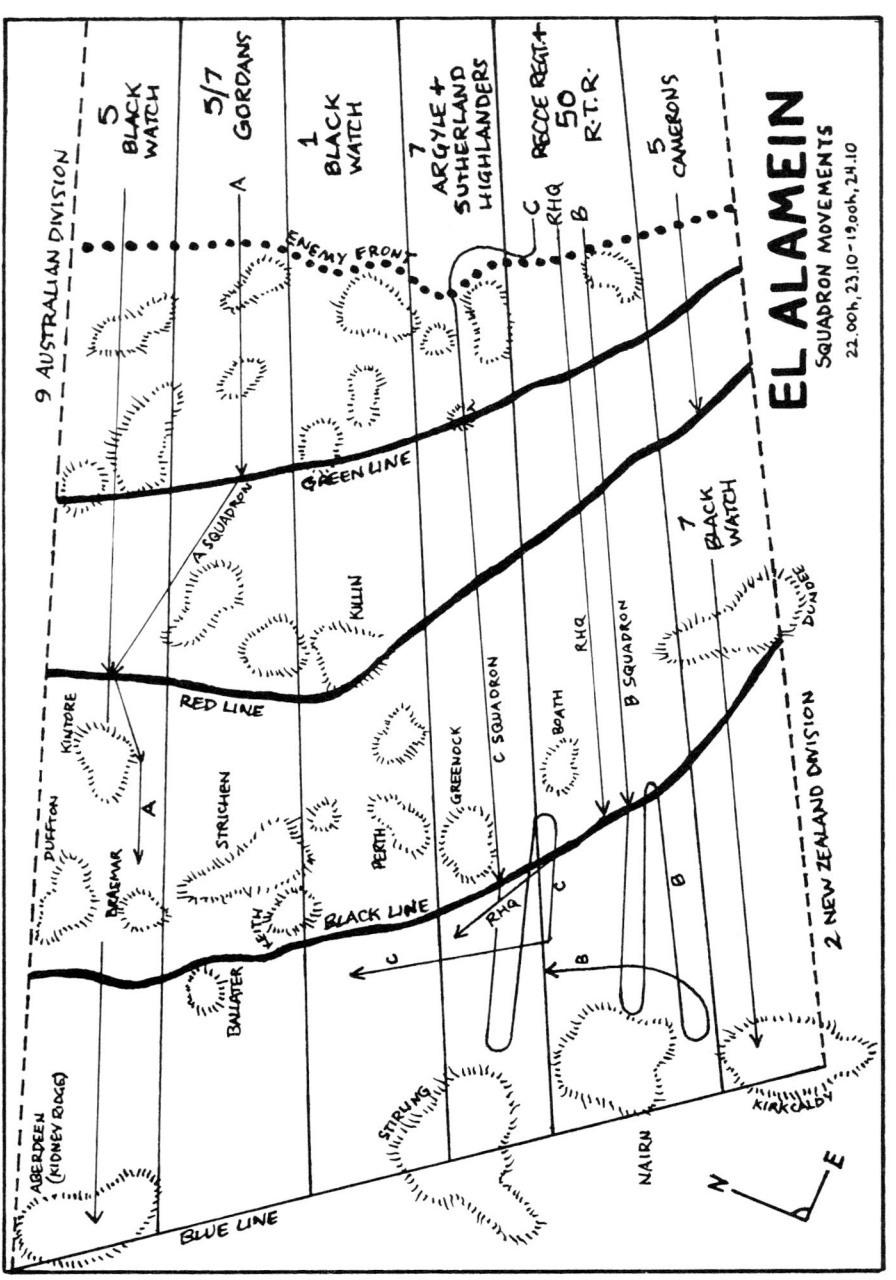

Map 2: 'El Alamein'. Dispositions of 51st Highland Division and movements of 50 RTR during the early stages of the battle. 23/24 October 1942.

two stretchers fixed on top – and taking them to the nearest dressing station.

The assault troops and gapping party now pushed forward, lighting the route as they went, but they struck a second minefield only a few hundred yards further on. This was much shallower in depth, and they succeeded in forcing a gap through it by 0400 hours. They were under fire the whole time and still suffering casualties. The tanks were able to go through and suffered only one casualty in the approach to this particular lane, a B Squadron tank having its track blown off by a mine at the second gap.

B Squadron put in an attack on NAIRN from a position approximately on the BLACK Line. At this stage 50 RTR were still under heavy enemy artillery fire and were so close to their own barrage that some of these shells fell amongst the tanks and infantry. Although the moon was still up, visibility was poor, because of the smoke and dust raised by the barrage.

Regimental Headquarters remained in B Squadron's forming-up place, whilst the squadron advanced on NAIRN with the remaining troops of the Reconnaissance Squadron riding on the tanks. The shelling from both Allied and Axis guns, however, was so bad that the infantry had to get off the tanks and walk. Major Peter Carter, Commanding B Squadron, was convinced there was no opposition from NAIRN, but there was heavy shelling, machine-gun fire and sniping coming from the direction of STIRLING, a strongly defended locality which had not, apparently, been taken by the Argylls.

Major Carter had just given the order to 'form line abreast and overrun the guns' when he noticed a low wire just in front of his tank and asked the infantry commander to investigate and try to find out whether or not it was a minefield. The infantry commander said he thought it was safe to advance, so Major Carter's tank went forward and was nevertheless blown up on a mine, as were two other tanks in the squadron which now blocked the route for the remaining tanks of the squadron and who, of course, could not now comply with Major Carter's order.

At this time the infantry were suffering casualties from their own shelling because they were so close to the barrage. Since the aim of the attack was to overrun NAIRN and there did not appear to be any opposition there, it was decided not to risk any more tanks in the minefield and from the shelling on STIRLING, but to rally to the rear and take up positions in readiness for any enemy counter-attack which might develop at daybreak.

NAIRN, as expected, was found to be clear, but STIRLING was still held by the enemy. Their tanks were seen forming up for a counter-attack but they did not come within range of 50 RTR's guns. Major

*Figure 13: Officers of RHQ, Alamein, October, 1942. (from left to right) Capt John Orbach, Capt A G Atkinson, Capt Gerald Chapman, Adjutant, Lt-Col John Cairnes C.O., Major Geoff Russell, 2nd in command. (J Orbach)*

Carter, with his remaining five tanks, went forward to the high ground between NAIRN and KIRKCALDY, where he contacted troops of the 7th Battalion The Black Watch on their final objective. It was from this position that he reported enemy tanks milling around west of 50 RTR's final objective, but showing no signs of putting in an attack.

There remained scattered mines in the NAIRN area and Major Carter lost one more tank, its suspension being damaged. The presence of the tanks behind the final objective at dawn enabled the infantry to consolidate and dig in their anti-tank guns.

At first light C Squadrons Ten Troop, led by Second-Lieutenant Vic Senior's 'point' tank, were roughly on the BLACK Line. They had had a difficult night but managed to get through the minefields to a lying-up position. Having gone through the Argylls' gap in the first enemy minefield, they had contacted a detachment of divisional sappers with one Scorpion and had forced a way through the second field under heavy shell fire. After this, progress was very slow. They advanced at walking pace behind the Engineers. Numerous trip wires attached to large mines were encountered, and several exploded, destroying one Bren carrier. Heavy shell fire was experienced during the advance. Progress was so slow that Major Williams, temporarily commanding C

Squadron, decided to dispense with the engineer reconnaissance party and continue at a faster speed in the path of the Scorpion. A minefield was encountered and the Scorpion began to sweep but was blown up. Despite this the sappers forced a gap.

While waiting for the gap to be made, C Squadron had made contact with the Black Watch to the north and a party of the Argylls, who were trying to get a message through to brigade headquarters. This party offered to lead C Squadron to GREENOCK, where the Argylls' regimental headquarters were situated, then about twenty minutes' walking distance away.

One of C Squadron's tanks, commanded by Lieutenant Cliff Wykes, was hit while travelling through the gap and two infantrymen riding on the back were killed. The advance continued and a further minefield was encountered on the forward slope of the high ground leading up to STIRLING. This field was covered by enemy artillery, machine-guns and snipers. A party of infantry went forward through the minefield to cover the sappers while they forced a gap for the tanks, but were forced to retire under very heavy fire.

The chief difficulty at this stage was that neither Major Williams nor the commander of his infantry company could contact the main body of the Argylls for the final assault on STIRLING. But for the additional minefield this might have been done.

The position at this time (about 0500 hours), was that the infantry were unable to establish a bridgehead to cover the sappers, and Major Williams was not prepared to advance blindly through the minefield since he wished to conserve his tank strength for any enemy counter-attack which might have developed at dawn. However, an attack was ordered, but subsequently cancelled when Sergeant Nash's Ten Troop tank was blown up on a mine. The infantry commander decided to dismount his men from the tanks, take them through the minefield and work round to try to join the main body of the Argylls, should they be having difficulty in the neighbourhood of STIRLING. Dawn was now breaking and C Squadron, who were attracting considerable artillery fire, rallied to a forward lying-up position, ready for any counter-attack. The enemy did not attack and the Squadron remained in this position in support of the infantry, under heavy shell fire, until it was ordered to rejoin Regimental Headquarters and B Squadron later in the day.

A Squadron on the right, commanded by Major Styles, got through the minefields on 153 Brigade's front with less difficulty. They were warned at 2359 hours that the gap in the first minefield encountered had been made, although the sappers had suffered fairly heavy casualties from accurate enemy mortar and artillery fire, where the gap was being made. This indicated that some enemy observation posts must have escaped unnoticed when the forward infantry went through.

At 0140 hours Major Styles was told the gap in the second minefield was clear.

Captain Barker, from the 1st Gordon Highlanders, met the squadron on the GREEN Line and guided them to the RED Line, where they linked up with the Gordons in the area west of KINTORE. At 0310 hours Major Styles met the Gordons' commanding officer, who said he was out of touch with his two leading companies. The infantry were being harassed by enemy machine-guns firing from the direction of BRAEMAR and DUFFTOWN, so A Squadron launched an attack with D Company of the Gordons, with the object of clearing the machine-guns. Having advanced about 400 yards, however, they struck a minefield and the leading tank was blown up. Major Styles halted the squadron and tried to find a way round, but they was no gap. Sergeant Ellery commanding a tank in Four Troop, was informed by his driver that the tank was stuck and would not move.

Ellery dismounted to discover barbed wire wrapped around the tracks; after removing the barbed wire with wire-cutters he found himself standing next to a German sign for mines. After consulting with his driver Trooper Clifford, they decided to reverse the tank back exactly on their own track marks. Guided back by Ellery, Clifford was able to reverse the tank out safely, allowing them to get clear.

Corporal Eddie Prett, in A Squadron's One Troop that night, recalls:
Our objective was a machine gun post, on the way we hit a mine which took a track off. We sat tight for a while but soon became a practice target for friendly and enemy gunners.

I decided there was no future sitting there so we nullified the fighting capability of the tank, and attempted to trudge back through our own lines, after some hairy situations we made it and were ferried back to a unit of flail tanks.

At daylight it was decided to rally the tanks in support of the infantry in readiness for a counter-attack. The infantry were consolidating on a line based on BRAEMAR and DUFFTOWN. During the night Major Styles had three tank casualties, one of which was by shell fire and two on mines. At 0900 hours A Squadron reported 20 German and Italian tanks on the high ground, ABERDEEN, being engaged by Shermans of X Corps, which had come up on the right of the Squadron's position. Three enemy tanks were seen to be knocked out by the Shermans. No enemy tank attack developed on A Squadron's front, and they remained in that area all day under shell fire, until recalled to join the remainder of the regiment in the evening.

Regimental Headquarters, together with B and C Squadrons were shelled heavily during the early part of the morning, but there was a lull towards midday, when orders were received that an afternoon attack was to be put in against STIRLING, with the aim of putting X Corps armour through. The regiment, less A Squadron, were to create a diversion by advancing across the front of STIRLING towards BALLATER and engaging any targets which presented themselves.

The attack was mounted with C Squadron (nine tanks) leading, followed by Regimental Headquarters (four tanks), and with B Squadron (four tanks) in reserve. The regiment very soon ran into heavy shell and anti-tank fire from the direction of STIRLING, and one of C Squadron's tanks was penetrated by an armour-piercing shot, which killed Troopers Travers and Gee. C Squadron then ran onto a minefield and seven of their tanks were immobilised, but they continued to man the turrets.

In the meantime B Squadron and Regimental Headquarters had wheeled round and taken up positions from which they could use their Besa machine-guns on enemy infantry. The regiment attracted much of the enemy's attention in that area, thereby creating a diversion, while units of X Corps advanced on STIRLING.

C Squadron was under heavy fire in the minefield, so Major Williams eventually decided to evacuate the surviving crews. He succeeded in getting all of them back safely on foot; Troopers Travers and Gee were buried later on the battlefield.

By late afternoon a large number of X Corps tanks were behind and to the right of 50 RTR, and in the failing light the regiment was ordered to retire and leaguer east of Tel el Eisa railway station, where they were joined by the remaining tanks of A Squadron.

During these overnight operations, the regiment achieved its main objective in that it succeeded in reaching lying-up positions through heavily defended enemy areas and minefields, and was ready to support the infantry against any counter-attack at daybreak. The presence of tanks at all times had a very considerable stiffening effect on the infantry, but a frightening effect on enemy infantry and their isolated gun positions, since the noise of the tanks advancing through the night could be heard over a large area. The Corps Commander himself later expressed the opinion that the presence of tanks reduced casualties among his own infantry, and induced enemy prisoners to surrender much more quickly and with less resistance than they otherwise might have done.

The regiment's strength by 25 October was nineteen battle-worthy tanks, and others were being recovered; the operation had begun with only 40 tanks. Most of the casualties were on mines. There were an unusual number of mechanical breakdowns, due mainly to the fact that many tanks were received from workshops only just before the offensive began and had not had sufficient preparation.

On the morning of 26 October A Squadron was ordered to STIRLING, then in British hands. A Squadron remained there in support of the infantry, holding it all day and night under shell fire. During this period Trooper Welsby was killed and Lieutenant Woods and Trooper Frost were wounded by mortar fire while dismounting from their tank.

On 27 October the regiment came under command of 4th Indian Division, and were joined by A Squadron in the evening. On 28 October they reverted once again to 23 Armoured Brigade and moved back to their former position near the railway. B Squadron remained with the Indian Division on Ruweisat Ridge and rejoined the regiment on 29 October.

Between 25 and 30 October every effort was made to re-organise and repair as many tanks as possible. During this time 50 RTR were leaguered among their own artillery, which was incessantly engaging enemy positions. Enemy shelling of the gun positions at night was unpleasantly close but no vehicles or personnel were hit. The men got no undisturbed rest. It seemed that the German guns had unlimited supplies of ammunition. It was during this period that Stukas attacked the regimental leaguer. During one such raid, both the regimental Medical Officer, Captain Bishop, and his driver, Trooper Midwinter, were badly wounded, the doctor losing an arm and his driver a leg.

Colonel Cairnes wrote: 'A tragedy as he is a good surgeon and many on the battlefield owe their lives to him. He will be a great loss to us. His courage and guts under fire were a byword throughout the brigade.'

Captain Bishop's post was taken over by Captain Anderson, Royal Army Medical Corps, until January 1943 when Captain A R P Ellis was posted to the Fiftieth, from 12 Field Regiment RA, as medical officer.

50 RTR was warned on 30 October that a large scale New Zealand attack would be launched on the following night, with the aim of putting X Corps through further north. The plan was postponed for 24 hours to give more time for preparation; it was mounted on the Sunday night, 1 November. This was the beginning of operation SUPERCHARGE, the Eighth Army's final attempt to break Rommels line and break out into the desert beyond.

The regiment left its leaguer area at 2230 hours and moved on an axis lit and gapped entirely by New Zealand sappers. The journey to the final objective, where they were to support 152 Highland Brigade (2nd and 5th Battalions The Seaforth Highlanders, and 5th Battalion The Cameron Highlanders) was not as hazardous as the operations on the night of 23/24 October, since they did not experience the same difficulty with minefields. There was no moon until the small hours of 2 November and visibility was almost nil because of dust on the track. The tanks moved head to tail but, even so, commanders were losing sight of the vehicle immediately in front. Most vehicles switched their tail lights on but quite often these were obscured by blinding sand.

During the advance behind the infantry, Colonel Cairnes' tank was fired on by an anti-tank gun which had, apparently, seen the navigating officer's tail light. Colonel Cairnes was travelling behind the navigating officer and the gun opened up when the tanks made a right angled turn to get onto the route. The moon was coming up leaving the tanks silhouetted. Shells landed just short of the Colonel's tank. Light enemy shelling continued during the advance, but there were no casualties.

Dawn was beginning to break as 50 RTR approached the Camerons' objective, and B and C Squadrons fanned out into battle formation. Suddenly, in the half light, an anti-tank gun screen to the immediate left and front opened fire. It was difficult to see their positions, but armour piercing shot and machine-gun tracer were whistling all round the tanks. 50 RTR replied with their Besas and threw out smoke, while manoeuvring for good fire positions. Unfortunately, the C Squadron command tank was hit several times, wounding the gunner, and an 88mm shot holed the turret, just after Major Williams and his crew had baled out. Major Williams resumed command in another tank. Captain Jolley's tank was knocked out and another B Squadron tank was hit, killing Sergeant Essex. The Headquarter tanks came under heavy fire, which stopped after the Besa machine guns had opened up and the smoke had been laid.

At dawn, 50 RTR were in good fire positions behind the Camerons' objective and a large number of Sherman and Cruiser tanks of X Corps passed through. The enemy gave no indication of putting in a counter-attack of any consequence, although there was still desultory fire from anti-tank guns on the left.

Regimental Headquarters eventually positioned itself turret-down on the left flank. From here the area to the south, occupied by the enemy, could be watched and support given to the Camerons on their objective 1,000 yards to the west. A and B Squadrons went forward to contact the infantry and to protect them during their consolidation. C Squadron were in reserve. There were scattered mines and small unmarked minefields in this area and several tanks ran onto them and had their tracks blown off or suspension damaged. Tank strength at this stage was: Regimental Headquarters – four, A Squadron – seven, B Squadron – seven and C Squadron – six.

The regiment was shelled all that day; the enemy laying down his fire in short, heavy and accurate concentrations in obvious places such as the ridge from which Regimental Headquarters was lying back about 200 yards. This shelling did no damage. Stukas came over, but they chose to bomb the Shermans who were sitting back, at long range, and knocking out German tanks west and south-west of 50 RTR's position.

Colonel Cairnes was called to a conference with the Brigade Commander, at which he learned that his regiment was to attack and capture Point 38 that evening with the remaining troops of the 2nd

Battalion The Seaforth Highlanders, who had been fighting all night and had already lost one company. Tired and without rations, they were given a special reserve box of 80 battle rations, which 50 RTR had been keeping for themselves.

The attack was to be in the form of a set-piece infantry tank advance, B Squadron leading and supported by a detachment from 295 Field Company, Royal Engineers, with A Squadron as the second wave with the leading infantry, followed by Regimental Headquarters and C Squadron with the reserve infantry. The Seaforths were very scattered and some difficulty was experienced in rallying them in time for the start at 1800 hours, when seven regiments of artillery were to lay concentrations on given localities from which the attackers might encounter resistance. The attack was mounted a few minutes after H-Hour, when the barrage began.

It went according to plan. B Squadron was on its objective in a very short time, taking about 100 Italian prisoners, who had come out of their holes waving white handkerchiefs at the sound of the approaching tanks. A Squadron put the infantry on the objective, and both squadrons rallied back at nightfall into close leaguer with Regimental Headquarters.

Major Carter, commanding B Squadron, had to change tanks twice during the advance, one being damaged on a mine and the other being hit. Major Styles, commanding A Squadron, also had to change tanks, because his own was knocked out by high explosive shells. He also lost another tank on mines.

50 RTR then leaguered in their forming up area, and the following morning Major Williams took four C Squadron tanks and three tanks from A Squadron to support the Seaforths on the objective. The infantry were having difficulty in consolidating, because of enemy snipers and machine-guns, and they had had casualties during the night. Two A Squadron tanks were blown up on mines and Major Williams had to change tanks quickly, because his gunner, Trooper Ashwell, was killed beside him in the turret by shrapnel from an air-burst. With his remaining four tanks however, he succeeded in clearing the area by sweeping it with machine-gun fire, and the Seaforths were able to dig-in. These four tanks stayed under shell fire with the infantry the greater part of the day.

In the afternoon the regiment was ordered back to leaguer and here they re-organised, with a Regimental Headquarters of four tanks and a composite squadron of twelve tanks commanded by Major Carter, for an attack with 5 Indian Infantry Brigade (4th Indian Division) that night. They were joined by a squadron of 46 RTR, under Major Eric Offord, the whole composite regiment being commanded by Colonel Cairnes.

Colonel Offord of 46 RTR recalls:

We had suffered heavy casualties and were withdrawn to refit. I could only muster a squadron. We had less than 24 hours refit when we were recalled to the battle, we eventually joined The Fiftieth who had two squadrons fit. This joint 50/46 RTR served in operation SUPERCHARGE, which helped with the breakthrough to the open desert.

The aim of this attack was to capture a stretch of the Rahman track four miles south of Tel el Aqqaqir. This would widen the gap made by the New Zealand Division's thrust and let the armour through in the area of Kidney Ridge. The advance met with little opposition and was entirely successful, one complete armoured brigade being put through just north of the Ridge in the early hours of 4 November.

The journey from the start point to Kidney Ridge entailed advancing over five miles in the dark through scattered minefields. There was a good deal of dust, particularly in the area where the barrage had fallen. Orders had been received that in no circumstances were tanks to be lost unnecessarily, so Colonel Cairnes decided to advance well in the rear of the infantry, and to arrive on the objective in support of them at first light. Regimental Headquarters led the advance, but, despite all precautions, the navigating officer's tank went up on a mine. He changed tanks and continued the advance, but it was eventually decided that rather than risk any more casualties, they would halt and go flat out for the objective at dawn. This was done and contact was made with the infantry on the objective and astride the Rahman Track.

For the infantry, the move up to the forming up area was of extraordinary complexity, which involved pulling back from the front line followed by a twelve mile approach march, mainly by night and through soft sand. Their anti-tank guns and transport carrying the 3/10 Baluch Regiment were unable to negotiate the soft sand on their axis of advance and had to be left in the rear. The Baluchis however, continued the march on foot. Meanwhile, the remaining infantry of 5 Brigade went on to the objective, which they took in one dramatic hour, taking 351 prisoners for a cost of 80 casualties.

As dawn approached, as the infantry could see the dim shapes of their own Bren gun carriers and 50 RTR's Valentines approaching, they felt relieved. As one Essex officer remarked, 'It was getting lonely up there.' The 4th Indian Division History reads:

> The kidney-shaped ridge was in our hands. The 5th Brigade had gone clean through the enemy lines to a depth of over eight thousand yards. Then came thunder out of the east as rank after rank of tanks came roaring past, plunged through the infantry and turned north for the kill. The sun rose on the last of Alamein.

Until about midday 50 RTR was the infantry's sole protection against possible counter-attack. There was also the danger that isolated enemy

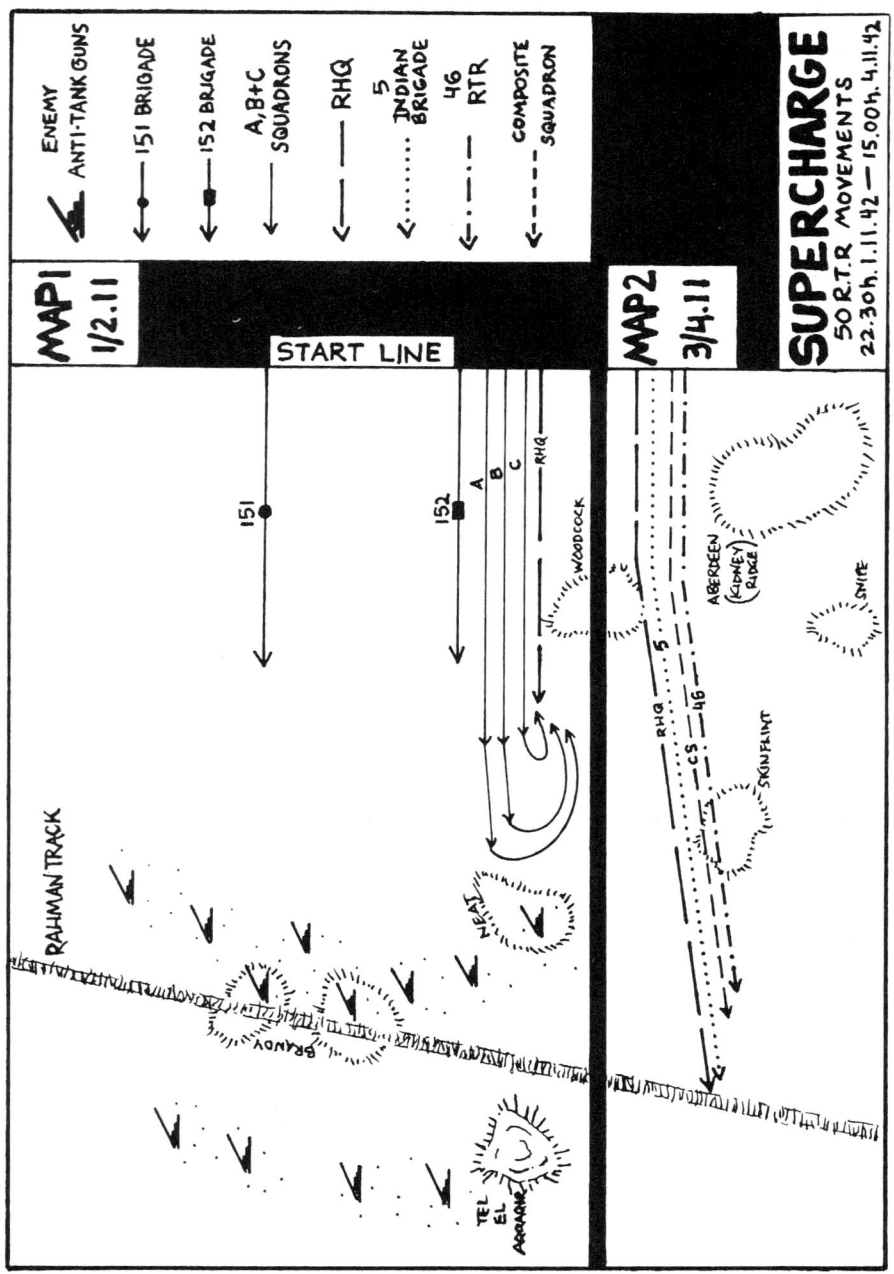

Map 3: 'Supercharge'. Final two attempts to break out into the open desert. 1/2 and 3/4 November 1942.

tanks which had been cut off might try to break through from the rear and so careful watch was kept against this, but no counter-attack developed.

Since the night of 23/24 October, the battle had been going badly for the Axis forces and news of this had by now reached Berlin. At 1330 hours on 3 November, Rommel received the following order from the Fuehrer:

> It is with trusting confidence in your leadership and the courage of the German-Italian troops under your command that the German people and I are following the heroic struggle in Egypt. In the situation in which you find yourself there can be no other thought but to stand fast, yield not a yard of ground and throw every gun and every man into the battle. Considerable air force reinforcements are being sent to C in C South. The Duce and Commando Supremo are also making the utmost efforts to send you the means to continue the fight. Your enemy, despite his superiority, must also be at the end of his strength. It would not be the first time in history that a strong will has triumphed over the bigger battalions. As to your troops, you can show them no other road than that to victory or death.

All along the line successes similar to that of 50 RTR and 5 Indian Brigade ensured that operation SUPERCHARGE and the breakthrough into the open desert was a complete success. It also made a mockery of Hitler's order.

In the afternoon of 4 November, 50 RTR returned to their old position beside the railway and spent the next few days re-organising. During this period and throughout the operation, recovery vehicles and workshops worked day and night to recover and repair damaged tanks. When the regiment moved up to El Daba on 9 November (by which time Rommel was in full retreat and X Corps were on their way to Bardia), they had 40 tanks and were ready to offer battle again. Throughout the Alamein operation Major W D Bazley and Squadron Sergeant-Major H.D. Price had ensured that the crews were never short of fuel, food or water. Often under fire and over difficult country the echelon never failed to reach the tanks.

It was now that Brigadier Richards chose to go on leave, leaving Colonel Cairnes in command of the whole of 23 Armoured Brigade.

On the same day the regiment received the following letter of thanks, from Lieutenant-Colonel K Mackessick, commanding the 2nd Battalion The Seaforth Highlanders:

> Dear Cairnes
> I am at last able to write you a short note to thank you for all you did for my battalion on the 3/4 Nov, particularly in helping us

out with food and other comforts. It was an extremely welcome gesture on your part and very much appreciated by us, who, as you know, were unable to get anything up that night.

I hope I shall be able to thank your Squadron Leaders personally very shortly, but, in the meantime, please believe we are all most sincerely grateful.

50 RTR's casualties during this history-making battle were one NCO and five other ranks killed, a further two men died of their wounds. Three officers and eleven other ranks were wounded. Two A Squadron crews and one from B Squadron were initially listed as missing; it was later discovered that after losing their tanks on mines they had joined ranks with the infantry, before rejoining their own regiment. Recommendations were made for one Distinguished Service Order, two Military Crosses, two Military Medals and eight Mentions in Despatches.

# Chapter 5
# THROUGH THE TAGURA GATE

## To Tripoli and Beyond

From 1 to 5 November, recovery units, brigade workshops and the regiment's own Light Aid Detachment and fitters had worked so well, both during and after the initial stages of the Alamein offensive, that by the time The Fiftieth had to move to the Bir Siheirat area on 9 November they had more tanks than when they went into action on the first night, 23 October. The regiment was again ready to offer battle, although at this stage X Corps were pushing into Cyrenaica and it did not appear likely 50 RTR would be called upon unless there was a serious hold-up of the advancing armour. The month of November was spent in training and re-organising.

On the night of 5th, some of the tank crews decided to celebrate Guy Fawkes' night, by letting off a number of flares. This attracted a German bomber, which then proceeded to bomb 50 RTR's position and put an immediate end to the celebrations. Fortunately for the regiment, none of the bombs exploded.

During this period 50 RTR moved gradually west and had reached a position south of Mersa Matruh by the end of the month. XXX Corps had been drawn into reserve but were aware they would be later relieving X Corps in the Benghazi-Agedabia area, and the regiment would probably be used to help crush the Axis resistance in the Agheila bottleneck, the most likely place for Rommel to make a stand.

While at Bir Siheirat, the regiment spent a number of days salvaging abandoned Italian and German equipment. The desert was littered with it. Priority was given to guns, vehicles and clothing. Many strange items were brought in, but the most peculiar item to grace any 50 RTR leaguer was driven in by the fitters: it was an enormous troop – carrying half-track, which had no less than eighteen wheels.

Leave began on the 16th, short periods of four days in Alexandria. By the end of the month the regiment was en route for El Adem. The tanks were to go by rail from 'Charing Cross'; it was also decided that 46 RTR were to lose their equipment and go back to the Delta, leaving the brigade with only two armoured regiments. There were at this time not enough Valentines in the Middle East for a complete brigade and a reasonable reserve. 50 RTR was then made up to full strength with vehicles from 46 RTR. One problem at this time was the number of men sick with jaundice; 50 during November, twelve of whom were officers, including the second-in-command, Major Russell and the next senior officer Major Bazley.

During December the three-ton lorry which carried most of the regimental documents and war diaries caught fire on the move and was completely destroyed.

Colonel John Cairnes wrote at the time:

My fly-proof office lorry went up in smoke the other day, (10th Dec). I lost my diary which I had kept for a year, and all my letters, photos, pay book and papers etc. and £8 in cash. Poor Gerald Chapman, my Adjutant, lost all his kit and bedding. On top of it all we lost a lot of valuable equipment including one of our wireless sets with which we got the BBC news. It is a bad time to have lost these things, as we are out in the blue and it will be ages before anything can be replaced.

December, however, turned out to be the most uneventful month 50 RTR had spent in the desert, except for a move from Matruh to El Adem, south of Tobruk, where they sat grounded from the 12th until the 31st. Colonel John Cairnes again:

We have been on the move a lot lately. Have had no mail for a month due to our moves. I fear a lot of the troops' mail may have been lost, as we hear all mail posted in England between 7th and 13th September was sunk. We have lagged behind in the chase after Rommel and have halted now about 20 miles south of Tobruk.

What our next job will be goodness only knows. Meanwhile my chief job is to keep the troops on their toes and prevent them from getting bored. They are in fine fettle at the moment and ready for anything.

I have arranged a programme of competitions up to the end of the month to cover all our activities and make everyone perform. The cooks' competition is to make a birthday cake for the CO!!

Strict rationing of fuel and lubricants, owing to Eighth Army's ever-increasing lines of communication and the urgency of getting supplies up to the forward troops, prevented the regiment from doing any training with tanks or B Echelon vehicles. During the stay at El Adem 50 RTR came temporarily under command of the 50th Northumbrian Infantry Division, but they could not train together because of the fuel shortage. A few days before the regiment moved on the 31st, all the tanks got a short run of ten miles, during which they practised the standard drill for an attack with infantry on a defended position.

During the last two weeks of the month, Colonel Cairnes organised a series of inter-squadron and inter-troop competitions, consisting of tank maintenance, radio procedure, navigation, small arms firing, squadron drill and turn-out, first aid, cooking, dramatics and several sports. The variety of these competitions was so wide that every man in the regiment found something in which he was interested. Colonel Cairnes' idea was to keep the men physically and mentally active during a very trying period. The title of Champion Squadron, which had gone to B Squadron on the voyage from England, went to A Squadron in this competition with C Squadron taking the wooden spoon.

The regiment had not received any mail during December, even though Colonel Cairnes had sent a truck 900 miles to collect it: for some obscure reason the postal authorities would not hand it over. So the Intelligence Officer, Captain John Orbach, flew from El Adem to 'Marble Arch' on Christmas Eve to collect it (Marble Arch, the *Arco Philaenorum* near Agheila, had been built by Mussolini on the site of an ancient Roman shrine, unlike 'Piccadilly Circus', 'Charing Cross' and 'Knightsbridge' which were originally just map references). John Orbach arrived back on Boxing Day with 46 mail bags, which made him very popular. Early in September, the regiment had ordered extra supplies from NAAFI in time for Christmas, but as these did not arrive, extra food was obtained from Tobruk. Everybody was in good spirits and Colonel Cairnes received a warm welcome when he visited the squadrons at dinner and the officers dined regimentally for the first time since leaving the UK. Orders were then received for the regiment's move forward, and on 31 December they left on the first leg of the journey to Agheila.

By 3 January 1943 adverse weather conditions caused the whole of the 50th Infantry Division, under whose orders 50 RTR were moving, to become bogged down fifteen miles north-east of Msus. By the 5th, the weather had improved slightly and the regiment managed to travel 30 miles to Solluch, moving slowly so that the lighter vehicles would not out-pace the heavier tank transporters.

After stopping to refuel at Agedabia, Agheila was reached in the late afternoon of the 7th; on the 8th, the transporters carrying the tanks were moving down the coast road towards the Sirte area. Crews were warned they would be rejoining their vehicles by the 10th. The regiment then lost 22 of its three-ton trucks to 22 Armoured Brigade for its march on Tripoli. After managing to get their vehicles through a water-logged desert, it was learned that they were not to be used in the forthcoming operations after all. So the regiment moved to Nofilia, passing through Marble Arch where the tanks had stopped and unloaded. 50 RTR was to remain there and await orders. 40 RTR had already moved forward

*Figure 14: 2nd in command, Major Russell (left) and the Adjutant Capt G Chapman en route to Tripoli, January 1943. (Dr Ellis)*

and were preparing, with the 51st Highland Division, for battle. Freddie August remembers the long desert journey:

> At El Adem we were on top of a plateau with nothing to stop the cold north wind blowing in from the Mediterranean. Were we glad when the transporters came early in the New Year to take us up to the front, then at Buerat – hundreds of miles on, across Cyrenaica and Tripolitania.
>
> I thoroughly enjoyed that eight or nine days' run along the coast road – to see the miracle of the green hills and the colonists' farms of Cyrene strangely reminiscent of the Downs on a misty day – what a change after months of the Western Desert!
>
> I remember vividly the first night we leaguered up among these hills – the first time for months we found difficulty in finding a flat space for our beds among the sweet smelling turf. It rained during the night and in the morning we had to off-load the tanks from the transporters, so that we could tow them to the road, as the rain had bogged them. Later that day we lost the convoy, as our progress was painfully slow. At every hill the trailer had to be unhitched, the unit going to the top and winching the tanks and trailers up behind them. We had had enough of the rain by then even though we had been praying for some for six months.
>
> It turned out for the best in the end though that we had lost the convoy, as that night the rains came again and the winds blew,

but we were safe and cosy in one of Mussolini's road houses, with a nice fire and a hot meal.

We caught up with the rest of the convoy about 11.00am the next morning, shortly after descending the breathtaking Barce Pass. They were trying to extricate themselves from a flooded field, they had misguidedly leaguered in the previous night. From there we entered the desert again passing through Benghazi and Agheila to our forward line at Buerat.

On 15 January, Eighth Army's offensive to capture Tripoli began. 50 RTR was ordered to the Wadi el Chebir to take up defensive positions astride the road and on the high ground west of the wadi, initially as Corps reserve, but also in a good position to stop any enemy armour breaking out and disrupting the lines of communication. On the 19th, C Squadron was ordered to move forward as replacements for 40 RTR as and when required.

Tripoli fell to Eighth Army on 23 January 1943. The first tanks to enter the city were C Squadron 40 RTR followed by C Squadron 50 RTR. Second-Lieutenant Senior was loaned to 40 RTR for the final entry into Tripoli and he, in fact, led the advance into the city in a 40 RTR tank called 'Dorothy', driven by Trooper Dignum, a 46 RTR driver. On arrival in the main square, they found a troop of armoured cars from 11 Hussars already there, they had beaten them to it by another route from the south. Commanded by Major Dicky Venn, C Squadron 50 RTR entered Tripoli by the Tagura Gate in brilliant moonlight, shortly after 0500 hours; their objective was the harbour, which they reached without opposition.

C Squadron had been first called upon three days after the march to Tripoli began. They were at full strength with sixteen tanks, taken forward on transporters up the main road, though many diversions had to be made when enemy rearguards blew up the road and bridges. This, and the danger of mines sown along the edge of the road, made the going extremely difficult for the transporters. By nightfall on the 20th, the column was two miles south of Misurata. Only one transporter failed to get there, having broken down. Major Venn contacted a scout car and was told the squadron must push on beyond Misurata if at all possible.

Meanwhile Colonel Cairnes had been at the front, at Leptis Magna, with Brigadier Richards and the leading squadrons of 40 RTR. Colonel Cairnes returned to C Squadron to order a push to Leptis Magna the following morning, where they would off-load and receive fresh instructions. He then returned to the front, where Brigadier Richards was commanding a pursuit force consisting of one squadron of 40 RTR, 1st Battalion The Gordon Highlanders, a battery of 25-pounder guns and a company of sappers.

The objective of this force, which left Leptis Magna at 1700 hours on 20 January, was Castel Verde. They expected to reach their objective before dawn on the 21st. However, they ran into an ambush shortly after leaving Homs; difficult countryside prevented the tanks from leaving the road; it had been breached in three places, and repairs took much longer than the sappers anticipated. It was not clear until 2230 hours that night.

Colonel Cairnes returned to Leptis Magna at 1500 hours to find C Squadron held up by 22 Armoured Brigade, who were going through. The squadron off-loaded and the men had a meal while Colonel Cairnes gave all tank commanders a picture of the battle. He told them they were to join the pursuit force commanded by Brigadier Richards and if 22 Armoured Brigade were not blocking the road, they would stand a good chance of catching them up.

In the meantime, the pursuit force was held up by another breach in the road. Brigadier Richards who had gone with them, returned to arrange for C Squadron to carry one company of the Gordons, and that they should move ahead of the other traffic on the road. This they did by double-banking for two or three miles. By the time the pursuit force was able to push on, C Squadron was in position behind them.

The force advanced through the night, despite several blown bridges and breaches in the road en route, but no considerable difficulty was experienced in constructing diversions. It was decided the tanks, with Brigadier Richards in his armoured car, and Colonel Cairnes in a scout car, should push forward without guns or lorried infantry. By 0800 hours on 22 January, the column had reached Castel Verde without any casualties and the Brigadier took over the town from the local chief of police. The tanks then went a mile west of the town to take up defensive positions. A troop of armoured cars of 12 Lancers overtook them, and made contact with the enemy. Surprised, the enemy opened fire with rifles, mortars and a 37mm anti-tank gun. The Valentines deployed for action, 40 RTR on the right and C Squadron 50 RTR on the left. Leaving the road was very bad going for the tanks and C Squadron had to deploy among soft sand dunes, where one tank shed a track. However, the enemy rearguard showed no signs of a fight and left in a great hurry under a smoke screen, before the tanks could get into action against them.

The crews rallied and brewed up for breakfast, when the Army Commander (Montgomery) arrived and told Brigadier Richards his force was to remain at Castel Verde and let 22 Armoured Brigade go through. However, at 1830 hours Lieutenant Ted Jenkin, who was acting liaison officer between Montgomery and Brigadier Richards, returned from Army Tactical Headquarters with orders for the pursuit force to go through the leading troops of 22 Armoured Brigade and take Tripoli harbour. The main body of the Brigade were to swing south and enter the city from the other side. Brigadier Richards left his orders and returned to Army Tactical Headquarters. Colonel Cairnes then marshalled the pursuit force. The column moved forward at 1915 hours. It was completely dark, and there was no moon. Progress was very slow because of the increased danger of mines and enemy ambushes near Tripoli itself; there were several enforced halts along the road.

C Squadron found the city deserted, with the local inhabitants barricaded inside their homes. The tanks had orders to open fire if they met any opposition, but they reached the harbour without incident and rallied in the main square near the entrance to the docks. Here Brigadier Richards set up his headquarters – armoured cars of 11 Hussars had beaten the tanks into the city by only a few minutes.

The entry into Tripoli is probably best described by Colonel John Cairnes in a letter he wrote on 25 January 1943:

> I was lucky enough to be amongst the very first troops to enter, and by mistake I was nearly the first British soldier to enter. I believe some armoured cars beat us by a few minutes but only because we took our time over the last few miles in case there were mines or booby traps about. Some of my tanks led the party with as many Jocks as they could carry riding on the outside. I was in a jeep and as we drew near the town I went ahead to see if the tanks were keeping in touch. In doing so I miscounted the number of tanks and thinking there were still some tanks ahead I speeded on towards the town. Ted Jenkins, a young subaltern, was with me. There we were speeding down the wide deserted street at 5am in the morning with nothing about us. Suddenly we realised there were no tank tracks on the road so we stopped and found the leading tanks behind us. It was nearly 5.45 when we finally pulled up in the square by the castle, facing the magnificent (but much battered) harbour, (bathed in moonlight it was magnificent), the Jocks soon got busy with their bagpipes.
>
> You wouldn't think a man could play bagpipes sitting on a moving tank. Well it could be if you ever see a newsreel of our entry into Tripoli. The Press were soon on the spot taking photos.
>
> All we wanted to do was wash and shave and sleep, for three days and three nights we had only snatched the odd few minutes sleep here and there, whenever one could find time. Funnily enough I didn't feel tired. It wasn't until I got down to a few hours sleep in the afternoon that I realised how tired I was. The tank drivers were magnificent the way they kept going day and night for 300 miles. The Bosche did everything he could to delay us, and some of the country we came through made this easy for him. All bridges and culverts were blown and some of those in the really hilly country made it very difficult for the sappers to

make a diversion, but they worked wonders and nothing they did could stop the tanks and my jeep. It slid down precipices and across great ravines or wadis and up the other side just like any mountain goat. A wonderful party which I wouldn't have missed for worlds.

Tripoli is an attractive town full of Italians, and natives with eyes popping out with hate at us. It is difficult to tell the natives from the Itie.

Some time later, during the victory celebrations in Tripoli, The Prime Minister, Winston Churchill made a speech to the victorious troops; one famous remark from that speech was: 'In days to come, when asked by those at home what part you played in the war, it will be with pride in your hearts that you can say "I marched with the Eighth Army . . ."'

Colonel John Cairnes tells us about one tank that never quite made it to Tripoli:

We have a tank called Rodney (A Squadron) which toured England to boost tank production, came out here, has been in every action, has done 3,000 miles, has been hit 11 times by German shells, 4 men have been wounded in her. She was hit at Alamein, was repaired under fire by the driver who brought her out, had her repaired by our workshops and then took her in again, when she stood up to another crack.

She was still going strong with her original driver, who has been with her all the time, and is now her commander. Poor old Rodney had to drop out short of Tripoli.

While C Squadron were advancing on Tripoli, the rest of the regiment had been engaged for over a week unloading supplies from landing craft, most of the time spent in the water, as the craft could not get up to the piers. The unloading of supplies at Buerat culminated with 445 tons of petrol in one day – which involved manhandling 1,200 drums – a feat which earned the men a tribute from their Commanding Officer. One B Squadron trooper wrote home: 'I did more hard graft in those few days, than I have ever done in my life before.'

At the beginning of February, the Regiment prepared to move from the Wadi el Chebir area to another area near Tripoli; by the 3rd they had reached Marconi, where they were to spend the next three days. This was the first time since arriving in the Middle East that the men had seen anything like a European city. It was here the regiment first learned that Winston Churchill would be reviewing Eighth Army troops in Tripoli. After arriving at a leaguer area south west of the city on the 6th, some of the men were allowed one day passes into the town C Squadron, however, moved out almost immediately. On 27 January, moving through steep sand dunes, C Squadron bogged down ten of their tanks in an effort to outflank the opposition. Zuara was entered on 1 February after a night attack was launched to shift the enemy rearguard.

Second-Lieutenant Senior of C Squadron wrote home:

At Zuara we were first in. It is a little one-eyed town of 4000 inhabitants mainly Arabs with an Italian administration.

We duly arrived and the officials were so anxious to hand the town over to us. Unfortunately, no-one could speak Italian, so eventually they produced the schoolmaster and I took the place over in bad French. This involved inspecting the Police, Town Hall, issuing orders and so on and eventually a drink with the Mayor and town officials.

Everything went well until the party scattered in disorder with the arrival of a couple of Messerchmitts.

On the 10th, the regiment was again on the move – this time southwest of Zuara, where they were put under command of 131 (Queen's) Infantry Brigade for the forthcoming attack on Ben Gardane, across the border in Tunisia.

The situation at this time was that 7th Armoured Division were pursuing and harassing the enemy in the north while 4 Light Armoured Brigade were patrolling in the south. Armoured cars had now crossed the Tunisian frontier, but 131 Infantry Brigade had been unable to make any progress along the badly damaged coast road. The frontier was marked by a long mud-pan running north to south, which was passable in only one or two places. It was therefore decided to withdraw 131 Infantry Brigade from the coast road and concentrate them in the El Assa area, with the intention of crossing the frontier and capturing Ben Gardane from the south-east.

On 11/12 Febuary the regiment rehearsed a night attack with the 7th Battalion The Queen's Regiment. The following day 50 RTR left El Assa, crossed the Tunisian frontier, and concentrated for the advance to Ben Gardane, which began at 1830 hours. The regiment advanced on the left of 131 Brigade, with B Squadron leading, followed by Regimental Headquarters, C and A Squadrons. Ben Gardane was captured without opposition at 1200 hours on 15 Febuary. The first troops into the town were B Squadron and a few sappers. C Squadron was sent round to the north to clear the area and capture the airfield, which they did without opposition. Regimental Headquarters entered the town from the south east and took up positions on the airfield. Shortly afterwards, an army film crew arrived. They managed to persuade B Squadron to leave the town and re-enter, so that the capture of Ben Gardane could be kept for posterity.

Tank troops were pushed out to the north western and western outskirts of the town to protect the infantry while they dug in. These troops were withdrawn at last light and the whole regiment leaguered near the airfield. Ben Gardane had been heavily mined and Major Peter Carter, B Squadron's commander, lost his tank on Teller mines while moving up the main Ben Gardane-Medenine road. There were no regimental casualties, but some sappers were injured clearing mines.

On the morning of the 16th, Messerchmitt 109s bombed the regimental leaguer to no effect, except for an Arab and his camel who were killed. Ken Bull, A Squadron's ammunition lorry driver recalls:

> These were rather persistent but gave us time to adopt defensive positions. Doug Tyler and myself were each nursing a Bren gun in the same slit trench, when we spotted an aircraft heading our way. We waited for it to get within range and opened fire.
>
> My gun fired about three rounds and jammed, so I acted as spotter for Doug. You can imagine how pleased we were when we saw the tracer hitting the 'plane. Smoke appeared and the aircraft crashed about two miles away.

The rest of the 16th was spent maintaining the internal security of Ben Gardane, pending the arrival of the 51st Highland Division, with whom the regiment would be fighting in attacks on Medenine and Mareth.

On the 20th the tanks advanced in column along the main road to a concentration area east of Medenine. B Squadron was ordered forward to support armoured car patrols of 12 Lancers, who were being shelled on the outskirts of Medenine. Colonel Cairnes had entered the town and reported it was clear of the enemy, but enemy observation posts in the hills west of Metameur, could bombard anything coming out of Medenine.

On the 21st, tanks of 50 RTR were once again the first to enter a former enemy stronghold, when with B Squadron leading, they advanced through Medenine to the Metameur area. One tank was lost to mines on the way. By now the enemy had withdrawn his forward observers from the hills west of Metameur, their posts eventually being occupied by British troops. A and C Squadrons also pushed forward to support 131 Infantry Brigade, forming a bridgehead in front of Metameur which was extended further westwards on the following day.

On the 24th, the regiment reverted to 23 Armoured Brigade command, while A Squadron went to support 152 Highland Brigade to secure the area west of the Wadi Zessar. The following day the remaining three squadrons joined A Squadron there, in a position which was to become known as the 'Fort George Bastion'. A and C Squadrons, in forward positions, were shelled later that afternoon, but no casualties were suffered. The Highland Division was now deployed along the line of the Wadi Zessar, with forward elements on Wadi Zeuss, and the Axis forces holding the Mareth Line and the mountains to the south. The Highland Division's task was to secure their position and patrol against possible counter-attack.

For the rest of the month 50 RTR remained at Fort George with 152 Highland Brigade. Except for artillery exchanges up and down the front, and the occasional enemy air raid, there was very little activity from either side.

Sergeant D G Ward of A Squadron recalls events at the Fort George position:

> Most of the tanks were dug into the sides of small sandhills dotted across a fairly level plain. Two or three hundred yards to our front was an infantry outpost, with a wireless vehicle by an abandoned farmhouse, but they withdrew behind us at last light, leaving us to guard the line and man the listening post each night. We were to retreat through a minefield if attacked at night and did we have a scare when the Highland Division sent up a machine-gun platoon to lay harassing fire over the enemy lines! But notice of this action did not reach us until some time after they started firing and we started retreating, although we didn't get very far.

The general situation in Tunisia now was: The British First and American Fifth Armies, who had landed in Morocco and Algeria in November 1942, had successfully advanced into the centre of Tunisia, threatening the Axis rear in the south and the capital, Tunis, in the north. Rommel, who had been constantly withdrawing his forces in Tunisia, now called a halt and prepared to counter-attack on both fronts.

By 1 March the situation had hardly changed. 152 Highland Brigade still held the line of Wadi Zessar from the coast to the main Medenine-Mareth road while 7th Armoured Division was operating in the south. 50 RTR remained at Fort George but as the enemy had good observation posts any movement brought down shell fire.

The regiment, warned of a possible counter-attack, were expected to hold out for four days. With this in mind they made themselves self-sufficient by dumping petrol and ammunition in the squadron areas. Their position was weakened when B Squadron was withdrawn to the east of the Wadi Zessar to act as mobile reserve to 23 Armoured Brigade.

The Highland Division had outposts well in front of Wadi Zessar. If the enemy attacked all forces were to withdraw into the wadi itself, leaving only the Fort George garrison on the western side. Each tank was allotted a position from which it could engage an advancing enemy while in a good hull-down position; all non-essential vehicles and personnel were sent to the 'Left out of Battle' camp in the Zarzis area.

On 4 March, as Axis forces were reported to be moving their armour for an attack in the south, the Fort George Bastion was mined, leaving the regiment just outside the minefield, with a gap left through which they could withdraw, should they be attacked at night. The expected attack came south of 50 RTR's position, on the morning of the 6th.

Rommel, having given the advancing Americans a bloody nose at Kasserine with his right, now turned to deliver a vicious left hook against the Eighth Army at Medenine. He was too late – Montgomery was prepared and waiting. After numerous attempts to break Eighth Army's line Rommel was forced to withdraw to the Mareth Line, leaving 52 tanks on the battlefield, 43 of which were knocked out by anti-tank guns.

This was Rommel's last battle in North Africa. He left for Germany shortly afterwards. He had been severely mauled by the New Zealanders, the Guards Motor Brigade and the 7th Armoured Division.

No major attack developed in the north where 50 RTR were situated, but the enemy did manage to infiltrate some infantry positions, enabling Italian troops to get into Wadi Melah, just forward of the regiment's position. Regimental Headquarters received mortar fire in the late afternoon, Colonel Cairnes' tank being narrowly missed.

Led respectively by Major Geoff Russell, Captain Ted Jenkin, Captain Les Williams, Lieutenant Vic Senior, Lieutenant Ted Howard and Lieutenant Ted Bond, a series of night patrols commenced, lasting until 20 March, in order to discover as much as possible about the approaches to the Mareth Line and about the Line itself. The early patrols succeeded in getting over a mile behind enemy outpost defences, while the later patrols penetrated to the Wadi Zigzaou and to an anti-tank ditch beyond. During one particular patrol, which lasted seven hours, Captain Jenkin who was on foot, was stalked by an enemy outpost. Evading his would be captors, Jenkin returned with sufficient information, to enable a route to the wadi to be mapped out.

On the 7th, C Squadron, commanded by Major Venn, was sent into Wadi Melah to clear out Italian infantry. The enemy were caught totally by surprise, some even folding their blankets. The squadron killed a large number with their Besa machine-guns. Fleeing Italians left their rifles and equipment behind. C Squadron then withdrew, under heavy shell fire, to their original battle positions.

After a couple of quiet days the regiment made its way to a new position, the Gourine, where they prepared to attack the Mareth Line. Over the next nine days, 10-19 March, the regiment rehearsed the operation with 7th Battalion The Green Howards and 6th, 8th and 9th Battalions The Durham Light Infantry of 50th Infantry Division.

The first Valentine tanks armed with six-pounder guns arrived during this period, and Major Russell left The Fiftieth to take command of 40 RTR – 'rather an awkward time to lose him,' remarked Colonel Cairnes – with Major G R A Maclaren joining the regiment from 40 RTR as second-in-command.

B Squadron's Major Carter, while outlining the regiment's part in the forthcoming battle on a blackboard, took the opportunity of reminding Eight Troop under Sammy Nixon that they were the only Troop to survive Alam Halfa and to set an example to the rest of the Squadron.

Although they did not know it at the time, 50 RTR were about to face their toughest test of strength and character to date. Colonel John Cairnes, always so very proud of his regiment, describes his own particular tank and crew prior to the forthcoming battle of Mareth, though he could have been writing about any one of his fifty-two crews:

> My war chariot goes by the name of 'Hawkins'. My tank crew are an amusing lot. Corporal Flaherty, the driver, is an Irishman from Wales and a great little talker. He knows his stuff and looks after my tank very well. My operator is a young corporal called Russell, very intelligent and a first class operator. The gunner is a cheery individual called Robins, also a first class operator as well as a good gunner. They are a cheery crowd even under the most trying conditions.

Eddie Prett, a tank commander in A Squadron's One Troop recalls:

> The weather in the area was delightful, warm sunshine, beautiful spring flowers and all sizes of tortoises basking in the sunshine. Idyllic – yet a nasty battle was just around the corner.
>
> As I understood the battle plan, 50 RTR were part of the frontal attack on the Mareth defences supporting an infantry brigade. As the General did not take us into his confidence we had to rely on the 'Grapevine' or 'Latrinograph' communication systems for any information.

# Chapter 6
# 'JOHN HAS GONE'

## Battle of Mareth

'I have no hesitation in saying there was no finer unit in the army than the one John led into action on 22 March; his was the star battalion of the brigade.' – Brigadier G W Richards, commanding 23 Armoured Brigade, March 1943.

22 March 1943 was one of the blackest, yet greatest, days in the regiment's long and arduous active service in Egypt and North Africa. On this day the commanding officer, Lieutenant-Colonel John Cairnes, last of the original 23 Armoured Brigade regimental commanders, was killed while leading his Regiment into action to repel a counter-attack by the German 15th Panzer Division. But, despite that grievous loss, and heavy casualties in tanks, the regiment fought most gallantly in the face of superior armour, anti-tank guns and a considerable weight of infantry which had overrun their position.

Had Colonel Cairnes survived, it would have been possibly the last time he led 50 RTR into action. He was to be promoted to second-in-command of a brigade.

This battle was the climax to the initial breaching of the Mareth Line defences on the night of 20/21 March. The plan was for the 50th Northumbrian Division to break through the Mareth Line in the north, allowing the 4th Indian Division to pass through, while the 51st Highland Division held ground to their left and the New Zealand Corps swept round the Matmata hills to the south, to threaten the enemy's rear.

The Mareth Line was a series of fortifications along the western bank of the Wadi Zigzaou, which stretched inland for twenty-two miles from the coast to the Matmata hills, the wadi itself forming a natural anti-tank ditch. Originally built by the French in the 1930s, to protect their interests in North Africa from Italian expansion in Libya, the defences were dismantled after the German armistice with France, and then hastily refurbished during the Axis retreat into Tunisia. In places the banks of the wadi were scarped (the sides cut vertical). However, the blockhouses were now antiquated and did not measure up to the standards of warfare in 1943. They could, therefore, serve little purpose other than for cover against artillery fire, and the defence proper would have to be fought from field positions between the blockhouses. The positioning of the line was also bad, for it lay immediately behind high ground which denied any long range artillery observation for the defence.

Rommel, who by this time had left North Africa, had on 26 January recommended abandoning the Mareth Line and concentrating their strength along the line of the Wadi Akarit forty miles to the north. He knew that the French Generals Catroux and Gautsch, with a lorried Sahara Company, had attempted a trial outflanking manouvre and decided that such a move was not possible. He also knew that the Eighth Army was far better equipped than the French had been and if Montgomery attempted such an operation the occupation and reconstruction of the Mareth Line would avail nothing.

Since January, Montgomery had been seeking a weak point in the defences; he even enlisted the help of a French engineer officer who had helped construct the defences. But there was no weak point. Montgomery's plan was boldness to the point of audacity. He was again taking the bull by the horns: direct frontal assault was the only answer, and the 50th Division, with 50 RTR in support, were given the dubious honour of leading the assault. They had to buy enough time to allow Freyberg's New Zealand Division to get around the southern end of the Mareth Line and attack the enemy in the rear. Montgomery knew that the Axis could not sufficiently defend against both attacks, and if he failed in one, he would succeed in the other.

The Italian General Messe (fresh from Russia, where he had commanded the Italian Expeditionary Force), commanding the Axis forces along the Mareth Line, had four Italian and two German divisions to defend it. Five miles behind these he had his reserve, fifty tanks of the 15th Panzer Division, which included the veteran tank men of 8 Panzer Regiment, one regiment of the 90th Light Division and the Ramcke paratroopers. On 19 March, Messe decided to reinforce the Italian Young Fascist Division (the best of the Italian troops available), whom 50 RTR and the 50th Division were facing in the northern sector of the line, with the 15th Panzer Division; a move which would have much significance later and which showed Axis awareness of Montgomery's intentions.

50 RTR, under command of the 50th Northumbrian Division, had three main tasks: first, to support the 8th and 9th Durham Light Infantry of 151 Infantry Brigade in breaching the Mareth Line and securing an initial bridgehead from Ksiba Ouest to Ouerzi; second, to support the 6th Durham Light Infantry, the reserve battalion of 151 Brigade, in enlarging the bridgehead thus made from locality 'X' to Ouerzi Ouest

(locality 'X' was an unnamed bastion); third, to support the 5th East Yorkshire Regiment, 69 Brigade, in exploiting 151 Brigade's success towards Zarat and the tower at Novamor.

Corporal Gordon Robertson, of D Company, the 6th Durham Light Infantry, describes the position about to be attacked:

> After crossing the wadi, up to your crutch in water, there was a 30 foot thick belt of barbed wire. Then an anti-tank ditch, a big one, and a minefield 30 or 40 yards deep, then a second lot of barbed wire. Once you had crossed this, you would be shaking hands with Jerry. Next there was the Zigzaou trench works with a pillbox on each end of each section of trenches, the trenches were three layers deep.

The first difficulty in this operation was to get all the tanks through the enemy minefield on the eastern bank of the Wadi Zigzaou, cross the wadi itself and to negotiate an anti-tank ditch, twelve feet deep and fifteen feet wide, along the western bank. This had to be done at night under a full moon, and it was imperative that all the tanks should not be caught out in the open on their own side of the wadi when dawn broke.

The mined wadi was about 50 yards wide where it was decided to force a crossing. Codenamed 'Sally', the daughter Colonel Cairnes never saw, it was originally an old French crossing place. The bottom was soft and sandy with a covering of water, but the banks here were not unduly steep and did not present a serious tank obstacle. The anti-tank ditch, however, was a definite hazard, and had to be breached by sappers of 9 Field Squadron Royal Engineers. There was a single row of 'dragons teeth' on the western side of the wadi, short lengths of railway line embedded in the earth and protruding about two feet. The enemy, apparently, had not had time to concrete them in and they did not present a serious obstacle.

However, since the reconnaissance patrols of a few days earlier, heavy rain in the Matmata hills had turned the wadi into a quagmire.

All tanks, except the four in Regimental Headquarters, carried fascines similar to those used in the tank assault on the Hindenburg Line in 1916. These were large bundles of brushwood, tied together and placed on the front of the tanks; as the tank approached a ditch too deep to cross safely, the fascine would be dropped into it, thus providing a path way for the tank to cross. A quick release device (a machete) enabled the tank commander to jettison it quickly when required. Drivers could see through their visors underneath the fascines, but the guns had to be traversed to one side and could not be used while fascines were being carried. It was proposed to cross the wadi by using some of the fascines to make a firm going for the tanks and then to jettison others into the anti-tank ditch. Under the circumstances, this alone was a very difficult and dangerous task to achieve. For each tank after dropping its fascine, would have to move back while another tank did the same. A drill had in fact been practised, but this of course was not under fire.

On the morning of 20 March, the regiment leaguered in the area, with 51 operational tanks, 43 with two-pounder guns and eight with six-pounder guns. Unfortunately, one remaining six-pounder tank commanded by Lieutenant Senior of Ten Troop had had to be evacuated to workshops the previous day with gear-box trouble; as this left the troop with only two tanks Senior took over his troop corporal's tank.

Colonel Cairnes attended a conference at 151 Brigade Headquarters in the morning and, having issued orders to all tank commanders they moved off to the forming up area in the Chet Meskine at last light, where Major Bazley, commanding Headquarter Squadron, delivered hot tea and rum to the crews before the attack.

On the approach to the forming up area, however, some of the Valentines were suddenly illuminated by unexpected bonfires, which began to blaze up on their fronts. These startling outbreaks were not due to the enemy, but to the huge fascines, ten feet long by eight feet high, resting on the tank's exhaust, which incidentally is at the front on a Valentine. The tank commanders concerned quickly jettisoned the burning fascines to the accompaniment of other commanders' verbal abuse; they were now well aware that their position would have been noted by the watchful enemy.

In the early evening of 20 March, Colonel John Cairnes wrote for the last time:

> These are very momentous hours and very similar to October 23rd last. All our chaps are in great heart and very proud to be in the van of things. John Hart held a delightful service last night in the dark. I couldn't attend it myself as I had a lengthy conference to attend, but I believe he had a large congregation. The troops love these services. John Hart always strikes the right note. He held a communion service this morning which I attended. I must end off now and get my supper and then we are off into battle.

50 RTR formed up in line ahead almost half a mile long on 151 Brigade's axis, with the two attacking infantry battalions on either flank (8 DLI on the left and 9 DLI on the right). The leading troop was to move close up to the barrage, level with the leading infantry on either side of it. The enemy must have seen the attack coming and they shelled the forming up area heavily from early in the evening until the British barrage began at 2230 hours. Freddie August recalls:

> I was surprised by the size of the fascines and where the stuff had come from—no trees in the desert! Guns were traversed to the rear and the poor old driver was more or less imprisoned in his compartment with the fascine resting on his hatches.

Our move up to the wadi was slow but uneventful, though we were accompanied by much shelling which continued all night. The tanks drew up nose to tail and the long hours of waiting began. Occasionally the CO came on the air enquiring about progress but couldn't get much satisfaction.

During the long wait our tank received a shell burst on the nearside rear. At first light I examined the damage and found a chunk out of the track and the rear drive sprocket, seeing that the track was not completely severed we managed to limp back to the start line.

The regiment formed up, One Troop of A Squadron leading with a troop of Scorpions from 41 RTR and a detachment from 9 Field Squadron Royal Engineers. Major Styles, commanding A Squadron, received the order to advance at 2315 hours, but there was some delay, owing to a breakdown in communications with the Scorpion troop. Lieutenant Ted Bond, commanding the leading troop, contacted the Scorpions on foot, and ordered them to advance; they were very slow in doing so, with frequent halts due to mechanical trouble. On striking the enemy's minefield wire the Scorpions began to flail, but had to stop shortly

*Figure 15: Lt Ted Bond, first into the Wadi Zigzaou. (Mr D Heeley)*

*Figure 16: Cpl E Prett, badly wounded at the very beginning of the Mareth battle. (E Prett)*

afterwards. A Squadron continued the advance, with the sappers clearing a gap with their detectors. At 0100 hours, the leading troop advanced into the wadi itself, while the remainder of the squadron halted on the west bank.

Lieutenant Bond's tank hit a mine and he went on foot to assist the engineer commander, Lieutenant Boynton. Fire from enemy anti-tank and machine-guns, both in the wadi and on the west bank, was now very heavy. Corporal Prett, Lieutenant Bond's troop corporal, while gallantly dismounting from his tank to lead his vehicle on foot and render all the help he could, had his leg blown off. Lieutenant Bond seeing that his corporal was wounded, dressed Prett's wounds and ensured that he was taken to the rear. Corporal Eddie Prett recalls:

On the way up to the wadi, our fascine caught fire, so Major 'Jock' Styles, our squadron commander, ordered me to take his. By this time the moon had risen behind us, silhouetting us against the skyline, a very dangerous situation to be in.

Major Styles complained over the air that JOHNNY ACK ONE (my tank) was not moving ahead fast enough, so I ventured out on foot to assess the position. While returning to the tank, I

*Figure 17: 'Ramillies', the A Squadron Valentine that blocked the crossing of the Wadi Zigzaou, March 1943. (Tank Museum)*

> stepped on a mine. End of my war, right leg blown off above the knee and severe injuries to my other leg and arms. Two sappers carried me out of the battle area on a stretcher, they were very brave as the area was being heavily shelled.

At the same time, two other A Squadron tanks received direct hits. Both drivers were wounded and had to be evacuated. The fire directed on the wadi crossing was now so severe, that every shell and bullet seemed to claim a casualty. To one observer at least, the wadi that night seemed like the mouth of Hell:

> The point of crossing was so obvious to the enemy that all his available fire, from artillery, mortars and machine guns, could be concentrated on it. No praise could be too great for the infantry, who fought through it to the relative peace of the enemy positions on the far bank, or, more particularly, for the steady courage of the engineers who could not cross but had to stay in mid-stream, trying to improve the route for tanks, until, as happened to a high proportion of them, they were wounded or killed.

Despite the perilous conditions under which they were working in the wadi, the sappers succeeded in gapping the minefield and breaching the anti-tank ditch on the other side. They reported that only two fascines would be required to allow tanks to cross the ditch. At about 0300 hours, Lieutenant Bond, now in his troop corporal's tank, crossed the wadi with Sergeant Gabe-Jones and dumped their fascines in the ditch, only to realise more fascines would be required. Two other A Squadron tanks then crossed, dumping fascines into the ditch, which they were then able to cross. Unfortunately, the next tank of Two Troop, Ramillies, attempting the crossing, bogged down in the middle of the wadi and sank almost up to its turret, and in doing so not only prevented the remaining tanks from getting across, but all other vehicles as well. The only exception to that fact, was the Daimler scout car of the regiment's medical officer, Captain Anthony Ellis. Despite the danger of mines on both sides of the wadi crossing, he and his driver, Trooper Watkin, managed to get across and set up a casualty collecting point under the lee of the western bank of the wadi close to the crossing place.

The senior engineer officer on the crossing told Major Styles it would take eight hours to prepare another crossing and it was useless to attempt to put across more tanks because the bogged one was also blocking the gap in the minefield. Receiving this information, Colonel Cairnes told Major Styles to try to get over further north where the 9th Durhams were attacking the Ksiba Est and Ksiba Ouest positions.

At this time, about 0415 hours, Brigadier D M W Beak, commanding 151 Brigade, ordered Colonel Cairnes to take his regiment, less A Squadron, back to the leaguer area behind the Chet Meskine, while A Squadron tried to cross the wadi. A Squadron's efforts to get reliable information about the crossing to the north failed, and since dawn was then breaking, Major Styles with his headquarters and two troops fell back to a covered position. The Squadron then had four tanks on the western bank of the wadi; they had contacted the infantry, then established on their objectives, and were in battle positions. They remained there throughout 21 March, under shell and mortar fire, maintaining communication by radio with Squadron Headquarters on the opposite side of the wadi.

During their long wait to cross the wadi, throughout the night of 20/21 March, the remainder of 50 RTR was subjected to heavy shell fire, and several tanks of B and C Squadrons were hit and temporarily disabled. A German 88mm gun firing into the moonlight from the western side of the wadi achieved several near misses on the tanks of Regimental Headquarters.

By dawn of 21 March, the infantry had formed a bridgehead over the wadi and were firmly established on the Ksiba Ouest and in the Ouerzi area. Corporal Robertson of the Durhams recalls:

> We attacked on Saturday and Sunday nights in succession, another weekend spoilt. We had been ordered to stay in the bridgehead for three days if we could. We penetrated about 1,000 yards in by 2,000 yards wide, that took us through the best part of the Line.

It was proposed to enlarge the bridgehead that night. A causeway over the wadi was to be built around the bogged tank by the strongly reinforced sappers, under the personal command of Brigadier Kisch (commanding Royal Engineers Eighth Army). The sappers used anything they could find, including oil drums and some of 50 RTR's fascines; this to some extent was successful. 50 RTR then moved forward under cover of darkness to cross the wadi, by first light on 22 March, the whole regiment had crossed. Corporal Bob Smallman, a tank commander in B Squadron's Six Troop wrote:

> We crossed over after a very rough ride just as daylight was breaking. The first feeling I had was one of relief at getting across, another thing that impressed me was the comparative stillness and quietness.
>
> We seemed to be in a shallow basin of desert with a few groups of palm trees growing near the wadi. There were quite a few bodies of our infantry boys lying still in the sand, obviously having been caught in the shelling of the previous night.
>
> Our tanks fanned out with a reasonable space between each one, we were then halted as nothing seemed to be happening. We climbed cautiously out of our turrets, still nothing happened, after a while we had a 'brew up' during which we noticed a few puffs of sand spurting up and realised we were being sniped from fairly long range.
>
> It seemed quite peaceful, however, after climbing back into the tanks and putting the headphones on, it began to dawn on us that things were moving.

Regimental Headquarters then took up battle positions near a small wood, immediately west of the crossing place, with A and B Squadrons forward protecting the leading infantry, and C Squadron watching the left flank. Enemy shelling and mortar fire was heavy and accurate, and the tanks had to jockey about throughout the morning. A Squadron were in the area of the Old Camp Site, where Major Styles contacted D Company, the 6th Durham Light Infantry. The Squadron used their Besas to good effect against enemy troops and transport from this position. At about 0700 hours, about 60 Italians surrendered, running fast towards the wadi crossing, but closely followed by their own or German mortar fire. No-one was hit.

Throughout the morning, A Squadron was under very heavy shellfire and Lieutenant Godwin, commanding Three Troop, was severely wounded in both legs while dismounting from his tank. The medical officer, Captain Ellis, came forward and evacuated him on a stretcher fixed to the back of his scout car. A shell landed under the troop leader's tank of Four Troop and blew an access plate off, damaging the engine and gearbox and jamming the steering brakes hard on. The crew continued to fight using the tank as a pill-box.

Meanwhile Major Carter's B Squadron had gone through on A Squadron's left and halted in order to silence enemy machine-guns.

They then pushed on north west towards Zarat and Novamor and took up positions on a ridge from which they could observe the enemy. At this stage, the leading tank, commanded by Lieutenant Kenneth Pillar, struck a mine and was immobilised. This left the squadron with thirteen tanks, one having been knocked out by shellfire the previous night and another having shed a track near the wadi crossing.

B Squadron reported seeing considerable enemy movement along the road running north-west from Zarat, but unfortunately out of range. This was thought to have been the German 15th Panzer Division, sent in as last minute reinforcements to stem the British advance. Later, two 50mm anti-tank guns and some half-tracked carriers were seen moving north east from Zarat. These were engaged and at least one carrier was knocked out by a six-pounder high explosive shell. Enemy anti-tank guns moved into the cover of the trees north of Zarat, and other guns were moving in close to and north west of Zarat. There was also considerable activity in the area of Novamor. Efforts were made to bring down artillery fire on these targets but the forward observation officer had not been able to get his vehicle over the wadi. Fire was eventually brought down using the radio link with 151 Brigade.

Lieutenant M M Morrison, of B Squadron, severely injured his arm in the recoil mechanism of his six-pounder gun and as Lieutenant Pillars's tank was immobilised, the latter took over Morrison's tank, leaving his gunner and driver in his own, with orders to stop and fight the tank while they still had ammunition. These two men, Lance Corporal Duffield and Trooper Wynn, fought on until the enemy overran the position. Trooper Gordon Wynn recalls:

> When Lieutenant Pillar left our disabled tank, George and I were instructed to remain where we were. In the late afternoon, it appeared that the rest of the squadron were ordered to retire and we lost contact. There was a ridge about 150 yards in front of us and we could see German helmets dodging about along the top. When darkness fell, before we could decide to stay put or to try to find our way back to British lines, we heard voices outside the turret and looked out expecting to see our own people but found we were wrong! The Jerries were quite reasonable and gave us five minutes to collect a few things. The one who marched us back couldn't speak much English, but managed to convey that he didn't think the Germans would be in Africa much longer.

The shelling and mortar fire on B Squadron became so heavy that they had to withdraw to a more covered position, from which they closed the gap between A Squadron in the Old Camp area and C Squadron protecting the left flank. C Squadron were also subjected to heavy shell and mortar fire throughout the morning and the crews were sniped at by rifles and machine-guns whenever they dismounted. On taking up their position on the left it was at once evident that machine-guns and snipers were also giving the infantry considerable trouble. The two leading troops, therefore, went forward and succeeded in quelling the machine-guns with their Besas. The enemy evidently saw an opportunity of using their anti-tank guns and very cleverly established a fire position without being noticed in front of the squadron. These guns suddenly opened fire together and before the squadron could withdraw under cover of smoke, three tanks had been knocked out. Corporal Taylor, Lance Corporal Evans and Trooper Butler were killed and Lieutenant Schofield was wounded. One tank commanded by Lieutenant Thompson, had both the driver, Trooper Worsfold, and the gunner, Trooper Tite, wounded. Sergeant Joyce, Thompson's troop sergeant, seeing the danger got into Thompson's tank and drove it back towards the wadi, placing both men in deep slit trenches. Shelling and mortar fire was very fierce at the time and dust made it impossible for the remainder of the squadron to pin-point the enemy anti-tank guns. Throughout the morning, Regimental Headquarters were subjected to heavy shell and mortar fire, and the navigating officer's tank received a direct hit on the front near the driver's visor, which split the armour and broke the driver's leg.

Towards mid-day, it was confirmed that the movement observed by B Squadron in the Zarat-Novamor area was indeed the 15th Panzer Division, commanded by Major-General Willibald Borowietz, forming up for a counter-attack. Quite by chance they had timed their move to perfection, leaving cover just as a heavy rainfall grounded the Royal Air Force, who were in the process of forming up for a heavy bombing attack on them. The rain also obstructed artillery observation and damaged the wadi crossing. Colonel Cairnes immediately told the rear link officer, the Adjutant, Captain Chapman, that six-pounder anti-tank guns were vital to the security of the position and that 151 Brigade must try to get some over the wadi before the attack came in.

Colonel Cairnes ordered Major MacLaren to go down to the wadi crossing and try and speed up the guns. MacLaren reported over the radio that there was the 'most indescribable confusion' on the wadi crossing, and there appeared to be no-one in control. In fact, not one single anti-tank gun ever crossed the wadi into the bridgehead.

Earlier in the day, Captain Ted Jenkin, the signals and reconnaissance officer, had had the greatest difficulty in getting his and other scout cars across the wadi, having been expressly forbidden by the 50th Northumbrian Division (who were on the crossing at the time) to tow vehicles across. The forward observation officer was also forbidden to cross, as already related, and was therefore unable to function.

From about 1230 hours onwards, shelling and mortar fire in the whole area became very intense, and it was evident that an attack was imminent, although there were no signs of enemy movement. At 1400 hours the Germans counter-attacked in three columns, one directed on Ouerzi Est, the second struck between Ouerzi Est and Ouerzi Ouest, the third along a shallow valley between Ouerzi Ouest and Ourzi. Within 30 minutes they had recaptured a position that the 6th Durhams had taken the night before, and then a company of the 9th Durhams was dislodged. The bridgehead was already beginning to crumble.

Then at 1530 hours, extremely heavy shelling and mortar fire came down on B Squadron's position; through the dust cloud created German tanks were seen advancing from the north west. In quick succession three tanks of B Squadron were hit and penetrated, Major Carter having a foot blown off inside his tank. His crew baled out and managed to get him to another tank, which then blew up on a mine on its way back. Captain Jolley, Major Carter's second-in-command, within minutes of taking command of the squadron was wounded in the leg by an armour-piercing shot. Lieutenant Garrett now commanded the remainder of the squadron, which stayed in their positions engaging the advancing infantry with their secondary armament; they witnessed a number of British infantrymen being captured, but they were unable to intervene. A Panzer Mark IV (Special) appeared on the ridge to the west of B Squadron and opened fire. Lieutenants Nixon and Pillar replied with six-pounders and hit the enemy tank, which then withdrew under cover. A short time later Lieutenant Garrett's six-pounder Valentine was knocked-out when a high explosive shell exploded under the tank. Trooper John Gibberd recalls:

> I was driving Dickie Garrett and we sat all afternoon with a tank burning on either side of us, wondering whose they were and how many of the crew got out and when our turn would come. We saw someone get out of one tank and start running in the wrong direction, towards the enemy lines. We hoped that he would be taken prisoner.

A Squadron, which had reported 20 German tanks forming up with infantry between Zarat and Novamor, had observed the German infantry advance into the dead ground just west of their position. The enemy tanks had halted out of range of the Valentines. Two, which had advanced to within 1,000 yards of the squadron, were engaged and hastily withdrew. A German Mark III then took up a hull-down position and scored a glancing hit on one of A Squadron's tanks. The shelling at this stage was intense, and the troop sergeant's tank of Two Troop, Sergeant Thomas, received a direct hit and was blazing. The Germans were advancing on the position and the infantry commander asked Major Styles for smoke cover to allow him to withdraw his men. The tanks laid smoke and the infantry withdrew in the direction of the wadi crossing. From his position on the right flank Major Styles could see that enemy tanks and infantry were working around the right flank under cover of the dead ground and soon afterwards opened fire with machine-guns. Corporal Gordon Robertson of the Durhams recalls:

> The enemy tanks were coming towards us, the infantry just in front. We opened up with everything we had. The infantry stopped, we got some of them, the rest went behind the tanks.
>
> The tanks were more determined they came forward and stopped about 300-400 yards from us, they were going to pick us off in their own good time. Just at that point, lo and behold one of 50 RTR's Valentines came up with some ammo to our trench, we were by now low on ammo, we got off three boxes of .303 ammo and some grenades.
>
> The Valentine then came up on our right and got cracking with his Besa machine-gun and his tank gun. We gave the tank commander a cheer for good luck and got on with it. The tank was now coming under heavy fire; when it got too hot she backed down for a few minutes and then returned, doing some good shooting each time.
>
> After about half an hour or so we looked back and saw an officer talking to the tank commander–where did he come from? Then the officer walked away, the tank commander jumped down and followed him, they were then talking again. There was a sudden movement from both of them and the tank commander shot the officer dead with his .38 revolver. The tank commander then gave us the Nazi salute with two fingers to the nose, indicating that the officer was a German.
>
> Things were now getting pretty hot for us, the enemy tanks were shooting at us, it was hectic and we were getting short of ammo again. Just then the Valentine got hit. We heard the clank of steel as it was hit high on the turret, it went back down the slope as if it was out of control and came to a stop, we thought they'd had it. But no, the crew got out though one was wounded. They gave us a wave and we gave them a cheer and they made their way down to the wadi.

Colonel Cairnes then ordered A Squadron to fall back on the right of Regimental Headquarters to prevent any enemy infiltration from that direction into the Regiment's position. He also ordered Major Venn to bring C Squadron to the left of Regimental Headquarters and advance to the ridge in front of them. Trooper J. Greaves recalls:

> I was with Major Styles, in the middle of the battle, an empty cartridge wouldn't eject from our Besa, so I climbed out of the turret and pushed the cartridge out woth a cleaning rod. It was a stupid thing to do as I didn't know if the bullet had fired, luckily it had. Then I saw Colonel Cairnes' tank hit, it was a nightmare.

*Figure 18: 'Hawkins', the remains of Col Cairnes' Valentine, taken a few years after the battle of Mareth. (Tank Museum)*

Colonel Cairnes then ordered the three remaining tanks of Regimental Headquarters forward to engage German tanks and infantry which were overrunning the position just vacated by A Squadron. He himself led, with the Adjutant, Captain Chapman, on his right and Major MacLaren, the second-in-command, on his left. There was a large number of German infantry on the ridge in front of them which Colonel Cairnes and Captain Chapman engaged with their machine-guns.

Five German tanks suddenly appeared on the ridge; Colonel Cairnes, who had swung west and was firing his guns in that direction, suddenly received a direct hit on the turret. This was followed by several other direct hits about the hull. The turret appeared to blow up and was very soon in flames. Captain Cliff Walters wrote:

> John had called us on the wireless to go up to the ridge to meet the German counter-attack. I was in the rear of C Squadron with Dicky Venn on the left of Regimental Headquarters. Shortly after I heard the order to go up to the ridge, I looked to my right and saw what I am convinced was a German tank just dropping below the skyline about 1,000 yards away. He had just fired at John's tank and I saw smoke rising as Corporal Flaherty jumped out of his driving seat and leapt on to the turret. He told me afterwards that John and Robbins, his gunner, were both dead, and he managed to drag Vic Russell, the operator, out and lean him against the side. I saw all this distinctly from about 50 yards away and as Corporal Flaherty got onto the tank again another shell

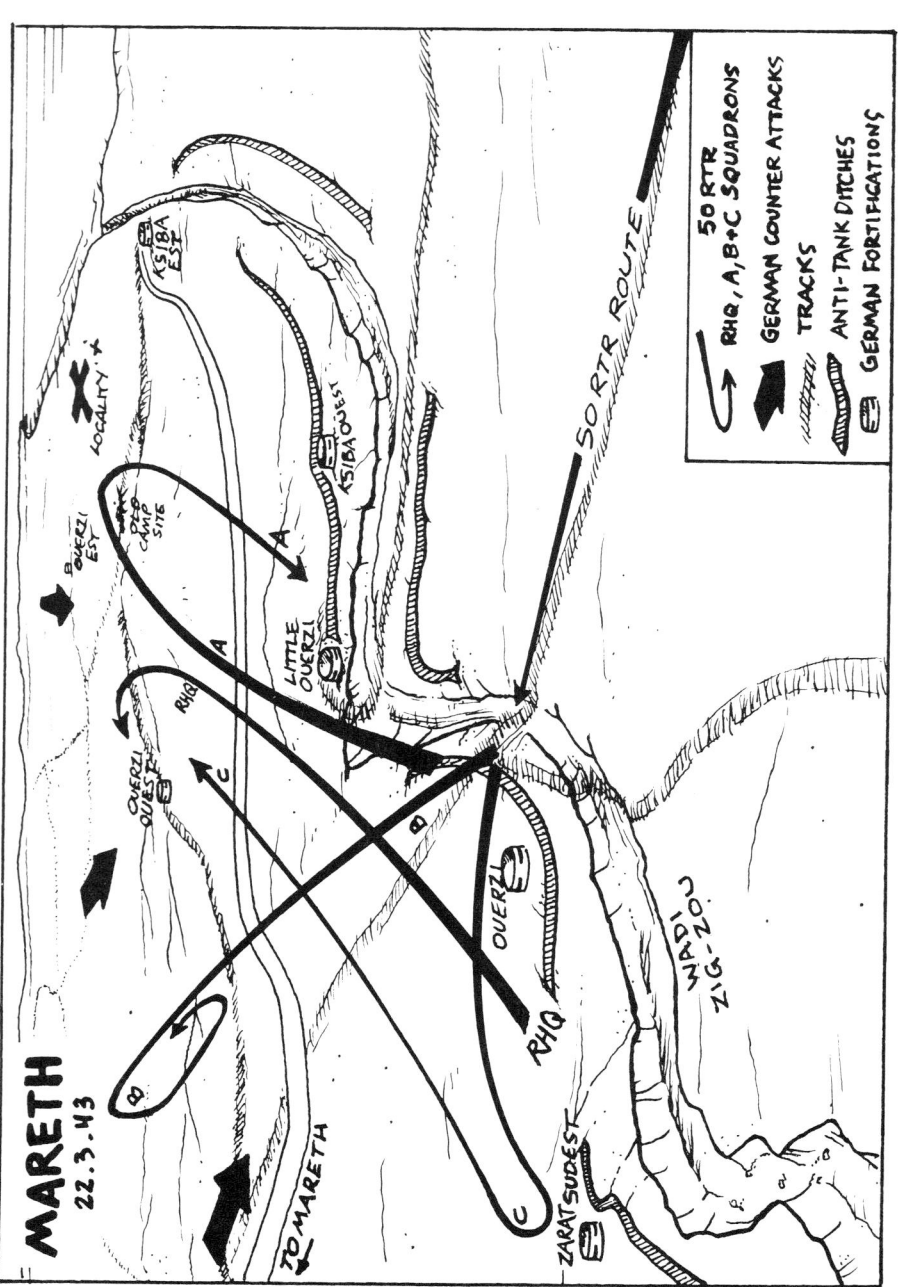

Map 4: 'Mareth'. Battle of Mareth and squadron movements on 22 March 1943.

*Figure 19: 'Hood', the remains of Major MacLaren's Valentine after the Battle of Mareth. (Tank Museum)*

hit the gun and mantlet.

Captain Chapman brought his tank close to the now burning tank of Colonel Cairnes and fired over 30 rounds of smoke to cover the rescue of Russell, but the wind was too strong and quickly blew the smoke away. Lieutenant Senior then ordered Sergeant Nash to move his tank over and give what fire support he could. Meanwhile, Trooper Lewis, Captain Chapman's driver, left his driving seat to assist the now wounded Corporal Flaherty in his gallant rescue attempt. Major MacLaren's tank came too near Colonel Cairnes's tank and received a hit on the turret which eventually set the tank on fire. Fortunately Major MacLaren had at the time dismounted and the remainder of his crew managed to get out unhurt. The Adjutant's tank was now the sole remaining of the four Regimental Headquarters tanks, and it withdrew to the wood near the wadi crossing, carrying Corporal Flaherty and Corporal Russell. Russell was so badly wounded that he died on the adjutant's tank before they reached the wood. By now every surviving tank of 50 RTR had been driven off every position they had occupied.

In the meantime, Major Styles took command and formed a defensive perimeter around the wood and the wadi crossing, with tanks forward on the right, left and in the centre. Major MacLaren quickly took over another tank and assumed command of the regiment. At this stage, 50 RTR had eighteen battleworthy tanks out of the original 51 which went forward on the night of 20/21 March.

Trooper John Gibberd recalls his thoughts after learning of the death of Colonel Cairnes: 'If anyone deserved a posthumous VC he did. I well remember the shock when it came over the air–"John has gone".

Tanks started moving back until Major Styles called them to order.'

C Squadron, as you will recall, had been ordered to come up on the left of Regimental Headquarters before Colonel Cairnes was killed and they had been able to fire at the enemy infantry. They had spotted enemy tanks which were out of range of their two-pounder guns, but which were able to engage the squadron. Corporal Boyt and Trooper Hannon were killed by a shot which penetrated their turret. Meanwhile, Sergeant Stan Nash, commanding a tank in C Squadron's Ten Troop, realising that enemy infantry were about to overrun his squadron's position, took his tank to the top of a small ridge from where he could observe enemy movement and pass back vital information, which he hoped would bring support for his squadron. This ridge was known to be covered by an enemy anti-tank gun, which had already knocked out several Valentines. However, Sergeant Nash remained on the ridge under fire until forced to withdraw. Meanwhile, Captain Walters was ordered to move forward and take command of C Squadron's Twelve Troop but when he got there he discovered that two tanks had already been knocked out.

C Squadron then received the order from Major Styles to rally. The Commander of 151 Brigade told Captain Chapman over the radio that the remnants of the regiment must stay and defend the wadi crossing at all costs. Major MacLaren formed the remaining tanks into a composite squadron commanded by Major Styles, which took up suitable defensive positions around the front of the wadi and prepared to stay there whatever happened. Darkness was beginning to fall and the worry was that the position would be overrun by enemy infantry. At this time a number of crews who had lost their tanks, but were unhurt, were fighting alongside the infantry with Bren guns and Thompson sub-machine guns. Sergeant Percy Lewis was one:

> It was a very hot night, the air was filled with fumes of gunpowder and the dust churned up burnt your throat. I was a tank commander in this battle. The bombardment from both sides was very heavy, deafening and frightening; again we lost many men and tanks, including my own. The three of us got out safely, taking our machine-guns and ammo with us and fell in beside the infantry and helped them. This lasted for about two days and we had very little to eat or drink, until finally the area was secured.

Shortly after midnight the divisional commander sent forward his liaison officer to report on the progress of the battle; he reported back: 'the whole area was lit up by the burning tanks of 50 RTR where they had been fought to a standstill by superior enemy armour.'

By 0200 hours, Montgomery saw that his attack had failed and the assault troops, those who survived, were ordered to withdraw.

Meanwhile, Major MacLaren went back to the Chet Meskine area to contact the brigade commander and try to find out exactly what the position was in relation to the defence of the wadi crossing. At this stage, the remaining tank crews were extremely tired and had been subjected over a period of three days to a very great strain, having had little or no sleep and having been shelled and mortared constantly. All the tanks needed refuelling and most of them were very short of ammunition. Major Styles informed Major MacLaren that he was taking his own and a few other tanks over the wadi to contact Major Bazley, commanding the echelon, on the other bank and ferry over fuel and ammunition.

Major Bazley, knowing how desperate the situation had become, had in fact, already ordered the echelon vehicles forward to the edge of the wadi. This now brought the echelon members right into the thick of the battle and under direct fire from the enemy, but despite losses to men and vehicles they were determined to help the tank crews as much as they could. One ammunition lorry hit a slit trench which caused the radiator hose to break away from the engine block. The driver, Trooper Bull, despite the enemy fire, calmly replaced the hose and refilled the coolant, before proceeding on his way. A fitter's lorry driven by Trooper Daw, which had been hit in the radiator and fuel tank and received three hits down the side of the vehicle, did not stop until it had been driven into a German gun pit. It was from this position that Trooper Daw discovered Trooper Garvin, who had escaped unhurt from his knocked out tank, wandering about in a minefield. Daw and another fitter successfully managed to get Garvin to safety.

Meanwhile Major Venn contacted the infantry commander and arranged an infantry defensive screen for the tanks during the night. The shell, mortar and machine-gun fire from the enemy throughout the night was very heavy and accurate, and the infantry commander told Major Venn that had the tanks not been there with their Besa machine-guns, holding the enemy infantry down, his men, in all probability, could not have remained.

With the infantry screen that night, was Jack Beldon, correspondent of the American *Time* magazine. Even in the midst of battle, humour was not forgotten, he wrote in his next report:

We were in a thin grove of palm trees, on the very bank of the wadi. Among these few trees were crowded a dozen or more Valentine tanks. Under fire, we scampered out of our carrier and crawled under a tank. My companions under the tank with me, in the fashion of British and American soldiers, began gibing at each other and at the situation.

'Tell them you marched with the Eighth Army,' said one, quoting one of Churchill's speeches.

'Yeah, tell them you marched under a tank,' the other laughed.

*Figure 20: Another casualty of the Mareth battle (quite possibly belonging to Lt Senior). (Tank Museum)*

In the meantime, Major MacLaren arranged for eight tanks to tow eight six-pounder anti-tank guns over the wadi before first light. Some of the tanks had difficulty securing and attaching the guns so that the lashings would not give when the tank turned. While a suitable method of pulling the guns was arranged, Major-General Nichols, commanding 50th Northumbrian Division, told Major MacLaren to withdraw the tanks to the eastern bank of the wadi and take up defensive positions there. Sherman tanks of 5 RTR, 22 Armoured Brigade were also to take up defensive positions in that area.

Until an hour before first light, Major Venn and his party remained in their positions covering the wadi crossing. They were subjected to machine-guns firing on fixed lines all night, and the enemy brought up an 88mm gun and some 50mm anti-tank guns, shooting by moonlight; but they were unable to reach the 50 RTR tanks without coming into the open. At 0330 hours, the order to withdraw was received. One by one the surviving tanks made their way down to the wadi, their tracks churning frantically, trying to get a grip on something solid. Lieutenant (now Colonel) Vic Senior recalls:

> At last we were ordered to withdraw to the other side of the wadi. We were making our way back when, somewhere near the crossing, we went up on a mine. None of us were hurt but the track and the suspension on one side of our Valentine was utterly destroyed.
>
> In this situation our Brigade Standing Orders were quite clear about what to do if a disabled tank was likely to fall into enemy hands–and ours certainly was! We were to immobilise the gun,

*Figure 21: RMO Capt Ellis, who played such a vital part in saving wounded tank members at Mareth. Both the doctor and his driver were decorated for bravery and devotion to duty for their part in the Mareth battle. (Dr Ellis)*

remove the small arms and such other essential equipment as we could carry, and destroy the tank by throwing a 36 grenade into the turret. Trooper Sydney Adams, my gunner, was getting some of his things out of the blanket box on the side of the tank but he gave this up when an anti-tank solid shot flew past the corner and missed the tank by a foot or two. He said it was like a moon flying past at chest level and it helped to speed his exit quite a bit. I threw the grenade into the tank and it was soon burning fiercely. We got a lift back to the echelon on another tank where Wally Bazley gave us a huge rum.

By 0430 hours they were on the eastern bank of the wadi and eventually the remnants of the regiment rallied and concentrated in the trees 800 yards east of the wadi with the intention of taking up hull-down positions on the ridge in front at first light. Enemy artillery was still very active, and they were using a six-barrelled mortar which had a most demoralising effect on the infantry. At first light on 23 March, two troops were sent forward to watch the northern flank, while Shermans of 5 RTR took up battle positions on the left. The Shermans attracted a great deal of attention and were shelled all morning by 88mms, two being hit and set on fire. 50 RTR reverted to 23 Armoured Brigade command at about mid-day, and Brigadier Richards ordered the tanks to return to their old leaguer area to reorganise and rest.

Throughout the battle for the bridgehead, the medical officer, Captain Ellis, and his driver, Trooper Watkin, had continually driven their scout car under heavy fire, attending to the wounded and carrying them to safety. This was only stopped when their vehicle was blown over by the force of a shell which landed nearby, badly wounding Trooper Watkin and peppering Captain Ellis in the leg. Undeterred the latter

*Figure 22: Tpr Watkin who drove the RMO throughout the Mareth battle. (Dr Ellis)*

obtained another scout car and continued his work until actually ordered back by Major MacLaren.

It is not surprising that after such an action, recommendations were made for five Military Crosses, six Military Medals and five Mentions in Despatches. Two of the awards were later upgraded to a Distinguished Service Order and Distinguished Conduct Medal, and the battle honour 'Mareth' was granted to the Royal Tank Regiment. Brigadier Richards also put forward a recommendation, that Colonel Cairnes be awarded a 'periodical' Distinguished Service Order for his actions throughout the North African campaign. This was turned down, not because Colonel Cairnes' action was unworthy of the award but because he was killed. At this time only the Victoria Cross and Mention in Despatches were awarded posthumously. The members of the regiment thought that this could have been an exception. Brigadier Richards obviously thought the same because he back-dated the recommendation in an attempt to get the award which Colonel Cairnes, without a doubt, deserved.

At this point, acting Lieutenant-Colonel Geoffrey Russell, who had left the regiment to command 40 RTR, returned to take over command and Major MacLaren returned to 40 RTR. Devastated on hearing of the loss of John Cairnes, a good friend and brother officer, Geoff Russell wrote a testimonial, a copy of which was handed to every member of the regiment. An extract reads: 'We have each lost a true friend. But his spirit and influence will remain. This is John Cairnes' Regiment and although his physical presence will be missing, his spiritual presence will be with us to guide us and fortify us in the battles ahead.'

50 RTR now reorganised on a two-squadron basis, each squadron with two troops and a headquarters of two tanks, and a Regimental

Headquarters with two tanks. Major Styles took A Squadron to the brigade 'left out of battle' camp to rest and refit. Throughout the operations from the night of 20 March 50 RTR had lost 33 tanks on the battlefield, 27 of which were irreparably destroyed. Personnel casualties were : one officer and seven other ranks killed, seven officers and 23 other ranks wounded, four other ranks posted as missing. As there was only 156 crewmen involved in the battle, this amounted to over 25% casualties.

On 24 March C Squadron, with nine tanks, and Regimental Headquarters with two, were ordered forward of the Highland Division. They were to expose themselves to the enemy as part of a deception plan to make the enemy think that a fresh attack was being made on the Mareth Line. This they did sufficiently well to get shelled and they withdrew under cover of darkness.

50th Division's attack on the Mareth Line had bought the time Montgomery had asked for; the New Zealand Division had reached its position in a long left hook manoeuvre, while the repositioned 4th Indian Division moved into the Matmata Hills to provide a link between the main force on the coast and the New Zealanders. The Axis forces were left with only one option, retreat.

The main part of the battle as far as the Division and 50 RTR was concerned was now over. They were tired and battered. North and west countrymen alike had attacked the enemy at his strongest point, they had driven a hole through it, and it is no discredit to them that they could not retain the positions which they had won.

Ronald Lewin in his book *Montgomery as Military Commander* wrote:
It happened that my battery position at Mareth was just behind the start-line for the attack, and I remember the Durham Light Infantry passing through our gun positions in high spirits and bursting with confidence. (I remember two days later seeing Brigadier Beak standing on the rim of the bowl in which we lay, endeavouring to rally the stragglers from the assault as they drifted back.) I remember spending a morning with 50 RTR a day or so earlier; no sign of hesitancy or doubt. The men were good but the plan was bad.

# Chapter 7
# BATTLE FOR THE GABES GAP

## Wadi Akarit and Sfax

In the new commanding officer Geoff Russell, the regiment had probably the best replacement for John Cairnes. An officer the men knew and trusted, brave in battle and determined to carry on the good work started by his predecessor. Born in Southport, where his family owned a cotton business, he was educated at Worksop College and had many sporting interests which included rugby, skiing and riding. There is a family story that on his way back to the stables after a ride, the horse, called 'Ginger', would stop at the local golf club and would not move another step until it had been supplied with a pint of beer. Geoff never married, but it is known he broke a few hearts in Southport. Would the men follow him as they did John Cairnes? Only time would tell.

From 25 to 27 March the regiment was rested and re-organised and was held in readiness to join a composite pursuit force, which was waiting to pass through the Mareth position and open the road to Gabes and Sfax, in order to maintain contact with the enemy, who were withdrawing very quickly from the main Mareth Line. 50 RTR, consisting of C Squadron and Regimental Headquarters, were ordered to join MACEFORCE, commanded by Brigadier G W Richards, on 28 March.

MACEFORCE consisted of 50 RTR and A Squadron 40 RTR, plus one battery of medium guns, two batteries of 25-pounder guns, two troops of six-pounder guns from 61 Anti-Tank Regiment, one troop of 9 Field Squadron Royal Engineers, 7th Battalion The Black Watch and one company of medium machine-guns from 1/7th Battalion The Middlesex Regiment.

The Highland Division were to clear the whole country from the coast to the main Arram-Mareth-Gabes road on the night of 28/29 March, as far as the Wadi Zerkine, and then MACEFORCE were to go through. This task was completed by dawn on 29 March, and MACEFORCE, which had crossed the Wadi Zigzaou during the night advanced on Gabes, C Squadron 50 RTR leading, followed by Regimental Headquarters; A Squadron 40 RTR were in reserve. Both squadrons carried infantry of The Black Watch. The country between Mareth and Gabes was scored with numerous wadis but routes were successfully found through them and MACEFORCE, with C Squadron leading, entered Gabes in the early afternoon without encountering opposition; the first troops of the Eighth Army to enter the town. C Squadron took up defensive positions on the northern edge of the airfield and Colonel Russell established his headquarters near one of the hangars. All the northern roads from Gabes had been blown by the enemy's rearguard, and the sappers were soon working on a crossing over which the New Zealanders passed a few hours after MACEFORCE had entered the town.

The regiment had leaguered by the sea near the airfield, and the tank crews had an opportunity of refreshing themselves with a bathe in the Mediterranean. A Squadron 40 RTR now returned to their own regiment, and 50 RTR moved to an area by the sea at Rhennouch on 31 March, where the men had a few days' welcome rest and were able to put in some thorough maintenance on the tanks.

By this time it was evident that the enemy was proposing to make a stand on the line of the Wadi Akarit, about 20 miles north of Gabes. The wadi and the high ground to the west of it formed a natural defensive barrier very similar to the Wadi Zigzaou in the Mareth Line position. Near the coast the flat land narrows to a few miles in width, known as the Gabes Gap. On the extreme eastern end of the Wadi Akarit rises a large hill known as Roumana, a few hundred yards westwards is the hill Fatnassa and still further west lie the hills of Zemlet el Beide and the great salt lake, Chott el Jerid, which cancelled out any repeat of the left hook manoeuvre performed at Mareth. An anti-tank ditch had been constructed between and in front of Roumana and Fatnassa, acting as a continuation of the wadi. This in turn was protected by a deep minefield. The minefield and the anti-tank ditch were both covered by a line of anti-tank and field guns. The line of the Akarit was also the start of the Tunisian Sahel (Plain); for the Axis forces there would be no further defensible position for almost 200 miles.

On 3 April the regiment was organised on a two squadron basis – C Squadron with three troops and a headquarters of two tanks, B Squadron with two troops and a headquarters of one tank and Regimental Headquarters with four tanks. It was hoped that more tanks would be received before the operations on the Wadi Akarit began. 50 RTR at this time had five Mark IX Valentines mounting the six-pounder gun, and were experimenting with a Browning machine-gun which fitted into the breech of the main armament and was fired through the barrel of the six-pounder. The absence of a machine-gun on the Mark IX was a most serious disadvantage, and the Browning had been produced by the Tank Reorganisation Group as a temporary substitute which, however, failed badly in the subsequent operations. Freddie August of B Squadron recalls his experiences with the six-pounder gun:

> Our tank had been pensioned off and we had been given another Valentine with the two-pounder removed and a six-pounder put in its place. This left no room for the machine-gun, so the bright idea was to weld an air-cooled Browning machine-gun into an empty six-pounder shell case, which in use would be thrust up the breech of the six-pounder cannon. Very ingenious in theory, but in practice, when I came to use it at the next battle – at Wadi Akarit – I found that after using one or two belts, the rounds were spraying everywhere like an old fashioned blunderbuss. Not only that but the gun itself got extremely hot, being air-cooled and, being confined in a gun barrel, it could not be extracted.

Vic Senior, newly promoted to captain and second-in-command of C Squadron was also detailed to conduct experiments with the Browning machine-gun. He recommended that it was not feasible when his Browning jumped out of the breech of the gun and continued firing inside the tank!

Experiments were also carried out to find the most satisfactory method of towing six-pounder anti-tank guns behind the tanks; eventually a large iron towing bar was fitted to the shackle holes at the rear. This proved to be most satisfactory in battle but a mistake was made originally in making the bars to a standard size. When the time came to fit them just before battle it was found that the width between the shackle holes in each tank varied and the bars had to be modified in a frantic last minute effort to fit them in time.

MACEFORCE had now been disbanded but a new pursuit force, SPEARFORCE, was formed to go through after the enemy line at Akarit had been broken. 50 RTR were warned, however, that they would be working with 152 Highland Brigade in the initial assault on the Wadi Akarit position and would probably join SPEARFORCE immediately after a hole had been made in the line. Colonel Russell and the squadron leaders, Major Venn (C Squadron) and Major Williams (B Squadron) attended a conference at the Highland Division Headquarters which lasted five hours, and returned with the tasks for the assault, which was to be made on the night of 5/6 April.

The general plan was for 201 Guards Motor Brigade to contain the enemy on the right of the main coast road, 51st Highland Division to attack Roumana and the line of the wadi to the main road, 50th Northumbrian Division to advance between Roumana and Fatnassa and 4th Indian Division to attack Fatnassa. 152 Highland Brigade, which 50 RTR were to support, were to attack the hill Roumana, in three phases: first, to capture and hold the Roumana feature itself; second, to capture and hold the high ground to the west of Roumana; third, to capture and hold the line of the wadi, from Roumana to the main road two miles to the east.

The infantry were to carry out a silent advance from 0330 hours to 0350 hours on 6 April, thereafter they would be supported by artillery. This was the first time the Highlanders had been called on to attack at night without a moon, to be followed immediately by an attack in daylight. 152 Brigade's advance was to be in conjunction with 50 Division attacking on their left.

50 RTR's role was, first, to supply two troops of tanks to support 275 Field Company, Royal Engineers in forcing two gaps through the known enemy minefield at the south western end of Roumana and breach the anti-tank ditch behind the minefield, which would allow armour and wheeled vehicles to pass through. The second task was to tow through one or other of the gaps sixteen six-pounder guns of 296 Anti-Tank Battery, as soon as the sappers had made a way. They were then to rally in a forward area ready to support the infantry in any possible counter-attack, and to watch for enemy infiltration on the flanks. Freddie August remembers preparations for the forthcoming battle at Wadi Akarit:

> Within a fortnight of the Mareth battle we had enough tanks and crews to lend a hand at Wadi Akarit. Sammy Nixon had got into the Major's bad books by running his tank over a mine while entering our first leaguer on the way, after being warned of unswept verges. He was given our six-pounder Vally with instructions not to damage it. Sammy told us this himself, when instead of leading our two troops into action as he always preferred, he sent his sergeant's tank to work point.
>
> We arrived at the lying up area and liaised with the Highlanders, then we got ready for the night action, cleaning, testing and loading our weapons. As there was no room in the turret for the smoke discharger, two three-inch smoke mortars were welded to the side of the turret and fired by cable from inside. I had found that the dust and sand thrown up by travelling had got into these and prevented them from being fired, so I used a piece of old gas cape to cover them. Standing outside the turret I loaded the discharger and carefully tucked this gas cape protectively around and wedged it into the back, I had forgotten that the firing mechanism was from the Lee-Enfield rifle and also carried the usual trigger.
>
> With a terrific crash and whoosh, a smoke bomb missed me by a fraction and went sailing down the infantry lines; with my heart in my mouth I followed its flight and saw it land, thankfully, in a clear space between two companies. I jumped down, seized the tank shovel and rushed over to where the smoke bomb had landed, shouting to all and sundry to bring more shovels. Many

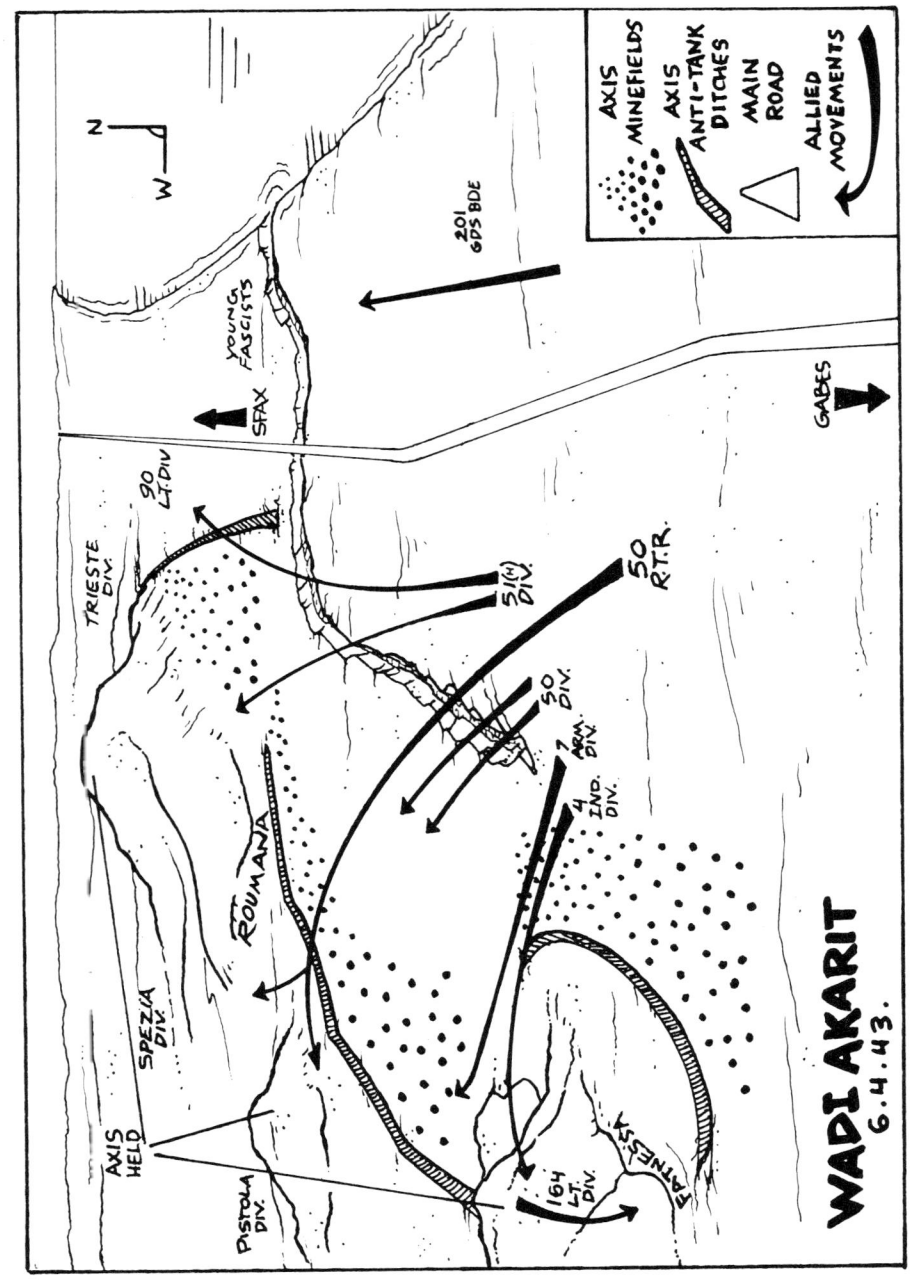

Map 5: 'Wadi Akarit'. Site of battle fought 6 April 1943.

came running to where it lay emitting a huge column of smoke like an erupting Vesuvius, a dead giveaway to any observant Jerry.

However we soon had it under control with a six foot pile of sand, I thought afterwards how lucky I was not to have been standing in front when I accidentally touched the trigger.

Early on 6 April, two troops of B Squadron, commanded by Lieutenants Vincent and Nixon, moved to the area with the sappers. The remainder of the regiment moved to an area on the main track, where contact was made with Major Semple commanding 296 Anti-Tank Battery; here the guns were hitched to the tanks. Apart from the two troops forward, there were only sufficient tanks in the two squadrons to tow fourteen guns. The other two were towed by the new second-in-command, Major Paton (formerly 4 RTR) and the navigating officer, leaving the command tank and the rear link tanks free to control the operation and give covering fire and smoke at the gap, should it become necessary. The previous afternoon Colonel Russell had addressed all tank crews and personnel of A Echelon, informing them of the plan and their own particular tasks. Since the initial phase of the attack was not due to begin until 0330 hours, it seemed unlikely that the gaps in the minefield would be ready before broad daylight and then not until 0800 or 0900 hours. All the crews, except those of the two forward troops, had a good night's sleep.

The two forward troops, with Lieutenant Strang of the Reconnaissance Troop in a scout car, moved forward with the sappers after the artillery had opened up at 0415 hours, providing covering fire until the gaps had been made and the ditch breached. The rest of the Regiment, towing the guns, moved forward to a position short of the gaps at 0830 hours. Lieutenant Vincent reported that the sappers had forced two gaps in the minefield and were breaching the anti-tank ditch at the right hand gap. The two troops had been under very heavy shell and mortar fire, and all three of Lieutenant Nixon's tanks had been knocked out, fortunately without any casualties. One of Lieutenant Vincent's tanks broke a track, leaving him with two tanks on the gaps. Lieutenant Strang's scout car received a direct hit from a mortar bomb and was destroyed but he escaped with a damaged ankle and his driver with a cut on the forehead.

By now the Highland infantry were involved in bitter fighting for Roumana and the surrounding area. The leading brigade found its initial advance up Roumana gradually being pushed back in a fierce, grenade-throwing battle among the rocks and crevices. The divisional reserve, 5th Battalion The Black Watch, were sent to reinforce them, which they did with spectacular élan, the leading platoon storming onto the crest in the nick of time to relieve a Seaforth platoon holding the summit. As night came, they worked their way towards the northern end of

Roumana, but found the enemy well dug in.

Meanwhile down by the road, 7th Battalion The Black Watch burst across the wadi into a bridgehead held by the Argyll and Sutherland Highlanders. Once across they made a right turn and headed for Roumana along the northern edge of the wadi; in doing so they lost all their officers and most of their sergeants, to extremely accurate enemy fire. However, by 0930 hours they had reached the foot of the hill. Heavy fire now forced them to take to the enemy trenches, where they settled down to fight it out. Enemy pressure at the foot of Roumana and the Argylls' bridgehead now began to get so heavy, that 1st Battalion The Black Watch was sent to reinforce both the Argylls and its sister battalion in the trenches. Freddie August recalls:

> Our six tanks had been ordered to advance, led by our Eight Troop sergeant's (Ken Jones') tank, with our six-pounder tank (Lieutenant Nixon's) an unaccustomed second. Being pitch-black we couldn't see if the track had been cleared of mines, as there were no markings we had to trust to luck. Unfortunately our luck was out and though Ken Jones got through OK we copped it and I experienced the trauma of running over a mine. Luckily our Valentines were stoutly built and the only damage was a disabled tank, the other four veered to pass us but only two got through unscathed, so that was half our force out of action.
>
> As it got lighter, away on our left was a range of hills in front of which was a wide scrub – covered plain, on our right was a hill called Roumana. As it got lighter still, we could see numbers of the enemy milling around, we decided to brass them up with some machine gun fire and Ken said to give them a few bursts.
>
> Just then we noticed some enemy troops approaching so we all drew our revolvers, but as they got nearer we could see that they were Italians, two of them supporting a third who was obviously wounded. Reaching our tanks, they asked in bad English to be taken prisoner. Rendering first aid and handing out fags we were suddenly startled by the other three tanks rushing past with their guns pointed rearwards. Panic broke out and a tentative move back was made, accompanied by the Italians crying, "Mamma mia, mamma mia". Not wishing to be left behind I joined in but I hadn't gone 100 yards when I realised we had left our driver, Trooper Crisp, sitting in his driving seat. We tagged on behind jogging along accompanied by some spasmodic shelling.
>
> The next day we went back with transporters and collected the tanks now with a few more dents but otherwise OK. After the tanks had been repaired we discovered that there was no suitable transporter to enable us to rejoin the regiment, which was

bombing up the coast road towards Sfax.

That last evening we had a visit from a stray Arab and with a smattering of French asked for the usual 'tchai' (tea), offering eggs in exchange. Not having had this delicacy for a long time, our French speaker, Ken Jones, asked for "six oeufs à sept heures" (six eggs at 7 o'clock) and kept repeating it to him, with our driver and me joining in the chorus "six oeufs a sept heures", the Arab kept replying "oui oui oui Monsieur", just like a pantomime. Of course no Arab appeared next morning – no idea of time and we left eggless.

At this stage the infantry had captured the Roumana feature but were no further forward and were having a lot of trouble from machine-guns, mortars and snipers on their left. As soon as the right hand gap was complete, C Squadron were ordered to unhitch their anti-tank guns and go through the gap in the minefield to silence the opposition on the left flank. As the leading troop, commanded by Lieutenant Cliff Wykes, were passing through the minefield, his tank ran onto a mine and was immobilised. As the crew baled out, a number of anti-tank guns on the left opened fire and killed the officer and his driver, Trooper Shillcross, as they were dismounting. The gunner, Trooper Boor, escaped with a cut under his eye.

The squadron pushed on over the ditch, and as soon as the tanks opened fire with their machine-guns over 300 Italians came out of their holes on the left and surrendered. There was a gap of over 3,000 yards between the left flank troops of 152 Brigade on Roumana and the right flank of the leading infantry of 50th Division to the west. Despite heavy shell and mortar fire in the area of the minefield, which badly wounded Lieutenant Inch and Trooper Hooton, C Squadron held this ground all day and throughout the night of 6/7 April. Both Inch and Hooton were evacuated to the regimental aid post but subsequently died of their wounds.

German Mark VI tanks were reported in the area and the squadron had pushed forward beyond the forward positions to get information about them. Unfortunately, Major Venn had no artillery observation officer with him and he was unable to contact those with the infantry, otherwise he could have brought fire down on a number of targets and neutralised the mortars which were harassing the gaps.

In the meantime, three tanks of B Squadron and two of Regimental Headquarters ferried anti-tank guns over the ditch to suitable positions behind C Squadron, taking over eight guns under the supervision of Major Paton. These guns were moved under heavy fire but their crews, riding on the backs of the tanks with their ammunition, worked magnificently and had their guns unhitched and in position within two or three minutes of the tanks arriving at their selected positions.

*Figure 23: B Squadron Valentine towing a six-pounder anti-tank gun across the anti-tank ditch at Wadi Akarit, April 1943. (IWM)*

In the late afternoon, Colonel Russell was ordered to send one troop of tanks to support 2nd Battalion The Seaforth Highlanders on the right of Roumana. The troop moved along the south eastern side of the hill until they contacted the infantry. They returned at last light, as the regiment went into close leaguer. C Squadron had to stay in the area of the gap all night, and replenishment was sent through to them. As previously stated C Squadron in their position were under heavy mortar fire; despite this the padre, Captain Hart, gallantly went forward with a burial party and buried Lieutenant Wykes and Trooper Shillcross.Trooper John Gibberd on the spare crews truck at this time recalls:

When tanks are knocked out as mine was at Mareth, survivors are put on a 'spare crews' truck which waits a safe distance from the fighting. Every now and again a jeep comes racing up with demands for a commander, gunner or driver according to requirements.

Late that evening I was taken to join Michie Thompson's troop, I remember passing one of our chaps lying on his back covered with desert dust looking as if he had been moulded out of the sand. It seemed all wrong that his face was covered and he wasn't doing anything about it – of course I knew he was dead.

I joined Michie after dark and the place was still under shell fire, so I wasted no time getting into the tank and didn't meet up with the rest of the troop. In the morning I learnt that instead of the rest I'd hoped for, my tank and two others were to spearhead

*Figure 24: C Squadron (part of SPEARFORCE) leaving the Akarit position for the main road and Sfax, accompanied by members of the 51st Highland Division. April 1943. (IWM)*

the advance into Sfax.
During the night enemy resistance slowly died down but it was not until the next morning that the full extent of the fighting could be seen. The German and Italian troops had pulled back leaving behind them a mass of guns and ammunition. General Tuker commanding 4th Indian Division had previously, with experienced foresight, commented 'Roumana will be a tough nut to crack'; he was right.

On the morning of 7 April, the Axis forces had withdrawn from the Akarit position and SPEARFORCE was formed. 50 RTR joined this force ready to advance through the Wadi Akarit and up the main coast road to Sfax, also accompanied by some 40 RTR tanks. 50 RTR had seventeen tanks and led the force onto the main road. There was a great deal of confusion at the two crossings, which were not suitable for wheels. Vehicles of 22 Armoured Brigade were also trying to get through at the same time, but SPEARFORCE had priority and Colonel Russell succeeded in holding other units back until the tanks were through. The covering Bren carriers were mortared by a small enemy rearguard and as the light was failing, they withdrew to a leaguer area a short way south down the road.

At first light on 8 April the advance continued, the carrier platoons leading the way with 50 RTR astride the road and to the right of it, with 40 RTR to the left. Contact was made with an enemy rearguard in the area of Achichina. Vehicles were seen moving about in the trees just south of the road junction, and, whilst the enemy were under observation, the road bridge over the Wadi Keibo was blown up, as was the railway bridge to the left. The enemy had at least two six-barrelled mortars mounted on half-track vehicles, which he fired accurately at the slightest movement.

Fire was eventually brought down, one half-track receiving a direct hit, bursting into flames and burning fiercely all night. The enemy had one or more anti-tank guns covering the position and these opened fire on the forward tanks when they tried to creep forward. It was impossible to attack the position anywhere but frontally. Two tanks attempted to go round on the right, but became bogged down. The leading tanks probed forward to try to bring their machine-guns to bear, but due to the light failing they were ordered to leaguer about 1,500 yards back. As the tanks were on a forward slope, they would be in full view of the enemy when dawn broke. The enemy after firing Spandaus on fixed lines for most of the night, withdrew before first light.

On 9 April, it was discovered that the Germans had mined the position well, and the break in the road at the wadi crossing had been very effective. A crossing was found to the left and with some difficulty all the tanks, preceded by carriers, managed to get over. This crossing was not fit for wheeled vehicles and it was some time before the artillery could catch up with the rest of the column. The Highland Division were supervising the traffic going through and allowed the column's rations through, but not the ammunition vehicles. Meanwhile the leading tanks had made contact with the enemy at about 1400 hours at the Wadi Chaffar some fifteen miles south of Sfax. The point troop, commanded by Lieutenant Michie Thompson of C Squadron got to within 100 yards of the position, before the enemy, with experienced patience opened fire. One tank was knocked out by a 50mm anti-tank gun, which penetrated the front armour, killing the driver, Lance Corporal Clifford. Trooper George Thomas was the gunner in the point tank and recalls the events of that day:

> Our crew was made up of Sergeant Stan Nash, Lance Corporal Paddy Clifford and myself. I am not sure, I think it must have been the reorganisation after the losses at Mareth and Wadi Akarit as this was, as far as I can remember, the first time I had been with this crew.
>
> On the morning of the 9th we continued the follow-up of the retreating German force, whose resistance was mainly rearguard. Our troop was on the right of the road, with the sea a short way to our right. As we approached the trees, into which the road disappeared behind a farmhouse, one of the Bren carriers proceeding up the road was hit and stopped with obvious casualties. Sergeant Nash ordered our tank to stop and he

*Figure 25: Pat Clifford (left), author's grandfather, killed in action April 1943. (author's collection)*

surveyed the front area with his field glasses from on top of the tank. Having some idea of the location of the Germans, he intimated that he was intending to attack the obstacle with the assistance of the other two tanks, which were 30 or 40 yards behind.

As we advanced, I was ordered to spray the front area from left to right with machine-gun fire. As we moved off and came from behind a small sandhill, we received a direct hit in the centre of the driver's compartment. The AP shell came into the turret at my feet, having spent itself. Sergeant Nash and I both immediately abandoned the tank, landing on the floor and made our way to the rear for protection. The Germans hit the tank in the turret from the right as we jumped out, and sprayed the tank with machine gun fire, setting fire to jerricans of diesel etc. on the sides. We remained behind the tank for a very long time until the other tanks came forward in their advance.

Once this had occurred we ascertained that Lance Corporal Clifford had, as we thought, been killed when the tank was hit by the first shell. We recovered his body from the tank and, with the help of a French farmer, buried Paddy beside his tank. After spending the night in the farm buildings and being fed by the farmer and his wife, we returned to the echelon, where I stayed for a few days whilst Sergeant Nash went on to rejoin the forward tanks.

Having been informed of the enemy rearguard, Brigadier Richards ordered 40 RTR to outflank the position on the left, with one squadron coming in directly in the rear of the enemy and another squadron from the north-east, while 50 RTR were to probe the position frontally. John Gibberd takes up the story:

> The gunner then turned his attention to me and I saw the AP shot, which are made of solid steel, bouncing off the ground too close for comfort. Michie Thompson, my tank commander, shouted something and I drove for cover without stopping to admire the scenery.

The column's artillery then put down a five-minute concentration of high explosive on the objective followed by smoke, and all tanks converged on the position overrunning it; 25 Germans surrendered. Three 50mm anti-tank guns, three 20mm Skoda guns and one 75mm Pak together with two half-tracks, were captured. Lieutenant Michie Thompson recalls:

> I jumped out of the tank and drew my revolver; several Germans appeared and I signalled them to get onto the tank. One was cheeky enough to get into the turret, leaving me to ride outside – the others, perhaps five or six in all, clambered onto the tank and around the turret. I recall one was an officer and I took his Zeiss binoculars from him – I later lost these in Italy.

Lieutenant Harry Haywood remembers the same action:

> As our troop was advancing down a slope towards the wadi a message came over the wireless telling us to pull out as the point troop had been ambushed. As the driver was turning the tank around, we were hit in the tracks and immobilised – the damage was repaired about six hours later. After the action I went to see the tank that had been knocked out and saw that the shell had gone through the front and into the turret. I had been in 6 Armoured Car Company in India with the driver before the war.

A French family living nearby had taken shelter under a small railway bridge during the attack and a young boy with them was killed by the column's shelling; the family was not discovered until the action was over. The position had been captured by 1730 hours and the tanks pushed on towards Nakta whilst the infantry mopped up and took the prisoners in hand.

John Gibberd recalls an incident at this time:

> The infantry came panicking up to us to say that there was a German tank in some woods – they didn't like German tanks. Michie fired a smoke shell and ordered me to charge through the

smoke – I couldn't see a thing – towards the tank. I didn't fancy our chances against a Jerry tank. When we got there we found the tank had been abandoned.

It was not long before the leading tanks were fired upon by mortars to their immediate front. Some 2,000 yards in front was a stretch of bare, open country. As the enemy strength was unknown it was too risky to push the tanks forward. Artillery support was called for but it had become too dark for observation, so the tanks rallied back and two defensive screens of infantry were put out ahead of them.

During the night of 9/10 April the enemy was very active on demolitions in the Sfax area. At first light on the 10th the tanks continued the advance and reached the town by 0810 hours without incident, despite a slight delay on two occasions while the sappers cleared mines sown across the road. C Squadron 50 RTR were the first elements of the Eighth Army to enter the town, and they took up defensive positions on the northern outskirts. John Gibberd, driver of the first tank into Sfax remembers:

We were waiting for orders and had just got the kettle boiling, when orders came through to pick up the infantry and drive into Sfax. We thought, or maybe just I thought, 'Blow that! We're going to have our tea first!' I cannot drink tea as hot as some can so for a few glorious minutes World War Two had to wait until I drank my tea.

A month or so later, I saw a copy of a newspaper which headlined on the front page 'at ten past eight this morning the British Army entered Sfax'. I thought if it had not been for our mugs of tea, it would have been eight o'clock!

Regimental Headquarters, followed by Brigade Headquarters and led by the pipers of the Highland Division, were mobbed by the local French population as they passed through the town; they insisted on climbing onto the tanks and riding through the main thoroughfare, brandishing flags of the Allied nations and singing the *Marseillaise*. Captain Gordon Atkinson marvelled at the spectacle of the adjutant 'being kissed by a variety of French maidens of all ages.' It was some time before the vehicles could get through to the northern outskirts of the town. Four Italians, who had been waiting to surrender, gave themselves up as the tanks were leaguering about eight miles north of Sfax.

Trooper E R Manwaring-White recalls the approach to Sfax:

For a few days, I had been detailed with thirteen others to travel in lorries and be up with the tanks (who were in hot pursuit of the enemy) when they leagured for the night.

We performed guard duties, to allow the tank crews to sleep at night. On 10th April we were aroused at 0430 hours and departed rearwards (guard duty over) to an area away from the front line.

We were soon back in the lorries and passed Mahares some 20 miles south of Sfax.

One of the leading tanks had been knocked out and one of the crew members, a chap named Thomas, was later taken into our truck and said, 'Poor Paddy, he was sure he was going to survive the war'. The irony of that remark caused it to stick in my mind.

Our truck reached Sfax late that afternoon and I noted in my diary at the time, 'cheering crowds, tanks had terrific welcome, plus flowers and wine.'

50 RTR had reached Sfax five days ahead of Montgomery's planned schedule. The rapturous welcome they received: was a welcome reward for some long days of hard work and fighting perhaps now they would have the chance to relax.

# Chapter 8
# 'WE MUST ALL BE TANK MINDED'

## The End in North Africa

On 13 April the regiment moved from its leaguer area north of Sfax to a new area, nearer the sea. The tank strength was now 30, B and C Squadrons having thirteen tanks each, including four six-pounders, and Regimental Headquarters had four tanks. Meanwhile A Squadron personnel were still at the Left out of Battle camp at Djorf, resting. It was on 1 April, during this rest period, that Lieutenant P J L Crooke was killed by an undiscovered enemy mine, while examining the Mareth battlefield.

On the 17th the regiment moved up the main Sfax-Sousse road, the tanks being taken off their transporters at M'saken and travelling the next 25 miles on their tracks. By 19 April, the regiment had leaguered south of Enfidaville. They were still operating on a two-squadron basis, A Squadron still being at 23 Armoured Brigade Left out of Battle Camp, now at Sfax.

50 RTR were to support 4th Indian Division (temporarily attached to the British First Army) for the assault on Enfidaville, the ground over which they were to operate having been reconnoitred two days previously by Colonel Russell and the squadron leaders, Major Venn and Major Williams.

The Enfidaville line was the Axis' last defensible position in Tunisia, from which to stop the Eighth Army advance on Tunis. With the British First Army and the Americans advancing from the west, the Axis forces would have to drive back the Allied thrust or surrender North Africa.

The coastal plain ended at Enfidaville, rocky hills known as Djebels, stretching from Pont du Fahs in the west almost to the coast itself. Five miles north of Enfidaville the plain was down to less than a mile wide, with one road to Hammamet running through it. There were two other roads that led to Tunis. In the centre, guarded by the hill and village of Takrouna, lay the road via Zaghouan; the other, running initially westwards below the hills to Pont du Fahs, was dominated by Djebel Garci.

The general plan for the attack was for 2nd New Zealand Division, with 8 Armoured Brigade, to assault and capture the prominent Takrouna feature, whilst 4th Indian Division and 23 Armoured Brigade were to attack the Djebe Garci and the high ground beyond it. The attack was to begin at 2130 hours on the 19th with an artillery barrage. 50 RTR were to move forward before darkness and be ready to support 7 Indian Brigade south of the Garci feature. Under command of 50 RTR were two troops of 513 Battery, 149 Anti-Tank Regiment, Royal Artillery, whose guns were to be towed by the tanks, should the ground prove too difficult for wheeled vehicles. The regiment moved from its leaguer at 0130 hours on the 20th, B Squadron leading, followed by Regimental Headquarters and C Squadron. At 0200 hours they crossed the start line and advanced to a lying up position. Just before first light they moved forward to form an anti-tank screen on the southern and south-eastern flanks of the Indian Brigade.

By first light the attack seemed to be going well. 5 Indian Brigade had advanced up and along the Djebel Garci against heavy opposition and the New Zealanders had surrounded Takrouna and were involved in bitter fighting for the peak. 50 RTR now crossed the Wadi Boul, the anti-tank guns being able to cross drawn by their own vehicles. Regimental Headquarters took up position on the edge of the wadi, with B Squadron a little to the left and front; C Squadron remained in the wadi behind Regimental Headquarters as reserve.

The village at the foot of Djebel Garci and in front of B Squadron began to receive heavy shell and mortar fire. Brigadier Richards ordered 50 RTR to link up with the New Zealanders, who were holding a strong point to the right of B Squadron's position. Three troops of C Squadron were sent forward to strengthen the gap between 50 RTR's right flank and the New Zealand left, and it was these tanks that made contact with a New Zealand brigade.

Meanwhile the section of scout cars operating in front of B Squadron had probed far enough forward to come under heavy mortar fire; they hastily withdrew. Another section of scout cars, commanded by Lieutenant E V Hibbert, managed to get well forward of C Squadron and the New Zealanders. They were able to pinpoint several positions from which the German artillery and mortars were firing.

B and C Squadrons were now ordered forward across the road which lay in front of their positions. C Squadron moved a little way before coming under fire; B Squadron came under heavy and accurate shell and mortar fire before they reached the road and were pinned down in their positions. It was during this shelling that Lieutenant Strang was severely wounded in the face by a shell splinter, which caused the loss of an eye. He was evacuated back on his own tank, which later returned to the squadron with a new commander.

During the afternoon 40 RTR came up on 50 RTR's right and joined

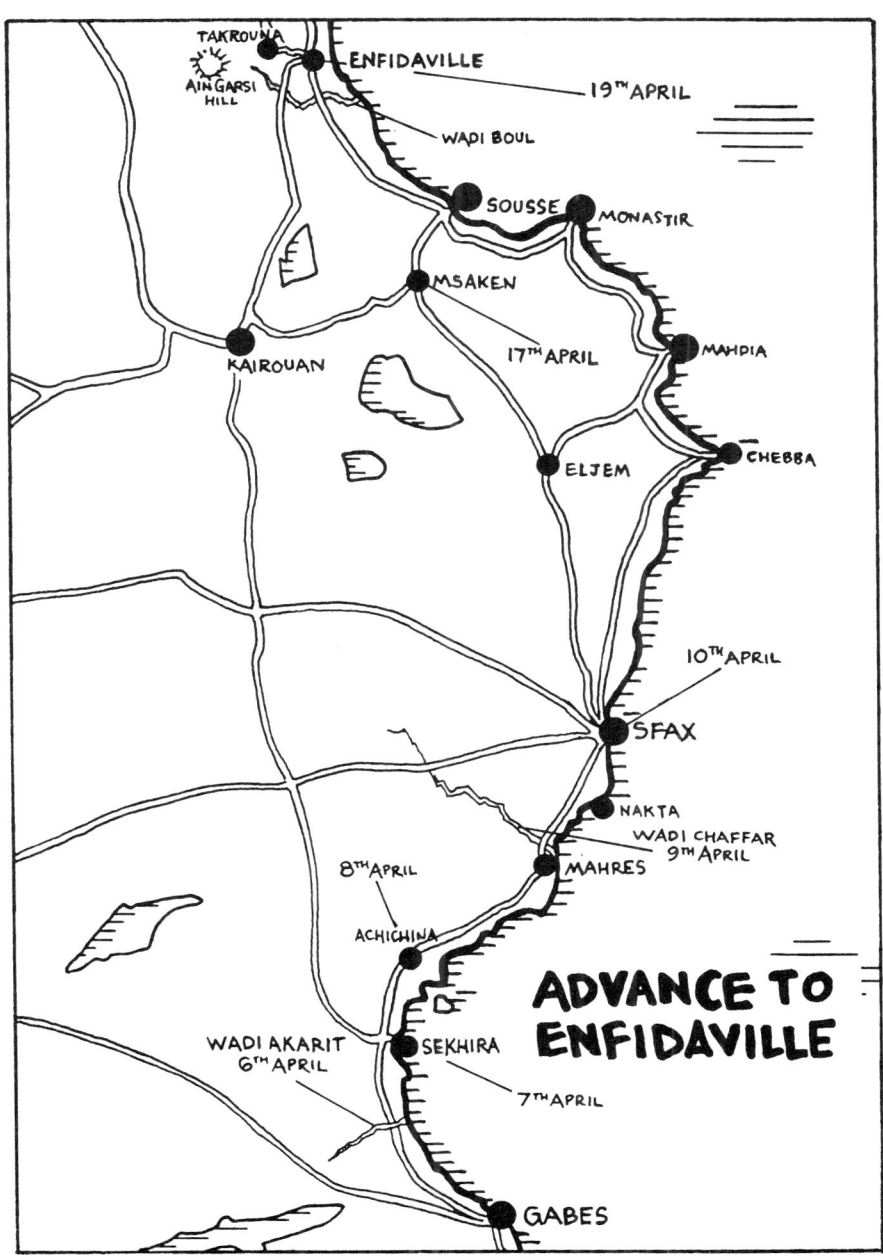

*Map 6: 'Advance to Enfidaville'. Advance from the Akarit position to Sfax and Enfidaville.*

up with the New Zealanders, thus relieving C Squadron who then moved to the left to strengthen B Squadron's front. By late afternoon all the anti-tank guns were in position, forming a screen south of the road. At dusk, infantry of the 1st Battalion The Royal Sussex Regiment came up to put out a protective screen for the guns and tanks during the night. The tanks had been ordered to leaguer by troops with the infantry and guns. Regimental Headquarters spent the night in the wadi. Leaguering by troops meant that replenishment would be difficult; however this was completed well before first light the next day.

At daybreak on the 21st the regiment advanced north of the road with B Squadron leading, followed by Regimental Headquarters and C Squadron. During the night Major Venn had fallen sick with dysentery and command of C Squadron went to Captain Jenkin. B Squadron now reached a bridge north of the road; there they halted in hull-down positions which were overlooked by Djebel Garci, still occupied by the enemy. This move allowed the enemy to engage B Squadron with mortars and 88mm guns. One 88mm high explosive shell landed on the front of Lieutenant Vincent's tank, killing his driver, Trooper Tatchell, instantly, and wounding the operator, Corporal Merriman. Lieutenant Vincent, who was dismounted at the time, was unhurt. The shell had split the front armour of the tank clean open; another tank of the same troop towed it back to the Wadi Boul, where Trooper Tatchell was removed from the vehicle and buried in the wadi by the padre, Captain Hart. Regimental Headquarters was also receiving attention from the German gunners, the second-in-command, Major W A Paton, being wounded in the head by shrapnel and Sergeant Broad of C Squadron was also wounded by shell fire.

At about 1530 hours, the enemy commenced a heavy and intense barrage on the part of Djebel Garci that was held by 5 Indian Brigade – this barrage was followed by an enemy infantry attack which, despite a spirited assault, was beaten off by the Indian infantry. One small party of German infantry succeeded in dragging a mortar onto a position which overlooked The Fiftieth's and very shortly opened fire on B Squadron's position. Major Williams opened up with his Besa, and at the same time Captain Garrett opened fire with his six-pounder gun, the target being some 1,300 feet above his position. High explosive shells were clearly seen to fall around the enemy mortar; this must have had the desired effect as it never fired again. At last light a detachment of infantry came forward to take over the ground that 50 RTR had held all day, and at 2000 hours the tanks moved back to leaguer near the Wadi Boul.

At daybreak on 22 April, B and C Squadrons dispersed a few hundred yards forward of the leaguer, Regimental Headquarters returning to their original position by the edge of the wadi. 40 RTR were similarly dispersed on the right of 50 RTR, and were subjected to artillery fire for the rest of the day. The next day the regiment moved back out of the front line and leaguered with 23 Armoured Brigade Headquarters, who were now back under command of 51st Highland Division.

On Easter Day, 25 April, the regiment was inspected on parade by Major General Wimberley commanding 51st Highland Division, who thanked them for all their help in the past desert battles. The following day the regiment was put under command of 56th (London) Division, who had come from Palestine to join the Eighth Army.

On 27 April, the regiment moved closer to the Enfidaville line, where they leaguered for the night in an olive grove. They were to attack at dawn the following morning with two companies of 3rd Battalion Coldstream Guards (201 Guards Motor Brigade) but the attack was postponed twice in the next 48 hours before being cancelled, and on 30 April the regiment was again moved away from the front line.

On 1 May, the regiment was facing the German 90th Light Division astride the main road to Tunis, just north of the village of Enfidaville, when Brigadier Richards brought the news that every man had been waiting for – 50 RTR was to be re-equipped with three squadrons of Sherman tanks.

May 1943 closed the first important chapter in The Fiftieth's war history; it was a chapter of hard and gallant fighting, of tremendous achievement, and inevitably of casualties. Everyone in the regiment was by now very tired, and all were resigned to the fact that they were not to be in at the final kill in North Africa, but they realised they had been chosen for other things.

On 2 May, the regiment handed over nine Valentines to 40 RTR – the crews went back to A Echelon and the remainder of the tanks pulled out under cover of darkness. The whole regiment leaguered that night near the village of Sidi Bou Ali, north of Sousse. The following day the men said goodbye to their faithful steeds, which had carried them so far through the desert, and handed in all their Valentines. The crews were then sent back to an area north of Sfax, where they rejoined A Squadron. The men were now to train with tanks with superior armament, giving them a better chance of survival against the enemy. Meanwhile, their Valentines would be handed over to the Free French forces fighting in Tunisia.

During this first week of May the regiment received 188 new recruits shortly after arriving one of these described his first impressions in a letter home: 'I am definitely happier here than anywhere else I have been in the army, not that I have been unhappy elsewhere, but here there is a different atmosphere. Everybody works together as a team.'

Sherman tanks began to arrive in twos and threes from 26 Armoured Brigade (Fifth Army), but no instructors. On 9 May, the padre held a

Memorial Service for the men from 50 RTR who had lost their lives since arriving in North Africa. Colonel Russell read out the Roll of Honour.

Trooper Ivor Sambells remembers The Fiftieth being reorganised at Sfax, as his particular workload was nearly doubled: 'I was the regimental barber – my former civilian trade – and as such, spent most of my time in A Echelon. I was kept very busy cutting up to 50 soldiers' hair a day. When the new Shermans arrived the numbers of personnel went from about 550 to 880.'

By 11 May, the regiment had fifteen Shermans on which to train, plus one Grant that somehow appeared; at least half of these tanks were defective and beyond repair. The following day the fighting in North Africa officially ended. After nearly two years the North African war was over. It had cost Germany and Italy almost one million soldiers killed, wounded or taken prisoner.

By the 17th, the regiment had 200 officers and men who could drive a Sherman tank and 24 had done the commanders' conversion course on the 75mm gun. On the 21st the men were each given 24 hours leave in Tunis, 20 all ranks at a time. On 30 May, after a month of training on their new tanks, the Commanding Officer, Lieutenant-Colonel Russell was proud to publish the following Regimental Order.

> On 7th May 1943, just before the regiment began individual training on the Sherman tank, I said we must all be tank minded, and in view of this every officer and man, whatever his employment, was given an opportunity of learning to drive a tank. Today, everyone in this regiment, clerks, cooks, storemen, lorry drivers and other employed men who do not normally fight in a tank, can drive. In an emergency, anyone of them could get into a tank and drive it away. This has been done in three weeks in the early mornings and late evenings and whenever our tanks could be spared from the specialist courses. It is a magnificent achievement and it is unlikely to be equalled by any other tank regiment. I wish to thank and congratulate all ranks.

June 1943 proved to be a very hard month for the regiment in terms of training and exercising; this lasted from sunrise to sundown on most days. Operational tanks arrived in small numbers, which meant the crews could not train as a squadron or regiment. The regiment, even if they had had the tanks to train on, could not have completed their final rehearsal for an invasion (the location of which was still secret) as the Highland Division, whom they were to fight alongside, were training at Djijelli over 400 miles away. On the 19th, during training carried out on the coast south of Monastir, a Sherman Mark III driven by Trooper Gibberd, was written off; drivers had been practising driving in and out of the sea in tanks that had been water-proofed. The exhaust chimney

*Figure 26: Shermans of 50 RTR aboard LCT 560, Sfax, July 1943, shortly before they left North Africa for Sicily. (IWM)*

(known to the men as a fish-fryer) on one of them had fallen off while the vehicle was in about six feet of water and 150 yards out; immediately the tank became waterlogged and the crew had to make a hurried exit. Another tank was then taken close enough to the stricken tank, to enable a rope to be attached between them.

By the end of the month, with 50 operational Shermans, the regiment was again ready for battle, whereupon they were sent to a concentration area near Sousse, ready for embarkation. Joe Heppell recalls:

> We went inland to avoid detection, dug slit trenches amongst the trees. On my 21st birthday, John Gibberd went to get some eggs from the natives. They refused 'V' cigs, so John gave them some 'Players'; we had a celebration of eggs and bread.
>
> A few days later during the final preparations for the invasion, we had to load a rocket-craft. Captain Vincent volunteered us to put the shells into the rocket-craft, as we were used to handling explosive shells.

In the first three days of July, the regiment was divided into three groups, ready for Operation BIGOT HUSKY (the location still, as yet, a secret). Group A: vehicles and personnel not required in the initial stages. Group B: all tanks, scout cars and transport required for the battle. Group C: a rear party consisting of all non-essential transport, plus the crews and first reinforcements, who were to follow up.

All planning for the invasion was done on coded maps, which later proved to be the topography of Sicily, with fictitious place names.

40 RTR, the last of 23 Armoured Brigade to come out of the North African battles, could not be re-equipped in time to participate, and only B Squadron of 46 RTR (who had re-equipped with Shermans in Egypt) would accompany 50 RTR. These in turn would be supported by the brigade troops consisting of – 11th Battalion The Kings Royal Rifle Corps (Queen's Westminsters), 331 Company Royal Army Service Corps, and 150 Light FieldAmbulance.

On 5 and 6 July all 50 RTR personnel were transported to Sfax and embarked on the 6th and 7th, rejoining their vehicles on the ships, which had been loaded the previous day. This was to be the first time that LSTs (Landing Ships, Tank) and LCTs (Landing Craft, Tank) were to be used to put tanks as well as troops ashore in the assault wave.

The regiment sailed in two convoys on 8 July.

# Chapter 9
# 'BLOODY ROUGH'

## The Fight For Sicily

For the invasion of Sicily in 1943 a vast fleet of 237 merchant vessels and troop transports, plus 1,742 motorised landing craft, were used to bring ashore the men, tanks, and supplies. These were protected by six battleships, two aircraft carriers, fifteen cruisers, 128 destroyers and 26 submarines, all under the command of Admiral Cunningham, with Admiral Sir Bertram Ramsay commanding the actual landings. This was an enormous concentration but, by the end of the first phase of the operation, 115,000 British and Canadians, and 66,000 Americans had been put ashore.

For the journey to Sicily, the regiment was distributed in twenty eight vessels of a new design, their tanks in LCTs and the Echelon vehicles in LSTs. Colonel Russell, the squadron commanders and liaison officers, accompanied the infantry in the leading assault craft.

50 RTR's War Diary records:

> The voyage to Sicily was uneventful, though in one way quite remarkable. The two convoys in which 50 RTR was sailing failed to attract the attention of enemy aircraft.

However, not everything was plain sailing. One unfortunate incident did occur, and that was when LCT 547 sank with two complete troops of C Squadron's tanks, a Daimler scout car and a recovery truck. Trooper Tom Wilson recalls:

> As the weather gradually became worse our craft slowly began to list to port as the day wore on. By nightfall it had a quite positive list, but, with our faith in the Royal Navy we all cheerfully bedded down for the night on the deck beside our vehicles. At daybreak we woke up to find that the port side of the LCT was just under water and the deck was at a very alarming angle. There didn't appear to be any immediate panic but we were told to put on our life jackets.
> 
> We had our breakfast and sat around for about an hour, suddenly the LCT's captain shouted "Abandon Ship" from the

bridge. I think everybody was somewhat shocked to say the least. As far as I know, like me, everybody just walked down the deck into the sea and swam a safe distance away from the craft and then did their best to keep afloat.

We could see the list getting worse and after about 30 minutes the six Shermans and a couple of support vehicles began to slide down the deck, the LCT then turned turtle and sank. After an hour in the water I was picked up by a Navy torpedo boat. I was helped aboard to only to discover that I had parted company with my slacks in the water, unfortunately I had put what valuables I had in the pockets. The sailors found us a few clothes and we were eventually put onto another LCT carrying stores and dumped on a beach in southern Sicily.

Ultimately, a search party from the regiment found us and we were taken to C Squadron's location, some time later we were fixed up with new tanks and personal gear.

All personnel were saved and picked up, but this was a great loss to the regiment as the possibility of obtaining more tanks was very remote.

Meanwhile aboard an LST, the A Squadron ammunition truck broke away from its shackles and began to slide from side to side and 'showed every desire to abandon ship, securing it was another of those happy times' (this same vehicle actually drowned during disembarkation). While aboard a B Squadron LCT, the ship's captain mistook the searchlights over Malta for the lights of Sicily and had the tank crews standing-to for most of the night.

When the ships left North Africa very few officers knew the destination; this relevant information was revealed to the regiment while at sea. The plan was for 51st Highland Division of XXX Corps to land on the south eastern tip of Sicily at 0245 hours on 10 July, secure a bridgehead and open up the beaches for support troops. All three squadrons of 50 RTR were committed with the Highlanders to the initial stages of the battle. 231 Malta Brigade were to land on the right of the Highland Division with B Squadron of 46 RTR. The Canadian forces with one armoured brigade were to land on the left, XIII Corps were to land on the right of 231 Malta Brigade and the Americans on the left of the Canadians. The allied air forces were to provide air cover and the Royal Navy were to carry out a bombardment programme.

The German forces in Sicily only amounted to two divisions; the reason for this was due to the work of British Intelligence. They had let false plans fall into German hands, which told the Germans that the next Allied thrust would come in Sardinia and Greece, and that the attack on Sicily was only a feint. The Germans, believing the plans to be authentic, strengthened the coastal defences in Sardinia and Greece. This operation by British Intelligence became known as 'The Man Who

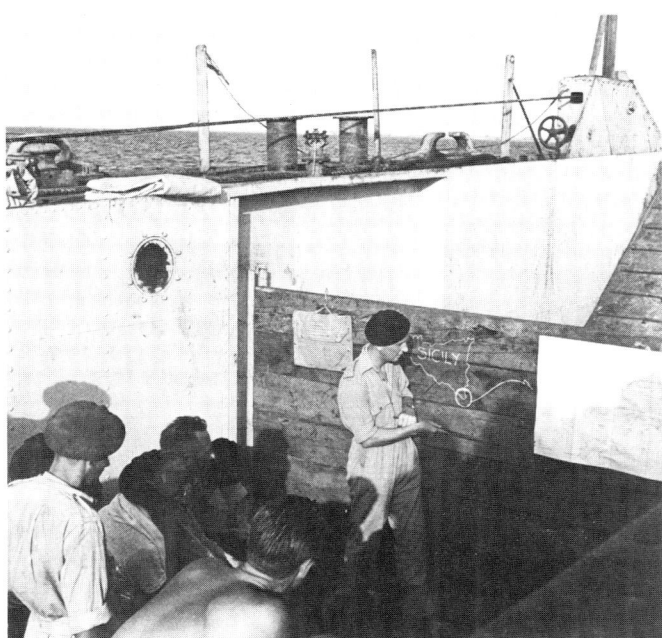

*Figure 27: Lt Ingham of C Squadron's Eleven Troop, after 3 hours at sea, reveals the destination as Sicily. (IWM)*

Never Was'.

The general topography of Sicily is very mountainous and movement off the roads and tracks was seldom possible. From the beginning of the operation it was evident that main roads would be fiercely contested and would play a major part in the forthcoming battles. 50 RTR's target after landing was the high ground known as Colorado Ridge.

During the last few hours at sea a force 6 wind blew up, reducing the speed of the convoy and, not for the first time, making many of the troops ill. However, the Tank Landing Craft reached the release point in good time and made their way to Portopalo Bay on the Pachino peninsula. The only signs of battle as they headed for the shore were the rocket ships pouring salvo after salvo across the beaches, sporadic machine-gun fire and enemy searchlights sweeping the sky. There was no moon, and all that could be seen of the Sicilian coast was a black blurred outline. The craft were guided in by the beachmaster, and the first to beach were carrying Colonel Russell's and the Adjutant's tanks with the two headquarter tanks of C Squadron. This craft grounded about 30 feet from the shore and the two leading tanks plunged into about eight feet of water, reaching the beach safely. These two tanks, the Adjutant's and Captain Vic Senior's, proceeded to the assembly area where the waterproofing was removed and the crews prepared for action. Meanwhile, there was some difficulty getting the remaining two tanks off.

*Figure 28: Capt Vic Senior (right) and Major Dickie Venn of C Squadron, Sicily 1943. (T Stanton)*

The landing craft had swung round, trying to get closer to the beach, because in front of the last tanks aboard were some carriers. These were shifted around in the well of the ship and the tanks got off, but into deeper water, which came right up to the turrets; however, they managed to get ashore safely.

Trooper Robert Blundell, of C Squadron aboard this first landing craft recalls:

> There were four tanks and a bulldozer on our landing craft and little else. The sea was like a mill pond. After two or three hours at sea we were told Sicily for the invasion. As we passed Malta in the distance we changed course and so did the sea; it was bloody rough.
>
> Our landing was quiet but not without a problem. As the bulldozer left the landing craft, the vessel swung round on a sand bank facing out to sea again. Captain Senior jumped naked in the water to test the depth and gave the OK to disembark. At this time we were all 'hatched down' and sealed in, still facing out to sea. I think we were the second tank off and the water was up to the top of the turret as we turned, or so we were told. It's an experience I shall never forget.

The Highlanders were by now on Colorado Ridge and waiting for C Squadron to support them. The beaches were a hive of activity with men and vehicles scrambling ashore at all angles; there was some difficulty getting the remaining two troops of C Squadron off their ship, so Colonel Russell formed a troop of Major Venn, Captain Senior and Captain Chapman, who then went up to support the Highlanders, carrying with them a platoon of The Black Watch – their intention was to capture the water tower, come up behind Pachino and block the northern exits from the town. While on their way to support the Highlanders, this composite troop was fired on by Italians with Spandaus and anti-tank guns, causing the infantry to dismount. After the tanks had destroyed two pill boxes, 200 Italians surrendered. When the move had been completed the composite troop made contact with Canadian troops on the airfield at Pachino.

On reaching the northern outskirts of Pachino, the infantry dismounted and swept into the town. Major Venn's two troops then arrived allowing Captain Chapman to return to Regimental Headquarters to resume his duties as rear link officer. C Squadron then formed a perimeter around the northern edge of Pachino.

Meanwhile, B Squadron, commanded by Captain Garrett, had an unopposed landing on the beaches. Since there was no opposition, the beachmaster decided to unload the landing craft that was carrying B Squadron's fuel and ammunition. The men of the Squadron were assisted in this task by some Italian prisoners left on the beach by the assaulting infantry. B Squadron's tanks then had their waterproofing removed and were sent straight up to the eastern end of Colorado Ridge to support 1st Battalion The Gordon Highlanders

A Squadron, commanded by Captain Jenkin, were the last of the regiment to come ashore; they assisted 5th Battalion The Black Watch to clear the beach and then took up positions around the radio station at the western end of Colorado Ridge. The regiment, 46 tanks strong, were now concentrated behind Colorado Ridge, less C Squadron, who were defending Pachino.

During the afternoon of 10 July Brigadier Richards landed and took over one of 50 RTR's Regimental Headquarter tanks, from which to command a composite force that was driving north westerly towards the high ground around Pihcazzi. This force consisted of Regimental Headquarters and B Squadron, some infantry carriers, 11 Regiment Royal Horse Artillery and one company of 1st Battalion The Dorset Regiment from 231 Brigade. This force pushed on through the night, though progress was slow. The terrain was very difficult for tanks, with deep ditches and wooded country on either side of very narrow track.

At first light on the 11th, B Squadron advanced towards the Tellaro river crossing at Paolo; the country was very hilly in parts, and on the plain approaching the river the tanks had to cross a network of irrigation ditches, in which several got stuck. The infantry carriers could not make any headway at all so the tanks had to go on without them and secure the bridge, which they did without opposition. They then took up a defensive position on the northern side of the river, directed on the town of Noto. Here the tanks had to wait for fuel as most of them were down to their last few gallons.

While the crews were brewing up, Trooper Holder of B Squadron was severely wounded in an accident with a two-inch smoke bomb, and died shortly after. Colonel Russell performed a burial service for him before they moved off again.

Having re-fuelled, the column advanced to Noto, where they took up positions on the high ground west of the town. Before the tanks leaguered for the night they were joined by their own A Squadron and B Squadron 46 RTR.

While Regimental Headquarters and B Squadron were advancing with Brigadier Richards, A Squadron had remained with 153 Brigade supporting 5/7th Battalion The Gordon Highlanders and 5th Battalion The Black Watch, advancing on routes east and west of Pachino. Except for a minor action by Two Troop, which resulted in 20 prisoners being taken, the squadron met little opposition and leaguered for the night of 10/11 July, five miles north of Pachino.

Meanwhile, C Squadron was under command of 152 Brigade who, on the morning of the 11th, were directed on Rosolini, fifteen miles north west of Pachino. The Squadron were in reserve but a strongly fortified line of enemy pillboxes and barbed wire was encountered three miles north-west of Pachino. An artillery barrage was put down on the position and it was attacked with infantry from the west, while C Squadron shelled the position from the south. The enemy fled very quickly after coming under shell fire abandoning 20 field guns, a variety of small arms and, surprisingly, 30 saddled horses.

By last light on 11 July, The Fiftieth had advanced 25 miles on varying routes meeting little or no resistance and assisting in the capture of a considerable number of Italian prisoners. There had been a number of tank casualties due to ditching and mechanical trouble but no battle casualties to either tanks or personnel.

On 12 July, Regimental Headquarters and A Squadron, with one squadron from 46 RTR, were given the task of capturing Palazzolo; B Squadron remained in reserve west of Noto and during the day C Squadron moved into reserve with 152 Brigade, three miles south of Floridia.

The column was now split in two – Regimental Headquarters and B Squadron 46 RTR advanced down the road north-west of Noto, and A Squadron down the road running due north in order to enter Palazzolo from the east. Both columns were supported by infantry and anti-tank guns. As the column, led by 46 RTR, neared the outskirts of Palazzolo they encountered a German anti-tank gun which was covering the road. Major Routledge, commanding the 46 RTR Squadron, could not locate the enemy gun. One of his tanks had overturned while crossing a small wall, so the crew tried to discover the whereabouts of the enemy gun on foot, while the remainder of the tanks retired to hull-down positions behind a ridge.

Meanwhile, A Squadron had been held up on the main road by heavy and medium guns, located on the ridge north of Palazzolo. The tanks deployed to the left of the road and any attempt to move forward resulted in heavy mortar fire coming from a thickly wooded valley through which the road ran. As the tanks could not advance in any sort of battle formation, they moved down the road in single file, firing from side to side. As the leading tank, of One Troop, commanded by Captain Graham Moss, rounded the first bend it was hit at short range by a 50mm armour piercing shot, which temporarily immobilised it. Captain Moss quickly changed vehicles, swung his guns round and knocked out the enemy anti-tank gun. Here the road was blocked with stones and timber, which had to be cleared before moving on. Captain Moss and his troop continued to advance down the road with all guns firing. As they approached the next road junction, they discovered they were behind the enemy positions and, as the remainder of the squadron came through firing their guns, 218 Italians surrendered, abandoning a number of guns and transport. During the action Sergeant Bovey and Trooper Mackintosh, of A Squadron, were killed when their tank received a direct hit from a mortar bomb.

By this time, the other column had succeeded in entering Palazzolo, but passage through the town was difficult as the streets were blocked with fallen masonry – the result of Royal Air Force bombing.

On entering the town the two columns linked up again and advanced on Vizzini, via the town of Buccheri. As they reached the high ground east of Vizzini, they were shelled and mortared, indicating that the town was held in some strength. The column then leaguered for the night.

By 13 July Hitler, now fully aware of the developments in Sicily, ordered two German divisions, 1st Fallschirm and 29th Panzer Grenadier, to intervene immediately. It had become apparent to the defenders that any hope of holding Sicily was futile. From the beginning there were not enough troops on the island, the coastal defences proved useless, 54th Napoli Division had been lost and, if the American II Corps' advance could not be halted, the Italian XII Corps was in danger of being trapped on the western side of the island. The Allies' plan to capture Messina as soon as possible, by the shortest route, was evident. The Axis' immediate solution was to stop Eighth Army's advance in order to give time to the Axis formations in the west to retreat and regroup in the north-eastern corner of Sicily. From there, they could be ferried across the Straits of Messina. Consequently two German parachute regiments and their support units were airlifted from Rome to the Catanian Plain.

On 13 July the column stood ready to advance into Vizzini, a scout

*Figure 29: Troopers Gill (left) and Crowther, Recce Troop, both killed by anti-tank fire on the outskirts of Vizzini, July 1943. (Mrs D Buttle)*

car patrol being sent down the road to see if the enemy had pulled out during the night. Half a mile from the town an anti-tank gun opened fire on the leading car but missed. The driver immediately reversed back up the road, but unluckily drove into a brick wall. As the crew dismounted, the enemy opened fire with a heavy machine-gun, setting fire to the car and wounding both the crew. Since the only approach to the town was down a narrow winding road covered by anti-tank guns, it soon became evident that the position would have to be taken by the infantry.

Both A Squadron and Regimental Headquarters were shelled periodically during the day, in their respective positions, and both had officers and men wounded while dismounted from their tanks. B Squadron replaced the squadron from 46 RTR during the day. Enemy shelling died down during the afternoon and the column was ordered to advance down the road again; A Squadron led, preceded by two scout cars. As they approached the bend in the road (where they had been held up in the morning), the same anti-tank gun opened fire and knocked out the leading scout car, killing the driver Trooper Gill, and wounding the commander Corporal McGough. Moments later, the second car was also knocked out and its crew, Troopers Brown and Crowther, were both killed. Trooper Alban Gould of the Recce Troop recalls:

> I had been detailed to drive the medical officer in my scout car to wherever we might be needed. Before long we received instructions to go up the road leading to Vizzini as two of the Recce scout cars had been hit by enemy fire and some injuries had been sustained by the crews.
>
> We duly set off on the narrow, rough road which offered plenty

of cover on both sides for snipers. Suddenly, as we rounded a bend, we saw two disabled Daimler Dingos in line ahead more or less blocking our passage to several squaddies lying on the right hand verge. We pulled up by them and the MO ordered me to get the two stretchers off the rear of the scout car whilst he gave first aid.

Then whilst I was turning the car around to go back, several bullets struck it and the radiator was punctured and the car thereby immobilised. I jumped out of the vehicle to join the MO and ran towards him but suddenly I remembered that I was not carrying my pistol. I rushed back to the car and grabbed my revolver. Once more I decided to join the MO but then more shots were fired and I saw him and one or more of the injured creeping back along the roadside ditch. I made by way to safety via a deep drain hole at the side of the road.

The destruction of these two scout cars seemed to be the signal for the enemy to open fire with every weapon they had. The tanks were trapped on the road with anti-tank fire to the front, shells falling behind and mortar fire falling accurately on the road, while snipers were firing from the high ground dominating the area.

A Squadron opened fire with their 75mm guns and machine-guns but with little effect. The leading tank was hit by an armour piercing shot but it did not penetrate the armour. It was impossible to destroy the enemy anti-tank gun as it was situated on a bend and protected by a bank. Regimental Headquarters opened fire on some transport 3,000 yards away on the left flank and knocked out two trucks, but the tanks were in a very bad position and, with the light failing, they slowly reversed back up the road to find cover behind the ridge they had just left. That night infantry of 231 Malta Brigade tried unsuccessfully to take the enemy position.

C Squadron had been ordered to advance on 13 July, with a mixed force of carriers and infantry. They had a long and difficult route through Canicattini Bagni, Palazzolo and Buccheri. Three miles from Francofonte, they ran into a regiment of German parachute troops. An anti-tank gun was covering the road and the close country prevented the tanks from leaving the road. German parachute troops had a reputation for being tough opponents, and this was borne out by the determined fight they put up. They stalked and sniped at the tank crews at every opportunity and whenever the crews dismounted they were fired upon from all angles. One company of 2nd Battalion The Seaforth Highlanders attacked the enemy anti-tank gun, but it had pulled back a further 500 yards down the road. A second attack was made by the infantry with C Squadron in support. This time the Germans pulled back to a ridge south of Francofonte. One more attack was made with tanks and infantry, but to no avail. C Squadron eventually leaguered for the night in this area; during the action Corporal Cole was wounded by a sniper and the Seaforths had considerable casualties. That night C Squadron had five battleworthy tanks left.

On 14 July, the Germans still held Vizzini. 231 Malta Brigade with two troops of A Squadron attacked in the afternoon. This failed to dislodge the enemy completely, but a renewed attack by 152 Infantry Brigade during the night, was successful.

On C Squadron's front, patrols had entered Francofonte and reported the town clear, but at first light on the 14th it was obvious that the enemy still held the ridge. The tanks engaged a number of targets and later learned that they had been effective. C Squadron were now ordered up the road to Francofonte. Sergeant Stump, commanding the leading tank, had advanced about half a mile when his tank was knocked out by a 75mm gun. This gun crew had waited until the tank passed their position before firing an armour-piercing shot into the rear of the vehicle. Sergeant Stump, Lance-Corporal Alford and Trooper Drew were killed instantly; the driver and co-driver escaped with severe wounds and burns.

As the column halted, the second tank was destroyed by a lone German paratrooper who stalked it with a magnetic mine, killing the driver, Trooper Malley, the remainder of the crew, with the exception of the co-driver, all being wounded. The following tank killed the German with a 75mm shell at point blank range.

The whole of this operation was carried out in extremely close countryside composed of orange groves, whose overhanging branches were lower than the cupola of a Sherman, so the remaining three tanks withdrew to more open ground. From this position they supported the infantry with shell fire throughout the day. By 1700 hours, there was only one fit tank left in the squadron. This was commanded by Corporal Maplesden, who continued to support the infantry until dark; on more than one occasion he took his tank forward to destroy pockets of enemy resistance and to silence the automatic weapons of the German parachutists. Shortly after 1700 hours the Seaforths launched another attack but met with little success. By dawn on the 15th, the Germans had pulled back, leaving a large number of their dead. Major Venn and the remnants of his squadron pulled back for rest and, as soon as tanks were made available, re-organisation.

On 15th July, orders came for Regimental Headquarters and A Squadron to advance through Vizzini at first light, taking the Militello road, while B Squadron moved on the Francofonte road – the joint objective was Scordia. About five miles from Vizzini the carriers leading A Squadron reported enemy mortars and anti-tank guns. The squadron deployed and destroyed the mortars and two 75mm self propelled guns.

The enemy also had troops in houses along the road but these were soon cleared when the tanks turned their guns on them. One tank from A Squadron had been hit by one of the self-propelled guns, but no damage was done.

The tanks then advanced towards Militello. They had been held up slightly by a crater blown in the road, the wheeled vehicles had to wait until the sappers who were travelling with the column had repaired it. As the tanks passed through Militello they were cheered by the local population. They carried on out of the town and on up the Scordia road. The tanks advanced unopposed through Scordia and met B Squadron and Brigade Headquarters, who had moved up the other road without interruption. Two troops of B Squadron were then ordered to head for the bridge over the River Gornalunga north of the town. As they approached they were fired upon by a 75mm self-propelled gun, which the tanks soon knocked out. They then discovered the Germans had destroyed one complete span of the bridge. While manoeuvring around the bridge Lieutenant Schofield captured two German officers of the 1st Parachute Regiment.

As the tanks could not cross the river at this point A Squadron was ordered to make for a smaller bridge on the left. On the way three of the remaining nine tanks broke down. As the squadron was crossing a deep ditch, Captain G Price's tank turned completely over, trapping him upside down in the turret. As the turret began to fill with water the two other members of the turret crew held up Captain Price's head and baled out the water with an empty shell case through the pistol port. The remaining tanks managed to pull the stricken tank onto its side. The crew escaped unharmed, except for a minor injury to Captain Price's arm.

After this delay and because of failing light, Colonel Russell took Regimental Headquarters forward to capture the river crossing. The Germans had turned some nearby farm buildings into strongpoints to protect the bridge. The tanks opened fire on these with high explosive shells. Regimental Headquarters then moved in and captured one German officer and ten other ranks, eight trucks and two staff cars. They were also able to release a number of British paratroopers who had been captured. It was noted at the time that the prisoners and equipment were all from the Hermann Goering Division.

Meanwhile, A Squadron had been ordered to the next bridge spanning the river west of Regimental Headquarters but it was not suitable for tanks. As darkness fell the whole area around the bridge where Regimental Headquarters were became lit up with burning haystacks, buildings and enemy vehicles. All squadrons remained in their positions for the night, protected by the machine-guns of 1/7th Battalion The Middlesex Regiment.

The following morning, 16 July, Regimental Headquarters, B and C Squadrons concentrated in the area of La Callura for rest and maintenance. At midday two troops of B Squadron were ordered forward to cover the withdrawal of some infantry, who were reported to be cut off. After a great deal of confusion the platoon were found, most of them asleep under a bridge. During this confusion Lieutenant Sammy Nixon's tank bogged down in the river and was exposed to anti-tank and machine-gun fire. The tank was finally dragged out and both troops rejoined the rest of the squadron towards nightfall.

At 0530 hours on the 17th the tanks were again split into two columns. They were to cross the river and advance towards the high ground south of the Catania-Ramacca road, B Squadron on the right and Regimental Headquarters and A Squadron on the left. Shortly after crossing the river B Squadron, temporarily commanded by Captain Senior, came under shell fire and they were ordered to turn north-west to capture the bridge spanning the river at Stimpata, where they ran into some enemy self-propelled guns, which they destroyed after a short fight. Both Lieutenant Nixon's and Corporal Snape's tanks were hit by armour-piercing shot but sustained no damage. The squadron took up positions west of the bridge, where they captured a number of trucks and four Germans. Lieutenant Nixon, armed with his Tommy-gun, dismounted and approached the four Germans; as he did so a burst of machine-gun fire from across the bridge hit him. He died a few minutes later. The 'rest of the Jerries didn't last long'. Lieutenant Nixon was buried beside the bridge.

As Regimental Headquarters and A Squadron advanced over the river they were fired upon by enemy mortars – these withdrew as the tanks advanced and took up positions north of the Catania-Ramacca road. A Squadron got into good fire positions south of the road and engaged a number of targets including two German Mark IV tanks. One tank from A Squadron was hit in the sprocket, which temporarily disabled it; as three of the crew dismounted to inspect the damage, they were all wounded by shrapnel. The squadron was now down to five tanks, which remained in position until last light, firing at enemy transport at long range. During the afternoon, an American bomber crashed near Regimental Headquarters and all but the radio operator baled out. His body was buried by the padre next day, next to the wreckage of the aircraft. At last light the squadrons pulled back to the ground they had been holding all day and leaguered for the night, responsibility for the river crossing at Stimpata being taken over by the infantry.

50 RTR were resting on the morning of 18 July and in the afternoon they were ordered to the Castellito area to take up positions to the right of 46 RTR. Here they leaguered for the night. On the night of 18/19

July, the Highland Division made attacks on Sferro and the important airfields at Gerbini. The regiment was ordered to advance and clear the ground between these places, and then make contact with the infantry on either flank, thus linking the whole position. A Squadron commanded by Major Jenkin led the way, preceded by carriers. Soon after they had crossed the river at Stimpeto they came under heavy shell and mortar fire. The ground here was a wide expanse of flat open country, which stretched from the river to the road and railway connecting the two villages. One of the carriers was destroyed and a scout car carrying Lieutenant Mike Waddell, who was the liaison officer between 50 RTR and the carriers, was also knocked out.

The tanks deployed for action and, as Gerbini was thought to be in friendly hands, Lieutenant Philip Mellor's troop was ordered to advance to the right of the village, while Lieutenant F Reed's troop went to the left. As these tanks approached the road and railway, a battery of German 88mm guns opened fire and within seconds all six tanks were knocked out; four of them brewing up, almost immediately.

Corporal Finch commanding one of the leading tanks, opened fire and continued to engage the enemy guns until his tank had been hit for the fourth time, and his driver killed. He then brought out the rest of his crew, picking up survivors on the way, and helping Lieutenant Waddell, who had come up to assist the wounded, to ferry them out. Lieutenant, now Doctor, Michael Waddell describes the action at Gerbini:

> I can remember thinking at the time that to send tanks across an empty open airfield to attack Germans dug in on the far side was going to be costly. I was acting as liaison officer at that time between 50 RTR and the Highland Division, and it was decreed that Bren-gun carriers of their reconnaissance unit should fan out across the airfield and proceed towards the enemy. Basically, of course, to see what sort of fire they attracted and from where it came. In my role I accompanied them in one of the Dingo scout cars to provide a wireless link between our tanks and their commander. As I recall, it was A Squadron, under Ted Jenkin, which was providing support, from hull down positions in undulating ground and amongst olive trees. A deep, wide, dried out river bed was on our left flank and away on our right flank, amongst thick olive groves, were German paratroopers armed with the latest anti-tank squeegee guns which had knocked out some of 46 RTR's tanks, and brought the attack going in there to a halt. Olive tree foliage is just the right height to blind a tank commander and their tanks had become sitting ducks to the well-armed and resourceful Germans. My carriers had advanced about half a mile when they were submitted to sustained and very

accurate heavy mortar fire. The Germans were so good and precise with their mortars that they were capable of hitting some carriers – which were by now scurrying off in all directions – on the move. I received a near hit which disabled my scout car. My driver and I were then subjected to some intense mortar fire which sent us scurrying into the river bed, or wadi, to seek cover, which we succeeded in doing by digging ourselves in to the sandy sides of the bank. We became separated and made our separate ways back to A Squadron Headquarters.

By this time two troops of tanks had set off across the airfield and had advanced about three quarters of a mile when the Germans opened up on them with 88mm guns.

One by one our six Shermans of A Squadron were hit and immobilised. Some crews started firing from their shattered tanks but were soon silenced. I had been given another scout car, driven by Ronald Greenfield, an excellent, brave and steady man. Standing up in this vehicle I had watched the decimation of our tanks, with horror. I saw that some of the crews, those left alive, had managed to run to a ditch or depression near the smoking tanks, and had gone to ground. Some were bound to be wounded and they were in a hopeless position as the Germans would fire on them as soon as they put their heads above cover. I passed the binoculars to Greenfield and without a word between us we mutually agreed to try and pick them up. I ran to Ted Jenkin's tank and told him we wanted to do this and he concurred, saying he would put some smoke down to give us some cover.

The smoke shells were sent over but they did not seem very effective and we expected an 88mm shell at any minute. Some mortar shells were fired at us but soon stopped, and we arrived at the ditch. I decided to take the worst of the wounded first and managed to get four of them onto and in the car. They all had bad flesh wounds with bone showing through, but reaction, shock and battle fatigue had not yet set in and they managed the bumpy, dangerous journey back to safety, well.

There were eleven survivors that we could find, and Greenfield and I made three journeys in all to collect them and ferry them back. We were in full view of the Germans all the time, and they could have shot us over open sights, so to speak, but they did not. It was as if they had decided we had enough punishment for one day and had decreed that we were to be allowed to pick up our wounded. Or because of events occurring on the left flank they had started to withdraw. Now we will never know, but we were very lucky.

The wounded, I cannot remember now how many there were

exactly, but I think there were six of them, were evacuated to the casualty clearing station as quickly as possible, some of them had frightening wounds, some were badly burned, and had lost enormous quantities of blood.

My experiences at Gerbini went some way into making me decide to study medicine after the war.

This had been Greenfield's first time in action; he described his thoughts to a military correspondent shortly after: 'It looked just impossible to me, but I thought to myself, "This is a queer job, but I suppose it is the sort of thing that happens." So we drove in among those shells and picked them up.'

Out of the thirty men that made up the crews of the two troops, thirteen were killed and a further three died of their wounds.

A Squadron was now down to two tanks, the remainder of the crews then being sent to B Echelon to rest. The regiment leagured that night near brigade headquarters at Castelitto.

On 20 July The Fiftieth had been ordered to exploit an attack by 153 Brigade, but the infantry attack had been unsuccessful. Major-General Wimberley arrived on the scene and ordered a troop of tanks to support the infantry at the Sferro river crossing, against a possible enemy counter-attack. B Squadron's Captain Vincent and his troop were sent down and ordered to open fire with their 75mm guns in the area north-east of Sferro. In return, they were heavily shelled by the enemy. The troop was then ordered back to its former position. C Squadron had now been re-formed and, under the command of Major Venn, the tanks headed for the River Dittaino, where a company of 7th Battalion The Royal Marines was to have crossed the river, with C Squadron leading. Colonel Russell went forward to contact the Marines, when his jeep was wrecked by a blast from an enemy shell. Both he and his driver were unhurt. Finally managing to get through to the Marines, Colonel Russell discovered that they were pinned down on the far side of the river, and that it was not possible for the tanks to go through. The regiment was then withdrawn and leaguered for the night at the crossroads at Mass Monaco.

One of those Marines was Lieutenant Michael Aldworth who, wrote: Our task was to advance across the Dittaino River and dig in. Later two fellow company officers and myself went up the track to make a recce and it was then that we saw that the enemy's defensive line was not merely held by Italian troops, as had been thought, but had formations of Germans there as well. However, nobody believed us and preparations were made for a night attack.

The action was an utter failure for us. When daylight came, everybody was pinned down by machine-gun, shell, mortar and rifle fire. Inevitably we had to withdraw to the foothills on our side of the river.

On the 21st the regiment was ordered to clear the ground where A Squadron had lost their tanks in the action on the 19th. Regimental Headquarters with B and C Squadrons took up positions west of the river. The 88mm guns that had caused so much damage two days previously were still there and very active. The tanks had not been in position very long when C Squadron was heavily shelled and Major Venn was wounded in the head. The shelling continued throughout the day and but no more casualties were suffered. Meanwhile, B Squadron had been ordered to the river crossing at Stimpata, taking positions on the right of the road. This was purely a feint to discover the enemy's fire power. It was now obvious that the enemy were there in strength, and only a full scale attack would dislodge them. That night the regiment was pulled back to leaguer west of Stimpata and the following morning they moved back to Landolina for a complete rest and reorganisation. The plan now was for XXX Corps to hold the ground already secured on the Catanian Plain with XIII Corps on the right, while the Canadian and American forces came up on the left.

For 50 RTR the move to Landolina ended a twelve-day period of heavy fighting and hard campaigning with a large number of casualties suffered. During this entire period the regiment's reconnaissance troop, commanded by Lieutenant E V Hibbert, was on duty for long hours, observing enemy movements and repeatedly leading the tanks through dangerous positions which were bound to result in casualties. Several scout cars were destroyed and the crews killed or wounded. A and B Echelons had the most difficult task they had faced to date; they had limited transport and all 50 RTR's supplies had been dumped on the beaches. The speed with which the tanks advanced and their separate routes all contributed to a most difficult task for the Echelons, commanded by Major Bazley. However, they were equal to the challenge and the tanks were never held up for want of fuel and ammunition.

Of the 52 tanks that left North Africa only nineteen were now fit for duty: six had been lost at sea, eight destroyed by enemy action; the remainder were in the unit or brigade workshops with mechanical trouble or damage from enemy gunfire.

On 22 July news came through that Brigadier G W Richards had left 23 Armoured Brigade, his successor being Brigadier R H B Arkwright. A Squadron received six new tanks from North Africa and with some from the workshops, the squadron was reformed. The new tanks had their weapons tested the following day and their sights adjusted. Meanwhile on the night of 21/22 July, C Squadron had moved out and were supporting 51st Highland Division at the bridgehead at Stimpata. The order for the day was now 'maintenance and rest'. During the night

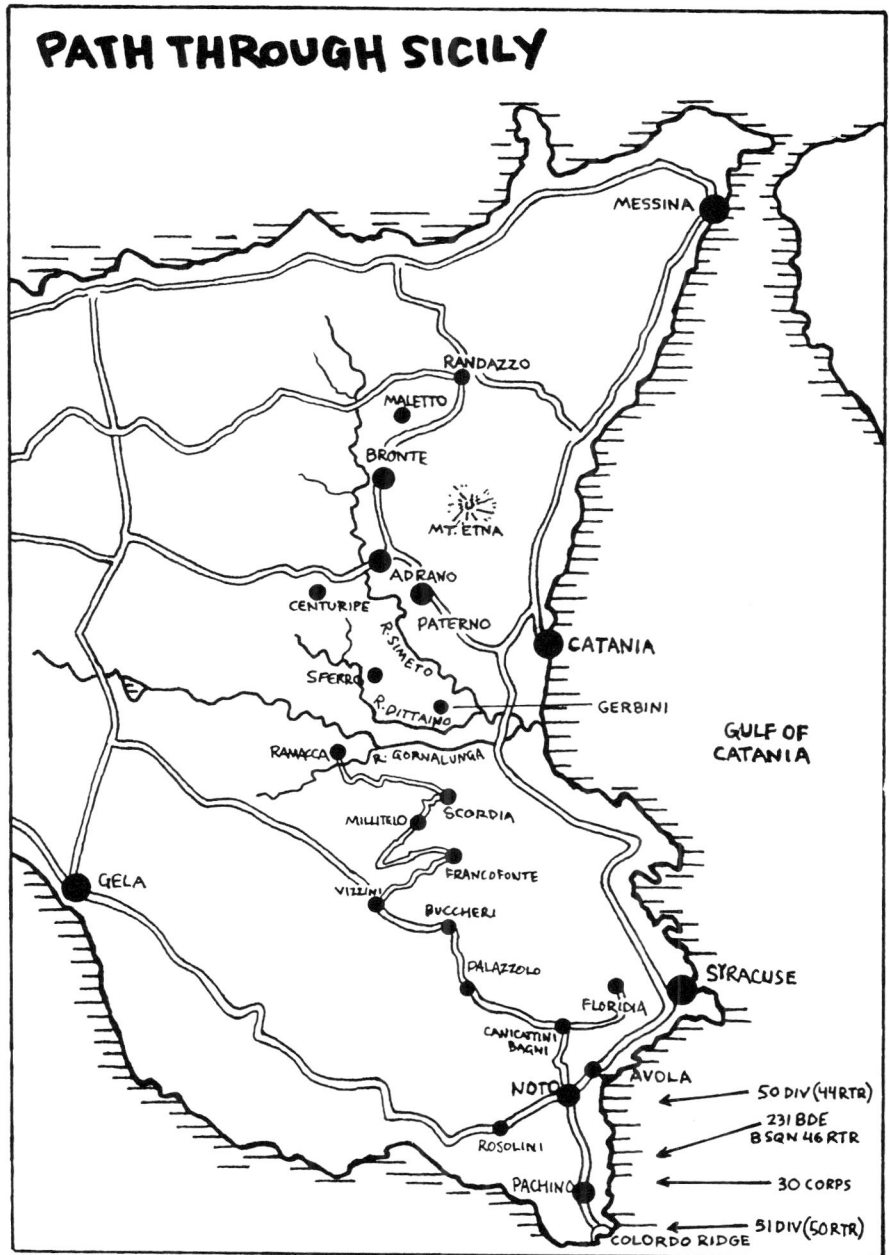

*Map 7: 'Path through Sicily'. General plan of Sicily showing route taken by 50 RTR during the campaign, July and August 1943.*

of the 23rd, A Squadron relieved C Squadron. XXX Corps then gave orders that the tank strength on 51st Highland Division's front should be increased. B Squadron moved up to Sferro, while A Squadron concentrated in the Stimpata area. Both squadrons were under command of the Highlanders. This move was short-lived. On the night of the 25/26 July both squadrons were relieved by 46 RTR, who were now up to fullstrength following the arrival of the remainder of their regiment from North Africa.

During the afternoon of 28 July, the regiment moved to a new leaguer area around Caruso, and a squadron leaders' conference was held that evening to discuss the forthcoming operation with 51st and 78th Divisions.

General Montgomery, commanding all British forces in Sicily, had asked which tank crew from the Eighth Army had performed the best in the Sicilian invasion. Corporal Maplesden and his crew were chosen for their work at Francofonte, where they alone supported the infantry against German paratroopers. Brigadier Richards, now at Eighth Army headquarters, presented the crew with a gift of five silver propelling pencils on behalf of the Army Commander. (These pencils had been sent to General Montgomery from an old lady in England, with the instructions that they be given to the best tank crew in Sicily.)

During the last two days in July, C Squadron were ordered to relieve 46 RTR supporting the Highlanders at Sferro. A Squadron, with eleven tanks, were in reserve to 78th Division. B Squadron, with twelve tanks, were standing by to join 152 Infantry Brigade. The remainder of the regiment, with fourteen tanks, were to remain with 23 Armoured

*Figure 30: Padre John Hart conducting Church Parade, Ramacca, Sicily. Note the Shermans of 50 RTR in open leaguer. (IWM)*

*Figure 31: Time for a 'brew up', Ramacca, Sicily, 1943. (IWM)*

Brigade in Corps reserve. Orders from Corps Headquarters required B Squadron to be as strong as possible for their operation with 152 Brigade, so one troop of C Squadron was put under their command. During the last days of July the regiment was in leaguer north of Ramacca, enjoying a period of rest and maintenance.

The general picture of the forthcoming attacks, as far as 50 RTR were affected, was that the regiment was to support both 78th Division in the Centruipe area with A Squadron and 51st Highland Division in the Sferro area with B Squadron; with Regimental Headquarters and C Squadron in corps reserve.

The attack on Hill 224 commenced on the night of 31 July / 1 August. B Squadron advanced at midnight to the village of Sferro, arriving there at 0130 hours on 1 August. At about 0330 hours, they were ordered to advance further but, due to a delay, they did not start until 0400 hours. They advanced out of the village, heading north-west along the road to Marsa Iazzovecchio Farm, where they halted so that the squadron commander could get a picture of what was going on. The enemy was holding the ground around Santa Angelico Farm and the wood above it contained both British and German troops. Just before daylight Five Troop from B Squadron was sent to support the infantry in the area of the wood. Eight Troop was sent to the centre of the position, and Seven Troop to cover the valley between 152 and 154 Highland Brigades; Squadron Headquarters in the meantime took up position west of Marsa Iazzovecchio Farm. Lieutenant Schofield's Five Troop contacted the infantry in the wood and disposed of the opposition. Seven Troop, under Lieutenant Grieve, moved forward to support the remnants of 5

*Figure 32: Signalman Schofield entertaining Messrs Furnival and Campbell, Ramacca. (IWM)*

Battalion The Cameron Highlanders, who were pinned down by snipers. When 75mm air burst shells were fired over the heads of the enemy they broke cover and ran, allowing Seven Troop to open fire on them.

On the left, Six Troop under Lieutenant Morrison took up positions at Massa Caponello Farm, where they opened fire on enemy guns that could be seen in the distance. Captain Vincent, B Squadron's second-in-command and Twelve Troop attached from C Squadron, also opened fire on these guns forcing the Germans out of their position. The guns and a nearby farmhouse were destroyed. With the advance of the infantry the position in that area became more stable. Regimental Headquarters and C Squadron, who had moved at first light, now came through Sferro and joined B Squadron.

During the day German mortar and artillery fire had been very accurate. As a result of this Lieutenant Grieve had been wounded while standing on the rear deck of his tank and, while Sergeant Oakes and his crew were making a meal outside their tank, a mortar bomb landed amongst them, killing Sergeant Oakes and wounding the other four. During that afternoon three German Tiger tanks were engaged by C Squadron, two of the Tigers being knocked out. During the action Lieutenant Mike Huth was killed by shrapnel when a shell exploded at the side of his tank.

Trooper Robert Blundell recalls some of his experiences during the Sicilian campaign:

To our dismay, at Francofonte we encountered the Herman

Goering Division. I think this was the first time we had anyone burnt to death, mainly due to carrying HE shells. At this place there was an irrigation channel running down from the hill and through an olive grove. Of course we needed water for a brew of tea, so I grabbed a two-gallon water can and filled it up, but going back through the trees a bloody sniper shot the can out of my hand, I moved very quickly thereafter without the water can. Before the day was over the infantry had sorted them out, I went back and looked at the water can, it was pierced with a small hole on entry, and on exit, a blast, I often wondered if that bullet had been a dum-dum bullet.

The next place was Scordia another small village, we were supporting the 78th Division and located next to a cemetery, shells were coming over left, right and centre, quite often landing in the cemetery which left a terrible smell in the air. At night they sent over their 'moaning minnies' mortars which came very close. At first light on 2 August the tanks moved up to the positions of the previous day. A Squadron still supporting the 78th Division, was having the most torrid time; the road on which they were travelling had been cratered by the enemy, there were numerous hairpin bends and it was very hilly. In the Sferro hills battle the infantry had thrown out a carrier screen, covering an advance they had made up the valley north of Sferro village. B Squadron had advanced with the infantry, mopping up a considerable area and taking prisoners. Enemy shelling had been rather spasmodic at this time – meanwhile A Squadron, together with 46 RTR were advancing on the right flank, where they lost two tanks on mines. At last light the regiment pulled back and leaguered in the same area as the previous night. The Echelon was brought forward but could not get through until after dark due to enemy shelling of the main supply

*Figure 33: The only known photograph of the whole of 50 RTR, on parade in Sicily, August 1943. (Dr Ellis)*

*Figure 34: Inspection by the Brigade Commander Sicily, August 1943. (Dr Ellis)*

route.

The following morning A Squadron broke leaguer at first light and returned to the previous day's position, where it was discovered that the enemy had pulled back. It was learned later that they were in full retreat, as their defensive line from Catania eastwards had been broken. The tanks remained in the same positions for the rest of the day. The plan of attack for the next few days was that the remainder of the regiment was to join A Squadron in support of 78th Infantry Division, of XXX Corps, for the final drive past the fortress town of Centuripp and on towards Mount Etna, thus cutting the enemy forces in two. The first objective was Adrano.

On the morning of 4 August, the regiment moved to an area southeast of Catenanuova. That morning an A Squadron troop had the hair-raising experience of one of their tanks almost falling over the edge of a very steep cliff. It was only recovered by the remaining two tanks acting as anchors. During that same morning the padre, Captain Hart, returned to the battlefield at Gerbini, where he conducted the burial service for 39 men, many of which had belonged to A Squadron.

The next day Colonel Russell and the squadron leaders reconnoitred the area. Colonel Russell then visited XXX Corps Headquarters and saw the Corps Commander, who said he realised that 50 RTR was the only unit continually in action since July, 1942, and that they would get a complete rest after the Adrano battle. Colonel Russell was also informed that the plan for the Adrano battle had changed slightly. B and C Squadrons would now followup the infantry, get onto the escarpment south of Adrano and support with fire from there. After

Adrano had fallen C Squadron, with a light reconnaissance force from other units, would move northwards along the west-face of Mount Etna to Bronte and contact the Americans.

On the morning of the 6th, the regiment moved to the bridgehead across the River Simeto, formed up and waited for the attack on Adrano, due to take place that night, to begin. The Royal Air Force had been bombing the town and had met with no opposition from enemy aircraft. It had been reported that the enemy had evacuated the town and had destroyed the only two bridges over the river.

During the night of 6 August, 11 Infantry Brigade of 78th Division had occupied Adrano and moved along the road northwards, where contact was made with C Squadron and the reconnaissance group. Demolition in the town and numerous road craters had made vehicle progress very slow, but by the evening of the 7th contact had once again been made with the enemy. An infantry attack of 1,000 yards' depth, supported by Twelve Troop, had carried them through the enemy rearguard. Corporal Hoare's tank ran over a mine and was immobilised, Troopers Lyons and Armstrong were concussed and had to be evacuated. The planned advance did not materialise, so the squadron pulled back and leaguered for the night. The rest of the regiment had remained in the previous day's position.

The enemy had occupied the high ground on C Squadron's front during the night of the 7th. On the morning of the 8th, C Squadron advanced along the road but were held up by three craters. Infantry from 11 Brigade had now occupied Bronte, and Ten Troop had engaged targets at a range of 2,500 yards. Lieutenant Freddie Kepple received a slight shrapnel wound from an enemy mortar bomb, which had been ranged on his troop. The rest of the regiment was now remaining in its present position for a few days and, in consequence, the rest of the Echelon was brought up, including four new tanks for C Squadron.

On 9 August 11 Brigade was relieved by 36 Infantry Brigade and C Squadron remained in support of them. The Germans – elements of 3 Parachute Rifle Regiment – had withdrawn to the high ground west and north-west of Bronte on the lower slopes of the volcano, Mount Etna. By mid-day, the road to Bronte had been opened and the tanks entered the town. The squadron commander, Captain (acting Major) Vic Senior, contacted the commanding officers of 5th Battalion The Royal East Kent Regiment (The Buffs) and 6th Battalion The Royal West Kent Regiment, who were to attack and occupy Mount Rivoglia, where the terrain was dreadful. It was impossible for the tanks to manoeuvre on the volcanic lava on the hillside itself, so the best way to provide support was by causing a diversion on the road while the infantry attacked from the south-east. The leading tanks attracted heavy shell and mortar fire while the infantry were able to advance up the slopes without attention from the enemy. A number of weapon pits were captured, and by nightfall the infantry were firmly established on the hill. During the action Lieutenant Ingham's tank was hit by a mortar bomb, but sustained no damage. The squadron spent the night on the road.

The next morning C Squadron was able to advance only a few yards up the road as six craters had been discovered. Because the road was under shell fire the sappers had great difficulty in repairing it and an unsuccessful attempt was made to by-pass the craters. This meant that the squadron had to remain on the road until nightfall, when the road would finally be cleared. A Squadron's Three Troop was still in Centuripe with one of its tanks on the edge of a cliff and it was not until then that the road could be cleared and the tank recovered. The troop re-joined the regiment that evening.

On 11 August, C Squadron were ordered to advance once the road was clear. Three armoured cars from 56 Reconnaissance Regiment were leading, and all were knocked out by a self-propelled gun firing from the slopes of Mount Rivoglia. A new attack was now to be made in the direction of Maletto, with 38 Irish Brigade, who had relieved 36 Infantry Brigade. Colonel Russell had also tried to get C Squadron relieved by a squadron from 46 RTR. This was refused, as 46 RTR were committed to another sector of XXX Corps' front. Also on the 11th the Adjutant, Captain G Chapman, left the regiment for the Middle East Staff School at Haifa. Lieutenant John D Masters was promoted to Captain and appointed Adjutant.

The following day C Squadron came under command of 38 Irish Brigade for the attack. The squadron had occupied Mount Macerone so that they could give covering fire to the infantry and attract some of the enemy's attention. The attack was only a partial success; the enemy was not on the high ground as expected. One troop of tanks was sent to support the 2nd Battalion London Irish Rifles who were attacking on the right, but they could not be reached. The ground which the tanks had to cross was covered by enemy anti-tank guns and they were forced to take cover when fired upon. While crossing a forward slope targets were engaged by the squadron at 4,500 yards and it was later discovered that a German Mark III tank had been knocked out. The squadron remained observing the position for the rest of the day and were subjected to spasmodic shell and mortar fire. Major John Sleeman (former staff captain of 2 Armoured Brigade) now joined the regiment as second-in-command though Colonel Russell had asked for Major Venn. Venn returned to command C Squadron and Major Senior to A Squadron.

During the morning of 13 August Major Venn took C Squadron to support the infantry of 11 Brigade, who were advancing towards Randazzo. After a few minor incidents they captured the town, the final

*Figure 35: Col. G Russell receiving his well earned DSO from General Montgomery. (Dr Ellis)*

objective of 78th Division.

On 14 August the regiment was able to relax for the first time since 10 July. C Squadron were finally withdrawn from the line and over the next few days award ceremonies were held and medals presented to officers and men who had distinguished themselves during the Tunisian campaign. Twenty reinforcements arrived on the 18th, and on the 20th Major Jenkin returned from hospital and took command of A Squadron. Major Senior reverted to captain and returned to C Squadron. News arrived on the 22nd that 50 RTR was to come under the command of 4 Armoured Brigade. This was for administrative purposes only. As 4 Armoured Brigade was located by the sea near Catania, the regiment prepared to move to that area. Two days later Captain J H Furness and Lieutenants T Howard, D Jackson, and E Wilcox rejoined the regiment from North Africa. On Sunday the 29th the padre conducted a memorial service for those of the regiment killed during the campaign. Meanwhile, Major L F Williams rejoined the regiment and resumed command of B Squadron, Major Garrett reverting to captain. The last few days of August were very quiet for the regiment, everyone having earned the rest. In little over a month, since landing in Sicily, they were now leaguered in the centre of what was once one of the enemy's main Mediterranean strongholds.

Unfortunately, conditions were far from pleasant. The summer heat was intense and the area was malaria infested with inadequate preventative equipment available. This had been lost in a ship which was sunk on the way. Many of the troops developed malaria which was suppressed, but not cured, by a bright yellow pill called mepacrine.

Thereafter this was taken daily until the regiment arrived in Palestine months later, when mepacrine was stopped and a more effective pill used to cure the disease.

After the regiment's first action with Shermans they discovered a number of defects. Although it was a better tank than the Valentine, the crews did not rate its performance in battle too highly. The Sherman had difficulty travelling in soft ground and diagonally across a slope; the hull and the turret were very high, which gave the enemy a larger target to aim at and it also made the tank top heavy; it was poorly armoured and, when hit, the tank brewed up too easily; the main armament was not sufficiently effective against the larger enemy tanks and, finally, the smoke from the exhaust pipes made concealment difficult when the engine was running.

In comparison to the German Tiger, Panther and Ferdinand tanks, the Sherman was out-gunned, and vulnerable. The best that the Sherman crews could hope for was to deploy more skilfully and load and fire faster and more accurately than their opponents thus limiting the ability of the German tanks to use their superior armament effectively

On 1 September 1943, orders were received for a move to Scordia along with 46 RTR, both regiments under command of 4 Armoured Brigade. The remainder of 23 Armoured Brigade was sent back to North Africa. Colonel Russell temporarily left 50 RTR to assist 40 RTR in their preparations for their forthcoming operations. The following day the medical officer, Captain Ellis, was posted to No 7 Casualty Clearing Station. He was succeeded by Lieutenant Brandon Lush, Royal Army Medical Corps. On 3 September the regiment was visited by its new brigade commander, Brigadier J C Currie, who brought news of a better leaguer area south of Paterno. On the same day the Eighth Army began a new offensive on the mainland of Italy. This was the first attack Eighth Army had staged since July 1942 which did not include 50 RTR. At 1000 hours on the 7th, the regiment moved to its new leaguer area near Scordia. On the way, one tank completely overturned when the road gave way: however no-one was injured. On the evening of the 8th, news reached them that Italy had capitulated; this was followed by an urgent message that no Italian aircraft were to be shot down, but the regiment had not seen any for months so the possibilty seemed very remote.

Over the next couple of days, the whole of 4 Armoured Brigade prepared and rehearsed for a parade and inspection by the Army Commander. After one or two hiccups the visit was finally cancelled. On the 14th, the Reconnaissance Troop received ten Universal carriers. Lieutenants B Chidell, L Macgregor and I C Macgregor joined the Regiment. On the 16th, A Squadron had been allotted the brigade firing range and a party was sent to reconnoitre the route to it. Sergeant Finch, in an 8cwt truck driven by Trooper Donnison went on this detail. During the reconnaissance, the truck hit a Teller mine and was blown in the air, landing upside down and bursting into flames. The occupants got out badly burned, and Trooper Donnison somehow managed to carry Sergeant Finch the three miles to Paterno.

From the 19th onwards orders began to arrive concerning the movement of the brigade for the next phase of the fighting, which would take place in Italy. Another chapter in the history of 50 RTR had closed, and another was about to open.

During the fighting in Sicily the total strength of the Axis forces was around 250,000 of whom 57,000 were German. They were facing two Allied armies – the American Seventh and the British Eighth, with a total of 450,000 men. The Germans, realising they had been duped with false invasion plans, had fought a gigantic delaying action with valiant military skill, still remembered and admired by allied forces today.

When the fighting finally finished, total casualties amounted to 4,278 Italian and 4,325 German dead, while on the allied side the losses were 5,532 dead, 2,869 missing and 14,410 wounded – a testament to the severity of the fighting over a comparatively short period.

The phrase 'brew up' has been used a number of times in this text, referring to either the destruction of a tank or the making of that great British institution, tea. This and general tank cooking, which the tank crews had perfected since their overseas service began, is described by Freddie August:

> Some sand or dirt in the bottom of an old tin with holes punched around the sides – a pint or two of diesel – a scrap of paper to start it and you've got a fire going in ten seconds.
>
> The only objection was the smoke and fumes which comes off in great black clouds if there is insufficient draught, giving the 'char' a peculiar taste and a thick black coating of soot on all our utensils.
>
> The 'brew can' consists of an empty potato tin with a wire through the top for a handle, a nice long handle so that you don't get burnt getting the tin off the stove – a tricky business sometimes. We had several tins like this – for such things as porridge, boiling vegetables, stews etc. and a frying pan or two scrounged from an abandoned house. The only thing we lacked was an oven, though when we were static for any time, we could soon knock these up with some bricks, an empty ammo box and some mud.
>
> We were supplied with a small petrol cooker, which took about half an hour to boil tea for five men so this was not used unless we were too far forward to risk lighting a diesel fire with its tell-

tale smoke. The petrol cooker came into its own when circumstances (in other words, when Jerry was about) made it necessary to cook inside the tank.

Our invasion rations consisted of 'Compo rations,' a box containing fourteen men's rations for one day, or one man's rations for fourteen days or what have you. The snag was we got a box to last us, five men, for three days, so if you work it out, you see we lost on the deal. We were told it was made up later so who were we to say different?

These rations were just the job – bacon and beans or sausages for breakfast; sardines, cheese spread, jam for toppers; stewed steak, meat and veg for dinner with an 'afters' consisting of a fruit pudding, treacle duff or milk rice pudding. Smashing! The biscuits too were eatable. Also included were seven cigarettes per man per day, chocolate, matches, salt, boiled sweets – even a packet of 'army form blanks' – toilet paper to you.

# Chapter 10
# 'STUCK IN THE MIDDLE OF MABEL'
## The Italian Campaign

50 RTR had been selected for the initial Eighth Army assault across the Messina Strait and into Italy on 3 September. However, it became apparent that the landings would be virtually unopposed and so, for the first time since their overseas service began, 50 RTR were left out of the assault force.

By 24 September 1943, now under command of 4 Armoured Brigade, the regiment had loaded 47 tanks and 20 B Echelon vehicles on two tank landing ships at Catania, ready for the short trip to Italy. By the 25th, Regimental and all Squadron Headquarters were at sea aboard LST 208. This was an American ship, and all ranks greatly enjoyed the

*Figure 36: 50 RTR's echelon vehicles waiting to be transported the short distance to Italy, 1944. (IWM)*

American rations. On the 26th, the ships docked at Taranto in Italy. Colonel Russell was the first ashore, expecting to find Brigade representatives with orders as to where to go. He met no-one, so he gave orders for the regiment to disembark. They then made the four-mile trip to the Brigade area – after having to turn round, when initially sent in the wrong direction. Early on the morning of the 30th the regiment was put on six-hours notice to move.

50 RTR having arrived in Italy, all ranks felt that the period of rest from battle was coming to an end. At the beginning of October they were leaguered seven miles outside Taranto, and early that morning orders were received to move the scout cars and nineteen tanks to the docks for embarkation and concentration further north. The remaining tanks were to leave later, at 1500 hours. That night an unexpected storm hit the area and three tanks spent the night acting as anchors for a landing ship in Taranto harbour. The B Echelon vehicles would travel the 450 miles to the new concentration area by road, and by 3 October they had made their way, via Messina, Reggia and Cartone, to Molfetta, with only five temporary breakdowns – a fine achievement as many of the vehicles had been with the regiment since May 1942. They were then ordered to an area south-west of Foggia. On the 5th the tank crews reached Foggia in their turn, followed a few hours later by their tanks, which had just arrived from Manfredonia where they had been disembarked. The whole 4 Armoured Brigade was non-operational on 6 October due to shortage of fuel. Later that night an order to move was received and the next day a reconnaissance party was sent towards Lucera.

On 8 October the B Echelon vehicles left by road, the tanks and Reconnaissance Troop, with artillery in support, starting for Lucera shortly afterwards. An exercise was carried out on the way. The Reconnaissance Troop carriers soon got bogged down in the soft soil, an experience all units suffered. After reaching the new leaguer area, all ranks had a full week resting and maintaining their vehicles. About this time 50 RTR was asked to supply a major as instructor in tank/infantry co-operation, at the Middle East (later Central Mediterranean) Training Centre for six months. Colonel Russell sent them one of his most experienced officers, V J Senior.

On the 16th the regiment received orders for its next operational task; this was to support 8th Indian Division, a new division in Eighth Army. Four days later sixteen new tanks arrived. On the 22nd, B Squadron were ordered forward in support of 17 Indian Brigade, who were in the area of Uriri. The remainder of the regiment had been ordered to follow on the 23rd, arriving there about midday. In the early hours of the 25th, B Squadron crossed the River Biferno and occupied Mount Grotolizzo. The following morning the remainder of the tanks were brought up behind B Squadron. The whole area was now becoming a quagmire due to the ever increasing rain, which was to last until the end of the month. Nearly all the tanks had become bogged down; the only vehicles to make any progress were the scout cars and these were used to bring up rations etc. The ground was so bad that at one stage all rations for B Squadron were brought up by mule train. On the 26th, 17 Indian Brigade was relieved by 19 and 21 Indian Brigades.

At the end of the month orders were received for 50 RTR, less B Squadron, to move to 78th Division's front near the coast to support the re-positioned 17 Indian Brigade. The plan was for 78th Division to capture San Salvo, Vasto and Cupello and clear the lateral road to Gissi. With Gissi captured, 17 Indian Brigade were to pass through and maintain contact with the enemy. The remainder of the Indian Division's centre line was to be in the Montefalcone area after 19 and 21 Brigades had cleared the River Trigno and resumed the attack from Gissi.

Here the Eighth Army was to meet the realities of the Italian front: the north bank of the Trigno was the Adriatic end of the Bernhardt Line. Twenty miles to the north was the Gustav Line along the River Sangro behind these were other lines culminating in the Gothic Line, the last before the Alps. All these lines would be stoutly defended and when one was taken, there would always be another.

Around this time Popski's Private Army, which had been operating in 78th Division's area, began seeking further recruits for their unit. 50 RTR's Corporal Jim Snape was one of the very few to be accepted by this band of daredevils. Vladimir 'Popski' Peniakoff wrote of him:

> A quiet man and the perfect clerk, who worked apparently day and night. I took him out on several operations as a patrol corporal, a role in which he enjoyed himself immensely. Between operations he returned to his clerking; equally a success in either capacity. He was killed at the end of the war.

At about 1400 hours on 3 November A Squadron, under Major Jenkin, crossed the River Trigno to support 46 RTR, who were already engaged in heavy fighting with 16 Panzer Division. The crossing was in a very bad condition and the going heavy. Shortly afterwards Regimental Headquarters, under Major John Sleeman, crossed the river while under attack from enemy aircraft.

A Squadron contacted 46 RTR and took up positions facing northeast. At 1600 hours news of an enemy counter-attack down the line of the railway was received. A Squadron moved towards the railway station and took up positions to protect the right flank of 17 Indian Brigade. As darkness fell C Squadron, under Major Venn, crossed the river and leaguered in the first available place.

Major Venn and Captain Bond walked forward to contact Regimental Headquarters and A Squadron, who were about a mile north of the river and east of San Salvo. Meanwhile 5th Battalion Royal West Kent Regiment attacked a position north of San Salvo at 2000 hours but retired when they ran into tanks. During the night C Squadron had two casualties – Lieutenant Brian Chidell, while sleeping, was run over by an infantry carrier and received stomach wounds, and Corporal Cole was injured by a tank which crushed one of his legs.

At dawn on 4 November C Squadron followed A Squadron and took up positions at San Salvo railway station. C Squadron were then ordered to support the Royal West Kents in an infantry attack, while A Squadron gave covering fire from their position at the railway station – the objective was a large hill on the far side of a small river. C Squadron had considerable trouble crossing the river and three of their tanks bogged down. The squadron dealt with some enemy infantry at the river and then advanced onto the hill behind the Royal West Kents. At this time the hill was being heavily shelled and mortared and the tanks kept below the crest. The infantry commander asked for the tanks to move closer to the infantry, so Major Venn ordered Nine and Ten Troops to move forward to the crest. Just as the leading tank of Ten Troop, commanded by Lieutenant Wilcox, reached the crest of the hill it was hit by two rounds, one of which pierced the co-driver's hatch, causing the tank to burst into flames and killing three of the crew, Troopers Cook, Heesom and Tye, and wounding the other two. Lieutenant Wilcox received serious leg wounds. The medical officer, Lieutenant Brandon Lush, took his carrier up to give assistance, accompanied by Colonel Russell. Shelling in the area was still very heavy. Lieutenant Lush, who had crossed the River Trigno under fire on the back of a tank, describes what happened next:

> We reached the leading tank, which had been hit, with only its commander and driver surviving, both badly wounded. Colonel Russell, together with an infantry private and myself, was tending the wounded. We dressed the wounds as best as we could and sent Lieutenant Wilcox back on a stretcher on the Bren carrier which returned safely.
>
> Before the rest of us could seek shelter, a mortar bomb landed just in front of us and I saw the infantryman fall. The Colonel and I both flung ourselves down and he said to me, 'That got me too, Doc.' He had received minor shrapnel wounds in both legs but before he allowed me to dress them he pointed to the infantryman and said, 'Attend to him first.' I told him that nothing could be done so he let me tend to him and insisted on staying while I took Lieutenant Wilcox's driver (who had been lying down) 'piggy-back' some half mile down hill to the infantry regimental aid post, where he could be better treated.

Despite his wounds, Colonel Russell remained on duty and continued to command. Lieutenant W Ingham's tank was also hit twice, but received little damage and there were no casualties.

After the capture of the hill, A Squadron moved forward to support 5th Battalion The Northamptonshire Regiment of 11 Brigade (78th Division) in their advance on the vital road junction south-west of Vasto. As the Squadron reached the first ridge along the way they engaged two Mark IV tanks and forced them to withdraw. First a troop, and later the whole Squadron, moved along the road to try and give closer support to the infantry. The two enemy tanks had withdrawn to the road junction itself but it was impossible for the Shermans to get at them due to the difficult ground. The infantry climbed the steep banks at the side of the road and dug-in at the top of the ridge. During the action, Captain Furness's tank was hit and knocked out, but he changed to another and carried on. At nightfall, A Squadron stayed where they were. C Squadron and Regimental Headquarters went into leaguer around the hill they had just captured.

The next day, the 5th, A Squadron again advanced towards the road junction but were held up by land mines. They did, however, manage to climb the steep banks to the left of the road and took up positions of all round defence. This allowed 44 and 46 RTR to pass through on their way to Cupello and Vasto.

At 0700 hours the next morning the regiment, less B Squadron, moved to support 17 Indian Infantry Brigade in the advance to Cupello, Furci and Gissi. C Squadron passed through A Squadron, who were in reserve, at the road junction, and pushed on through Cupello, covering the infantry advance. A large crater in the road had prevented the squadron opening up the road into Furci, but the infantry entered the town during the afternoon. C Squadron remained in the same position for the rest of the day. At 2000 hours 50 RTR were ordered to move in support of 78th Division for their advance on Casalbordino the next morning.

About this time, the first of many escaped British prisoners of war passed through the regiment's lines; disguised as Italians they had escaped during the Italian armistice. It was noted how cheerful they were. Colonel Russell was now beginning to feel the effects of his wounds but still refused to leave the regiment. However, the Corps Commander wanted Russell fit for the forthcoming operations and so ordered him out of the line for hospital treatment. Major Sleeman, the second-in-command, took over until Colonel Russell had recovered.

The regiment started a three-hour march at 2030 hours, passing through Cupello and Vasto. All went well until about midnight when the tanks had reached a small river crossing which had been demolished by the enemy. The tanks had to wait while the sappers built a Bailey bridge across the gap. During this time Major Sleeman contacted 36 Brigade headquarters. There, he was informed that at first light on 6

November 50 RTR were to support 8th Battalion The Argyll and Sutherland Highlanders in an attack across the River Sinello, on to Casalbordino and, if possible, across the River Sangro. One squadron of 46 RTR, now with the forward troops, was to come under command of The Fiftieth.

At dawn on 6 November, A Squadron, followed by C Squadron and B Squadron 46 RTR, advanced in support of the Highlanders across the River Sinello, but a halt was called due to demolitions west of Casalbordino.

At 1100 hours one troop of A Squadron set off with two carriers and some infantry, in the hope of getting to the high ground on the right of the Highlanders' position. By using narrow tracks and avoiding enemy mines the position was reached and the rest of the squadron followed. Now that the tanks were in place the infantry began its advance towards the village of Torino Di Sangro (at the mouth of the river Sangro); the tanks gave supporting fire and dislodged the enemy. Meanwhile, Regimental Headquarters and C Squadron moved to the monastery near Casalbordino.

The weather had now broken, there was torrential rain for several days and many vehicles bogged down; meanwhile the enemy had fallen back behind the River Sangro and blown the bridges behind him. Strong defences had already been constructed north of the river and the enemy settled down to enjoy Christmas behind this impregnable Winter Line.

In Italy the officers divided their maps into zones, each one with a girl's name. John Gibberd remembers one officer's reply to an order, when he had left the road, putting the tank out of action as it sank up to its belly in soft mud. The plaintive voice of the young one-pipper was heard, 'Afraid I can't move now; I'm stuck in the middle of MABEL.'

Elsewhere and earlier, various attacks had been made across the River Trigno by 19 Indian Brigade with B Squadron in support, the only result being a very small and insecure bridgehead west of the river. By 5 November, the enemy had shown signs of having withdrawn from the coastal sector, where Vasto had fallen. On the 6th, 1/5th Battalion The Essex Regiment pushed forward towards Palmoli with B Squadron's Headquarters and two troops in support. Using the main road to Palmoli they crossed the River Trigno easily and reached Palmoli late that afternoon. The next morning the Essex Regiment advanced to Carunchio with B Squadron again in support. No opposition was met and the squadron settled in here until the 12th.

The much talked of 'Winter Line' had now been reached, and Eighth Army were fast approaching the River Sangro. This meant a period of patrolling, reconnaissance and re-grouping of forces before an attack

on the Sangro position could be made. Trooper Alban Gould recalls:
> About the 10th November I volunteered for some liaison and reconnaissance work with an Indian Division. Here I was introduced to a very pleasant young home grown officer, Lieutenant Jackson. On the 12th, Mr Jackson was given some order as a result of which he and I were to proceed forward on our own. This we did, making our way across a broad valley probably a couple of miles wide.
>
> Although the day was fine, the ground was atrocious because of the previous rains and the awkward terrain. My scout car, like all the others in the Recce Troop, was a Daimler Dingo and, like all the others, did not have left the full complement of five forward gears and five reverse gears. This was due to the punishment they had received from the local ground conditions. I had three forward gears left when Mr Jackson and I set off but it was not long before we lost the first of these, whereupon I suggested that we should seek an alternative route instead of ploughing straight ahead but this was not agreed. Before long the remaining gears went. Dingos were excellent on hard surfaces but the cross-country conditions in Italy at that time were just too much for them.
>
> While we were grounded, it was decided that Mr Jackson would go on foot and seek aid to tow us out, I was to remain on guard with the scout car. After some while, a Sherman tank appeared on the crest of the high ground behind me. It then proceeded to travel directly towards me. Suddenly a shell exploded behind the tank and then another in front of it, this straddling continued, getting closer and closer to the target. Despite the range-finding, the tank continued to make a bee-line for me and eventually stopped by me. Members of the crew dismounted and began to get towing tackle prepared when, suddenly, I heard the scream of a shell and dropped to my knees clenching my fists over my eyes.
>
> After a few seconds, I opened my eyes and saw Lieutenant Jackson standing in front of me leaning against the scout car. When I asked him if he was all right I got no reply, I then through my blood-stained eyes took a closer look only to find that Mr Jackson was dead. I had been peppered from head to foot with shrapnel. The tank crew asked me if I wanted to go with them but I refused as I felt that they would be hit themselves at any moment. I dragged myself away from the abandoned scout car to a nearby ditch which offered a little protection. There I passed out until I was found by a party of Sikh stretcher-bearers.

The Winter Line was a strong natural position based on the River Sangro and strengthened by defence works which commanded the whole of the Sangro valley. At this time the river was in flood, the level of water being subject to wide variation depending on the amount of rainfall in the mountains; it could with great difficulty be forded at certain periods. On the south bank of the river, there was an escarpment stretching 2,000 yards down to the river, and to the north a low lying plain which gradually climbed to a steep-sided ridge, along which were the main German positions. Included in the defensive system on the ridge were the two villages of Mozzagrogna and Fossacesia.

Gradually, a plan was beginning to take shape. 8th Indian Division, with 50 RTR in support, had been chosen to lead the way and break into the Winter Line, thus allowing other forces, led by 4 Armoured Brigade, to exploit the breakthrough.

50 RTR's task was to avoid the only two roads, which were known to be heavily mined and commanded by the two villages on the ridge. Advance across country between them, descend the 2,000 yards into the valley, cross the river and form up on top of the escarpment 1,500 yards north of the river within a small bridgehead held by 78th Division, then advance 2,000 yards uphill in support of the infantry. The infantry were to attack on a two-brigade front, 21 Indian Brigade on the right and 17 Indian Brigade on the left, with A and B Squadrons supporting them respectively. The aim was to gain a firm base in the area of the Li Colli Ridge on the main San Maria-Fossacesia road. The tanks were to follow the infantry's centre lines as far as the ground and minefields would allow, and were to be up on the objective by first light to give close support. When this was achieved, 17 Indian Brigade, with B Squadron, would strike west and secure San Maria and Mozzagrogna, and later the road junction at Lanciano. The remainder of 4 Armoured Brigade would then pass through this position and roll up the enemy defences from the rear, eastwards to the sea. During this period of planning and reconnaissance rain fell continuously, which made the task of getting tanks over the river daily more difficult.

The regiment was handicapped at this period by the fact that the three fighting squadrons were all some distance from Regimental Headquarters. A Squadron was in covering positions above Torino Di Sangro (on what is now the site of the CWGC Cemetery), B was still with 8th Indian Division in the south and C Squadron moved during this time to help 17 Indian Brigade complete their task of reaching Atessa. On 14 November, B and C Squadrons reverted to regimental command and plans were made to assemble 50 RTR in the area of Scerni, taking over 46 RTR's old leaguer area. 46 RTR then returned to 23 Armoured Brigade on the Fifth Army front. As the maximum number of tanks was required to cross the river on the night of the attack, ten tanks from 46 RTR were sent to The Fiftieth, which gave the regiment a

*Figure 37: Typical conditions endured during the Sangro battle, November 1943. (IWM)*

strength of 61 tanks.

On the 16th the regiment assembled in the Scerni area. On the 17th, Major Sleeman learned that the Sangro attack would take place on the night of 19/20 November providing the weather held. The attack had to be made on this date because the moon was in its last quarter and, should the attack be postponed more than 48 hours, there would be insufficient light for the sappers to clear the minefields. During this planning stage the tank crews carried out extensive trials, towing six- and seventeen-pounder anti-tank guns – something the regiment had not done since their action at the Wadi Akarit, the previous April.

On the 19th November 50 RTR was ordered to move cross-country to the forward assembly area at Paglieta, less than a mile south of the River Sangro. Major Sleeman and the Adjutant, Captain Masters, remained behind with their tanks to complete final preparations with the Royal Engineers. The route chosen descended into a small valley, crossed the River Osento and climbed the other side. However, the leading tanks had 'churned up' the crossing so badly that at 2100 hours Major Venn returned to Regimental Headquarters to report that most of the tanks had bogged down in the river, as had been expected. However, twelve tanks of Major Jenkin's A Squadron had managed to get across country and had reached Paglieta overlooking the Sangro valley, but this could not be confirmed as radio silence was in force.

Major Venn then returned to 4 Armoured Brigade Headquarters to warn them of the situation. Despite this, the Brigade Commander ordered the remainder of the brigade to press on as planned. By morning, the two other regiments of the Brigade were also at the river crossing. The only redeeming feature of this sorry mess was that the enemy had no air patrols in the area. Had they found this sitting target they would have been able to do a great deal of damage. It took three days for the D8 tractors to tow all the bogged tanks out.

The bogged down tanks of 50 RTR were finally towed out to the road. They then made their way to Paglieta via Atessa, where they discovered only ten tanks of A Squadron and three from C Squadron. By this time 36 Infantry Brigade had moved across the River Sangro to form the bridgehead and, on 20 November, called for support from A Squadron. Major Jenkin refused because the ground conditions would not allow it; however, the Brigade Commander ordered the tanks forward. They attempted to comply and, as expected, became bogged. The following day A Squadron were again ordered across the river to support troops holding the bridgehead.

Ken Bull of A Squadron's One Troop explains what happened to the two missing A Squadron tanks:

After the disastrous cross-country approach and having regained the road, which was very narrow at that spot, A Squadron was then ordered into an adjoining paddock in order to leave the road clear for the wheeled vehicles of the infantry, whilst the situation regarding the remainder of the regiment was sorted out.

Our tanks took up position along one side of this paddock, backed in, ready to pull straight out when the order to move came. We were now waiting for the order to move, in that time and because the ground was so very soft most of the tanks bellied, when the order finally came to move only two tanks were able to reach the road. I was in the second one.

Going down the hill towards the river we were under enemy fire and copped a fair old stonking. In normal circumstances the road would have led directly on to the bridge, but this had been destroyed. We were supposed to meet an infantry guide, but no guide being obvious, we attempted to clear the road to allow infantry vehicles to pass, backing into a narrow track alongside a farm building.

When our guide was finally located we started to move forward and this caused the edge of the track to collapse. Our tank took on something like a forty degree list to starboard. By using our tow ropes and with the aid of the other tank we were able to regain the road.

Both tanks then set off to ford the river, our tank waited on the

'Stuck in the Middle of Mabel' / 173

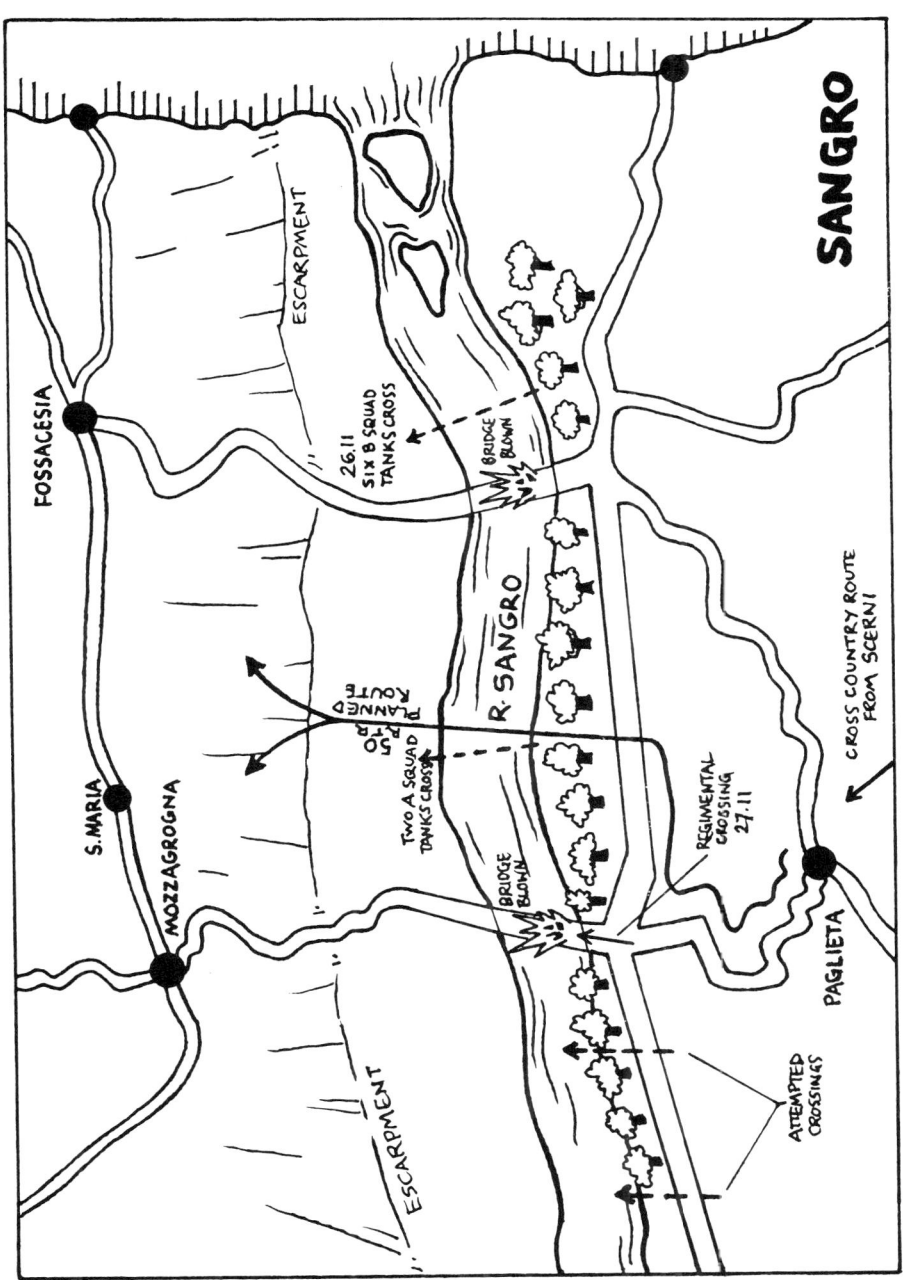

Map 8: 'Battle of the Sangro'. The regiment's attempts to cross the river, November 1943.

south bank until the other one had almost crossed and then we crossed. During our crossing we were strafed by a couple of ME 109s but they did no damage. However, as we approached the far bank, the other tank which was by then heading diagonally towards the road, hit a mine and blew a track off. By swinging around this tank, we were able to reach the road.

Having reported our position, we were ordered to move into the lee of an escarpment and wait. I think that, at this point, even Monty realised the limitations of having only one mobile tank. Our tank was the first one to make a successful crossing of the River Sangro.

The attempt was finally abandoned with tank strength slowly being whittled away. Twenty tanks were now off the road due to bogging. Patrols were immediately organised up and down the river to try and find another place to cross. There had been more rain and the ground was getting visibly worse by the hour.

On the 22nd, Major Sleeman joined the regiment at Paglieta. B Squadron, under Major Garrett, was ordered down to the River Sangro and Eight Troop started to cross. They got across, but the ground on the far side was too soft and the tanks bogged once more. B Squadron then leaguered by a mill which was situated near the crossing.

Lieutenant Gerry Keohane who had joined the regiment at Foggia and who was now commanding Eight Troop in B Squadron recalls:

In November 1943 having finally crossed the Sangro the three tanks forming my troop became hopelessly bogged down during the advance to Mozzagrogna. We could do little else while waiting for the D8 tractors to pull us out once more. The crews decided to cook a decent meal, having existed on hard tack for about five days. My driver, one Jock Smith, decided that having won some sugar and flour from a visiting Canadian truck, he would make pancakes for the whole troop while the others busied themselves with bully-beef stew and dumplings.

At this point, I was called away to do a liaison job with the infantry and didn't return to the troop for a couple of hours. By this time Jock had about a dozen lovely thick pancakes keeping hot on our fire whilst he proceeded to build up the stock on the others. The stew was bubbling away and the aroma from the stew and the pancakes was making everyone's mouth water.

It was at this point that I became conscious of the sound of an aircraft flying overhead. As the Royal Air Force had won superiority in the air, and we hadn't seen an enemy aircraft for weeks, vigilance had become very lax, as everything passing overhead had been RAF This one wasn't.

A Messerschmitt with a bomb under its wing was beginning a

dive on us. I called out to take cover. As I looked up I saw the bomb begin its descent. There was a gap of about eighteen inches under the front of the nearest tank and fifteen of us trying to be the first into that comparatively small space.

The bomb struck, almost equal distance from all the tanks, and luckily for us plunged to the bottom of the bog the tanks were trapped in, before exploding. Huge clouds of mud rained down and flew everywhere. There were odd shouts from crew members who had been unable to reach cover, as they were struck by these very solid chunks of mud.

Slowly and rather sheepishly we all pulled ourselves off the ground. Sheepishly, for there had been a fair bit of pulling and kicking to get to the underside of the tank before the bomb went off, but in the end no-one was hurt, not seriously anyway.

As we collected ourselves, however, we saw our full loss. One clod of mud, a huge piece, had caught the plate of pancakes fair and square and covered them in goo, and yet another had knocked over the billy with the stew and dumplings in, so that we had lost the whole of our lovely hot meal – our first for days – and with no prospects of an immediate repeat as we had used up all available ingredients.

It was then we had one of those moments which tanks crews the world over will recognise. A fair bit of swearing and cursing going on, when above it all came Jock's voice, 'What the hell is the matter with you lot. We still have our hard tack and jam, haven't we?'

The original plan now had to be altered. The new line of attack for 8th Indian Division was up the main road to Mozzagrogna, a key position in the Corps objective. 17 Indian Brigade, with B Squadron in support, were given the task of capturing this position. 21 Indian Brigade were to swing to the right with A Squadron and secure the Li Colli position.

Repeated patrols were sent out to find a new crossing that was suitable for tanks, but without success, so Major Sleeman decided to construct one himself. He planned to make use of the main Paglieta-Mozzagrogna road and all that was required was an estimated four hours' work with a bulldozer. During the night of 25/26 November the sappers carried out the job, but there had been heavy rain in the mountains during the day and the river level rose by four feet. All this extra water and the work done by the sappers altered the main current of the river from the middle to the far bank, thus making the crossing impassable. One tank of B Squadron tried to get across at 0300 hours but got stuck and blocked the bulldozed gap. Further attempts were made before daylight but all met with the same result. On the morning of the 26th Major Sleeman asked for Bailey bridges to be built, but the men and materials were not available so an alternative crossing was selected a few hundred yards to the right.

The whole attack now depended upon the tanks of 50 RTR getting across the river. Attempts were unending, but every time something would happen to prevent success. By 1300 hours on the 26th, it not having rained for twelve hours and the ground starting to dry out, B Squadron tried to get across yet again; this time with a little success. Six tanks got over and made for the lying-up area below the escarpment on the main road. As the seventh tank made the attempt, the river crossing was shelled and put out of action. The water which had become diverted from the river caused the ground to become so soft that the tank became bogged when nearly clear. Another tank going around the obstacle also bogged down. During the night, 626 Field Squadron, Royal Engineers worked on the alternative site. The bank on the far side of this new crossing could not be completed due to the risk of noise and sparks from exhaust pipes, which could have brought down enemy shell fire. The work was only half completed when Major Sleeman decided to attempt a crossing.

By 0400 hours on the 27th the remnants of B Squadron were across the river and able to give 8th Indian Division support. At first light, A Squadron followed, then Regimental Headquarters and C Squadron. One tank of A Squadron was lost on a mine during this move.

At 1000 hours 50 RTR were in the lying-up area under the escarpment. At 1030 hours A Squadron moved forward to support 21 Indian Brigade in their advance up the Roman road towards Mozzagrogna. At midday Colonel Russell rejoined the regiment as commanding officer, after discharging himself from hospital, against medical advice. The site where the tanks had been lying-up had been shelled all day, though without casualties.

At 2100 hours on 27 November the artillery barrage opening the main attack on the Winter Line began; it had by now well earned its name.

The infantry had attacked Mozzagrogna and the town was captured by 17 Indian Brigade at 0120 hours on 28 November. They had found it a much harder task than anticipated because the enemy had used flame-throwing tanks. Supporting weapons which included the tanks, had been unable to reach the infantry in the town due to a stretch of road, one and a half miles long, being saturated with mines of all descriptions and covered by mortar fire from the village of San Maria. As a result, at 0800 hours the infantry withdrew to their bridgehead positions. The tanks of 50 RTR had not been engaged, though B Squadron lost one vehicle on mines while moving forward.

At 2100 hours another attack was launched on Mozzagrogna to secure the road, thus allowing the sappers to remove the mines and permit tank support to pass through before first light. The attack went in under a barrage. Two companies of infantry reached the town and found covering positions, while two other companies provided close support for the sapper working parties, who worked hard, although they were receiving casualties from mines, shell and mortar fire. By now, the 29th, time was more important than the quality of the work that the sappers were doing; so Major Sleeman ordered one troop of B Squadron to advance to Mozzagrogna at 0530 hours, followed by the remainder of the Squadron.

B Squadron advanced, with Seven Troop, commanded by Lieutenant Teddy Grieve, in the lead. Following the leading tank was one of the regiment's carriers carrying a section of Engineers. This ran over a mine and blew up killing the driver, Trooper Hodge, and badly wounding Trooper Charlton, who died of his wounds later that day; several of the sappers were also wounded.

At 0600 hours Colonel Russell left his headquarters and went forward in a scout car to see B Squadron. The medical officer, now Captain Lush, describes what happened next:

> While I was tending to some wounded by the road, along which we were attacking a familiar voice said, 'Do you need any help Doc?' It was Colonel Russell. I said 'No thanks.' So he asked his driver to proceed in their jeep. They went around the next corner and there was an enormous explosion and a huge black cloud arose. His vehicle had gone over a large mine. I ran to the scene, having to press myself to the ground once when a 'moaning minnie' came down all around me.
>
> There was little left of the Colonel's jeep and he and his driver were lying on the ground. His badly injured driver said 'The Colonel's bought it!' Regrettably, he was right. The driver had both legs broken and other injuries, but I was able to get him back and he survived the war.

Major Sleeman again took the command, which he had relinquished only 36 hours earlier, with Major Venn taking over as second-in-command.

In spite of the gallant work done by the sappers the road was not clear of mines by first light. However, Lieutenant Grieve took his troop up the ridge and on to the objective. The leading two tanks were put out of action by mines and each time he transferred to the tank behind. As it became light Grieve, in his third tank, managed to get through and into the town. Another troop tried to get through to support him but this troop was also put out of action. As it was now daylight it became essential for the tanks to get into the town before the enemy were able to consolidate. Lieutenant Grieve therefore went on alone ahead of the infantry. As he swept through Mozzagrogna, overrunning

*Figure 38: One of the German tanks knocked out by Lt R Willson and his crew on 30 November 1943, Mozzagrogna, Italy. (T Stanton)*

and killing the enemy, they soon became scattered and confused.

Restricted in the narrow streets of the town, Grieve was unable to bring his guns to bear, so he got out of his tank and, standing on the turret, engaged the enemy with his tommy-gun. After reaching the far side of the town, Lieutenant Grieve returned to the infantry and assisted them in mopping up what was left of the enemy troops. More tanks of B Squadron had by now got through but during their advance from the escarpment to Mozzagrogna nine had been lost on mines. Captured German engineers said that they had laid every mine they had.

During the remainder of the day all three squadrons were in support of 8th Indian Division, winkling the enemy out of houses and the close country about the town. Mozzagrogna had been captured, the initial objective had been taken against formidable opposition, but the exploitation troops did not pass through that day as expected.

At 0610 hours on 30 November 44 RTR, the exploiting armour, began to pass through B and C Squadrons, who covered their left flank as 44 RTR swung down the road towards Possacesia. A Squadron was then sent to support 1/12th Battalion The Frontier Force Regiment, who were to locate and destroy enemy positions north-east of the town, allowing 44 RTR to overrun the Sangro position from the rear. The country was very close and it was difficult to deploy the tanks. Lieutenant Reginald 'Willy' Willson, commanding the leading troop, moved his vehicle 100 yards further along the road, hoping to get a better fire position. As he pulled round a corner and into 'what proved to be a perfect hull-down position', he came face to face with three brand new German Mark IV

Specials and a self-propelled gun belonging to the 26 Panzer Division, which were firing to his left in the direction of Mozzagrogna. Lieutenant Willson immediately engaged the leading enemy tank with the high explosive shell that was already in his gun and it caused two of the crew to bale out. Two more rounds of armour-piercing shot finished this tank off; he then fired three rounds into the second tank and knocked this one out also; the third tank he knocked out with two more rounds. He then hit the self-propelled gun with three more rounds; this vehicle managed to limp away, but was later found abandoned.

Lieutenant Willson's tank was then subject to heavy gunfire but he continued to support the Frontier Force Regiment until 1215 hours and later supported 5th Battalion The Royal West Kent Regiment's attack on Romagnoli. He then knocked out another enemy tank, which had been lurking in the woods to the north of the main road. Willson's action had eliminated the enemy armour in the immediate vicinity, thus allowing the exploiting forces to advance unimpeded.

A Echelon had moved over the river the previous night and were harboured below the escarpment. During the morning German Focke-Wulf 190s attacked them, and hit three trucks. One of these was the water truck belonging to C Squadron. While being machine-gunned, Squadron Sergeant-Major Tom Stanton, realising the danger to neighbouring vehicles, dashed to an ammunition truck and drove it to safety. He then returned to the burning vehicles and organised the remaining drivers in clearing the area and getting the fires under control. Enemy air activity was now on the increase, operating every few hours.

At midday C Squadron advanced forward to support the Royal West Kents in their advance on Romagnoli, which they had to do with their right flank completely exposed. A Squadron, now with 21 Indian Brigade, advanced with them up the axis road to join up with 17 Indian Brigade. The advance was led by 1st Battalion The Mahratta Light Infantry heading for a key position overlooking the whole Sangro valley. While in close support of the infantry, Four Troop, commanded by Lieutenant Kenneth Pillar, was dealing very effectively with mortar and machine-gun positions. Near the top of a ridge, and while still in front of the infantry, Lieutenant Pillar's tank was hit by a shot from a German tank which was sited 400 yards away. Without pausing, Pillar continued to advance and fight his tank; it was then hit a second time, putting the gun out of action. As the crew baled out, they were fired upon by tank and infantry machine-guns. One of the crew was wounded in the process and, in spite of the intense fire that was directed on them, Pillar returned to the wounded man and carried him to a more sheltered position. Lieutenant Pillar then realised that his driver, Trooper Timm, was still in the tank, so he returned yet again to the vehicle, which was still under fire from the enemy and in danger of being set on fire. While he was climbing onto the vehicle it was hit a third time by an armour-piercing shot, the force of the impact throwing Pillar to the ground. Undaunted, he again climbed onto the front of the tank and began to open the driver's hatch, but just as the hatch was opening 'a fourth shot hit the 75mm gun and gouged a large groove out of the barrel, before ricocheting downwards, killing Pillar instantly.'

For Pillar's self-sacrificing act of heroism, he was recommended for a posthumous Victoria Cross.

Lieutenant Pillar's troop originally consisted of only two tanks, the other being commanded by Sergeant Ned Taylor. At this stage, the infantry had run short of ammunition and had temporarily fallen back some 200 yards to await further supplies. This left Sergeant Taylor out in front, on his own, and facing a ridge over the top of which he knew were enemy tanks. He held his ground and continued firing at enemy positions, keeping his squadron commander informed of the situation. When One Troop, commanded by Lieutenant Keane came up to support him, Taylor dismounted and, by crawling some distance, located three of Lieutenant Pillar's crew and dressed the wound of the one who was hurt. Sergeant Taylor continued to crawl forward to the knocked out tank, but realised that it was hopeless to try and get into it as the enemy still had it covered. He therefore returned to the crew and helped them back to his own tank, put Lieutenant Keane in the picture and brought back the wounded man on his own vehicle.

Meanwhile, the medical officer, Captain Brandon Lush, had been dealing with other casualties. When he heard about the events concerning Lieutenant Pillar's tank and realised that there was still a wounded man inside, without consideration for his own safety he ran towards the knocked out vehicle, which was 300 yards ahead of the infantry positions. Enemy fire was heavy at first but Captain Lush carried on and mounted the front of the tank. He opened the driver's hatch and found the driver, Trooper Timm, still inside alive but badly wounded. Injecting Timm with morphia and waiting until it took effect, he then pulled the man out and onto the ground, where, with assistance, he got him back to an ambulance. As Lieutenant Pillar's tank was still in full view of the Germans, it may have been that Captain Lush was recognised as an medical officer by the watchful enemy, fire having stopped when he reached the Sherman. Nevertheless, the doctor had made a gallant and successful bid to save a wounded man in an extremely difficult and dangerous situation. Dr Lush recalls:

> I heard a plaintive cry over the radio from Trooper Timm saying that he was alive and badly wounded. He cried for help, so I got together some volunteers from the Friends' Ambulance Unit and we set out with a stretcher towards the German lines.
>
> We passed the last infantry outposts, who warned us that the

area ahead was mined. Nevertheless, we passed through unscathed and found the destroyed tank with Trooper Timm still alive and conscious within it. The body of Lieutenant Pillar was lying alongside.

We were all wearing Red Cross armbands and the German infantry watched us from a distance while we got Trooper Timm out with difficulty and took him back to an infantry regimental aid post. Unfortunately, he died on the way back.

Ken Bull takes up the story:

As the light faded we were ordered back to the squadron leaguer. In the process of doing so our Sergeant Hookway's tank ran into a gully and became stuck at an angle of around 45 degrees. Lieutenant Keane, realising that it would be impossible to salvage the tank in the dark, sent our troop corporal's tank back to Squadron Headquarters for fuel, ammo and food whilst we, in our tank, took up a guard position 25 yards from the disabled tank.

At that time it was still unclear what had happened to Lieutenant Pillar, so the Squadron Commander, Major Jenkin, ordered Lieutenant Keane to take two men and investigate. By this time it was pitch dark.

This left me and one other crew member on our tank and, with the enemy prowling around in the woods 100 yards away, the situation was very unhealthy. Lieutenant Keane returned later having had a fruitless search. It was then decided that the other crewman and myself plus the entire crew of Sergeant Hookway's tank would do sentry duty during the night. At the end of my stint I went over to wake the other crew; this took a few minutes.

I was just about to start back to our tank when there was a series of gun flashes from behind our lines. I thought some poor bugger was in for one hell of a stonk. Not half, the gunners had been tipped off about the Jerries in the woods. The only trouble was their range was a trifle short so we copped it. Things got a bit hectic, those inside the tanks closed down sharpish and I was stranded outside, so I stretched myself on the ground next to Sergeant Hookway's tank, there I stayed for what seemed an awful long time. A short break in the artillery fire gave me the chance to cover the short distance to our tank.

During the night our troop corporal returned with the 'goodies'. Having re-fuelled, re-ammoed and had some hard tack we got a few hours kip. Half an hour after first light, while supporting the Indian infantry working their way towards Lanciano, we were walloped by an anti-tank gun, Brew Up!

4 Armoured Brigade commander informed 50 RTR that they must have

more tanks and that arrangements had been made for the regiment to receive these as soon as they became available, as an enemy counter-attack was expected from the Lanciano area. All tanks damaged by mines were repaired and spare crews made up ready to accept the new vehicles – the regimental tank strength on 30 November was 25.

All this changed on 1 December, when 14 Canadian Tank Regiment (The Calgary Regiment of Dieppe fame) were to relieve 50 RTR, so the issue of new tanks was postponed. Despite this both A and C Squadrons were in action in support of the infantry throughout the day. It was then found that the Canadian tanks could not cross the river, so the expected relief could not take place as early as it should have done.

Meanwhile A Squadron had been pressing on with 21 Indian Brigade, the line of advance being an old Roman road, which was densely wooded on either side and also lined with numerous houses, the majority of which contained enemy machine-guns. The One Troop tank commanded by Lieutenant Keane was knocked out by an anti-tank gun and brewed up. Keane then transferred to his troop corporal's tank – the troop sergeant's tank had still not been recovered at this time. During the day the road junction just outside Lanciano had been reached and German tanks engaged. Three were claimed as hit; this was later confirmed by the Mayor of Lanciano, who said they were taken away, damaged, on transporters.

A and C Squadrons were now in direct contact, and 17 and 21 Indian Brigades had linked up also. B Squadron had covered the left flank throughout the day and had engaged various targets at long range, a number of enemy anti-tanks guns being claimed as destroyed.

On 2 December A and C Squadrons took up positions overlooking Lanciano, while B Squadron resumed left flank protection. No further forward progress could be made due to a deep obstacle, strong enemy action and lack of artillery support.

On 3 December, the 3/15th Battalion The Punjab Regiment, assisted by C Squadron and covered by A and B, entered Lanciano at first light and reopened the road. One squadron of 14 Canadian Tank Regiment passed through and on to Treglio – where they discovered that none of the vital bridges had been destroyed.

50 RTR now reverted to 4 Armoured Brigade. After 3rd County of London Yeomanry (Sharpshooters) had cleared the road, The Fiftieth followed and halted one mile from the town. At 1140 hours B Squadron was called forward to deal with enemy machine-gun positions that had been by-passed by the leading troops.

The whole Sangro operation was a battle against nature; the tanks had never fought in conditions so bad. The ground turned into a gum-like substance after every drop of rain, making tank movement very difficult. During the crossing of the Sangro and while giving support to the infantry, 50 RTR had 31 tanks bogged down and only by 'the spirit shown by all ranks' was the regiment able to maintain fighting efficiency. During the Sangro battle 50 RTR had lost fifteen tanks, including nine on mines, two knocked out, and one drowned. The eight day postponement of the battle had enabled the enemy the reinforce its position, bringing 26 Panzer Division from the Fifth Army front, 90 Panzer Grenadier Division from Venice and the 334 Infantry Division from Genoa. These units would continue to oppose 50 RTR for the next four weeks.

The regiment had by now fought in every major battle with the Eighth Army since July 1942 – the only armoured unit to stay the course. At the conclusion of the Sangro operations the following message was received by Brigadier J Currie commanding 4 Armoured Brigade from V Corps Commander:

> I write to congratulate you and the whole of your brigade for the wonderful way they have fought during the last battle. I think it is true to say that the success of the Sangro battle was mainly due to the dash and fighting qualities of your brigade.
>
> The difficulties of the country and the going made the task extremely difficult, but they were determined to overcome both.
>
> Thank you so very much, and I envy you your command, of which you must be really proud.

Just to put things in perspective, the battle of the Sangro River took place just a year after the battle of Alamein, and for 50 RTR to have advanced with the Eighth Army such an enormous distance in that time – embracing every sort of terrain and climate, from the heat and dust of the desert to the mountains in snow – will always remain an incredible achievement.

On 5 December 1943, 50 RTR were in 4 Armoured Brigade reserve. The German Winter Line had been broken, but the exploitation had not been as successful as had been expected. In the planning stages of the Sangro battle it had been proposed that the exploitation to Pescara should be without any artillery support, relying on tank guns. However, the eight-day postponement had allowed the enemy to be reinforced, and in consequence the advance was now held up along the line of the River Moro.

The 1st Canadian Division relieved 78th Division in the coastal area. It was decided that the Canadians would attack on the night of 5/6 December on a two-brigade front, their objective being Ortona. 3 County of London Yeomanry and 44 RTR would be in support and 50 RTR in reserve. 50 RTR were to be ready to move at first light on 6 December with 35 tanks, but no call came for the regiment following the attack by the Canadians. Later in the morning of the 6th, the Commanding Officer, now Lieutenant Colonel John Sleeman, went forward to 4 Armoured

Brigade tactical headquarters, where he learned that the regiment was to return to support 8th Indian Division, who were south of the River Moro on the left of 1st Canadian Division. This move was to enable 14 Canadian Tank Regiment, who were supporting 8th Indian Division, to move to the coastal sector and re-join its own brigade, which would in time relieve 4 Armoured Brigade.

The intention on 8 December was for C Squadron to move up to support 21 Indian Infantry Brigade, which was holding a very limited bridgehead across the River Moro. It was impossible to get tanks across until a bridge had been built but good covering fire could be given from the south bank. On the morning of the 8th, C Squadron were in position on the south bank of the Moro. 8th Indian Division then put in a diversionary attack in order to attract enemy attention away from the Canadian sector.

On the 9th, 50 RTR learned that a Bailey bridge over the river should be completed by first light on the 10th, enabling C Squadron and the rest of the regiment to cross into the bridgehead held by 21 Indian Brigade. This bridge had been built in an almost unbelievable operation in the face of intense fire. It had to be assembled on the enemy side, since there was no room on the British side, so precipitous was the approach to the river; no progress could be made by infantry or armour until it had been built.

The regiment's B Echelon suffered from a Luftwaffe bombing raid during the morning of the 9th, resulting in the medical officer, Captain Lush, and Second Lieutenant Pritchett among others being severely wounded. Pritchett died later that day. A Squadron had rejoined regimental headquarters and during the night their leaguer area was heavily shelled, resulting in Troopers Bailey and Freer being killed and others wounded; one, Trooper Hallmark, died of his wounds the next day. Dr Lush recalls:

> I was running out of medical supplies so I went back with my driver to B Echelon some miles back to collect them.
>
> For several days previously the Luftwaffe had sent twelve Junker 87s to dive bomb our forward positions at exactly the same time every day.
>
> I looked back from whence we came and saw six planes bombing our forward positions. I thought, 'Where are the other six?' and looked up to see them hurtling down at us, so I shouted 'Down, everybody,' and flung myself down in the soft mud. I then lost consciousness (I don't know for how long) before I heard my driver's voice saying 'Christ! Look at that bleeding crater!' I was totally unable to move but I remember saying 'What crater?' and found that there was a large bomb crater eighteen inches in front of my head.

Had the ground been hard, I would have been blown to smithereens but as it was the bomb had penetrated deeply and I had simply been peppered with some eighteen fragments – one of which had traversed my left forearm, penetrated my cap badge and cut across my scalp from front to back. The others inflicted trivial superficial wounds elsewhere.

Captain Lush was eventually replaced by Captain L Feinmann, Royal Army Medical Corps, who volunteered to remain with 50 RTR while his unit returned to the United Kingdom.

By first light on the 10th the Bailey bridge over the River Moro, which by now had earned the name 'Impossible Bridge', had been completed and C Squadron were able to get first one troop across then, by midday, the rest of the Squadron. The leading troop had to clear the road north of the River Moro of derelict vehicles before progress could be made. B Squadron then moved up into the position vacated by C Squadron on the south bank. Forward movement of Regimental Headquarters and A Squadron to Frisa was halted at Lanciano as the Canadians had been held up. B Squadron were still supporting the infantry at the bridgehead with great success, despite the enemy having turned each house into a stronghold. On one occasion the tanks put the infantry into one house three times before they could finally hold it. The 3/15 Punjab Regiment, though receiving heavy casualties, successfully held the bridgehead for three days; this was very difficult as the enemy held the dominating ground.

During the night of 11/12 December the bridgehead was counter-attacked. This attack was repulsed and further ground was gained. A Squadron 44 RTR, who were in Roalti, now came under command of 50 RTR.

On the 12th the second-in-command, Major Venn, went forward to contact 21 Indian Brigade and sent back orders for Regimental Headquarters to move forward. An attack by 1/5th Battalion The Mahratta Light Infantry was to be made to try and extend the bridgehead further west. B Squadron were to support this attack at first light on 13 December.

To ensure the tanks would reach the objective, Lieutenant Gerry Keohane was detailed to accompany the infantry on foot and reconnoitre the tank route. Keohane and his driver took their carrier as far as possible and then he dismounted with a No. 38 radio to maintain contact with the carrier, which would then relay any information back to headquarters with a No. 19 radio. Soon after leaving the carrier, the 38 set was put out of action and runner was now the only means of communication. The infantry attack despite numerous losses had been successful, but pockets of resistance were by-passed. Moments later the whole area came under heavy artillery fire and Keohane's driver

*Figure 39: C Squadron tea-party with members of the 8th Indian Division, Italy 1943. (T Wilson)*

brought the carrier up to him. But, seeing that it was pointless doing a recce from a carrier, Keohane ordered the carrier back to a safer place. While examining a track, Lieutenant Keohane ran into the crew of a German 75mm anti-tank gun, who were in the process of spiking their gun. As the enemy took up their arms, Keohane dived for cover, but two Germans worked their way around and captured him. Keohane made as much noise as possible and succeeded in attracting the attention of a section of Indian infantry, who came on the scene and took all three men prisoner. Lieutenant Keohane had a difficult time persuading the Indian troops who he was, after which he was able to take prisoner the remaining gun crew. The enemy had by now started to mortar the area but Lieutenant Keohane continued with his task of checking the road, accompanied by the section of infantry that had rescued him. As the mortar fire increased, one of the Indian soldiers ducked to avoid shrapnel and wounded Lieutenant Keohane in the leg with his bayonet.

Despite this misfortune Lieutenant Keohane completed his reconnaissance and walked back to his carrier to find that it had been knocked out and the driver badly wounded. After ensuring that the driver was taken to a First Aid post, Keohane made his way on foot back to the tanks, who were ready and waiting, and reported to his squadron leader. He was then able to lead them into their positions with the minimum delay. They arrived just in time to beat off an enemy counter-attack.

B Squadron crossed the river at 0300 hours, passed through C Squadron and into the forward lines of the Mahratta Light Infantry. Regimental Headquarters remained in position above the river and A Squadron moved into the position just vacated by B Squadron. B Squadron spent 12 December shooting up enemy positions on the left of the Mahrattas, one group of houses being totally destroyed. Over 20 dead Germans were later discovered there. A counter-attack that afternoon on the same flank was broken up by fire from the tanks.

At 2300 hours on the night of the 13th, A Squadron supported an attack by 17 Indian Brigade in the direction of Caldari, the squadron crossing the river at 2330 hours. A sapper reconnaissance party had cleared the route of mines but several derelict vehicles had to be towed off the road by the leading tank. Regimental Headquarters crossed over at 0245 hours and remained under the escarpment on the north bank until daylight. A Squadron reached the road junction just outside the town at 0300 hours, but the infantry were not getting on as well as was hoped. Colonel Sleeman, realising the effect that armour had on infantry morale, ordered A Squadron to send some tanks forward. Three Troop was detailed for this task, moving towards Caldari, where the infantry was held up by machine-guns near the cemetery. The tanks dealt with these and followed the infantry into the town, which was then heavily shelled. Three Troop remained in the town for several days, before being relieved. A Squadron, less Three Troop, were now sent to support 1/5 Battalion Royal Gurkha Rifles, who were also held up short of their objective.

The Germans had by this time introduced a weapon that was new to this theatre of war – a tank-mounted flame-thrower. This device had the infantry very worried. At first light, enemy tanks on the main Ortona-Orsogna road had opened a wild fire with their machine-guns and flame-throwers. In the half light, several rounds of armour-piercing shot were fired by the leading troop and the enemy tanks retreated. To strengthen A Squadron a troop from C Squadron was sent to Caldari to relieve A Squadron's Three Troop, so that the latter could return to their squadron.

During 14 December 50 RTR were subjected to heavy shell and mortar fire – one salvo of *nebelwerfers* landed in the Regimental Headquarters area killing Trooper Baker and causing other casualties. In the afternoon the forward infantry reported an enemy tank behind a house on the northern side of the road. As the house was not more than 700 yards from the leading tank, the tank commander decided to fire at the intervening wall until a hole had been punched through it. He then fired eight rounds of armour-piercing shot through this hole, through the back wall of the house and into the enemy tank. Later examination of the target showed that enough damage had been done to force the crew to abandon their vehicle. The leading troop also managed to hit a half-track, an anti-tank gun and two ammunition trucks.

On the 15th, A and B Squadrons took up their positions of the previous day and observed troop movements on the upper reaches of the River Moro, but they could not tell if they were friend or foe; they were later discovered to be German. During the previous three days B Squadron had inflicted considerable damage on the enemy in the surrounding houses, counting over 40 German bodies. The regiment was now down to 29 tanks, so A Squadron of 3 County of London Yeomanry were put under command. They were to support B Squadron, who in turn were supporting the Royal West Kents in their attack on the main Ortona-Orsogna road, with the aim of cutting off the enemy and denying him the use of the road.

At 0400 hours on the 16th, A Squadron 3 County of London Yeomanry advanced. The going was very difficult but, by 0600 hours, they were in position and at 0800 hours they met and knocked out two German Mark IV Specials. Meanwhile at 0530 hours, Eleven Troop of C Squadron, commanded by Lieutenant Ingham, had attacked a group of houses north of the road, while Twelve Troop went around the houses to prevent the enemy escaping. All went well until Eleven Troop were 100 yards from their objective, when they were fired upon by numerous anti-tank guns. The infantry went to ground – smoke was put down by the enemy and two of their tanks advanced from behind the houses. The infantry and Eleven and Twelve Troops now withdrew. The Germans held the dominating ground and had the advantage.

At 1045 hours Colonel Sleeman came up and ordered Eleven and Twelve Troops back into the attack. The two troops went round to the left of the houses and knocked out a half-track on the way. Another troop closed in from the south and knocked out a Mark IV Special. Two other vehicles were destroyed and a number of prisoners taken. A Squadron reported that they had knocked out one enemy tank and three ammunition trucks on the same day. This brought the total bag for the day to six enemy tanks – a fact that at the time went unnoticed.

Colonel E Mitford, second-in-command 4 Armoured Brigade, then ordered the Yeomanry to be withdrawn from the battle and only to be used in an emergency and ordered fifteen tanks from 44 RTR to be given to 50 RTR, who after three weeks of fighting were very much below strength, so that they could carry on.

On 18 December A Squadron were supporting 6/13 Battalion Frontier Force Rifles of 19 Indian Brigade – the country was very close, the ground waterlogged and there were very few roads capable of taking tanks. Approaching a valley with houses on the far side containing enemy troops, they found the only way across was a narrow track which was mined. One tank attempted to get over but ran onto a mine, the

'Stuck in the Middle of Mabel' / 189

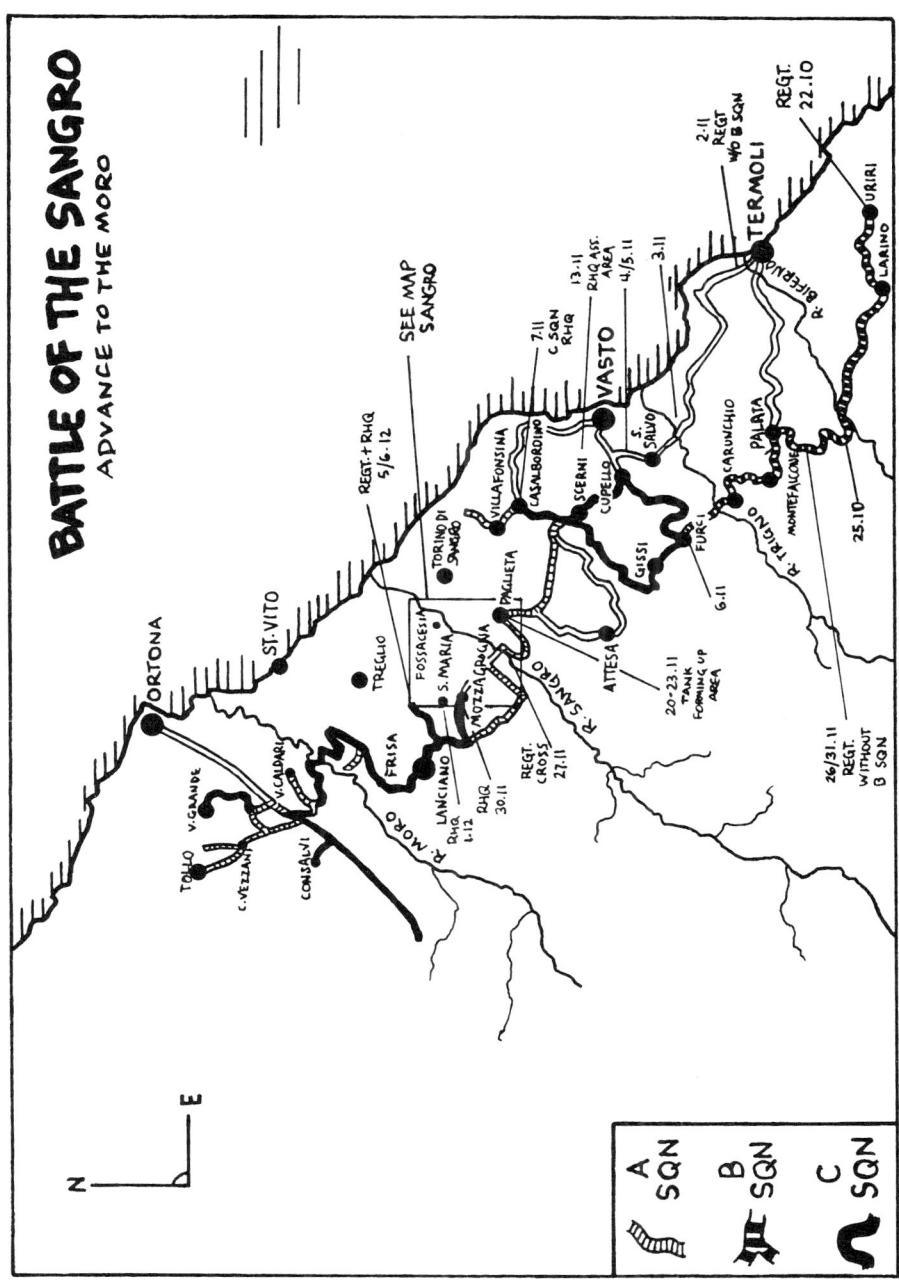

Map 9: *The Battle of the Sangro and Moro Operations. The routes followed by the regiment in these operations, November and December 1943.*

South African tank commander Lieutenant L Macgregor being killed in the resulting explosion. After this failure it was decided to engage the enemy position by fire. Later the infantry got across during darkness while the mines were cleared by the sappers, the tanks going over at first light. Also on the 18th, a German Mark III flame-throwing tank was captured intact during the attack on the Ortona-Orsogna road. Markings and documents showed that it was from 2 Battalion 26 Panzer Regiment.

On the 19th, while B Squadron were supporting 1/12 Battalion Frontier Force Regiment, one tank of Eight Troop was knocked out and burst into flames. Four of the crew were badly dazed but managed to get out of the burning vehicle. As they dismounted they came under machine-gun fire; Lieutenant Keohane, who had been wounded by the armour-piercing shot was now in danger from the flames. The troop sergeant, Eric Butcher, left his own tank and crawled across, first dragging his troop leader away from the fire and then getting the four dazed men back to a safer place. He again crawled forward and dressed Lieutenant Keohane's wounds; returning to his own tank, he sent for medical assistance and continued to fight with the rest of the troop until the infantry had reached their objective. Freddie August recalls:

> Our troop was on the extreme right with Sergeant Butcher's tank in front, mine behind and to the left and Lieutenant Keohane's on the extreme right flank. Rather a dangerous position, as there seemed to be some desultory fire coming from that way.
>
> Suddenly I saw Lieutenant Keohane's tank receive a direct hit with no explosion but with bits of metal flying off in all directions from the strike, so I knew it was an AP shot. It was some seconds before the fire took hold, which enabled the crew to evacuate safely. The turret then blew up which was a truly awe inspiring sight – shells and bullets exploding all over the place amid flames erupting like a huge blow torch from within. Bill Nicholas, Keohane's driver, came across to my tank and asked me to administer an injection of morphia to Lieutenant Keohane who was lying not far from the tank. When this was done – his leg was already dressed with a shell dressing – he was helped into the turret of my tank which I had just brought over to him. I went over to Major Garratt's tank to ask permission to take Keohane to the RAP, to my surprise he was closed down. The only way I could attract his attention was to batter on the turret flaps with my revolver, up popped the Major and gave me the OK.
>
> Arriving at the regimental aid post (me sitting by the driver's hatch and Bill Nicholas on the other side) we found the gunner, Geoff Moms, and the wireless operator, Jack Hurn, were already receiving attention. By now the tank was only smouldering so I

went over for a 'shufti' and found the small round hole where the shot had penetrated, below the track and right into the turret, where it must have ricochetted about the place creating mayhem.

Its a wonder they were not all killed.

During the night of 19/20 December, Regimental Headquarters, A and B Squadrons had withdrawn to separate leaguers and were all shelled heavily. Troopers Robers and Rudd were killed, several others were wounded and six tanks were temporarily disabled. Plans were made on the 20th for C Squadron to support 1/5 Battalion The Essex Regiment. From first light on the 21st, A Squadron was scheduled to relieve C Squadron in the area of Consalve – the tank strength of 50 RTR was now down to 20.

The 21st was a quiet day and this enabled extra effort to be made to get as many replacement tanks as possible up to the Regiment. C Squadron, under Major E Vincent, was given priority as they were to support the Essex Regiment in their attack on Villa Grande, known to be held by the German 1st Parachute Division, on the next day.

Corporal Smale had got his tank bogged down on the south side of a valley when, on the other side, he noticed some wounded Indian troops, so he and his crew went to assist them. As they approached the wounded one of the crew stepped on an S mine. Two of his crew, Troopers Haft and Sinclair and one other soldier were killed and Corporal Smale was severely wounded.

On the same day one tank of B Squadron received a direct hit from a mortar bomb, which landed just above the co-driver's seat, killing the co-driver Lance Corporal Edwards, who was writing a letter home, and setting the tank ablaze.

On the 22nd the attack on Villa Grande commenced at 0600 hours with a barrage on the village. The village itself was about 1,000 yards long, running north and south, its very solid old stone houses lining the narrow road to Tollo. The only available approach was down a poor track flanked by woods and two small rivers, the village being protected on the west side by a steep slope and one of the rivers. At 0615 hours the infantry advanced and the tanks were asked to deal with some machine-gun nests that had been set up the previous night. The tanks went forward along the road but one was lost on mines before the machine-guns were destroyed.

One company of infantry went forward at 0645 hours and was badly shot up by machine-gun fire. Two troops of C Squadron supporting this company pushed forward over an open field, where the ground was so soft the tanks could only move at a snail's pace. At 0839 hours the troop leader's tank was brewed up by an anti-tank gun that had been set up in the doorway of a small cottage in the village. Shortly after this another tank was knocked out by the same gun. One other

*Figure 40: Members of C Squadron, Italy 1944. (from rear left to right) Tpr Knowles, Tpr Tom Wilson, Sgt unknown, Sgt George Boor, Tpr Ken Skillcorn, Tpr Jim Christie, Tpr Nobby Newbury, Tpr Halsey, unknown. (T Wilson)*

troop was sent to reinforce the left, and they lost one tank to the same gun but the two remaining tanks destroyed the gun immediately afterwards.

When the leading tank of the troop was knocked out and set on fire, the shot had penetrated the right wall of the turret, killing the gunner and radio operator outright. The tank commander, Lieutenant Cyril Spence, although badly wounded in the thigh, managed to get away from the burning vehicle, but broke his arm in doing so. The driver and co-driver, Troopers Wilson and Bowen, managed to get clear unhurt. Trooper Bowen went to help Lieutenant Spence, while Trooper Wilson went to Sergeant Woodcock's tank to call for help. Sergeant Woodcock grabbed his first aid kit and, with Trooper Wilson, crawled across to Lieutenant Spence and dressed his wounds. All this movement had attracted enemy machine-gun fire and snipers. The three men now had to get the wounded officer to safety, but because of the heavy firing they all had to crawl. This they did by placing Spence on the back of Trooper Bowen who then acted as a crawling stretcher. They succeeded in getting back to Sergeant Woodcock's tank, where Spence was taken on board and then sent to the rear for medical attention. Lieutenant Spence died of his wounds the following day. Also killed during this action were Lance Corporal Unsworth and Troopers Dance, Jackson and Turner.

On the 23rd, C Squadron were still involved with the Essex Regiment, trying to capture Villa Grande. By that morning, the infantry had only captured one house. Colonel Sleeman arrived and organised an attack for 1200 hours. Two troops of tanks, covered by the remainder of the squadron, were to give close support to the infantry by going round on the right flank. One other tank was to get alongside the house that had already been captured and establish communications. But although the tanks carried out their task the infantry could not get forward and the attack failed in the face of heavy enemy fire.

On the 25th, Christmas Day, everyone felt that this particular day would be rather quieter than usual on both sides. Quite the contrary; the artillery fire was fiercer than had been experienced for some time. Regimental Headquarters was heavily shelled on a number of occasions. A Squadron supported the Punjab Regiment on the left flank and claimed one enemy tank north of the Villa Grande-Tollo road. At 1415 hours another attack on Villa Grande went in; this time it went according to plan and the infantry got into the village. C Squadron's Ten Troop, commanded by Lieutenant Freddie Kepple, knocked out one Mark IV Special on the way; his troop also captured seventeen prisoners, who were fighting from trenches and camouflaged pits to the east. Everything seemed to be in order as the tanks withdrew to their leaguer area. One troop was left in the village to encourage the infantry, but at 1830 hours this troop reported that the infantry were not, in fact, in control of the village and no contact had been made with the Essex Regiment, which had been expected to take over and secure it. Though the regiment was in action during Christmas Day, the men did manage to get their special ration consisting of pork chops, one mince pie and one orange.

On the 26th, the battle to reach the River Arielli continued. C Squadron again tried to capture Villa Grande and eventually, after they had heavily shelled the village, it was thought that the infantry had finally got a grip on the place. One troop again remained overnight in the village with the infantry, as there still seemed a certain amount of doubt as to whether they would hold. The German parachute troops had been ordered to hold out to the last man and this they were doing very effectively.

50 RTR were now due to be relieved by 44 RTR, one squadron at a time. But heavy rain fell and the tank route to the forward area was made impassable; no other route was found, thus the relief by 44 RTR was delayed. During the day Regimental Headquarters were heavily shelled and a number of casualties were suffered.

On the 27th it was decided to end the resistance in Villa Grande once and for all; 400 rounds of high explosive on delayed fuses were fired into the village during the course of the morning. In the afternoon, the remaining tanks of C Squadron supported a final attempt to secure

*Figure 41: Cooking arrangements 50 RTR style, Italy 1943. (T Wilson)*

the village. The infantry commander rode in the co-driver's seat of the lead tank and directed fire on houses known to contain the enemy, but it was not until 1530 hours that the infantry reported the village secure and that the tanks would no longer be required. By the end of the action C Squadron had fired over 1,000 rounds of high explosive into the village. Ken Bull recalls:

That morning our tank commander had been taken from us, which left me and another A Squadron bloke, two from B Squadron, all in a C Squadron tank. So there we were, four rankers sitting in the tank, bitter bloody cold, wet, hungry, fed up, stonked to buggery and wondering what would happen next. Then an officer (new and in-experienced) wearing a leather jerkin, which effectively covered his rank insignia, dropped into the turret. He was easily recognisable as an officer by his collar and tie; he told us that we were going to blow the village apart.

Three troops were organised, two of three tanks and one of two tanks. The idea was that we should approach from different directions, take up firing positions and open fire on the nearest building; when that building collapsed we were to move on to the next and repeat the exercise. When our ammo started to run low we would signal the next troop, who would then come up and open fire, while we went back to replenish. The third troop would then follow suit, we would then after re-arming return for another bash.

The three tanks detailed off to form the first troop (of which ours was one) were ordered to take up hull down positions behind a slight ridge, range and open rapid fire with our 75mms. Our tank commander then ordered us forward to the top of the ridge exposing us to the enemy, who immediately began to stonk us with mortars, one bomb actually hitting the offside track where it went around the sprocket.

Only a day or so previously we had lost a tank and crew member in a very similar situation (a mortar bomb had landed on the periscope mounting) and as our position was very unhealthy, I, being the next senior rank, told the officer in no polite way what I thought of him, so we backed down behind the ridge again.

Two days later when he took off his jerkin, instead of a pip on his shoulder, as I had thought, there was a crown – oh dear a Major! I apologised for the language and harsh words. To his credit he assured me that no offence had been taken and that I was to put him right should he commit any further errors. He subsequently became second-in-command of the regiment.

The following day the Royal West Kents, with B Squadron in support, advanced north of Villa Grande, but met no opposition. The heavy shelling of the previous day had made the position too hot for the Germans to hold. The village and surrounding area were now under complete control; a position of great value to the Allied armies had been established ready for their forthcoming operations west of the River Arielli, two miles away.

At 0510 hours on 29 December, B Squadron supported 1/5 Battalion Mahratta Light Infantry in an attack across a valley one mile from the River Arielli. The bridge over the valley had been destroyed the previous day but the sappers had got to work on it during the night. On the approach to the bridge the first tank became bogged, but by 0715 hours all had got across. The Mahrattas had by this time taken their objective and had six tanks of B squadron in support.

Meanwhile, A Squadron were supporting Punjabi patrols, who were trying to make contact with the Mahrattas from the left flank. This was not completely achieved, due to enemy fire across the flat open stretch of countryside south-east of the valley and nearby road junction. It was on this day, the 29th, that 4 Armoured Brigade received a new commander, Brigidier H J B Cracroft.

On the 30th, B Squadron took up positions within the bridgehead formed by the Mahrattas, having spent the night in the forward defence line.

The weather had now cleared and the Royal Air Force were able to take to the air again; but at about midday one flight of bombers mistook their target and bombed Regimental Headquarters, luckily without casualties. One can only imagine the obscenities that came from the mouths of the Regimental Headquarters personnel – 'it is bad enough being bombed by the enemy, never mind your own bloody side.' To avoid a recurrence 50 RTR was allocated an air contact team.

Arrangements had now been made for 44 RTR to take over all 50 RTR's bogged and unfit tanks and assume their front line commitments. However, as darkness fell snow also began to fall and by daylight on the 31st all mechanised movement was at a halt. A and B Squadrons were still in their forward positions; they had received orders to hold their ground and make no further advance. Snow in the B Echelon area was up to four feet deep in places and all vehicles were immobilised because of the waterlogged ground. The night of the 31st, New Year's Eve, was one of the most miserable that 50 RTR had ever spent, with little or no cover from the rain other than the tanks. At about 2100 hours a bitter wind got up, the rain turned to snow and the ground began to freeze.

With the coming of 1944, 50 RTR was still in the front line and had been separated from B Echelon since 22 October. Winter had finally arrived and with it the difficulties of supply and maintenance increased. The regiment were to move shortly to another army front but, with all three fighting squadrons in the front line, this made any move even more difficult.

On 1 January 1944, the regiment woke up to a blanket of snow covering the countryside – every slit trench was running with water, sunken tracks were more like rivers and the small valley which lay between A Squadron's leaguer and its daytime positions was running four feet deep. The enemy were equally affected by the weather and hardly a shot was fired all day.

On 3 January the second-in-command, Major D P Venn, was evacuated to hospital and Major Jenkin temporarily took over. Final arrangements were now being made for the long-awaited relief. All tanks that were bogged, mined or awaiting recovery were handed over to 44 RTR and the regiment, less one squadron, withdrew to the B Echelon area, leaving the tanks in the forward area with skeleton crews until the roads became passable. The remaining squadron under Major Vincent was later relieved by 14 Canadian Tank Regiment. By the 5th all personnel of 50 RTR were out of the front line and rest was the order of the day. 'We,' wrote Colonel Sleeman, 'celebrated Xmas Day on the 6th.'

Trooper Harry 'Tiny' Dorras of C Squadron remembers a quiet period in Italy:

Stanley Nash was our troop officer; I was the co-driver on his tank, which also meant batman. I remember on one of the rare occasions we got fresh meat and I attempted to cook it, he remarked how good the mustard was. When things got really quiet he and I used to take a good stock of wine up and play chess in an abandoned shepherd's hut.

Trooper Les Garland of the echelon says:

On the Sangro I had a little Jewish boy named Cohen, he guided me over the river; we had to follow a wide bend and keep in the centre; he walked in front of us and kept us in line. One morning a few weeks later (we were near Lanciano, where there was snow on the hills) he called me early on and said that an elderly Italian woman was outside crying; he had given her a tin of corned beef but she blessed him and still cried. He took me to her and we discovered that she wanted a little salt. I had a tin in my tool box from our time in the desert, it was a bit musty – a great relief to her; she blessed me and went off happy in the snow.

The regiment was now back in 23 Armoured Brigade as 4 Armoured Brigade was about to leave for the UK. They were to move to X Corps on the American Fifth Army front. On 10 January Colonel Sleeman wrote:

Up to and including the operation in Sicily, this unit formed part of 23 Armoured Brigade, but in Italy we have been proud to serve under and add to the fighting record of the old well known brigade of 7th Armoured Division – 4 Armoured Brigade.

Our operations with the Eighth Army are now temporarily concluded. It is interesting to note that our arrival in and departure from the Eighth Army coincided in each case with the posting of our great leader, General Sir Bernard Montgomery.

On the 11th, 50 RTR started its journey to Fifth Army and that night was spent by the railway station at Castelbordino. On the 14th they arrived at Teano in 23 Armoured Brigade area, where they were informed that it was hoped they would have at least three weeks' rest from battle. The following day 47 tanks from the Royal Scots Greys were taken over, the Greys also being on their way back to Britain. The next day the regiment moved into the billets just vacated by the Greys. The rest of the month was spent in training and all ranks were promised four days leave in Salerno. On the 18th, the regiment learned that the popular officer, Major D P Venn, had died in Barletta on 16 January from the effects of a poisoned neck.

The medical officer now had time to evaluate the condition of tank crews exposed to long periods of action. The following is an extract from his report:

The maintenance of the unit in the line for a prolonged period produced less physical disease than expected, but strain and exhaustion, with resulting loss of efficiency and morale were observed. Many men had to live in their tanks for 24 hours a day, for many days on end and under adverse weather conditions. This did not produce the acute exhaustion seen in infantry cases, but it is possible that the effects of such prolonged exposure require equal, if not more prolonged, rest if the soldier is to be restored to full efficiency. It is noteworthy that under these severe conditions no cases were evacuated for neurosis.

At the end of the month Colonel Sleeman was selected to take up the post of GSO I Instructor at the Staff College in Camberley. John Sleeman's time with the 50th had not been a happy one for him or the regiment. In a Territorial regiment Sleeman's qualities as a regular officer were not appreciated by the men of the 50th. He had been imposed on the regiment from the start and had replaced the much loved and respected Geoff Russell. He never seemed to appreciate the special effort he needed to make when replacing a man like Russell. In addition his priorities when the regiment was withdrawn from action were very much resented and sadly he never gained the respect or trust of the regiment.

To be fair, Sleeman's first command could not have come at a more difficult time than at the height of the Sangro battle; the pressure on him to succeed and to follow orders which he did not always agree with, must have at times been very severe. On reflection, the men of the 50th may well feel they treated him badly, as after the war John Sleeman became a very efficient high grade staff officer.

Lieutenant Colonel Anthony Lascelles, ex-second-in-command of 46 RTR, now arrived from the Anzio beachhead and assumed command. The future Major General Lascelles recalls:

> I was second-in-command of 46 RTR who were part of the force landing at Anzio. As I was embarking, I got a message that I was to command 50 RTR. I could not leave 46 RTR at such a time, but after about a week in Anzio, nothing much was happening. I joined 50 RTR who were then on the east coast near Ortona. I had only been with them for ten days or so when I had to return to 46 RTR whose CO, Eric Offord, had been badly wounded, and of course he had no second-in-command. I stayed 5-6 weeks with 46 RTR until I was relieved and again joined 50 RTR.
>
> 50 RTR was my first command and I liked them very much. It so happened that I spent only a short time with them, a few months, and during this time we were not involved in any major operation.

Other officers who left the regiment at this time were Major Bill Williams, promoted to Lieutenant Colonel as an instructor in North Africa. Major Garratt went to the Royal Armoured Corps Depot and the padre,

Captain Hart, was sent to a new Eighth Army leave camp at Bari. Of these outstanding officers only Major Garratt would rejoin the regiment.

Since May 1943, when the regiment converted to Sherman tanks, only ten per cent of all reinforcements had been trained on that vehicle. Of the 37 other ranks who joined 50 RTR on 8 January, all had had only two weeks' Sherman experience. The first ten days of February were therefore taken up with intensive training on and firing from the new tanks. Then news came that the regiment were to relieve 40 RTR in the next few days.

After two postponements, 50 RTR finally relieved 40 RTR on the night of 15/16 Febuary. All the tanks completed the journey to their new location and were in battle positions by 0130 hours on the 16th. One troop of A Squadron went under command of 46th Infantry Division, the rest of the regiment were under 5th Infantry Division command; at this time 50 RTR had 51 tanks.

From 17 to 28 Febuary very little activity took place on the regiment's front so that over 1,000 seats at various concerts and theatres were allocated to the regiment. At the end of the month, the American 88th Infantry Division took over from 5th Division in the sector from the sea to Castelforte and 50 RTR came under the command of the Americans. Fresh from across the Atlantic, this unit was known as the 'Cloverleaf Division' from their shoulder badge until after their attack on the Gustav Line, became they were known as the 'Blue Devils'.

C W 'Doc' Waters, of 100 Battalion, 442 Regiment, 88th United States Infantry Division, recalls:

> Teano was the railhead for supplies coming in through Naples, and was probably the location of the Headquarters of 50 RTR. The front lines were north of the Garigliano, with our area running from Minturno to Castelforte. The Garigliano valley is as flat as a pool table and our Bailey bridge and the artillery emplacements had to be heavily camouflaged and deeply dug in. The Germans had observation posts over much of the valley. Due to these circumstances, I seriously doubt that there was any armour forward of the rear slopes of the hills on the south edge of the valley. I saw none during three trips back and forth. Our positions on the Garigliano bridgehead were precarious, to say the least, the armour was needed south of the river to prevent a breakthrough by an armoured thrust through Castelforte, Minturno or Ausente Creek. All of the above could only succeed if we and 50 RTR were overrun first. I am sure we all appreciated the back up by the 50th.

During this period, 1 to 5 March, 50 RTR were on the north side of the River Garigliano; this section of the front was very quiet with only the odd shell being fired into the regiment's position despite it being overlooked from the hills behind Castelforte and Minturno. Only two squadrons were deployed over the river while B Squadron trained with the Echelon near Teano. Trooper Ernest Wills of C Squadron recalls one exciting moment in this quiet period:

> I suppose the greatest sight was Mount Vesuvius erupting. We were at Teano at the time and across the valley at night, through a large pair of German field glasses one of our chaps had got hold of, you could see the lava flowing down the sides of the mountain.

The 6th to the 12th was another quiet period, but the weather had turned for the worse, although the regiment did take advantage of two fine days to relieve A Squadron, B Squadron going over the river with thirteen tanks. The troop of tanks that was with 46th Division could not be relieved, so three crews from B Squadron were sent to take over.

On the 15th the weather allowed the Army to commence a fresh assault on Cassino; the area was bombed heavily and great destruction was caused. X Corps had no major role in this attack, which was designed to push the enemy back towards the Hitler Line. 23 Armoured Brigade were assigned the task of defending the left flank of the main attack. A strong mobile force was to be used, consisting of 40 RTR with A Squadron 50 RTR under command. On the 18th news was received that the Brigade would shortly be moving to the Adriatic coast to relieve 1 Canadian Armoured Brigade. On the 22nd Major Vincent left the regiment to take up a staff appointment; after a little reshuffling, Major G Price took command of C Squadron and Major E Scott B Squadron.

By 23 March, all tanks were back and out of the line. That night A Squadron moved to Caserta railway station, but were not entrained until the 26th. On the way one tank was lost when it fell over the edge of a raised road and turned on its side; all efforts to recover it failed. The regiment was now moving back to the area where it had been at the beginning of the year. They were to support 8th Indian Division in the Orsogna area with two squadrons, the third forming a Corps reserve. 40 RTR were to be on the right of The Fiftieth. At this time Colonel Lascelles received the following message from General Sloan, commanding the American 88th Division:

> During the period 2nd March to 22nd March, the 50th Royal Tank Regiment has been in support of front line units of this division. This service has been marked with a fine spirit of willing co-operation and efficient performance of duty. It is my desire to express my appreciation for the splendid manner in which your officers and men have worked together with the officers and men of this division. It is felt that the association has been mutually beneficial and we would look with satisfaction on future orders assigning us to service together.

From the 25th, the tanks – one squadron per train – were taken to St Vito railway station for transport to Scerni. The main road party left Teano for the same destination on the 26th, where the regiment took over from the Canadians. By the 31st they had completed the move and fully taken over the Canadians' position at the front. At 0700 hours eight small calibre shells fell in the Regimental Headquarters area, knocking out a three-ton truck and damaging two scout cars and a staff car.

On 1 April, the whole Corps front was very quiet and both Allied and Axis forces dug in, with the only activity being patrols from both sides. 50 RTR were directly supporting two brigades of 8th Indian Division. A Squadron was in the Eusanio del Sangro area; One Troop was in a position forward of the squadron, this troop being subjected to heavy shell fire by a large calibre gun at certain times of the day. B Squadron was in the Poggiofiorito area, while C Squadron were in reserve at Castelfrentano.

For the next eight or nine days Colonel Lascelles made extensive tours of the forward areas. While with B Squadron he got caught in an enemy barrage. A Squadron made a number of attempts to quieten the gun that was firing on them, but without success. Two members of a German patrol were captured in the Regimental Headquarters area, having been sent to make notes of the vehicles using the road near Castelfrentano, known as the 'Mad Mile', a long, steep stretch of road climbing past the brickworks to Castelfrentano. No-one lingered on the 'Mad Mile'. It was under German observation and throughout its length was a constant target for shot and shell.

On the 10th, 4th Indian Division took over from 8th Indian Division on the ridge south of the Moro, and B Squadron was relieved by 40 RTR and moved to a ridge north of the river.

A few days later it was discovered that Russians were in the enemy lines opposing the regiment. These turned out to be Ukrainians who had been captured in earlier operations by the German Army. They had been given the choice of fighting for the Third Reich or remaining in prison. Each battalion was called Ost (east). The one facing 50 RTR was 412 Ost Battalion and on the night of the 18th fifteen deserters crossed into the regiment's lines.

On the 20th, an ENSA show was in progress in the town of Lanciano. A large number of soldiers were present and the town's population had also come out to see the show, which was disrupted when eighteen German fighter bombers attacked the town at 1130 hours. Six members of 50 RTR were killed and seven wounded. Total casualties were very high and included 45 civilians. Sergeant Joe Hart of the Intelligence Section recalls:

We were to have a treat – a concert party in the Lanciano Theatre (or Opera House). Those who were not on duty piled into a 3 tonner and off we went. Well we got to Lanciano and found that the 4th Indian Division were running the town, even had an Asian traffic policeman on point duty. The show was fine and all seemed well.

Afterwards we had a bit of time to wander around the town, it was about noon. We were in a quite narrow street – Ray Corran, Scotcher and myself – when we heard the unmistakeable sound of diving Messerschmitts. Then all hell broke loose, cannon fire and bombs – all three of us dived into a church doorway. After it was all over we managed to get back to the main square which was a shambles, Italian women were leaning over the balcony of the theatre streaming blood and shrieking.

We pushed on and found the traffic policeman we had seen earlier lying dead in the road, with a Catholic priest administering the last rites! We eventually got back to where we had parked the 3 tonner. No one was to be seen! Then we noticed the shrapnel holes in the body and canvas of the vehicle, worse, the blood dripping to the ground out of the tailboard. Six of our chaps had been killed – and the date: Hitler's birthday.'

For the rest of the month, the regiment remained in the 'Impossible Bridge' area, protecting the river crossing against possible enemy counter-attack. At the end of the month it was learned that they would be relieved by 7 Armoured Brigade, and all equipment was to be handed over or sent to Ordnance; this was to be completed during May.

During the first week in May, preparations were made for the handover, advance parties having arrived by this time. From the 8th to 12th the handover continued, to be completed by the 18th. During the night of 11/12 May the C Squadron area was shelled by a self-propelled gun and Trooper Plant from the Squadron was killed when his tent received a direct hit. Two days later, the 14th, the enemy advanced in battalion strength from the area of Orsogna and overran the forward positions of the 1/12 Battalion Frontier Force Regiment. B Squadron, who were in Poggiofiorito, stood to and at 0845 hours advanced towards Orsogna to support a counter-attack to regain the lost ground. The counter-attack took place in full view of the enemy at a range of 1,500 to 2,000 yards. The tanks advanced with the infantry – the enemy met this with mortar fire and by the time the counter-attacking infantry had reached 100 yards from their objective their casualties were so severe that the tanks could get no further due to lack of infantry support. Lieutenant George Lindley of B Squadron was killed by a mortar bomb in the attack and both Major Scott and Captain Bond were wounded.

During the action, one tank got into difficulties and required a tow, Sergeant Hunter bringing his tank up to help. His driver, Lance Corporal

Connah, positioned the tank, dismounted and fixed a tow rope, remounted his tank and pulled the stuck tank out. He then got out of his own vehicle again and removed the tow rope; all this he did in full view of the enemy snipers and mortar crews. Later in the day, Sergeant Hunter's tank hit a mine, which broke the track in five places; again in full view of the enemy the crew got out and managed to repair the track enough to allow them to get the tank back. Another counter-attack was made at 2000 hours, without tank support, and was a complete success.

On the 15th, the relief could begin again and the first group of tanks were handed in to D Army Delivery Squadron at Torino. By the night of the 18th all remaining personnel were relieved by 2 RTR.

It was then that the men learned that relief was not just a break from the front line; the regiment was being sent back to North Africa. On the 19th the Corps Commander talked to all ranks and thanked them for the fine work they had done in Italy. From the 22nd to 26th, all personnel were in a staging area at Taranto, where leave was granted into the town.

Not forgetting the part played by the regiment's support personnel, 50 RTR's War Diary records:

> The ability of the Echelons and the administrative and technical staff, amongst whom were the Adjutant, Captain Masters, Major Bazley commanding Headquarter Squadron, Captain Walters of B Echelon, Captain Hall, the Regimental Technical Adjutant, Quartermaster Captain Dromey, Captain Davis of the REME and the Regimental Sergeant Major John Cowe, kept the fighting squadrons fully supplied during the campaign, playing a vital part in its success, had it not been for the hard and sometimes gallant work carried out by the Echelons, the tank crews would surely, had an even harder time.

One essential supply, or lack of it, that did cause the tank crews dismay was the issue of rum. In Italy, more often than not, it arrived very late in the day, when all the crews had turned in for the night, making the issue more of a nuisance than a boon. It was argued that the crews should carry sufficient quantities, to last them three or four issues!

On the 27th, the regiment embarked on *HMT Banfora*, leaving Taranto the following day. 50 RTR had been in Italy for exactly eight months, during which time they had been continually in action with various divisions, including 8th Indian, 4th Indian, 78th Infantry, 46th (North Midland) Infantry, 5th Infantry and, for three weeks, the American 88th.

On many occasions the tank crews of 50 RTR mixed freely with the men from India One tank crew whose vehicle had been knocked out in the Sangro battle, were very well entertained despite the language barrier: 'They were quite fantastic, nothing was too much trouble; it was very obvious to us that these infantrymen had a very high regard for tank crews.'

To their credit, the Indian armed forces formed the largest volunteer army in World War II and 87,000 lost their lives. Although India was under British rule, there was no conscription, every Indian that served in the armed forces was a volunteer and enlisted as a matter of honour.

The regiment's own casualties during their time in Italy were – eight officers killed and thirteen wounded; 28 other ranks killed and 51 wounded – a total of exactly 100 casualties.

## Chapter 11
## 'THE THIN RED LINE OF BLACK HATS'

### Action in Greece

After two days at sea, HMT *Banfora* arrived at Port Said, Egypt, on 1 June, 1944. The regiment was to have a period of rest and reorganisation. At 0430 hours the following morning 50 RTR disembarked and entrained for the base camp at Qassassin. Colonel Lascelles, who had been sick and in hospital in North Africa, met the ship as it docked.

On the 3rd, 50% of the regiment were sent on leave. During the next five days tanks and vehicles began to arrive and preparations were being made for training with 56th Indian Division. Rumours were also about concerning a move to Palestine. From now until the end of the month things were quite relaxed; the remaining 50% of men went on leave. All new tanks were checked over, the guns fired and training with the infantry started. It was confirmed that the regiment would be going to Palestine (despite new rumours of an interesting move to Syria) at the end of training. At the end of the month Colonel Lascelles was posted to command 2 RTR in Italy; Major J O Collins assumed temporary command.

At the beginning of July, 50 RTR was training at Beni Yusef, Maadi and Helwan, south of Cairo. Arrangements were also being made for the move to Palestine, to the brigade camp at Beit Jirja, north of Gaza. On 2 July, A Squadron's tanks were on the way by rail from Maadi. En route, at Ismailia, Corporal Saunders from A Squadron was accidentally killed by the discharge of a pistol.

On the 7th, the remainder left Helwan under the command of Major Vic Senior, arriving at the Beit Jirja camp at 1730 hours the following day, the Echelon vehicles travelling by road through the Sinai Desert. The new camp, by the sea, looked promising, but the men had to be on their guard from pilfering and, as a precaution, extra guards were posted and a searchlight system set up for use at night. It was during this early part of July that the attempted assassination of the High Commissioner, Sir Harold McMichael, occurred.

Squadron training now started, eight hours a day with one day off per week. At the end of the month news of the new commanding officer was received – it was to be Lieutenant Colonel J R D Carlton MC (formerly of 2 RTR), who was already on his way from England and would be with the regiment in early August.

For the first three weeks of August the regiment was hard at work training near the towns of Aslou and Gaza. The new commanding officer had arrived on 3 August and during the following week had inspected the squadrons and met every man. On the 17th orders were issued for the whole of 23 Armoured Brigade to move back to Egypt and advance parties were to be sent to Mena. The sudden end of training and orders to move immediately were signs that action could not be too far away; the men could only guess where.

After all the preparations for the move had been made the regiment left Palestine on the 21st – that night being spent in the Sinai desert. They reached Mena the following day to find that the advance parties had done their job well; all tents were erected and a hot meal was ready. B Squadron 46 RTR also arrived at Mena and was put under command of 50 RTR, to be known as D Squadron. For the rest of the month the regiment went through an extensive training programme.

Only Colonel John Carlton knew of the regiment's final destination but there were indications in the training programme, which was undertaken without tanks. Instructors from infantry units were brought in to train the regiment in their new role as infantry. They learned how to patrol streets supporting each other; to search buildings always being aware of booby traps; and crowd control – much the same as our modern forces in Northern Ireland today.

It was originally planned for the regiment to move by air and 86

Figure 42: Relaxing in Palestine, Sergeants McNaught, Flaherty, Cowan and Gabe-Jones. Tel Aviv August 1944. (Flaherty Family)

*Figure 43:* HMS Aurora, *who had one of the best gunnery teams in the Mediterranean, carried 50 RTR from North Africa to Greece, 1944. (Author's collection)*

aircraft were made available for this. However, on 5 September plans were changed and the move would be by sea. On 7 September the regiment moved to Amirya, where they learned the plan of operations, but still not the destination. Planning with the Royal Navy now started, to arrange the loading of vehicles, etc. At the beginning of October Colonel Carlton held a squadron leaders' conference outlining the final plans. But the destination would not be known until arrival.

On 10 October, all ranks were confined to camp, the first real indication that the regiment would soon be on its way. On the 12th orders were received to move to Alexandria for embarkation. They arrived at the docks at 0700 hours on the 13th and marched straight on to the ships. 50 RTR were assigned to *HMS Aurora*. All loading was completed by 1030 hours and the ship sailed at 1100 hours.

The small convoy carrying the force consisted of *HMS Black Prince*, *HMS Aurora* and three destroyers. They travelled at 22 knots, making for Poros Island, part of the Peloponnese group east of the Greek mainland. The convoy reached Poros at 1200 hours on 14 October, where it awaited a small convoy from Italy. First light on the 15th revealed the arrival of *HMS Orion* and *HMS Ajax* (of River Plate fame) with some minesweepers and tank landing ships. The ships now headed for the Piraeus on the Greek mainland. On the way they had to pass through an enemy minefield, where *HMS Lyon* was damaged and a tanker carrying water sank within three minutes.

It may be an opportune moment to explain why 50 RTR were aboard *Aurora* and heading for Greece. One of the greatest problems facing the allies in the Mediterranean theatre was the future of Greece. Long before the defeat of the Germans in southern Europe, it was clear that Greece would be celebrating her liberation with a full-blooded civil war between the Communists and the lawful Greek government. Churchill determined to prevent a Communist takeover, despite opposition from America and Russia; the result was operation MANNA, the British intervention in Greece, which was to plunge British troops into the bitter strife of Greek politics

On 23 August the German forces occupying Albania, mainland Greece and the Aegean islands came under the command of General Lohr – amounting to around 330,000 men in total. Within a few days of Lohr taking command he was given orders to evacuate Greece. He was to retreat to a line running along the Bulgarian/Yugoslav borders.

The evacuation of the Peloponnese gave rise to clashes between the German 41st Division and Greek guerrillas, who were reinforced by the British 2 Airborne Brigade. However, losses to the Germans were very light and no serious delays were encountered.

Mention should be made here that in 1947, the Greek government revealed to the United Nations the text of an agreement made between 11th Luftwaffe Division and the ELAS (Communist) partisans, according to the terms of which the men of the 'People's Army' agreed not to hinder the German retreat on condition that they were given a certain quantity of heavy arms and other military equipment for their forthcoming war with the government. These weapons were soon to be used against 50 RTR and other British units in Greece.

The task allotted to British troops was to prevent ELAS from overturning the established Greek government. The Greek Prime Minister, George Papandreou, gave this regime a liberal and democratic aspect which was acceptable to the Western Allies. However, the threat of subversion was growing daily and, summoned by the Liberation Committee of Communists (EAM), armed units of ELAS converged on Athens, passing the retreating Germans without clashing.

Meanwhile, the convoy carrying 50 RTR reached the Piraeus just as night was approaching on the 15th. Mines had been laid in and around the harbour, which delayed the unloading of troops until the 16th. At first light on the 16th, the regiment was formed up into squadrons and disembarked at 0700 hours, landing at Irakleous Bay. Greek trucks and buses were formed up along the road to Athens, which saved the men a six-mile march to the city – they had finally learned their destination.

The plan of operations was for 2 Parachute Brigade to land and take the airfields south of the city; 11 Battalion King's Royal Rifle Corps (60th Rifles) transported by British cruisers would land and secure the port, 50 RTR would then pass through and occupy the town; twelve hours later 40 RTR would land and become force reserve.

The streets were lined with people cheering and clapping and the regiment halted for lunch at the Old Palace Gardens. The squadrons were then sent to take over the various vital points in the city, which were being held by 2 Parachute Brigade. Regimental Headquarters remained in the Palace Gardens for the night. Lance Corporal Percy Wadey recalls one moment of panic in Athens:

> We were the first troops to land in Greece and marched through Athens to the British Embassy for guard duty. One event I remember well was when Nine Troop was responsible for the 24 hour guard, with Sergeant Neal as guard commander and myself as second-in-command. At dusk the British flag was lowered with full military honours. The following morning with all the guard present, I hoisted the flag.
>
> Later that morning a staff officer entered the guard room and asked who was responsible for hoisting the flag and as it was my responsibility I admitted I was the one. Needless to say the flag was the wrong way up which was, of course, a sign of distress. When I offered to right it I was told it would cause quite a stir and he advised me to leave it, hoping it might pass unnoticed, which fortunately, was so.

On the 17th, Regimental Headquarters was set up next to the railway station. B Squadron, who were guarding the Greek broadcasting station at the Zappion building, captured three Germans in civilian clothes. A

*Figure 44: C Squadron's Nine Troop providing the Guard at the British Embassy Athens, October 1944. (G Thomas)*

*Figure 45: Adjutant Capt John Masters (5th from the left), being made welcome in the Sergeant's Mess, Athens, October 1944 (from left to right) Sgts McNaught, Gabe-Jones, Puddick, Ellery, Capt Masters and Sgt Flaherty. (Flaherty family)*

*Figure 46: Demonstration in Omonia Square, Athens, December 1944. The tanks belong to 46 RTR. (IWM)*

number of similar incidents occurred during the day. On the 18th, the commander of the allied forces in Greece, Major General R M Scobie, and the Greek Prime Minister, landed at the Piraeus, a guard of honour being provided by men of B Squadron. Over the next few days a considerable number of German documents were discovered and six more Germans, including a woman, arrested; the Greek police recognised the woman as a spy.

On the 22nd two troops of C Squadron, under command of Captain H B O'Sullivan were sent to support the Greeks guarding the dockyard on the island of Salamis. Two days later they reported that armed ELAS had landed on the eastern side of the island and were looting civilian property. At this time the Communist controlled ELAS (People's National Army of Liberation) had been disarming the local police force, but the allied occupation force had not the power to disarm ELAS, so arrangements were made to re-form the police with sufficient strength to deal with them.

By the beginning of November, some of the tension that was present when the landings took place had disappeared and the troops began to relax a little. On the 5th the brigade football team including eight men from The Fiftieth played a local Greek team. This was the official beginning of football in the Athens area. Regimental Headquarters and B Squadron held a party in the men's mess on the 7th, and another football match was played on the 8th. A Remembrance service was held on the 11th, for all those who fell in the 1914-18 war. A further football match was played on Salamis Island the following day in which the two sides scored one goal each Captain O'Sullivan was elected as Honorary President of Salamis Football Club.

The only incident to spoil these happy days happened on the 10th, outside C Squadron's Headquarters. Two corporals from the 3rd Greek Mountain Brigade complained of being jostled by the civilians. One of the Greek soldiers drew his pistol and the other a hand grenade. The crowd quickly dispersed, but not before one had been struck by the pistol butt. Major Senior, commanding C Squadron, turned out the guard and arrested the two corporals, much to the delight of the crowd. The two men were detained and then escorted back to their barracks.

Information was now being received that ELAS were about to attempt a *coup d'état*, and that there was a threat of widespread disturbances; the regiment was to be alert at all times. All the signs of an uprising were there – the Communists had started painting slogans in vivid red paint on buildings, and a huge Communist parade was held on 19 November. If the Army or Royal Air Force mounted a parade the Communists would put on a counter-demonstration – all this was building up to a confrontation which would not be long in coming.

By the end of the month crisis after crisis erupted in the Greek

*Figure 47: Officers of the regiment outside Manna Barracks, October 1944.*
*Back row – Lt Hall, Lt Hallowes, Lt Keane, Lt Glashen (SA), Lt Sheppart, Lt Lewis MM, Lt Chidell, Lt Conlin.*
*3rd row – Lt Gardiner, Lt Nash MM, Lt Neethling (SA), Lt Murray, RMO Capt Fienmann, Lt Waddell MC, Lt Thomas, Lt Willis MC, Capt (QM) Dromey MBE.*
*2nd row – Capt Furness, Capt Lee, Capt Bond MC, Capt Hibbert, Capt Walters, Capt Price, Capt Kepple, Capt Moss MC, Capt O'Sullivan, Maj Garrett.*
*Front row – Maj Jenkin MC, Maj Scott, Maj Collins, Lt Col Carlton MC, Capt Master, Maj Bazley MBE, Maj Senior MC.*
*SA denotes South African Officer. (J Masters)*

Government – the main worries were from ELAS, who might attempt a military coup at any time; the Communists would offer resistance to any new government. In this event, martial law would be proclaimed and 50 RTR, based in Athens, would have three main tasks: to arrest certain politicians; to occupy Communist political and military headquarters; and to take over ELAS arms and ammunition dumps.

These tasks would be carried out firmly but quietly, the troops acting as police rather than soldiers. However, should the situation warrant it, aggressive action would be taken.

On 2 December 1944 the Greek Communist Party started active resistance to the Government. Early on the 3rd the regiment received orders to stand-to and all ranks were confined to their billets. B and C Squadrons, who were quartered in the city centre, reported firing in Constitution Square, the main square of Athens. It was discovered that the police had opened fire on a large Communist demonstration which had defied the Government's ban on marches through the city. It was not until tanks of 46 RTR arrived on the scene that any kind of order

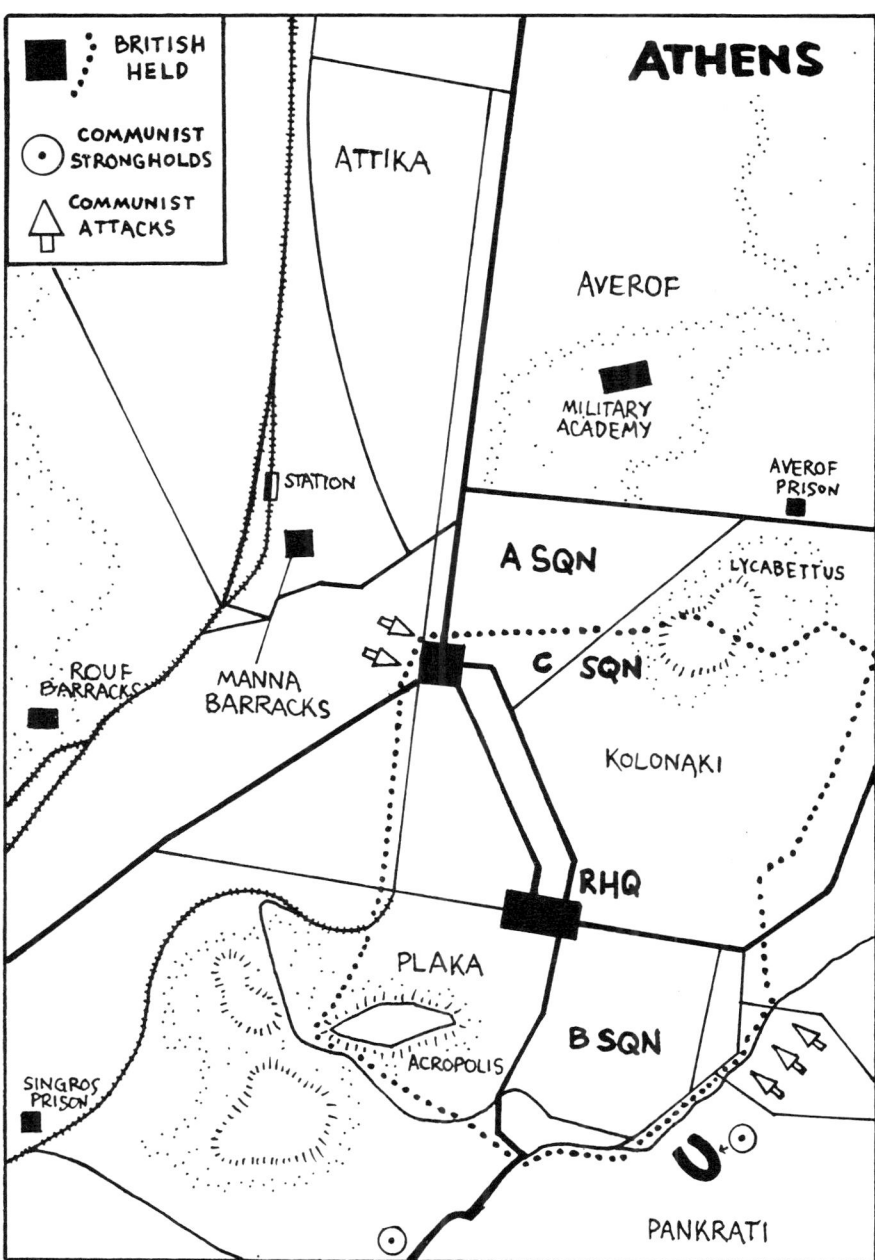

Map 10: 'Athens'. The Thin Red Line of Black Hats.

was restored. Late in the afternoon the first fighting broke out between ELAS and the Nationalists – this was high above the city on the Acropolis.

The following day ELAS attacked a number of city police stations. The police station in Ippocratous Street was surrounded and only the arrival of a patrol from C Squadron prevented ELAS from doing further damage. On at least two occasions Colonel Carlton and the Regimental Sergeant Major, John Cowe, armed with only swagger canes, managed to disarm members of ELAS, so avoiding unnecessary bloodshed, though this would be the last opportunity. Following this and other minor incidents, martial law was proclaimed on the evening of 4 December.

Guard duty at night had always been an unfavoured task, but now it began to take on a new meaning and many of the men from the regiment would suffer traumatic experiences because of it.

During the afternoon of the 5th, Colonel Carlton informed all squadron leaders that a state of war now existed between the British troops and ELAS. As a result of this the regiment was re-grouped during the night. A Squadron withdrew from the Rouf area and occupied Omonoias Square with three troops, one troop remaining in occupation of the telegraph office just south of the square. B Squadron remained at the Zappion Building, less one troop which remained at Goudhi Barracks. C Squadron, less the two troops on Salamis Island, concentrated in Korai Street. D Squadron was very much split up; one troop at the radio station at Neo Liosia, one at Marathon Dam and one at Pallini radio station, and the fourth in reserve at Manna Barracks with Headquarter Squadron. Regimental Headquarters moved to join the troop of D Squadron at Neo Liosia. One troop from 40 RTR was sent to guard the Criminal Record Office in the centre of the city. All this re-grouping and movement was carried out without incident, but everybody knew that hostilities would commence the next day. Not only were the British fighting against their former allies but they would often be unable to distinguish between civilian and guerrilla.

During the morning of the 6th two troops of C Squadron and one troop of B Squadron, sent from the Zappion building, attacked EAM Headquarters (the political wing of ELAS) which was situated in the offices across the road from them in Korai Street. The only entry was through a heavy steel grille and a pair of strong double doors; a tank from 46 RTR made short work of this by driving straight through the steel grille and firing its 75mm gun at the doors, making a tremendous noise that reverberated right through the building. The attack was successful and 30 prisoners were taken though Trooper Newns from C Squadron was killed during the attack. Meanwhile, a company from 2 Parachute Brigade joined A Squadron in the defence of Omonoias

Square. ELAS also showed their contempt for the Red Cross when, on the same day, two grenades were thrown at the medical officer's vehicle.

The ELAS attack on the MO's vehicle was not an isolated incident; it had already happened to RAMC personnel in other units. From now on, ELAS would continue to disregard the Red Cross and the Geneva Convention. It now became necessary, for the first time in World War II, to arm RAMC personnel.

During the 7th, 50 RTR had to clear the area surrounding Ermou, Athinas and Stadium Streets. Until this was completed ELAS would still control the centre of the city. Two troops each from A and B Squadrons formed a strong point at the junction of Ermou and Athinos Streets. Once in position they were frequently attacked with dynamite, ELAS making excellent use of the narrow streets for cover from which they could attack the 50 RTR position. ELAS suffered heavy casualties and 50 RTR had a number also including Corporal Faulkner and Trooper Coady who were both killed.

At the end of the second day of fighting it became obvious to ELAS that the British troops in Athens only amounted to a handful of units, and these were dangerously separated. In the north of the city a large and well armed ELAS force had securely established itself, while in the south the Greek Mountain Brigade was meeting fierce opposition from ELAS armed with German Spandau machine-guns.

On the evening of the 9th the troops posted at Neo Liosia were ordered to destroy the radio station and withdraw. Trucks were sent for them under the command of Captain Freddie Kepple. On the return journey the column was ambushed just north of Athens, but the leading vehicles did not stop and drove through the ambush, two soldiers being wounded. The rear of the column had seen the ambush, so turned their vehicles round and returned to the radio station. Two tanks were sent out to escort them back to their base in the city. On the outward and inward journeys the tanks shot up the ambush area and claimed casualties. Ernest Wills recalls:

> At first we went into action with our lovely white webbing and it took some civilian to point out what lovely targets we made with our white cross straps on our backs, just right for a sniper to set his sights on. So we were told to blacken our webbing, by foul means if necessary, so with great joy black boot polish or some soot from a chimney was soon put on them.

During the night of 10/11 December, the troops at the junction of Athinas and Ermour Streets were subjected to increased ELAS activity and by morning it was discovered that ELAS had advanced closer to the regiment's perimeter. Captain Bond, commanding the troops at the road junction, was wounded by a rifle grenade, which landed in the room he was occupying. For several days following, the situation remained critical, but all ELAS attempts to dislodge the troops failed. At one stage the opposing forces were only 30 feet apart. This determined action prevented ELAS from entering the centre of the city in strength.

On the 11th an ELAS officer carrying a white flag approached a 50 RTR position. He said he had orders to attack any British soldiers in his way. He was told, politely, that The Fiftieth would be quite happy to take them on, should they decide to try. During that afternoon Lieutenant Reginald Willson of C Squadron was investigating reports of ELAS occupying the hospital buildings. While he was on the steps of the hospital he was shot and died instantly. Occupation by ELAS was then confirmed – they dragged Willson's body inside and removed his battle dress and pistol.

By 12 December the perimeter around the city centre was completed and held by British troops. Nevertheless elements of ELAS were still able to reach the city centre and had to be dealt with by what troops were available.

Major-General Scobie, commanding the British troops in Greece, referred to this perimeter as 'the thin red line of black hats'. The line was tenuous and had a concentrated attack been made by ELAS, then the perimeter would have collapsed; as it was, no major attack took place. It was now that substantial reinforcements were on their way to Greece and tank reinforcements were the topic of the day, which might mean the re-equipping of the entire regiment for, although much experience had been gained in the infantry role, tanks and tank work was still what the regiment had been trained for.

However, in the early hours of the 13th, ELAS mounted their largest assault on British positions to date. On the outskirts of the city, the infantry barracks which housed 23 Armoured Brigade's rear headquarters and signal squadron, the artillery's gun lines and was also the main supply depot for Athens, was heavily mortared. After blowing a large hole in the barrack wall, almost 1,000 ELAS poured through to destroy the telephone exchange, killing all but one of the operators. In the fighting that ensued 60 of the defenders were killed or wounded and over 100 taken prisoner. ELAS casualties amounted to 30 killed and 40 taken prisoner. Though they had struck a major blow for their cause, they had failed to locate and destroy the field guns which had been their main objective.

Throughout all the operations, civilian reports continually reached the regiment. Some were undoubtedly accurate and some most alarming, but it was impossible to give every one the attention which was warranted had they all been true. For example, at this time one building which the regiment occupied in the north of the perimeter was reported as due to be blown up by ELAS every night.

By early evening on 14 December, B Squadron was relieved at the

Zappion building and took over the left flank, between Omonoias Square and Likavittos. Meanwhile, the regimental Light Aid Detachment were ordered to Rouf Ordnance Depot to service some vehicles. The depot was located outside the perimeter and was held as a separate position. The fitters were given an armoured car escort, but the escort, apparently thinking that a heavy recovery vehicle could do 30mph, made off far too quickly and did not maintain contact with the column behind. They were accordingly attacked very heavily from all sides as soon as the armoured cars went on ahead. Had the control by Captain Bert Rothwell been anything other than excellent, there would have been heavy casualties. However, with no panic the column of trucks made their way through ELAS-infested neighbourhoods and eventually arrived at the depot with only a few casualties. In the weeks that followed the fitters performed admirably, and although over 400 shells fell in their area, completed their work. The following extract is taken from a diary kept by Captain H Rothwell of the regiment's REME (Royal Electrical Mechanical Engineers) detachment:

15th Dec. – Rough journey, took wrong street and we got shot up. Three casualties.

16th Dec. – All day under fire from ELAS. Many radiators with bullet holes repaired with chewing gum. Lt-Col. Badcock and myself blown through doorway by direct hit from French 75mm.

17th-22nd Dec. – Got over 70 vehicles back to Piraeus.

23rd Dec. – Hard going, with little sleep. In three days over fifty 75mm shells land on park. Most vehicles very much perforated.

By 15th December ELAS pressure at the road junction of Ermou and Athinos Streets had grown less, due to actions on either flank by two battalions from 2 Parachute Brigade. It was decided that the two troops of A Squadron there should be relieved by two platoons of the Greek National Guard, several platoons of which 50 RTR had under command. Further, it was decided to hand over this section to 11 Battalion The King's Royal Rifle Corps, (60th Rifles), in whose area it was. Except for small posts, that part of the regiment in Athens would be concentrated on one section of the front. Command passed to the 60th Rifles at midday, and A Squadron came into reserve behind C Squadron. This was primarily to give them a rest but had the secondary effect of giving depth to the line. The troop of A Squadron in occupation of the telegraph office was also relieved by a platoon of the National Guard, under command of, and supported by, a section of Headquarter Squadron.

During the evening of the 15th, the regiment heard that the first squadron of tanks would be arriving very shortly, and at a squadron leaders' conference the next day B Squadron, by winning a ballot, received the allocation. It was decided to withdraw them from the line and replace them with A Squadron. It was now necessary to relieve the troop of B Squadron at Goudhi and this was done by sending the troop of D Squadron still left in Athens. This troop had been under command of C Squadron.

50 RTR patrolled most actively at night during this period. Although untrained for this type of work, much aggressiveness was put into it. This fighting patrol work was very necessary; it was impossible at this stage to put in an attack of any size so patrols continually harassed the ELAS lines, giving them no rest. ELAS were kept continually on their guard, never knowing where fighting patrols would strike next.

During 16 December C Squadron's right flank was relieved by a company of the 2nd Battalion The Highland Light Infantry, and they in turn relieved the troop of 40 RTR which had been serving under their command, this troop returning to its own regiment, which had now arrived. The regiment's sector now extended from Asklipiou Street on the right to Tatission Street on the left, a front of about 700 yards through very narrow streets, with ELAS often only the width of a street away.

On the morning of 17 December the relief of B Squadron by A Squadron started. A troop of A Squadron passed through the main position with a tank in support and established themselves in a building. This relief was completed without any major incident, although Corporal Gaunt of B Squadron was killed by an ELAS sniper.

It was on the 17th that Captain O'Sullivan was at last able to report the latest situation on Salamis Island. The total British force there was about 35, but the soldiers under O'Sullivan had built up so much goodwill, having secured for the people all the relief they needed, that a force of 250 armed men now existed, all having placed themselves under command of the British. They were confident of being able to deal with any emergency which might arise and they considered the island secure: a most notable feat, accomplished by the personal initiative of the commander.

After last light on the 17th, B Squadron were relieved by A Squadron and went into reserve, awaiting the arrival of their tanks. When these arrived the squadron was to come under command of 4th British Infantry Division, who were all now ashore, and whose task it was to clear the road from the coast. Colonel Carlton decided to give A and C Squadrons one tank each, to use in close support of infantry, and to have two tanks as a regimental reserve at Regimental Headquarters. Major Senior gave C Squadron's tank to Sergeant Maplesden who, readers will recall, had done so well in the Sicilian campaign.

On the morning of 19 December, an unfortunate accident took place in B Squadron, which resulted in the wounding of eleven soldiers. During an arms check a 36 Mills grenade exploded in a room where a troop was assembled. Due to the presence of mind of their troop leader,

Lieutenant K Hallowes, who himself was wounded, no-one was killed. During the four seconds which elapsed from the time the fuse was ignited all got on the floor. The grenade exploded on a table and set off a smoke grenade, which wounded some by burning.

During that afternoon, B Squadron were ordered to move to the coast at Phaleron to take over their tanks. They were then to go into billets in the same area. They collected their tanks, as did the crews from A, C and Regimental Headquarters, which later returned to the regiment in Athens. Up until this date all tank support had been provided by 46 RTR.

For the first time dynamite throwers now made their appearance on the regiment's northern front. A Squadron, using borrowed tanks and armoured cars, put down fire on a building known to all as the 'unfinished building', which was located in Kaningos Square and was an ELAS position. Armoured cars were placed in Pattission Street to stop any ELAS attempting to escape through the back of the building and dynamite was thrown at one of them from an upstairs window. The charge consisted of a German stick grenade with additional blocks of dynamite tied to it, making a very effective demolition charge. A later model used took the form of a tyre packed with dynamite, a fuse worked into the charge and the whole bound with rope. It would then be lighted and rolled to the target, usually a wall. This was used both in an effort to destroy positions and as a terror weapon.

20 December was quiet for 50 RTR, but marred by another unfortunate accident. Sergeant Tebbutt out with a line party from the Royal Corps of Signals was shot dead by a Greek sentry at the telegraph office. On the same day the Royal Air Force Headquarters north of Athens had been attacked and overrun by ELAS, many RAF personnel being taken prisoner. This resulted in a reassessment of the situation at both Pallini and Marathon, at each of which 50 RTR had two troops with D Squadron Headquarters also at Pallini. The regiment was warned that these troops would probably be withdrawn. On the 21st a patrol was carried out from their location to the sea at Loutsa, via Sparta. The patrol met a road block manned by two ELAS men, who were made to remove the road block. On the return journey the patrol was fired on in Sparta, but no casualties were suffered. The beach at Loutsa was found to be suitable for embarkation and free of mines. On this day also Trooper Percival of C Squadron was killed by a sniper during the afternoon.

On 22 December, a plan was evolved which required the use of two of the regiment's tanks, with a Bren carrier and sappers able to deal with mines. Much ELAS activity had been reported in the area surrounding the prominent feature named Lefes Strefi, which was in the rear of the Communist lines facing 50 RTR's positions. Very little aggressive action had been taken against ELAS in this area, except for patrol activity, the force commander not being prepared to push forward in the north until the south and the lines of communication were secure. It was felt that ELAS were possibly under the delusion that they dominated this section of the front and, in order to shake them out of any such complacency, Colonel Carlton decided to take a small armoured force north along Pattission Street and then turn east along Leoferes Alexandras, in the direction of the Averof Prison. Road blocks had been reported on this route, but not of a very substantial nature, although they were known to contain mines. With Colonel Carlton commanding one tank and Major Jenkin the other, this small force set out into ELAS territory and made havoc of all they met. The crew of the carrier did fine work. When the road blocks were encountered they dismounted and, covered by the tanks, removed the numerous mines. This operation was performed satisfactorily three times, but Corporal Mattock and Trooper Hough were killed by a sniper at the fourth road block, which was in the vicinity of the prison. The force returned along the same route and were engaged by ELAS dynamite throwers. This sweep certainly made ELAS think hard, for they went to great trouble to ensure that a repetition did not occur.

This day also saw the first of the official ELAS representatives who, from now on, were to present themselves regularly at the regiment's post in Themistockleious Street. Their visits were so regular that this became known as 'negotiation barrier'. Some things that passed over this barrier included dirty pieces of paper addressed to the British Prime Minister.

In the early hours of the 23rd, Lieutenant M Sheppard took a patrol of A Squadron into ELAS lines. They lay up for a long time and waited for the enemy to appear. Eventually a small group of ELAS was seen in a doorway, slightly below ground level. The patrol crept up, threw grenades and killed four or five, with no loss to themselves. This was typical of the minor actions fought by the regiment during this period, never giving the enemy rest or a feeling of security.

On the 25th, Christmas Day, all was comparatively quiet in the Athens area, any activity being overshadowed by the presence of the Prime Minister and Foreign Secretary in the city. 50 RTR provided the guard of honour for them both at the British Embassy. This did not mean that there was no fighting, which was certainly not the case, as can be seen from the following account of an action fought by troops of D Squadron at the Pallini radio station.

Major R Andrewes, commanding D Squadron at Pallini, received a report from a civilian that there were some British prisoners of war being held by ELAS in the village of Paiania, about four miles south of Pallini. A fighting patrol was sent out under the command of Lieutenant Butt, whose orders were to investigate this report and, if true to attempt the release of the prisoners.

The house in which the prisoners were being held was pointed out by a civilian. Lieutenant Butt left a section to cover any withdrawal while he took the other two sections to the house, surrounded it and called for the occupants to surrender. This they did without resistance, the nine British soldiers held inside being released. Their ELAS guards were taken into custody. The released soldiers were found to be from the 60th Rifles and had been captured during an attack by their battalion on Ardittes, south of the Zappion building. Lieutenant Butt withdrew to the covering party and, while crossing the square, was fired upon. Fire was returned as the patrol made their way from the village.

The return journey was made cross-country and all went well until the troop attempted to cross a road, half way back to their own lines. An ambush was encountered and heavy small arms fire was directed upon them; unfortunately the ELAS prisoners escaped in the confusion. To disengage, Lieutenant Butt decided to withdraw small groups one at a time. This was successful, and by twos and threes the patrol returned to Pallini. Two of the released soldiers failed to return, and it was assumed that they had been recaptured. The result of this action was that seven very grateful British soldiers were released from captivity. They could not, however, return to their own unit in Athens as the road was not open, except to a large force. They were therefore rearmed and remained at Pallini.

At 0530 hours on 26 December firing broke out around the science laboratory of the Athens University, which was occupied by a troop of C Squadron. It was a key position in the sector and attacks by ELAS were predicted daily by civilians. In fact, 4 inch mortar bombs used to land on the roof of this post regularly but without great effect. On this occasion, however, a dynamite attack was launched on the south-west face of the building, which did little damage but, apparently through sympathetic detonation, all the booby traps laid by 50 RTR around the building exploded. This must have frightened away any ELAS, as no bodies were found and the attack did not develop.

On 27 December the regimental medical officer, Captain Feinmann, was wounded while returning from treating Trooper Allen, who had himself been wounded in a forward position. Trooper Allen was to be carried back by a party of which the doctor was one, when they were fired upon, Trooper Allen was hit again and killed and the doctor badly wounded by an explosive bullet.

On the morning of the 28th the half squadron of D Squadron at the Marathon Dam started their withdrawal. It had been decided to destroy or render unserviceable all heavy equipment, which included a three-ton truck. A scout car was to attempt to reach Pallini along a road round the north of the dam, then south down the coast through Makri to Pallini. The crew of this car were the driver, Trooper Youldon (50 RTR), who could not walk due to illness, and Sergeant George Magee of D Squadron (46 RTR), who had a septic foot. Tom Youldon recalled what happened in a statement made shortly after:

> Marathon Dam was evacuated in two parties, the cross-country party under command of Captain Denby, and Sergeant Magee and myself in the scout car. We left the dam at 0615 hours, for Pallini, by way of Boyatti, Capandrittou, Grammatico, Marathon and the open coast road to Pallini.
>
> The first village, Boyatti, where there were two blown bridges, and the second village of Capandrittou were both successfully negotiated and, apart from some shooting on the part of the ELAS at the blown bridges, where we think we killed one of them and presumably had our aerial shot away, there was very little or no trouble.
>
> It was after the village of Capandrittou, about one mile the other side, travelling towards the third village of Grammatico, that we experienced our real headache. This was in the form of an immense road block, which was absolutely impassable to a scout car, and made us realise why the ELAS had not put up the fight that we more or less expected.
>
> When we realised that we were in a tight spot Sergeant Magee tried to send another message over the air and it was then that we discovered that our aerial had been blown away. We next consulted the map and discovered that by doubling back on our tracks for about half a mile we would come to a track on the left side of the road and, as anything was better than remaining a sitting target and eventually being captured or killed, we decided to take a chance on it. Before doing so, however, we threw a revolver, the head of a rifle bolt and the ammunition for both arms, together with some 36 and 77 grenades, into the stream that ran alongside the road, so if we were captured or killed, and it seemed obvious that we would be one of the two, we would be carrying the minimum of arms, and the ELAS would not benefit so very much.
>
> We took to the track, and then observed the ELAS trying to surround us. Eventually we got stuck and the ELAS, who were waiting for such an opportunity, opened up on us with everything they had, and we did not stand a chance. After dislocating the wireless set and rendering the arms and grenades harmless, we surrendered and were taken to Capandrittou for interrogation. All they got from us were numbers, names and ranks.

One hour before first light the walking troops left, striking due south across the Pendelikon mountains to Pallini. At 1630 hours this force arrived with only three men missing. These had fallen out due to exhaustion and their intention was to rest, lay up and then move on the next day. They were unfortunately captured by ELAS, however, but subsequently released during the truce which followed. Of the scout car nothing was heard until several weeks later, when the crew returned.

During the night of 27/28 December it was found, through civilian information, that ELAS were attempting to mouse-hole through a row of buildings in Solonos Street, in order to dominate a new area. When troops were sent to deal with this it was found that ELAS had succeeded in their plan to such an extent that only one wall still required attention. The ELAS men made off when attacked, leaving behind them much evidence of their work. Following this, C Squadron, the troops involved, made a strong point to counter any similar move and by 1030 hours five kills had been made from it. Captain Brian Chidell recalls this eventful night in Athens:

> I was in command of the force housed in the Chemical Laboratory, a key position on the corner of two streets in Athens. We had the roads covered by machine-guns, but one night the trooper on guard heard ominous banging noises from the terraced houses a few yards from us. He woke me up and I telephoned for our one and only tank, which arrived pretty quickly and the banging noises stopped at once. On investigation, we discovered that ELAS had been mouse-holing through the walls of the houses and they got pretty near to us. But for the vigilance of my chap on guard we would surely have been blown up.

It was on the 28th also that civilians reported that ELAS intended to make an attack on the regiment's sector in Athens that night. This was not a new rumour or report, but nevertheless, Headquarter Squadron were ordered to put out positions in the front and rear of the line to deepen the defences; no attack developed. During the same night, in a bout of over-enthusiasm, Pallini was shot up by fighters of the Royal Air Force. They had apparently seen a light and judged it to be ELAS. Luckily apologies were sufficient, as no one was hurt, but it did recall memories of Italy and no doubt the same verbal abuse.

During the night of the 29/30th a large fire broke out in the block of buildings in A Squadron's sector near Pathission Street. The fire very soon engulfed the only exit and the bottom of the stairs was a mass of flames. It was now that Trooper Hall took control of the situation: he calmly climbed out of a fourth floor window, around the corner of the building and onto an adjoining roof. Satisfied that an escape route was possible, he returned towards the window and hooked his fingertips into a crack in the masonary. Hall then proceeded to literally drag his comrades out, one at a time around the corner and onto the adjoining roof. He even made sure the men brought their arms and rations with them. This fire burned so fiercely that some of the forward posts on the other side of the road had to withdraw. Unfortunately, just prior to this a building was dynamited and as a result three men (Trooper Sprackland from the regiment and two National Guardsmen) were killed. Earlier that evening, Svolos, a former ELAS cabinet minister, presented himself at 'negotiation barrier' under a white flag. He said he wanted to see the Archbishop. He was immediately handed over to Brigade Headquarters for interrogation.

The following night an attack by the ELAS was made against one of the most forward post in C Squadron's sector, under the command of Corporal Edwards. Despite a determined assault the post held firm and suffered no casualties, though inflicting a number on the ELAS. The next morning Corporal Edwards realised that the enemy had occupied the house across the road from his post. Taking two men with him Edwards attacked the ELAS position; breaking into the house they discovered that the ELAS had 'mouse holed' from the rear of the building and were preparing to put the house into state of defence. Determined to clear the position Edwards pressed home his attack. Subsequently two ELAS were killed and a third wounded. Due to Corporal Edwards' aggressive leadership, arms and ammunition had been captured and the ELAS never again attempted to occupy a house near his position.

During the early morning of 31 December, a report reached the regiment through the Cable and Wireless Company (whose installations the troops at Pallini were guarding) to the effect that they had been attacked during the night. Telephone and radio communications were put out of action, thus preventing the garrison from making contact with Regimental Headquarters. Later that morning contact was re-established and Pallini confirmed that they had been attacked at midnight by 50 or more ELAS, supported by an armoured car, automatic weapons and an anti-tank gun. The armoured car was one which had previously been captured from the Royal Air Force at Kifissia. This vehicle was attacked with great determination by one of the riflemen released from ELAS a few days previously. He crept up very close to the car and scored a direct hit with a PIAT (Projector Infantry Anti-tank). After a few moments the car blew up. The attack was finally beaten off at 0130 hours; one officer and four men were wounded; one, Trooper Jamison, died of his wounds shortly after. ELAS left behind a substantial number of dead.

Although the force at Pallini was now unnecessary, it was considered unfortunate that it had to be evacuated at this stage in the operations, for it was apparent that ELAS were beginning to weaken in Athens, and to have a force there would have blocked any ELAS withdrawing in that direction. D Squadron were dismayed that they had been withdrawn, for they had excellent positions and were confident that they could have withstood a powerful attack.

B Squadron, now re-equipped with tanks, had moved down to the coast near Phaleron on 19 December. Their tanks had come straight off the ship from Italy. They appeared to be in a bad condition, as one of them burnt out a clutch in the first few hundred yards. However this was a false impression, for in the weeks that followed no major mechanical fault was encountered.

The Squadron was placed under direct command of X Corps, who had recently arrived to take over operational command of the land forces in Greece. On 20 December the Squadron prepared for the next day, when they would commence operations with battalions and brigades of 4th Infantry Division.

The main task accomplished during the 20th and 21st was the evacuation of a large force of Royal Electrical and Mechanical Engineers that had been cut off in a factory area at Imittes. This was carried out by two troops of B Squadron under command of The King's Dragoon Guards.

The securing of the Phaleron-Athens road had by this time started. It was necessary to clear and dominate several hundred yards on either side of the road, which was wide and straight, and so gave every opportunity to snipers firing from long range. 4th Infantry Division tackled this task by advancing along both sides of the road to a depth of 600 yards, with the main thrust coming from the south. Other units of the division, in the centre of Athens, worked down from the city to meet the oncoming forces. The tanks of B Squadron supported these drives from 20 December onwards, which provided them with excellent shooting, the operations proceeding favourably against strong opposition. Formidable road blocks were encountered which withstood all efforts on the part of the tanks to blast them down with fire. These road blocks were covered by ELAS positions immediately behind them. To enable the infantry and sappers to reach the blocks, to demolish them, the tanks fired high-explosive ammunition with delayed fuse, bouncing the rounds off the ground about ten feet in front of the blocks, so that the explosion took place in the air over the heads of the defenders. The ground being far more open than had previously been the case in the fighting, the tanks were able to engage the enemy at long range. This took ELAS by surprise and their reaction was to panic and run, thus giving B Squadron easy targets.

Up to 28 December B Squadron had been operating by troops' on the scale of one troop per battalion. This, in normal circumstances, would have been inadequate, but no more tanks were available and, although it meant no rest for the crews, support was given to the infantry on every occasion it was asked for. On the 28th, the squadron was able to operate on a more liberal scale; large areas had been cleared and the

Phaleron road was now open. The Division turned its attention to the districts south of Athens, which were known to be ELAS-infested. It had been assumed that this area would prove difficult, but this was not so, and district after district rapidly fell to the advancing troops. By this time it was apparent that ELAS resistance in the southern part of the city had crumbled, and large areas fell without trouble. At the end of the year 4th Infantry Division had completed its task in the south and was preparing for future operations, the first being a drive from east to west across the northern front of the perimeter. B Squadron were to continue their support in this new attack, and the last two days of the year were spent in maintenance and rest.

At the beginning of 1945 the campaign in the city of Athens was reaching its final stages. The situation now was that what had previously been a perimeter defence around the centre of the city had become a salient striking up from the coast at Phaleron and embracing most of Athens. The head of the salient had been the northern section of the perimeter line, and this section was being held by 23 Armoured Brigade, of which 50 RTR formed a part.

The regiment still had under command one squadron of 46 RTR who had been attached prior to leaving the Middle East and who, readers will recall, had been re-designated D Squadron. Also attached at this time were units of the Special Boat Service who, throughout their time with the regiment, did excellent service. 50 RTR was now complete, less B Squadron with their tanks, who were still under command of 4th Infantry Division.

On the first day of the New Year, therefore, the situation on the part of the front held by 50 RTR was very much as it had been for the previous two or three weeks. An attack had not been possible through lack of troops, as a successful attack would have involved the winning of ground and extra responsibilities for the troops available, every street corner having to be covered or occupied if infiltration by ELAS was to be prevented. During 1 January 1945, with another regiment from the brigade having been relieved in a different part of the city, it was decided to attack frontally the enemy defences facing 50 RTR's positions. The success of this action would mean the final removal of any threat to the centre of Athens for, though large areas had been cleared by this time, ELAS were only 500 yards from the force's main headquarters.

The assault was to take the form of a two-regiment attack, with 50 RTR on the left, to a depth of 400 yards. Upon the penetration and capture of the enemy line, the 60th Rifles were to pass through 50 RTR's lines and, before the enemy could respond, would establish themselves 300 yards further forward, with the front facing Pattission and Stournara Streets, and then south, along Arakhovis Street to Likavittos, which had for many weeks been the right flank protection. The attack was to

*Figure 48: Jack Hedley, C Squadron's Medical Corporal, described by Col. Carlton as 'outstanding'. (J Hedley)*

be supported by tanks without previous artillery fire.

The force commander decided to use all three squadrons, dividing the area into three parts, each to contain one of three known strong points in the area. The plan was to go straight for these objectives with maximum force and then, when firmly established, to clear backwards, using in addition National Guards and City Police, who were attached to the regiment in large numbers. Each squadron was to have two tanks in support. A and C Squadrons, who were in the line, were to withdraw from it early on 2 January, leaving it held by the National Guard, and concentrate for the attack, which was timed to commence at 0700 hours.

Before first light on 2 January, Regimental Headquarters moved to a forward position, and at 0700 the attack commenced as planned. C and D Squadrons had the two hardest objectives to capture. The first was a hospital, which was just inside ELAS territory and which was being used for both ELAS and civilian patients. Had this been its only use it would have been by-passed, but ELAS were using the building as a defensive post. It was decided that the hospital would not be engaged by tanks unless resistance was met. The enemy did not remain silent for long, as a Teller mine was thrown from a balcony, despite the fact that a red cross flag was being displayed upon the building. From that moment its status was forgotten, and C Squadron launched their assault after the tanks had shelled it. Though suffering casualties, including Lieutenant 'Bish' Thomas, C Squadron soon effected an entry and captured the place. The patients, although suffering from shock, had not sustained injury as they had all been in the back of the building. The hospital staff quickly went round the beds and marked those containing ELAS. One nurse was arrested as she was found to be wearing a pistol under her skirt.

A few minutes later D Squadron reported themselves in the telephone exchange and it was apparent that the completion of the regiment's task was only a question of time, the two main centres of resistance having already fallen. Slowly, throughout the morning, the regiment continued their clearing operations, with prisoners passing through Regimental Headquarters all the time on their way to the cages. There were casualties but they were light compared to those sustained by ELAS.

By 1230 hours the whole area was clear, with the exception of one building in which fanatics still held out. This was completely surrounded and with the regiment firmly established on the line of Thonistokleous and Netaxa Streets, it was considered safe for the 60th Rifles to pass through and on. On the right, 2 Battalion The Highland Light Infantry had completed their task and were up on 50 RTR's right flank.

During the action a tank commander asked a passing civilian if he could speak English, 'Yes, very well,' was the reply. The officer then asked the man if he knew which house ELAS were firing from. The man pointed to a house at the end of the street and the officer promptly ordered two rounds to be fired at this target. It later turned out that the man could not speak English very well and he thought the officer had asked him where he lived!

As had been expected the attack had knocked the complacency out of ELAS in this area, and the 60th Rifles had a comparatively easy time and were quickly on their objective and, by dawn on 3 January, the centre of Athens was safe.

During this attack 50 RTR had taken approximately 200 prisoners and suspects in addition to many rifles and light machine-guns. Casualties suffered by the regiment were two men killed, both from D Squadron, and two officers and eleven men wounded. Fifteen ELAS bodies were found in 50 RTR's area.

On 3 January, the regiment organised patrols of the National Guard to search the captured area. One patrol captured a further seven ELAS members. These were the same men who had refused to surrender the previous day. The platoon of National Guard who had been guarding their only escape had withdrawn for no apparent reason, the commander being placed under arrest when he failed to obey an order to go back.

Although the line had been driven forward in the area just vacated by the regiment, 2 Parachute Brigade, on the left, with their right flank on Omonoias Square, had not moved. Their attack took place on 4 January, supported by two tanks of C Squadron 50 RTR, one of which was quickly knocked out by a hidden double-Teller mine. The crew were badly burned and had it not been for the commander, Lieutenant M Brooke who, in full view of the enemy, opened the driver's hatch and got the driver out, the latter would most certainly have been killed.

Lieutenant Brooke was also wounded.

The second tank continued to support the Brigade during the rest of the day and claimed ten ELAS killed and a similar number wounded. The attack was a success and this, coupled with 50 RTR's attack and the drive of 4th Division from the east, did all that was necessary to encourage ELAS finally to clear out of the districts around the centre of Athens. On 5 January the action against ELAS became far more mobile and hastily-formed columns were organised and occupied communication centres in outlying districts. All that was left to do in Athens and its suburbs was to complete an extensive search for ELAS personnel and arms, an operation which went on methodically and without further incident. The major portion of this task was completed by units of the National Guard; the regiment, like other British units, co-ordinated the search operations of one of these National Guard battalions.

More Sherman tanks were now beginning to arrive in Greece and on 5 January D Squadron reverted to their own regiment (46 RTR) to be re-equipped. During their stay with 50 RTR they had become very much part of The Fiftieth and their attachment had created a new understanding between the two units. C Squadron also discovered that they were to receive fourteen tanks in the next few days.

All this time B Squadron had remained under command of 4th Division. On 3 January, the squadron supported 28 Infantry Brigade in their attack on the Averof Prison area. They attacked from the east with three battalions, troops of the squadron supporting each battalion. Heavy opposition was met and many casualties were inflicted on the enemy. An estimated 50 ELAS were killed by tanks, the majority of these occurring when a large body of ELAS tried to break off the action and run across open country to the north. During the day, the brigade took over 350 prisoners. Three tanks were lost on mines but without casualties to personnel. During the 4th the attack continued and the prison area was captured. Two troops of the squadron were ordered to the other side of the city to join a force moving north along the western edge of Athens.

During the 5th, ELAS resistance weakened dramatically and it became apparent that they were withdrawing from the city. Towards midnight, the Adjutant, Captain Masters, and Major Scott, commanding B Squadron, were called to Brigade Headquarters and told that a squadron had been ordered to go to Patrai, better known as Patras, a port on the north western coast of the Peloponnese. B Squadron were to go, and their task was to support BLOCKFORCE, which consisted of two battalions and 139 Infantry Brigade Headquarters, commanded by Brigadier Adam Block, an officer of whom it was said he 'would take no nonsense'. The squadron had to be ready for loading, with its tanks and Echelon vehicles, at the Piraeus by 1015 hours the following day. This required the maximum effort from all ranks; it was accomplished without incident and B Squadron embarked in a tank landing ship during the early evening of 6 January. They disembarked at Patras on 10 January at 0900 hours and by the afternoon had been allocated to various infantry battalions.

Throughout the fighting in Athens a small British garrison had occupied Patras, composed of 11 Indian Infantry Brigade, from 4th Indian Division. Although fighting had never broken out the garrison had had a most uncomfortable ordeal, as ELAS were alongside them in the town in far greater numbers than they themselves and they had been unable to take any action. It was necessary, therefore, to reinforce this position as soon as possible, in order for ELAS to be told to get out or fight. BLOCKFORCE was accordingly despatched.

Meanwhile, during 6 January, the Brigade Commander visited 50 RTR and informed Colonel Carlton that a further squadron would be required at Patras. The squadron was to go without vehicles and would take over a complete squadron of tanks from Italy at the other end. This was another rush move and, as C Squadron still had a troop on Salamis, it was decided to send A Squadron under Major Jenkin with a tactical Regimental Headquarters.

The second-in-command, Major Collins, remained in Athens to command C and part of Headquarter Squadron. The force for Patras was to load at the Piraeus on the following day.

By 1800 hours on the 7th all had embarked on the Norwegian liner *Bergensfjord*. It was a ship of about 12,000 tons, clean and by far the best troopship in which any part of the regiment had ever travelled. The ship sailed early on the 8th. It was understood that she would arrive at Patras on 9 January but they did not put into port on that day, the Captain having received orders to keep out of sight of land. However, on the 10th they arrived off Patras and anchored three miles off-shore. On 11 January the ship went alongside the quay and after some delay the regiment received orders to disembark. An old tobacco factory was to be the regiment's billet and by the evening all had settled in. B Squadron, who had arrived the previous day, reverted to being under command of their own regiment.

The situation in Patras now was that the force commander considered he was sufficiently strong to dictate terms to the ELAS garrison in the town. He therefore ordered them to be out by 0600 hours on 11 January. In the meantime British troops had formed a small bridgehead around the harbour in preparation for an attack on ELAS positions on 11 January; B Squadron were to support the infantry in this attack. Surprisingly, ELAS obeyed the order and, by the time A Squadron and Regimental Headquarters had disembarked, all ELAS troops were out of the town and the surrounding area. The force commander informed

A Squadron that, due to the new situation in Patras and the failure of their tanks to arrive, it was likely that they would return to where they had come from. Nevertheless, during 12 January, B Squadron, in support of the 2/5 Battalion The Leicestershire Regiment, opened the road in the direction of the airfield, some 20 miles along the coast from Patras. There were no major incidents, and by nightfall the force had reached the River Kato Akhaia.

Early that evening 50 RTR learned that a tank landing ship had arrived with their tanks and that A Squadron would be expected to unload their tanks that night and be available to 11 Indian Infantry Brigade the following morning. The squadron of vehicles, plus additional ones for Regimental Headquarters, were all from 17/21 Lancers (26 Armoured Brigade). All tanks were disembarked by 2200 hours. A Squadron worked for another four hours getting them ready for action, so had little sleep before being sent to the various battalions by first light.

The intention of the force commander at Patras was to worry ELAS as much as possible between 12 January and the date of the agreed truce on 15 January, in order that as many as possible of the Communists, and their equipment, could be captured. In addition to the force sent along the road to the south-west, a further three thrusts were to be made, each in battalion strength, one north and then east along the coast road in the direction of Corinth, supported by two troops of tanks, the second to strike inland along the road which went south and then south-west from Patras, supported by a troop from A Squadron, and the third to make an attempt to capture a large force of ELAS known to be in the foothills in the immediate vicinity of the town.

The main event during 12 January was an attack by 2/7 Gurkha Rifles on a large ELAS force in the area of Kiang. This force, which had only recently left the town, were in the foothills to the south-east of patras, based on the Klaus wine factory. The plan was that an infantry battalion would march cross-country during the night, so that at first light they would be behind and above the ELAS troops. When this movement was completed a mobile column, supported by a troop from A Squadron, was to attack the ELAS force from the front and drive them on to the infantry.

The attack did not go altogether as planned, the infantry being observed by the enemy while trying to work their way to the rear; the enemy then withdrew further up the mountain into a more commanding position. Had it not been for the timely arrival of the tanks, severe casualties would have been inflicted on the Gurkhas. As it was, the wine factory was captured and the ELAS force disintegrated: a large number of ELAS had been killed by the fire of the tanks. E D Smith, a subaltern in C Company of 2/7 Gurkha Rifles wrote in his own book

'Even The Brave Falter':
> Then began a long walk over difficult country. It was a dark night but the men in front set a stirring pace which got our circulation going. Before the morning light came, a tired footsore company was sitting in platoon positions overlooking one of the possible valley exits from the Plain of Patras.
>
> Soon the early rays of light revealed a large body of men moving towards us. Not daring to let them get near enough to overrun us by sheer weight of numbers, we opened fire at long range, hoping that many would waver, throw down their arms and evaporate back into their peaceful occupations.
>
> I sat by two Gurkha riflemen who were manning a Bren gun, watching as they fired at a group of ELAS working their way through a cemetery; the little dots appeared to fall like ninepins. Did they want to attack us or were they trying to escape from the British tanks that had landed behind them in the Bay of Patras?
>
> That day I learned a lesson; even if men go to ground under fire, and they appear to be sitting ducks it does not necessarily mean they are dead or wounded – and to assume so is the height of folly. We did this only to find ourselves under severe pressure in less than an hour. Those Greeks had courage but fortunately for us their leadership was poor, many of their weapons were antiquated and ammunition was in short supply. Gradually we assumed control, disarmed many and captured scores of sullen and dejected men.

The truce arranged between ELAS and the British troops in Greece was scheduled to come into force at 0001 hours on 15 January. At this time fighting was to stop and the enemy were to be given every opportunity of carrying out their part of the agreement to withdraw to certain specified areas of the country. The operations based on Patras were designed to ensure the deaths of as many ELAS as possible before that time, after which there would be a brief halt, and then, when ELAS had completed their moves, operations would continue to search for any stray dumps of arms etc. still left in 50 RTR's area.

By evening of 14 January the two troops on the north road moving with 3/12 Royal Frontier Force Regiment had reached Aiyion. In other areas operations had continued satisfactorily against little opposition, but in the face of foul weather. Troops to the south and south-west had cleared as far as the village of Katarraktis, and the airfield to the south-west was clear and in use, while a battalion of infantry with one troop of B Squadron in support was based in the village of Kata Akhaia.

On 16 January Colonel Carlton and the Adjutant returned to Athens to see the rest of the regiment. The Adjutant was attempting to obtain the release of tank spares as, up until now, the only spares available were those taken from other tanks.

During 18 January a parade of British troops took place in Patras: two troops of B Squadron led it. The other half of B Squadron, commanded by Captain G E Price, was on the Corinth road *en route* to the Frontier Force Regiment, who were pushing on to Stomion to meet units of 46th (North Midland) Division's Reconnaissance Regiment.

From 18-23 January all was quiet, and on the latter date all troops with the exception of those at Corinth reverted to 50 RTR command, returning to Athens and subsequently going into 23 Armoured Brigade reserve to train with a brigade from 46th Division.

On 9 January the troops were withdrawn from Salamis. This force had been in occupation for a very long period, having done great things on the island, and had become loved and respected by the people there. The 35 men under Captain H B O'Sullivan had taken control of the island before hostilities with ELAS commenced and established law and order and distributed food and fuel amongst the local population. When hostilities commenced on the mainland over 50 ELAS were arrested. Captain O'Sullivan recruited 200 dockyard workers as a temporary police force, and established outposts and patrols throughout the island. ELAS twice attempted to secure the island, but without success. Thanks to the foresight of Captain O'Sullivan, Salamis remained inviolate throughout the civil war. The population now regarded him as their saviour.

It was a great pity that the regiment was not together on 17 January, when the Supreme Allied Commander Mediterranean Theatre, Field-Marshal Sir Harold Alexander, came to see them while on a visit to Athens. He stayed some time and after Colonel Carlton, who luckily was in Athens that day, had introduced all the officers, Field Marshal Alexander addressed the regiment as follows:

> I realise you have had a particularly difficult task, which you have done extremely well. A tank man without a tank is like a cavalryman without a horse. You are all highly skilled tank technicians, but the experience you have gained will prove very useful, I am grateful to you.
>
> It is now very obvious, and as the Prime Minister has said in the House, if British troops had not taken the action they did, then there would have been large scale massacres in Greece. A good stout-hearted brigade on the spot prevented this. The Greek people are grateful to you. I will not discuss the politics of the thing, because you know as much about this as I do.
>
> The test of a good soldier is if he can overcome a difficult situation however he is equipped. You all proved yourselves to be good soldiers. I know you are all very glad to get to tanks again, and I hope to have you back with me again.

*Figure 49: Sergeants of 50 RTR, with the commanding officer and the adjutant, Athens, November 1944.*
Back row – Stan Hookway, Syd Williams, Jack Northover, Ted Terry, unknown, Norman Chick, Stan Rudman, Jimmy Hall, Wilfred Mitchell.
4th row – Godfrey Tebbett, Tim Cole, Vic Law MM, Jock McNaught, Frank Smith, unknown, Frank Puddick, Don Neal BEM, Ray Joyce, Fred Maplesden MM.
3rd row – Fred Wenlock, Don Ellery, Ted Hadrell, Harold Pillinger, Alf Webley, Tom Hunter MM, Jim Pearce, Jim Taylor, Bill Clark, Joe Hart.
2nd row – Ted Tiley, Charlie Hague, Eric Butcher, Joe Larkin, Frank Thompson, Bill Sewell, Ernie Perkins, Ray Gabe-Jones, John Humphries, Eric Hadley, Chris Cawthorne.
Front row – Bill Millington, George Edge, Jock Menzies, Hubert Price MBE, John Cowe, Lt Col. J D Carlton, Capt J D Masters, Cyril Smith, Wyn Snape, Malcolm Budd, Roy Corran.
*(W Green)*

The best of luck to you all.
Apart from the occasional sniping from ELAS die-hards, who were severely dealt with, the situation in the Athens area remained quiet until 26 January. On that date Brigade Headquarters informed Major Collins that C Squadron, who still had only one tank, would be required to go to the Thebes area to take over Shermans from a squadron of 46 RTR. On the 27th advance parties of C Squadron accordingly left Thebes, the remainder of the Squadron moving the following day. There they came under command of 4th Division and were located with three troops in Thebes, two troops in Levadhia and one troop at Khalkis.

The last day of January is an appropriate one on which to sum up the regiment's activities during operations in Greece. On 6 December, when the fighting first started, the regiment was completely infantry, with a squadron of 46 RTR attached to it. It was a period in which the regiment fought as infantry and, although completely unaccustomed to this role, everyone felt that their task had been well and truly completed. Despite this, the regiment was to be denied the battle honours 'Athens' and 'Greece 1944-45', which was subsequently awarded to every other unit involved in the Greek Civil War including the Royal Dragoons, the

Casualties suffered by 50 RTR during those operations were as follows: one officer killed, ten wounded; seventeen other ranks killed, 62 wounded and two captured.

# Chapter 12
# HOMEWARD BOUND

## Victory and Disbandment

'I believe that most of the trouble is over out here now and the civilian population is beginning to settle down once again. They are a very unlucky people – due to a too excitable interest in politics.' So wrote Major Walter Bazley in January 1945.

Now that the Greek civil war was temporarily over, the regiment returned to less demanding work. The fighting may have been over, but the pressure on ELAS had to be maintained.

On 6 February the regiment was moved to the Corinth Canal area, Regimental Headquarters and B Squadron to Loutraki, C Squadron to Corinth. The troops of B Squadron who had been in Patras now rejoined

*Figure 50: Staghound armoured cars of 50 RTR. On the right is Tpr Thomas, who was with the author's grandfather when L/Cpl Clifford was killed. (G Thomas)*

the squadron. On the 12th a four-week training programme was started, including tradesmen courses in radio, driving and maintenance and gunnery; these were to take place at the school that had been established in Loutraki. The Secretary of State for Foreign Affairs, the Right Honourable Anthony Eden, visited Corinth on the 17th, meeting and talking to some of the men.

For several weeks life was uneventful. Training and sport were the main occupations of the troops, a strange contrast to the many preceding months of overseas service spent amid great excitement and changes. Highlights of this period were the partial re-equipment of the regiment with 20 Staghound armoured cars and the rugby win of 46 RTR.

On 2 May, patrols began to cover the area around Kalamata, with the purpose of visiting the various small towns and villages. This area had been isolated from the fighting, but it was feared that armed bands of ELAS were hiding there. The regiment welcomed this change from the settled way of life at Loutraki – each troop was to spend five days in the patrol area before being relieved and this was to carry on until mid-July. After one of these patrols had returned, the patrol commander reported to Captain Chidell: 'All quiet, except for some local throat slitting.'

On the 8th the regiment heard the news that Germany had capitulated and that the war in Europe was over. This was celebrated by all ranks spending the day in Athens, dancing and drinking. Amidst all the jollification one thing stood out more than anything else – being out of it all; once again 50 RTR had missed out at the final kill. The brigade commander reminded the men that '...their record of achievement, was closely followed by another, that every man should be proud of – that though we didn't reach Berlin, the victories, the determination and courage of the regiment in history-making battles, started those who did get there off on the right foot.'

The victory celebrations continued until the 13th, when sporting activities again took place, ending a week later with the final of the inter-troop soccer competition, which was won by Lieutenant Thompson's Troop from B Squadron. The winners were presented with a cup and £10 to spend.

On 1 June a motor-cycle trial was held; this proved to be very popular with outriders from other units but the regiment's ace, Trooper Statham, won the individual event. The weather at this time was perfect and bathing was the main occupation, closely followed by boating. Some members of the regiment managed to obtain a motor launch, *Salamis*, which travelled faster backwards than forwards. However this was quickly rectified and many a long hour was spent joyfully cruising along the coast. There is a story that this launch somehow managed to find its way to England.

*Figure 51: Officers and men of C Squadron (front left to right) SSM Snape, Lt Knaggs, Capt Chidell, Capt O'Sullivan, Major Senior, Capt Kepple, Lt Waddell, Lt Glashen, SQMS Webley, St Sgt Coutts (REME). (G Thomas)*

Two weeks later the regiment lost an officer who had become known as the 'Grandfather' of the regiment, not by virtue of his age, but because he had been with 50 RTR longer than any other member. Major Walter D Bazley was appointed to command No. 30 Reception Camp in Athens on promotion to Lieutenant-Colonel. Throughout his service abroad he had commanded Headquarter Squadron and the Echelons in battle and never had the troops gone hungry or short of supplies.

The rest of the month saw more sporting events, plus the 'Loutraki Carnival' which raised £200 for the RTR Benevolent Fund; the success of this was primarily due to Major Senior's inspiration and organisation. Here the men and the local population could bowl in 'Phil's Joint' or play hoop-la with 'Honest Bill'; a netball competition and donkey races were also amongst the variety of sideshows. Brigadier Arkwright rode in one of the races, with C Squadron providing the bookies.

In the first week in July the regiment's stay in Loutraki came to an end, and they were moved to new quarters near Salonika, where they met old friends of 4th Indian Division. On 20 July 125 places on the next LIAP (Leave in Advance of Python, Python being discharge) home were allocated to the regiment; these were drawn out of a hat, with the majority going to C Squadron. The lucky men were to leave on the 27th. As a result of this, C Squadron was temporarily disbanded.

On 3 August came news that the regiment had won its first double Military Crosses, both Major Jenkin and Major Senior receiving bars to

*Figure 52: Greece 1945.*

their medals for their gallantry in Athens.

Twelve days later news that Japan had surrendered came through. Again, this victory seemed a little detached from the regiment, stationed in a country that always seemed to boil over. Nevertheless, all ranks took the opportunity to have a riotous evening. The following day 50 more men left on leave. A week later, two South African officers, Lieutenants Glashen and Knaggs left the regiment for South Africa and release.

At the end of the month Colonel Carlton and Major Senior visited the Turkish border to add Turkey to the list of countries seen, if not visited. The Turkish guards looked even more disreputable than the Greeks, and even appeared a little trigger happy. September was another very uneventful month, apart from the rain, which turned the regiment's area into a quagmire and earned the camp the name 'Belsen'. Brigade Headquarters again decided to switch the regiments around, thus permitting 50 RTR to occupy the most sought-after billets in Athens, Kifissia.

In the first week of October, 150 men returned from leave in the United Kingdom and the weather had broken into glorious sunshine. The move to Kifissia was completed on the 14th, taking over from 40 RTR.

During November, the regiment was getting very low on personnel, due to leave and release, so when 21 other ranks joined from 4 Reconnaissance Regiment they were made most welcome. However, the next day a further nineteen men left the regiment. On the 20th,

Cambrai Day was celebrated, and treated as a holiday, with the officers serving lunch to the troops. In the evening a dance for all ranks was held in Kifissia Stadium. Four days later a further 120 men returned from leave in the United Kingdom.

December had begun with men coming and going and replacements arriving from units that had been disbanded, including a new Regimental Sergeant-Major. On the 17th, the Hallowing Service of Phaleron British Military Cemetery (now Phaleron War Cemetery) took place, led by the Bishop of Portsmouth. One hundred all ranks under Major Garrett attended.

On Christmas Eve Captain Chidell conducted carol singing in the 'Black and Green' club – Christmas Day being celebrated in the usual Army fashion. On Boxing Day a mock football match was played, a very muddy and wet pitch adding to the amusement of the spectators. Afterwards the officers played the sergeants – the referee decided to play for the sergeants and laid a heavy smoke screen down across their goal; it was a very amusing game, but impossible to reckon the score.

It was obvious by now, that the regiment was to be disbanded and that this was to be in Greece and not in the United Kingdom. This came as a surprise to the more traditional soldiers of the regiment, but to the majority of the other ranks it meant they were going home for good. Up until now the regiment, by being in Greece, had missed early disbandment; thus the men avoided the trauma of cross-postings to other regiments, allowing them to finish their time with the regiment.

1946 began as a holiday – no sporting activities – and unlike Christmas life was taken very easily, although within a week Captain Grieve broke his leg playing rugby. The middle of January saw the real

*Figure 53: B Squadron firing demonstration for the Greek General Staff, February 1946. (Tank Museum)*

*Figure 54: Members of the Sparta patrol March 1946. (author's collection)*

start of all ranks going home on release. A few were replaced to fill the more important duties. One event which affected everybody occurred on the 26th – the drachma went up in value to 20,000 to the pound. February followed much the same pattern as January. A farewell party was held for Colonel Carlton, who was leaving the regiment, and B Squadron, who still had their tanks, gave a demonstration for the Greek General Staff.

By 1 March, Major I C Moyans had taken command of the regiment. While men were still leaving for home, 110 replacements arrived from 46 RTR, which had already been disbanded. On the 5th, a patrol led by Captain Conlin discovered a mass grave in the area of Sparta. It had been reported that up to 250 people had been murdered by ELAS and thrown in the pit. Amongst this number there was also reputed to be five or six British soldiers, killed by ELAS in 1943.

On the 14th a patrol left for the Kalamata area to observe the local conditions and hand out Red Cross parcels. On the 13th, Lieutenant Colonel L G Hynes arrived from England to take over command of the regiment from Major Moyens. The end of the month saw the first general election that Greece had had for ten years and The Fiftieth was put on standby. Patrols were sent out to assist local Greek forces in quelling any trouble should it arise – a few shots were fired, but this was dealt with by the local police. April was a month in which more work was done in administration than at any other time.

The day of disbandment was drawing near and farewell messages were arriving from other units of the brigade. Captain Grieve got married at Salonika and the Regimental Headquarters officers mess was broken into. The regiment was again reduced in strength to one tank squadron and one armoured car squadron. Captain Conlin got engaged to a local girl and married within a fortnight, with B Squadron providing the guard of honour.

On 30 April 1946 Captain M O Waddell made the final entry in the War Diary for 50 RTR. It reads:

> A Squadron handed in their armoured cars to 140 RVP Athens. One other rank (Argentine volunteer) was despatched to the UK for repatriation to the Argentine. The Brigade held a farewell parade at Loutraki – General Crawford taking the salute at the March Past.

The regiment that had been born and raised in Bristol was now ending its life under the sun in Greece. The men started to go home – overland through Italy and Switzerland, later by air transport – back to the country they had risked life and limb for. Some thought it was a job well done – but most were disillusioned – had it been worth it? Is any war worth it?

Trooper Douglas Stockall of C Squadron remembers the comradeship that he found within the regiment:

> The great thing, and I know this is a much over-worked cliché, was the remarkable spirit of comradeship. That this persists to the present day is shown by the numbers attending the Old Comrades reunion each October and also, as in my case and probably others, by the number of old comrades who remain in touch with each other as personal friends. Though sadly the number dwindles each year as we grow older, and death takes its toll.

*Figure 55: Two of the regiment's casualties, Phaleron War Cemetery 1945. (Author's collection)*

There was a remarkable family atmosphere about 50 RTR I am told that people who were sent back to hospital were filled with apprehension at the possibility that when the time came for their discharge, the regiment might have moved so far ahead that they might be posted elsewhere.

I believe that this sense of 'belonging' was general in units of the Eighth Army.

Some of the men enjoyed the army and its way of life. Sergeant Jack Adams, known as 'Tash' to his friends, continued his service for another ten years, only to be invalided out due to wounds received in the Mau Mau uprising, while serving with the King's African Rifles. We will let 'Tash' Adams and others end this story with their thoughts and memories of 50 RTR.

50 RTR was a very fine regiment, and C Squadron was a squadron I was always proud to be a member of. The Royal Tank Regiment is the finest outfit one could wish to be with, and The Fiftieth was the cream.

Sergeant Major Percy Lewis:

I served with The Fiftieth for nearly six years. We were a mixed crowd, bankers, teachers, bus drivers, factory workers etc. but we all got on very well together. The Army was a great leveller of people and promotion was open to anyone irrespective of civilian status.

Trooper Robert Blundell:

I left The Fiftieth to go into hospital, hoping to be back within a week or so. Instead I was flown to North Africa and physically regraded. I did go back to Italy with a vehicle maintenance unit, – much safer – but I wouldn't swop my years with The Fiftieth for anything. It was an honour to have served with every man.

Edward Burtonshaw:

I was in RHQ, working in the CO's operational office, and while I travelled with the tanks, I did not, thank God, have to go into action with them. I never lost sight of the fact that I only had canvas around me and so my first task on going up to a battlefield was to find somewhere to hide and it is marvellous how secure you can feel behind a cactus hedge.

The real tank soldiers were the crew members, I suppose some 200 out of a total of 650. A lot of the latter had vital jobs to do, of course, but they were in less danger of having their ears torn off. I used to see at close hand some of these chaps immediately after a battle, and very often found that they had suddenly aged ten years.

John Gibberd:

My C Squadron troop sergeant was Sergeant Kew, a large, cheerful type. Corporal Boyt, our troop corporal, was as good natured a chap as you could wish to meet. Once, when I was late on parade (laziness), he told the officer he'd sent me to the stores for something, so spared me the 'fizzer' I deserved. On our last evening in England I remarked, 'I wonder how many of us will come back alive.' Jeph was very annoyed. 'You didn't ought to say that Gibby, we'll all come back alive,' he said. He was right, of course, we were probably all thinking it, but I shouldn't have said it.

Actually, nine of that troop were killed. Others in the troop were Lance Corporal Mitchell, a driver, killed in Greece, married with two children I believe.

Troopers Davies and Joyce – drivers – I remember in one pretend night battle when a halt was called near a pub. Officers were trying to sort things out and Joyce, with or without permission, nipped into the pub for a pint – and of course we were liable to be told to move at any minute.

When I said 'a pint' it was an understatement. I had to follow his tank – no lights of course – which, perhaps to 'avoid enemy action', careered from one side of the road to the other. The trip ended when his tank ended up with one side track down the gap between the station platform and the flat truck he'd been attempting to drive onto – causing a major holdup in the battle. I think they got a crane to lift the tank out.

Others were Troopers Shillcross and Ashwell, both killed – nice blokes. 'Perc' Wadey, Trooper Pritchard, Trooper Broad, a good-natured married man, and John Norton, my particular pal. We were both equally bad at snooker and used to play in the Working Men's Club or the Conservative Club – for free. Soon after we arrived in Egypt he had to be sent back with incurable dysentery and I lost track of him.'

Jim 'Jock' Lowe:

I was always concerned in keeping the tank guns in tip top condition, increasing my wireless knowledge and improving my morse transmissions and reading, under the instruction of Ginger Sarginson – a very clever sparks.

I recall the night when Guy Schofield and I sat in the alcove at the side of the Imperial Hotel and saw off a bottle of scotch and a bottle of brandy in the dark. We then went to bed in the bath, happy days! The last I saw of Guy was in Athens, where we were both on the receiving end of a Mills bomb.

# POSTSCRIPT

In 1949, 44 RTR who, together with 50 RTR had been disbanded in 1946, were reformed at the Drill Hall in Old Market Place, Bristol, under the title of 44/50 Royal Tank Regiment. In 1947, 23 Armoured Brigade was brought off suspended animation with 40 and 41 RTR.

Within a few years the Territorial Army had gone through many changes and The Royal Gloucester Hussars were incorporated into 44/50 RTR. This was followed by an amalgamation with the North Somerset Yeomanry, and 50 was dropped from the title. As for the Liver Bird, this was still to be seen right up until 1967 when the brigade was disbanded.

Every year, on the Saturday nearest to 23/24 October, old comrades of 50 RTR hold their annual reunion in Bristol to recall their experiences together and to remember fallen comrades. The 50th Royal Tank Regiment may have passed into history, but not before writing their own pages into the annals of war with their gallantry and tenacity.

# Annex A
# ROLL OF HONOUR

Information in this annex is arranged as follows: Name, number, rank, squadron (at time of death), date and place of death. Commonwealth War Grave Commission Cemetery, or Memorial for those with no known grave.

In certain cases, men went missing in one theatre of war, were found to have been captured and later died and were buried in another theatre of war. In these cases date of 'reported missing' and 'date of death' are shown.

The Roll has been compiled from the following records:- 50 RTR War Diary 1939-1946; Roll of Honour, Royal Armoured Corps Headquarters, Bovington; Commonwealth War Grave Commission Cemetery Registers.

Where there has been a discrepancy in the date of death, both are shown and from which source. It is assumed that the War Diary is to be believed, as this was written at the time or shortly after.

During the research for the Roll, it was discovered that a number of names, formerly thought to have been members of 50 RTR, were not members of 50 RTR at all. For example, the War Diary states: 'On Jan 2nd 1945, two other ranks from this regiment were killed in action.' This entry actually referred to two members of 46 RTR attached the regiment. Also, a number of names were incorrectly added to earlier lists of 50 RTR casualties, having been entered under 50 RTR instead of 51 or 40 RTR.

A Roll of Honour does more than just list the dead and missing of a regiment, it can tell its own stories, for example:

three young men joined up together, became good friends, did their training together, all posted to the Royal Armoured Corps, then to 50 RTR and all posted to the Reconnaissance Troop, died within moments of each other at the same place, all have no known grave, length of combat duty 3 days and their army numbers – 7959586, 7959588, 7959590.

This Roll contains 153 men with an average age of 30.
The following key may be helpful when reading through the Roll:
\* Before name denotes 'in RTR on 1 September 1939'.
**Killed in action** – Killed while in direct contact with the enemy.
**Killed by enemy action** – Killed by enemy action while away from the front line.
**Battle Accident** – Unfortunate accident while away from the front line and direct contact with the enemy.

**ALFORD**, Edward G. 7896626, Lance Corporal C Squadron, formerly of the RAC. Killed in action 14 July 1943, Francofonte, Sicily. Son of Mr and Mrs E G Alford. Buried in Syracuse War Cemetery, Sicily. Grave 8 A 9. (Born Bristol.)
**ALLEN**, Arthur F. 14319833, Trooper. Killed in action 27 December 1944, Athens, Greece, aged 21. Son of Arthur Ambrose and Emma Allen of Barnes, Surrey. Buried in Phaleron War Cemetery, Greece. Grave 19 E 20. (Born London SW.)
**AMBROSE**, Harry F. 7914923, Lance Corporal C Squadron. Killed by enemy action 20 April 1944, Lanciano, Italy, aged 35. Son of Richard Francis and Hetty Ambrose, husband of Marjorie Ambrose of Exeter. Buried in Sangro River War Cemetery, Italy. Grave 14 D 41. (Born Devon.)
**ASHWELL**, Frederick W. 5574299, Trooper C Squadron. Killed in action 2 November 1942, El Alamein, Egypt, aged 28. Son of Frederick William and Florence Mary Ashwell of York. Buried in El Alamein War Cemetery, Egypt. Grave 18 F 24. (Born York.)
**BAILEY**, Herbert H. 7934297, Trooper A Squadron. Killed by enemy action 10 December 1943, Lanciano, Italy, aged 38. Son of William and Blanche Bailey. Buried in Sangro River War Cemetery, Italy. Grave 14 D 18. (Born London N.)
**BAKER**, Albert E. 7897320, Trooper A Squadron, formerly of the RAC. Killed in action 16 July 1943, Scordia, Sicily, aged 22. Son of Mrs V Baker of Tooting, Surrey. No known grave, commemorated on Panel 1 of the Cassino Memorial, Italy. (Born London SW.)
*****BAKER**, Reginald. 5184822, Trooper RHQ Squadron. Killed in action 14 November 1943, Caldari, Italy, aged 23. Buried in Sangro River War Cemetery, Italy. Grave 14 E 42. (Born Bristol.)
**BINNS**, Douglas A. 7956678, Trooper A Squadron. Killed in action 19 July 1943, Gerbini, Sicily, aged 22. Son of Frank and Lilian Binns, husband of Catherine Binns of Dagenham, Essex. Buried in Catania War Cemetery, Sicily. Grave 1 C 17. (Born Salford.)
**BOWKER**, William H. 3535751, Trooper, Died of wounds 12 August 1942, Hill 26 Egypt, aged 28. Son of William and Gertrude Bowker, husband of Phyllis Bowker of Whitefield, Lancs. Buried in El Alamein War Cemetery, Egypt. Grave 4 A 28. (Born Lancashire.)
**BOVEY**, Frederick G. 7912490, Lance Sergeant A Squadron. Killed in action 12 July 1943, Palazollo, Sicily, aged 30. Son of George and Annie Bovey of Newton Abbott, Devon. Buried in Syracuse War Cemetery, Sicily. Grave 4 B 4. (Born Devon.)
**BOYT**, Jephannah E. 7897102, Corporal C Squadron, formerly of the RAC. Killed in action 22 March 1943, Mareth, Tunisia, aged 23. Son of Edwin Andrews and Flora Boyt of Thornbury, Glos. Buried in Sfax War Cemetery, Tunisia. Joint Grave, 14 E 3. (Born Gloucestershire.)
**BROWN**, Albert. 7959586, Trooper Reconnaissance Troop. Killed in action 13 July 1943, Vizzini, Sicily, aged 20. Son of Albert and Clara Brown, ward of Mrs E. Turner of Barnsley, Yorks. No known grave, commemorated on Panel 1 of the Cassino Memorial, Italy. (Born Barnsley.)
**BUTLER**, Leslie J. 5575578, Trooper C Squadron. Killed in action 22 March 1943,

Mareth, Tunisia, aged 26. Buried in Enfidaville War Cemetery, Tunisia, Grave 5 E 14. (Born London, domicile Wiltshire.)
*CAIRNES, John E. 31902, Lieutenant-Colonel. Killed in action 22 March 1943, Mareth, Tunisia, aged 38. Son of Frederick and Lucy Barbara Cairnes, husband of June Cairnes of Howth, Co. Dublin. Buried in Enfidaville War Cemetery, Tunisia. Grave 5 E 17. (Born Eire.)
CAOLA, Edward V. 7906331, Trooper. Killed in action 27 July 1942, Ruin Ridge (Miteiriya), Egypt, aged 23. Son of Mr and Mrs G. Caola of Bristol. Buried in El Alamein War Cemetery, Egypt. Grave 20 A 21. (Born Bristol.)
CASSIDY, Eugene. 5502808, Corporal A Squadron, formerly of The Hampshire Regiment. Killed in action 19 July 1943, Gerbini, Sicily, aged 36. No known grave, commemorated on Panel 1 of the Cassino Memorial, Italy. (Born Glasgow, domicile Southampton.)
CHARLTON, Cecil. 4541193, Trooper Reconnaissance Troop. Died of wounds 29 November 1943, Sangro Valley, Italy, aged 25. Buried in Sangro River War Cemetery, Italy. Grave 14 E 45. (Born Derby, domicile Derby.)
CHEESE, John I. 7917480, Sergeant B Squadron. Killed in action 4 September 1942, Munnassib (Alam Halfa), Egypt, aged 31. Son of James and Hannah Cheese, husband of Joan Cheese of Folkstone, Kent. Buried in El Alamein War Cemetery, Egypt. Collective Grave 27 D 17-19. (Born Monmouth.)
CLAYTON, John. 3532413, Lance Corporal B Squadron. Killed in action 3 September 1942 (CWGC states 4th), Munnassib (Alam Halfa), Egypt, aged 23. Son of Alfred and Florence Clayton, husband of Constance Clayton of Manchester. Buried in El Alamein War Cemetery, Egypt. Collective Grave 27 D 17-19. (Born Manchester.)
*CLIFFORD, Patrick. 7881367, Lance Corporal C Squadron, formerly of 6 ACC RAC, 2nd RTR. Killed in action 9 April 1943, Wadi Chaffar, Tunisia, aged 33. Son of Frank and Molly Clifford, husband of Gladys Amy Clifford of Burton on Trent, Staffs. Buried in Sfax War Cemetery, Tunisia. Grave 13 F 7. (Born Eire.)
COADY, Dennis J. 14231878, Trooper. Died of wounds 7 December 1944, Athens Greece, aged 21. Son of John and Marie Coady of Surbiton, Surrey. Buried in Phaleron War Cemetery, Greece. Grave 17 E 6. (Born London SW.)
COLLIE, Alexander. 7955219, Trooper C Squadron, (RTR RoH gives rank as Pte.) Killed in action 11 December 1944, Athens, Greece, aged 21. Son of James and Lucy Collie of Bramhall, Cheshire. Buried in Phaleron War Cemetery, Greece. Grave 17 C 16. (Born Manchester.)
COOK, Thomas E. 7943957, Trooper C Squadron. Killed in action 4 November 1943 (CWGC states 2nd), San Salvo, Italy, aged 34. Husband of Beatrice Maud Cook of Hull. Buried in Sangro River War Cemetery, Italy. Grave 2 D 15. (Born Hull.)
*COOPER, Thomas C. 7887688, Lance Corporal B Squadron. Died of wounds 24 October 1942, El Alamein, Egypt, aged 22. Son of Charles and Mary Cooper of Sneiton, Notts. Buried in El Alamein War Cemetery, Egypt. Grave 5 A 18. (Born Nottingham.)
COWAP, William T. 7922815, Lance Corporal. Killed by enemy action 21 August

1942, Alam Baoshaza, Egypt, aged 35. Son of William and Ellen Cowap, husband of Dorothy Cowap of Newton Abbott, Devon. Buried in El Alamein War Cemetery, Egypt. Grave 3 A 2. (Born Plymouth.)

*CREASEY, Edward C. 7885432, Sergeant. Killed in action 22 July 1942, Ruin Ridge (Miteiriya), Egypt, aged 26. Son of William and Norah Creasey, husband of Glenys Creasey of Felixstowe, Suffolk. Buried in El Alamein War Cemetery, Egypt. Grave 9 A 11. (Born Hertfordshire.)

CRESSWELL, George E. 7914268, Lance Corporal. Killed in action 27 July 1942, Ruin Ridge (Miteiriya), Egypt, aged 28. Son of Escourt and Alice Cresswell, husband of Eileen Cresswell of Rainham, Essex. Buried in El Alamein War Cemetery, Egypt. Grave 9 B 7. (Born London E.)

CROOK, P J L. 177283, Lieutenant A Squadron. Battle accident 1 April 1943, Mareth, Tunisia, aged 22. Son of Edward Arnold and Mary Crook of Fulham, London. Buried in Sfax War Cemetery, Tunisia. Grave 10 D 20. (Born London SE.)

CROWTHER, Geoffrey. 7959588, Trooper Reconnaissance Troop. Killed in action 13 July 1943, Vizzini, Sicily, aged 32. Son of George and Ethel Crowther, husband of Helena Crowther of Great Horton, Bradford. No known grave, commemorated on Panel 1 of the Cassino Memorial, Italy. (Born Bradford.)

DANCE, Leonard. 4947319, Trooper C Squadron. Died of wounds 22 December 1943, Villa Grande, Italy, aged 21. Son of Mrs P E Dance of Addlestone, Surrey. No known grave, commemorated on Panel 1 of the Cassino Memorial, Italy. (Born Hampshire.)

*DAVIS, Clifford J. 7894236, Trooper, A Echelon. Killed by enemy action 7 August 1942, Hill 26, Egypt, aged 23. Son of James Miller and Mabel Davis of Crossways, Glos. No known grave, commemorated on Column 22 of the El Alamein Memorial, Egypt. (Born Gloucestershire.)

DEMPSTER, John J. 7902200, Corporal A Squadron. Killed in action 22 July 1942 (CWGC states 23rd), Ruin Ridge (Miteiriya), Egypt, aged 26. Son of John James and Ethel Dempster, husband of Doris Dempster of Lancaster. Buried in El Alamein War Cemetery, Egypt. Grave 24 D 3. (Born Lancashire.)

DREW, Henry. 7952349, Trooper C Squadron. Killed in action 14 July 1943, Francofonte, Sicily, aged 19. Son of George Ernest and Elsie Drew, of Knaphill, Surrey. Buried in Syracuse War Cemetery, Sicily. Grave 8 H 5. (Born Surrey.)

DUNKLEY, James W. 7904016, Corporal. Missing in action 22 July 1942, Ruin Ridge (Miteiriya), Egypt. Died 4 August 1942 while prisoner of war in Italy. Son of Thomas and Winifred Dunkley of Kislinbury, Northants. Buried in Caserta War Cemetery, Italy. Grave 6 A 13. (Born Northants. RTR RoH gives place of death as Middle East.)

*DUNSMORE, John S. 7888431, Trooper. Died of wounds 24 October 1942, El Alamein, Egypt, aged 23. RTR RoH has no record of day of death. Son of Daniel and Eliabeth Dunsmore of Glasgow. No known grave, commemorated on Column 22 of the El Alamein Memorial, Egypt. (Born Glasgow.)

EDWARDS, George J. 7912519, Lance Corporal B Squadron. Killed in action 21 December 1943, Villa Grande, Italy, aged 31. Son of Wilfred and Laura Edwards, husband of Clarice Olive Edwards of St George, Bristol. Buried in Sangro River War Cemetery, Italy. Grave 14 E 28. (Born Bristol.)

**ESSEX**, Ronald W. 7917459, Sergeant B Squadron. Killed in action 2 November 1942, El Alamein, Egypt, aged 30. Son of George E. and Louisa Essex, husband of Frances Essex of Dorchester. No known grave, commemorated on Column 21 of the El Alamein Memorial, Egypt. (Born Dorset.)

**EVANS**, John. 7917511, Lance Corporal C Squadron. Killed in action 22 March 1943, Mareth, Tunisia. Husband of Elsie Evans of Brown Edge, Staffs. Buried in Enfidaville War Cemetery, Tunisia. Grave 5 E 15. (Born Staffordshire.)

**\*FAULKNER**, Frank. 7895838, Corporal. Killed in action 7 December 1944, Athens, Greece, aged 25. Son of Samuel and Emmie Faulkner. Buried in Phaleron War Cemetery, Greece. Grave 17 B 3. (Born Manchester, domicile Oldham.)

**FERRIS**, Frederick A. 5184561, Private, Army Catering Corps, attached 50 RTR. Died of wounds 21 April 1944, Lanciano, Italy, aged 24. Son of Mr and Mrs John Wiltshire Ferris, husband of Sylvia Ferris of Winterbourne, Glos. Buried in Sangro River War Cemetery, Italy. Grave 14 D 42.

**FIELDON**, Harold. 7957526, Trooper. Died of injuries, accident, 26 July 1945, Athens, Greece, aged 37. Buried in Phaleron War Cemetery, Greece. Grave 20 A 9. (Born Yorkshire, domicile Yorkshire.)

**FORD**, William G L. 555636, Trooper, formerly of the RAC. Died in railway accident 16 July 1943, Egypt, aged 27. Son of William and Mabel Ford, husband of Annie Ford of Abbotts Langley, Herts. Buried in Tel el Kebir War Cemetery, Egypt. Grave 4 L 7. (Born Brighton.)

**FREER**, William H. 7945650, Trooper A Squadron. Died of wounds (enemy action) 10 December 1943, Lanciano, Italy, aged 23. Son of William and Elsie Freer of Chesterfield, Derbyshire. Buried in Sangro River War Cemetery, Italy. Grave 4 E 33. (Born Derbyshire.)

**GARDNER**, Herbert. 1439153, Trooper B Squadron. Died of wounds 29 January 1945, Athens, Greece, aged 21. Son of Samuel and Margaret Gardner of Corsham, Wilts. Buried in Phaleron War Cemetery, Greece. Grave 17 C 10. (Born Wiltshire.)

**GAUNT**, John J. 922175, Corporal B Squadron, formerly of the Royal Artillery. Killed in action 17 December 1944, Athens, Greece, aged 28. Son of John and Constance Gaunt of Gamlingay, Cambridgeshire. Buried in Phaleron War Cemetery, Greece. Grave 17 E 4. (Born Bedfordshire.)

**GEE**, Eric E B. 7915025, Trooper. Killed in action 25 October 1942 (CWGC states 24th), El Alamein, Egypt, aged 24. Son of Cecil Bruce and Sylvia Agnes Gee of Carhampton, Somerset. Buried in El Alamein War Cemetery, Egypt. Grave 16 F 2. (Born Brazil.)

**GILL**, Cooper L. 7959590, Trooper Reconnaissance Troop. Killed in action 13 July 1943, Vizzini, Sicily, aged 20. Son of Cooper and Elizabeth Gill of Yeadon, Yorks. No known grave, commemorated on Panel 1 of the Cassino Memorial, Italy. (Born Leeds.)

**HAFT**, Harry. 3460673, Trooper C Squadron. Killed in action 21 December 1943, Villa Grande Italy, aged 31. Son of Morris and Leah Haft of Liverpool. Buried in

Sangro River War Cemetery, Italy. Grave 14 B 22. (Born Liverpool.)

**HALLMARK**, Henry J. 3460674, Trooper A Squadron. Died of wounds 11 December 1943, Lanciano, Italy, aged 31. Buried in Moro River Canadian War Cemetery, Italy. Grave 13 B 13. (Born Manchester, domicile Manchester.)

**HANLEY**, James. 180459, Second Lieutenant, formerly of the Royal Army Service Corps. Killed in action 22 July 1942, Ruin Ridge (Miteiriya), Egypt, aged 27. Son of James and Annie Hanley of York. No known grave, commemorated on Column 21 of the El Alamein Memorial, Egypt. (Born Glasgow.)

**HANNON**, G J. 7939644, Trooper C Squadron. Killed in action 22 March 1943, Mareth, Tunisia, aged 32. Buried in Sfax War Cemetery, Tunisia. Joint grave 14 E 3. (Born Liverpool, domicile Liverpool.)

**HARDING**, Frederick V. 7917416, Corporal B Squadron. Killed in action 4 September 1942, Munnassib (Alam Halfa), Egypt, aged 32. Son of Frederick John and Sarah Lucy Harding of Coombe Martin, Devon. Buried in El Alamein War Cemetery, Egypt. Collective grave 27 D 17-19. (Born Southampton.)

**HARGREAVES**, Eric. 7934990, Trooper A Squadron. Killed in action 19 July 1943, Gerbini, Sicily, aged 26. RTR RoH has no record of day of death. Son of James and Emma Hargreaves, husband of Joan Hargreaves of Milnrow, Lancs. Buried in Catania War Cemetery, Sicily. Grave 2 G 33. (Born Lancashire.)

*****HARTLEY**, William. 7888700, Sergeant. Died of Wounds 24 October 1942, El Alamein, Egypt, aged 32. Son of Mark and Ellen Hartley of Blackburn, Lancs. No known grave, commemorated on Column 21 of the El Alamein Memorial, Egypt. (Born Blackburn.)

**HARVEY**, Frank E. 7958993, Trooper A Squadron. Killed in action 19 July 1943, Gerbini, Sicily, aged 20. No known grave, commemorated on Panel 1 of the Cassino Memorial, Italy. (Born Sheffield, domicile Sheffield.)

**HEESOM**, Sidney. 329140, Trooper C Squadron. Killed in action 4 November 1943, San Salvo Italy, aged 27. Buried in Sangro River War Cemetery, Italy. Grave 14 E 40. (Born Cheshire, domicile Cheshire.)

**HEWINS**, Robert E. 7917464, Sergeant Reconnaissance Troop. Killed in action 22 July 1942, Ruin Ridge (Miteiriya), Egypt, aged 30. Son of George and Alice Hewins, husband of Kathleen J Hewins. No known Grave, commemorated on Column 21 of the El Alamein Memorial, Egypt. (Born Lincolnshire.)

**HILLIER**, Neville M. 7932593, Corporal Regimental Headquarters. Died of wounds 6 January 1945, Athens, Greece, aged 30. Son of Harry and Mary Hillier, husband of Mollie Hillier of Johannasburg, South Africa. Buried in Phaleron War Cemetery, Greece. Grave 19 C 6. (Born Middlessex.)

*****HOBBS**, Gerald L. 113709, Captain A Squadron. Killed in action 22 July 1942, Ruin Ridge (Miteiriya), Egypt, aged 27. Son of Langley and Evelyn Hobbs, husband of Annette Hobbs of Ealing, Middlesex. Buried in El Alamein War Cemetery, Egypt. Grave 4 B 8. (Born London W.)

**HODGE**, Albert G. 5508361, Trooper B Squadron. Killed in action 29 November 1943, Mozzagrogna, Italy, aged 27. Son of Murial L Hodge, husband of Grace Hodge of Christchurch, Hampshire. Buried in Sangro River War Cemetery, Italy. Grave 14

E 43. (Born Devon.)

HOLDER, Arthur J. 7946640, Trooper B Squadron. Battle accident 12 July 1943, Paolo, Sicily, aged 20. Son of Charles and Hilda Holder of Wolverhampton. Buried in Syracuse War Cemetery, Sicily. Grave 1 H 9. (Born India.)

HOOTON, Paul R. 7952059, Trooper C Squadron. Died of wounds 6 April 1943, Wadi Akarit, Tunisia, aged 20. Son of Frederick R and Olga A Hooton of Rushden, Northants. Buried in Sfax War Cemetery, Tunisia. Grave 14 C 25. (Born Northants.)

HOUGH, William F. 7900204, Trooper Reconnaissance Troop. Killed in action 22 December 1944, Athens, Greece, aged 25. Son of Benjamin and Charlotte Hough of Cardiff. No known grave, commemorated on Face 1 of the Athens Memorial, Greece. (Born Glamorgan.)

*HUGHES, Alan P. 68692, Major B Squadron. Killed in action 4 September 1942 Munnassib (Alam Halfa), Egypt. Son of James and Florence Hughes, husband of Elizabeth Hughes of Bebington, Cheshire. Buried in El Alamein War Cemetery, Egypt. Collective grave 27 D 17-19. (Born Wallasey.)

HUTH, Michael S. MM, 269304, Lieutenant C Squadron. Killed in action 1 August 1943, Masa Monaco, Sicily, aged 28. Son of Sydney and Ruby Huth of Culmstock, Devon. No known grave, commemorated on Panel 1 of the Cassino Memorial, Italy. Awarded Military Medal when a sergeant with 44 RTR. (Not on RTR RoH.)

INCH, Charles B R. 198591, Lieutenant C Squadron. Died of wounds 6 April (CWGC states 5th) 1943, Wadi Akarit, Tunisia, aged 28. Buried in Enfidaville War Cemetery, Tunisia. Grave 6 F 13. (Born Edinburgh, domicile Worcester. Originally reported to have been killed in road traffic accident while on duty. Eye witness accounts place him at the Wadi Akarit.)

JACKSON, David C. 240869, Lieutenant Recce Troop. Killed in action 12 November 1943, Scerni, Italy, aged 22. Son of Stonewall and Alsie Jackson of Wallington, Surrey. Buried in Moro River Canadian War Cemetery, Italy. Grave 9 H 3. (Not on RTR RoH.)

JACKSON, John P. 7961234, Trooper C Squadron. Killed in action 22 December 1943, Villa Grande, Italy, aged 20. Son of Harold Ewart and Florence Jackson of East Kirkby, Notts. No known grave, commemorated on Panel 1 of the Cassino Memorial, Italy. (Born Nottinghamshire.)

*JAMES, George H. 7896990, Lance Corporal B Squadron. Killed in action 4 September 1942, Munnassib (Alam Halfa), Egypt, aged 21. Son of Alfred and Beatrice James, husband of Daisy James. Buried in El Alamein War Cemetery, Egypt. Collective grave 27 D 17-19. (Born Bristol, domicile Bristol.)

JAMISON, John. 2824879, Trooper A Squadron. Killed in action 31 December 1944, Athens, Greece, aged 33. Son of John and Annie Jamison of Blackhills, Morayshire. Buried in Phaleron War Cemetery, Greece. Grave 19 A 14. (Born Moray.)

*JENNINGS, James. 94921, Captain B Squadron. Killed in action 4 September 1942, Munnassib (Alam Halfa), Egypt. Buried in El Alamein War Cemetery, Egypt. Collective grave 27 D 17-19. (Born Manchester, domicile Cheshire.)

JOHNSON, Frank L. 7914938, Corporal. Killed in action 27 July 1942, Ruin Ridge (Miteiriya), Egypt, aged 32. RTR RoH have no record of day of death. Son of Maurice and Minnie Johnson, husband of Enid Johnson of Cheltenham. Buried in El Alamein War Cemetery, Egypt. Grave 9 B 9.(Born Gloucestershire.)

**JONES**, Cyril R. 7912502, Lance Corporal A Squadron. Died of wounds 19 July 1943, Gerbini, Sicily. Son of Edwin and Kathleen Jones of Ilford, Essex. Buried in Catania War Cemetery, Sicily. Grave 1 G 47. (Born London E, domicile Bristol.)

**KEILY**, Edward W. 7945118, Lance Sergeant. Died of wounds 10 January 1944, Bari Hospital, Italy, aged 37. Son of Major General F P C and Kathleen Keily of Redhill, Surrey. Buried in Bari War Cemetery, Italy. Grave 10 D 27. (Born India.)

*****KEW**, Hubert S. 421018, Sergeant. Died on active service (illness?) 30/31 October 1942, El Alamein, Egypt. RTR RoH have no record of day of death. Son of Henry and Mabel Kew of Falfield, Glos. Buried in El Alamein War Cemetery, Egypt. Grave 3 E 4. (Born Gloucestershire.)

**LEWIS**, James E P. 7915322, Corporal C Squadron. Died of wounds 18 July 1943 received at Francofonte, Sicily, aged 33. Son of James and Elizabeth Lewis, husband of Mabel Lewis of East Ham, Essex. Buried in Enfidaville War Cemetery, Tunisia. Grave 2 E 21. (Born London E.)

*****LIDGLEY**, Douglas B. 420964, Corporal A Squadron. Died of wounds 7 August 1942, Alexandria, Egypt, aged 23. Son of William and Florence Lidgley of Fishponds, Bristol. Buried in Hadra War Cemetery (Alexandria), Egypt. Grave 3 E 16. (Born Bristol.)

**LINDLEY**, George. 302474, Lieutenant B Squadron. Killed in action 14 May 1944, Orsogna, Italy, aged 24. Son of Ernest and Beatrice Lindley, stepson of Margaret Lindley of Leeds, Yorks. Buried in Sangro River War Cemetery, Italy. Grave 14 D 34. (Not on RTR RoH.)

**MACDONALD**, William. 7924991, Trooper A Squadron. Died of wounds 17 July 1943, Stimpato, Sicily, aged 23. Son of William and Mary MacDonald, husband of Jessie MacDonald of Ruchill, Glasgow. Buried in Syracuse War Cemetery, Sicily. Grave 6 A 9. (Born Glasgow, name spelt McDonald on RTR RoH.)

**MACGREGOR**, L. 1103116V, Lieutenant, South African Armoured Corps, seconded to 50 RTR, A Squadron. Killed in action 18 December 1943, Tollo, Italy. Buried in Sangro River War Cemetery, Italy. Grave 14 E 26. (Born South Africa)

**MACKINTOSH**, John G. 3318064, Trooper A Squadron, formerly of the Highland Light Infantry. Killed in action 12 July 1943, Palazollo, Sicily, aged 23. Son of John and Lucy Mackintosh, husband of Margaret Joan Mackintosh of South Benfleet, Essex. Buried in Syracuse War Cemetery, Sicily. Grave 4 B 2. (Born Yorkshire.)

**MALLEY**, Wilfred J. 4462336, Trooper C Squadron. Missing believed killed 14 July 1943, Francofonte, Sicily, aged 30. Son of Joseph and Ann Malley, husband of Catherine Malley of Liverpool. No known grave, commemorated on Panel 1 of the Cassino Memorial, Italy. (Born Flintshire.)

**MANDERS**, John J. 7946656, Trooper A Squadron. Missing believed killed 19 July 1943, Gerbini, Sicily, aged 20. Son of John and Annie Manders of Wednesbury, Staffs. No known grave, commemorated on Panel 1 of the Cassino Memorial, Italy. (Born Staffordshire.)

**MATTOCK**, Harold W C. 7923079, Corporal Reconnaissance Troop. Killed in action

22 December 1944, Athens, Greece, aged 37. Son of William and Elizabeth Mattock, husband of Alice Mattock of Wallingford, Berks. No known grave, commemorated on Face 1 of the Athens Memorial, Greece. (Born London E.)

**McARTHUR**, Roy. 7952285, Trooper. Killed in action 17 December 1943, River Moro, Italy, aged 29. Son of Percy and Nellie McArthur of Crouch End, London. Buried in Sangro River War Cemetery, Italy. Grave 2 B 35. (Born London.)

**McCULLOUGH**, Brian. 7915874, Trooper A Squadron. Killed in action 19 July 1943, Gerbini, Sicily, aged 23. Son of James and Mary McCullough of Marton, Lancs. Buried in Catania War Cemetery, Sicily. Grave 1 A 14. (Born Manchester.)

**MELLOR**, Philip B J. 220696, Lieutenant A Squadron. Killed in action 19 July 1943, Gerbini, Sicily, aged 23. Son of William and Sussanah Mellor, husband of Mavis Mellor of Humberstone, Leics. Buried in Catania War Cemetery, Sicily. Grave 1 A 13. (Not on RTR RoH.)

**MITCHELL**, Wilfred L. 7914942, Sergeant C Squadron. Battle accident 20 December 1944 (CWGC and RTR RoH state 12th) Athens, Greece, aged 34. Son of Edward and Leah Mitchell, husband of Beatrice Rose Mitchell of Dorchester, Dorset. Buried in Phaleron War Cemetery, Greece. Grave 17 C 17. (Born Dorset.)

**MORLEY**, John T. 3864578, Trooper A Squadron. Killed in action 19 July 1943, Gerbini, Sicily, aged 22. Son of Michael and Jane Morley. No known grave, commemorated on Panel 1 of the Cassino Memorial, Italy. (Born Wigan.)

**MURPHY**, Albert D. 7917489, Lance Corporal B Squadron. Missing in action 22 July 1942, Ruin Ridge (Miteiriya), Egypt, aged 31. Died 17 August 1942 during sinking of the Nino Bixio. Son of William and Alice Murphy of Brighton, Sussex. No known grave, commemorated on Column 22 of the El Alamein Memorial, Egypt. (Born Brighton.)

**NEWNS**, Norman K. 7902908, Lance Corporal C Squadron. Killed in action 6 December 1944, Athens, Greece, aged 34. Son of George and Elizabeth Newns, husband of Dorothy Evelyn Newns of High Wycombe. Buried in Phaleron War Cemetery, Greece. Grave 17 C 20. (Born Buckinghamshire.)

**NIXON**, Cecil B G. (Sammy) MC. Mentioned in Despatches. 179928, Lieutenant B Squadron. Killed in action 17 July 1943, Stimpato, Sicily, aged 28. Son of Cecil and Gertrude Nixon of Bosham, Sussex. Buried in Catania War Cemetery, Sicily. Grave 1 B 32. (Born London W.)

**OAKES**, Harold. 3857775, Sergeant B Squadron. Killed in action 1 August 1943, Sferro, Sicily, aged 25. Son of Thomas and Ellen Oakes, husband of Emma Oakes of Bolton, Lancs. No known grave, commemorated on Panel 1 of the Cassino Memorial, Italy. (Born Bolton.)

**ORAM**, Arthur P. 7932886, Trooper A Squadron. Missing believed killed 19 July 1943, Gerbini, Sicily, aged 22. Son of Henry and Margurite Oram of Southampton. No known grave, commemorated on Panel 1 of the Cassino Memorial, Italy. (Born Southampton.)

**PATEFIELD**, Norman B. 7941731, Trooper. Missing in action 22 July 1942, Ruin Ridge (Miteiriya), Egypt. Died 17 August 1942 during sinking of the Nino Bixio, aged 30. No known grave, commemorated on Panel 23 of the El Alamein Memorial,

Egypt. (Born Yorkshire, domicile Yorkshire.)

**PEARCE**, Thomas V. 7906320, Trooper. Died on active service (illness?) 3 July 1943, Moascar Military Hospital, Egypt, aged 23. Son of Henry and Ellen Pearce of Bristol. Buried in Moascar War Cemetery, Egypt. Grave 1 B 14. (Born Bristol.)

**PERCIVAL**, Edward V. 7952450, Trooper C Squadron. Killed in action 21 December 1944, Athens, Greece, aged 23. Son of William and Ruth Percival of Codsall, Staffs. Buried in Phaleron War Cemetery, Greece. Grave 17 C 2. (Born Birmingham.)

**PICKTHALL**, Leonard. 7941496, Trooper. Missing in action 27 July 1942, Ruin Ridge (Miteiriya), Egypt. Died 17 August 1942 during sinking of the Nino Bixio, aged 28. Son of Harold and Elizabeth Pickthall, husband of Edith Mary Pickthall of Brighton, Sussex. No known grave, commemorated on Column 23 of the El Alamein Memorial, Egypt. (Born Cheshire.)

**PILLAR**, Kenneth J. Mentioned in Despatches. 222658, Lieutenant A Squadron. Killed in action 30 November 1943, Romagnali Italy, aged 23. Son of James and Greta Pillar of Barrow in Furness, Lancs. Buried in Sangro River War Cemetery, Italy. Grave 14 D 21. (Not on RTR RoH.)

**PLANT**, Basil. 14388695, Trooper C Squadron. Killed by enemy action 11 May 1944, Poggiofiorito, Italy, aged 19. Son of Harold and Minnie Plant of Longton, Staffs. Buried in Sangro River War Cemetery, Italy. Grave 14 E 37. (Born Staffordshire.)

**PRITCHETT**, Kenneth N. 262388, Second Lieutenant B Echelon. Killed by enemy action 9 December 1943, River Moro, Italy, aged 21. Son of Henry and Ethel Pritchett of Tunbridge Wells, Kent. Buried in Sangro River War Cemetery, Italy. Grave 14 E 34. (Not on RTR RoH.)

**PUDDICK**, Frank E. 3459411, Lance Sergeant. Died of wounds 28 December 1944, Athens, Greece, aged 29. Son of Frank and Rose Puddick of Islington, London. Buried in Phaleron War Cemetery, Greece. Grave 17 C 9. (Born London N.)

*****PUGH**, Eric. 7893037, Lance Corporal B Squadron. Killed in action 4 September 1942, Munnassib (Alam Halfa), Egypt, aged 21. RTR RoH has no record of day of death. Son of Richard and Elizabeth Pugh of Maesbury Marsh, Salop. Buried in El Alamein War Cemetery, Egypt. Collective grave 27 D 17-19. (Born Shropshire.)

*****REED**, F.N. 12165, Lieutenant A Squadron. Killed in action 19 July 1943, Gerbini, Sicily, aged 26. Son of Albert and Dorothy Reed, husband of Veronica Reed of Harrow, Middlesex. Buried in Catania War Cemetery, Sicily. Grave 3 L 32. (Born London NW.)

**RILEY**, John E. 7894001, Sergeant B Squadron. Missing in action 27 July 1942, Ruin Ridge (Miteiriya), Egypt. Died 17 August 1942 during sinking of the Nino Bixio, aged 25. Son of John and Ellen Riley of Preston, Lancs. Buried in Phaleron War Cemetery, Greece. Collective grave 7 D 1-10. (Born Preston.)

**ROBERTS**, Thomas H. 7956659, Trooper B Squadron. Killed by enemy action 19 December 1943 (CWGC and RTR RoH state 18th), Tollo, Italy. Son of George and Mary Roberts. Buried in Sangro River War Cemetery, Italy. Grave 14 E 25. (Born London E.)

**ROBINS**, Kenneth I. 7902759, Trooper Regimental Headquarters. Killed in action 22 March 1943, Mareth, Tunisia, aged 30. Son of William and Mabel Robins of

Ilfracombe, Devon. Buried in Enfidaville War Cemetery, Tunisia. Grave 5 E 16. (Born Devon.)

**RUDD**, Norman R. 7941500, Trooper. Killed by enemy action 19 December 1943 (CWGC and RTR RoH state 18th), Tollo, Italy, aged 22. Son of Reginald and Maisie Rudd of Tunbridge Wells, Kent. Buried in Sangro River War Cemetery, Italy. Grave 14 E 27.(Born Kent.)

*****RUSSELL**, Geoffrey E. DSO. TD. 32082, Lieutenant Colonel. Killed in action 29 November 1943, Mozzagrogna, Italy, aged 37. Son of Mr and Mrs Ernest Russell of Birkdale, Southport, Lancs. Buried in Sangro River War Cemetery, Italy. Grave 14 E 44. (RTR RoH states born in Manchester.)

*****RUSSELL**, Victor A. 7891847, Corporal Regimental Headquarters. Killed in action 22 March 1943, Mareth, Tunisia, aged 22. No known grave, commemorated on Face 3 of the Medjez el Bab Memorial, Tunisia. (Born Burma, domicile Bristol.)

**SAUNDERS**, Alfred T. 7916173, Corporal A Squadron. Died in accident 3 July 1944 (CWGC state 2nd) Ismailia, Egypt, aged 31. Son of William and Helen Saunders, husband of Lilian Saunders of Hammersmith, London. Buried in Moascar War Cemetery, Egypt. Grave 3 A 11. (Born London W.)

**SCOURFIELD**, Colwyn. 7933318, Trooper A Squadron. Missing believed killed 19 July 1943, Gerbini, Sicily, aged 27. Son of Thomas and Elizabeth Scourfield of Milton, Pembrokeshire. No known grave, commemorated on Panel 1 of the Cassino Memorial, Italy. (Born Pembrokeshire.)

**SHERRETT**, William. 7933092, Trooper. Missing in action 22 July 1942, Ruin Ridge (Miteiriya), Egypt. Died 17 August 1942 during sinking of the Nino Bixio, aged 31. Son of James and Alice Sherrett, husband of Esther Lees Sherrett of Oldham, Lancs. Buried in Phaleron War Cemetery, Greece. Special Memorial C, 9 B 14. (Born Liverpool.)

**SHILLCROSS**, George W E. 7939650, Trooper C Squadron. Killed in action 6 April 1943, Wadi Akarit, Tunisia, aged 33. Son of George and Ruth Shillcross of Kegworth, Leics. No known grave, commemorated on Face 3 of the Medjez el Bab Memorial, Tunisia. (Born Derbyshire.)

**SINCLAIR**, David. 7951413, Trooper C Squadron. Killed in action 21 December 1943, Villa Grande, Italy, aged 25. Son of David and Isabella Sinclair of St Margarets Hope, Orkney. Buried in Sangro River War Cemetery, Italy. Grave 14 B 23. (Born Orkney.)

**SKILLCORN**, William K. 3781539, Trooper C Squadron. Killed by enemy action 20 April 1944, Lanciano, Italy, aged 23. Son of William and Effie Skillcorn of Isle of Man. Buried in Sangro River War Cemetery, Italy. Grave 14 D 40. (Born Isle of Man.)

**SMITH**, Arthur Q. Lance Corporal B Squadron. Missing in action 27 July 1942, Ruin Ridge (Miteiriya), Egypt, died while prisoner of war in Italy 27 October 1942, aged 33 RTR RoH states died in Middle East. Son of Arthur and Emily Smith, husband of Margeret E Smith of Warwick. Buried in Caserta War Cemetery, Italy. Grave 4 D 1. (Born Berkshire.)

**SMITH**, Robert. 7946640, Trooper A Squadron. Killed in action 19 July 1943, Gerbini,

Sicily, aged 21. Son of Thomas and Martha Newton Smith of Steeton, Yorks. Buried in Catania War Cemetery, Sicily. Grave 3 L 31. (Born Yorkshire.)
**SNAPE**, James. 3536135, Corporal, formely B Echelon. Killed in action 23 May 1945, Austria, on temporary service with Blitz Patrol of No. 1 Demolition Squadron (Popski's Private Army), aged 34. Son of William and Sarah Snape of Chorley, Lancs. Buried in Klagenfurt War Cemetery, Austria. Grave 2 A 2. (Born Lancashire.)
**SNOW**, Douglas. 7909339, Trooper. Died of wounds 22 April 1944, Lanciano, Italy, aged 28. Son of George and Annie Snow, husband of Doris Snow of Sileby, Leics. Buried in Sangro River War Cemetery, Italy. Grave 14 E 36. (Born Leicestershire.)
**SPENCE**, Cyril J. 300108, Lieutenant C Squadron. Died of wounds 23 December 1943, Villa Grande, Italy, aged 26. Son of Alfred and Rosetta Spence of Dursley, Gloucs. Buried in Sangro River War Cemetery, Italy. Grave 14 D 29. (Not on RTR RoH.)
***SPRACKLAND**, George H W. 7897125, Trooper. Killed in action 30 December 1944, Athens, Greece, aged 24. Son of Henry and Louisa Sprackland of Ashton Vale, Bristol. Buried in Phaleron War Cemetery, Greece. Grave 17 B 10. (Born Bristol.)
**STABBINS**, Francis R. 7912530, Trooper B Squadron. Killed in action 4 September 1942, Munnassib (Alam Halfa), Egypt. Buried in El Alamein War Cemetery Egypt. Collective grave 27 D 17-19. (Born Somerset, domicile Bristol.)
**STANSFIELD**, Leslie J. 7917441, Sergeant A Squadron. Missing believed killed 19 July 1943, Gerbini, Sicily, aged 28. RTR RoH have no record of day of death. Son of Albert and Florence Stansfield, husband of Edith Mary Stansfield of Horswell, Woking, Surrey. No known grave, commemorated on Panel 1 of the Cassino Memorial, Italy. (Born Surrey.)
**STEIN**, Albert. 7937950, Trooper A Squadron. Missing believed killed 19 July 1943, Gerbini, Sicily, aged 31. No known grave, commemorated on Panel 1 of the Cassino Memorial. (Born Rumania, domicile London WC.)
**STONE**, William. 7903879, Trooper. Missing in action 22 July 1942, Ruin Ridge (Miteiriya), Egypt, died of wounds received during sinking of the Nino Bixio 26 August 1942, aged 34. Son of Percy and Emma Stone of Pilsey, Derbys. Buried in Phaleron War Cemetery, Greece. Collective Grave 7 D 1-10. (Born Derby.)
***STUMP**, Harold J. 5183375, Sergeant C Squadron. Killed in action 14 July 1943, Francofonte, Sicily, aged 22. Son of Alfred and Beatrice Stump of Chipping Sodbury, Gloucs. Buried in Syracuse War Cemetery, Sicily. Grave 8 A 10. (Born Gloucestershire.)
**STYLES**, William S. (Jock) 134837 Major. Died in the UK. 15 August 1945, aged 32. Son of William and Janet Simpson Styles, husband of Barbara Jeanne Styles of Bournemouth, Hants. Buried Wool (Holy Rood) churchyard ext. Dorset. Grave 72. (Born Bumbarton).
**SUMMERS**, Harry A J. 7917567, Corporal. Died of wounds 7 August 1942, Ruin Ridge (Miteiriya), Egypt, aged 29. Son of Harry and Florence Summers, husband of Kathleen Summers of Balsall Heath, Birmingham. Buried in El Alamein War Cemetery, Egypt. Grave 4 D 22. (Born Birmingham.)
**SYMMONS**, John K. 7959034, Trooper Symons on RTR RoH. Killed by enemy action

20 April 1944, Lanciano, Italy, aged 26. Son of James Dilling and Doris Ivy Symmons, of Merton, Devon. Buried in Sangro River War Cemetery, Italy. Grave 14 D 43. (Born Devon.)

**TATCHELL**, William J. 7917475, Trooper B Squadron. Killed in action 21 April 1943, Wadi Boul (Enfidaville), Tunisia, aged 32. Son of James and Ethel Tatchell, husband of Ellen Tatchell of Bath, Somerset. Buried in Enfidaville War Cemetery, Tunisia. Grave 6 D 11. (Born Somerset.)

**TAYLOR**, Vernon G. 7914945, Corporal C Squadron. Killed in action 23 March 1943, Mareth, Tunisia, aged 32. Son of Albert and Annie Taylor, husband of Juaneta Taylor of Redruth, Cornwall. Buried in Enfidaville War Cemetery, Tunisia. Grave 5 E 13. (Born Swansea.)

**TEBBUTT**, Godfrey D. 5509056, Sergeant Headquarter Squadron. Battle Accident, 20 December 1944, Athens, Greece, aged 31. Son of Samuel and Annie Tebbutt of Paignton, Devon. Buried in Phaleron War Cemetery, Greece. Grave 17 C 1. (Born Yorkshire.)

**THOMAS**, John H. 7912387, Trooper. Missing in action 27 July 1942, Ruin Ridge (Miteiriya), Egypt, aged 29. RTR RoH have no record of day of death. Son of Charles and Elizabeth Thomas of Chudleigh, Devon. No known grave, commemorated on Column 24 of the El Alamein Memorial, Egypt. (Born Cornwall.)

**THOMPSON**, Ian C M. 180475, Second Lieutenant. Killed in action 27 July 1942, Ruin Ridge (Miteiriya), Egypt, aged 25. Son of George and Hilda Thompson of Oaken, Staffs. Buried in El Alamein War Cemetery, Egypt. Grave 9 B 8. (Born Wolverhampton, formerly of the Royal Artillery.)

**THOMPSON**, Norman J. 79177570, Trooper. Missing in action 22 July 1942, Ruin Ridge (Miteiriya), Egypt. Died 17 August 1942 during sinking of the Nini Bixio. aged 28. Son of John and Annie Thompson, husband of Elsie Thompson of Tamworth, Staffs. Buried in Phaleron War Cemetery, Greece. Special Memorial 9 B 15. (Born Birmingham.)

**TIMM**, James R. 5050917, Trooper A Squadron. Died of wounds 30 November 1943, Mozzagrogna, Italy, aged 25. Son of Mr and Mrs J W Timm of Little Longstone, Derby. Buried in Sangro River War Cemetery, Italy. Grave 14 E 32. (Born Derbyshire.)

**TRAVERS**, Hugh J. 7945483, Trooper C Squadron. Killed in action 25 October 1942 (CWGC and RTR RoH state 24th), El Alamein, Egypt, aged 32. Son of Major Hugh and Margaret Travers, husband of Francis Travers of Mayfield, Sussex. Buried in El Alamein War Cemetery, Egypt. Grave 26 F 4. (Born Halifax.)

**TURNER**, Harry. 7937861, Trooper C Squadron. Killed in action 22 December 1943, Villa Grande, Italy, aged 23. Son of William Henry and Fanney Turner. No known grave, commemorated on Panel 1 of the Cassino Memorial, Italy. (Born Staffordshire.)

**\*TYE**, Wiliam J J. 7896332, Trooper C Squadron. Killed in action 4 November 1943, San Salvo, Italy, aged 22. Son of Mr and Mrs W J Tye of Easton, Bristol. Buried in Sangro River War Cemetery, Italy. Grave 14 E 41. (Born Bristol.)

**UNSWORTH**, William B. 7940818, Lance Corporal C Squadron. Killed in action 22 December 1943, Villa Grande, Italy, aged 29. Son of Joseph and Janet Unsworth, husband of Margaret Unsworth of Salford, Lancs. Buried in Sangro River War Cemetery, Italy. Grave 14 D 30. (Born Manchester.)

**VENN**, Douglas P. 164146, Major C Squadron, formerly of the RAC. Died of illness 16 January 1944, Barletta, Italy, aged 30. Son of Vivian and Ida Venn of Westbury on Trym, Bristol. Buried in Sangro River War Cemetery, Italy. Grave 14 E 31. (Born Bristol.)

**WALKER**, Charles G. 7931775, Trooper B Squadron. Battle accident 26 August 1942, Alam Baoshaza, Egypt, aged 30. Son of William and Florence Walker of Bengeo, Herts. Buried in El Alamein War Cemetery, Egypt. Grave 12 E 11. (Born Hertfordshire.)

**WATKINS**, Andrew. 3598856, Trooper A Squadron, formerly of The Border Regiment. Died of wounds 22 July 1943, Gerbini, Sicily. Buried in Catania War Cemetery, Sicily. Grave 1 G 32. (Born Bolton, domicile Bolton.)

**WATT**, W. 2353918, Lance Corporal, Royal Corps Signals attached 50 RTR. Killed by enemy action 26 December 1943, Tollo, Italy, aged 37. Son of William and Beatrice Watt, husband of Dora Watt of Leeds, Yorks. Buried in Sangro River War Cemetery, Italy. Grave 10 D 27.

**WELSBY**, Terence. 3534812, Trooper A Squadron. Killed in action 26 October 1942 (CWGC and RTR RoH state 27th), El Alamein, Egypt, aged 22. Son of John Harry and Gertrude Welsby, husband of Alma Welsby of Withington, Manchester. Buried in El Alamein War Cemetery, Egypt. Grave 22 H 23. (Born Salford.)

**\*WILLIAMS**, Edmund. 7895690, Corporal. Killed in action 22 July 1942, Ruin Ridge (Miteiriya), Egypt, aged 23. Son of Mr and Mrs J A Williams of Horsefield, Bristol. Buried in El Alamein War Cemetery, Egypt. Grave 17 G 15. (Born Bristol.)

**WILLSON**, Reginald L. 182343, Lieutenant C Squadron. Killed in action 11 December 1944, Athens, Greece, aged 23. Son of Albert and Nora Willson of Hertford. Buried in Phaleron War Cemetery, Greece. Grave 17 C 6. (Not on RTR RoH.)

**WOOD**, Geoffrey W. 117570, Lieutenant A Squadron. Died of wounds 26 October 1942 (CWGC and RTR RoH state 27th), El Alamein, Egypt, aged 30. Son of John and Edith Wood, husband of Margaret Joan Wood of Little Chalfont, Amersham, Bucks. Buried in El Alamein War Cemetery, Egypt. Grave 11 C 4. (Born Kent.)

**WOOD**, Robert C. 7917449, Corporal. Killed by enemy action 20 April 1944, Lanciano, Italy, aged 33. Son of Earnest and Florence Wood of Ingatestone, Essex. Buried in Sangro River War Cemetery, Italy. Grave 14 D 45. (Born London SW.)

**WYKES**, Clifford. 184006, Lieutenant C Squadron. Killed in action 6 April 1943, Wadi Akarit, Tunisia, aged 25. Son of George and Emily Wykes, husband of Ruth Wykes of Shildon, Co. Durham. No known grave, commemorated on Face 3 of the Medjez el Bab Memorial, Tunisia. (Born Nottinghamshire.)

**YANEZ**, Lucas. 7932545, Trooper. Died in accident 9 June 1945, Greece. Son of Catherine Yanez of Penydarren, Glam. Buried in Phaleron War Cemetery, Greece. Grave 5 C 5. (Born Glamorgan.)

**YEOMANS**, Ernest G. 7931396, Trooper. Killed in action 22 July 1942, Ruin Ridge (Miteiriya), Egypt, aged 36. Son of Richard and Florence Yeomans, husband of

Phyllis Yeomans of Leeds. Buried in El Alamein War Cemetery, Egypt. Grave 9 A 12. (Born Northamptonshire.)


Former members of the Regiment known to have died while serving with other units:

**BALLANTINE** James DH. 52518 Major. Died of wounds sustained at Maltot, Normandy while serving with 9 RTR 10 July 1944.

**CHAPMAN** Gerald. 162105 Major. MBE. Died while serving with 2 RTR 14 January 1946. Buried Naples War Cemetery, Italy. Grave 4.O.9. (Former Adjutant.)

**CHAPMAN** JA. 170277 Second-Lieutenant. Killed in action while serving with 8 RTR in Egypt 10 July 1942. Buried Alamein WC. Grave 17.E.20.

**GILES** John F. 68678 Captain. Killed in action while serving with No 3 Commando, Vaagso Island, Norway. 27 December 1941.

**TURPIN** Henri F. 166266 Lieutenant. Killed in action while serving with the 6th (Airborn) Armopured Recce Regiment in Northwest Europe 17 April 1945.

**WESTON** Eric CK. 58963 Major. Killed in accident while serving in Palastine 22 March 1945, aged 32. Buried Khayat Beach War Cemetery grave B.A.6.

# Annex B
# HONOURS AND AWARDS

The roll of awards has been compiled from the following sources: Mr Bill Green of Bristol, who has been invaluable; The Tank Museum at Bovington; Imperial War Museum; War Diary; members of 50 RTR; and the London Gazette. The announcements in the Gazette can be misleading; the recipient's name may not be 'gazetted' until many months after the action, in which time the unit concerned may have moved to a new theatre of war.

The majority of the awards can be read in the narrative. All recommendations 'Granted' and 'Not Approved,' have been included.

## DISTINGUISHED SERVICE ORDER
Lieutenant-Colonel J E Cairnes, recommended for operations in the Western Desert October 1942 – March 1943 (Not Approved)

Captain R A P Ellis, Royal Army Medical Corps, for 20/23 March 1943, Battle of Mareth. Original recommendation was for Military Cross. London Gazette 28 May 1943.

Major (acting Lieutenant-Colonel) G E Russell, recommended for 23/24 October 1942 at Battle of Alamein (Not Approved). Awarded June 1943 for operations Akarit-Sfax April 1943. London Gazette 10 July 1943.

## ORDER OF THE BRITISH EMPIRE
Lieutenant Colonel John C de F Sleeman, Awarded January 1944 for operations in Italy.

## MEMBER OF THE BRITISH EMPIRE
Major Walter D Bazley, for operations in Italy while commanding the Headquarter Squadron, awarded April 1944.

Regimental Sergeant Major John Cowe, for operations in Greece, awarded 29 December 1945.

Lieutenant Reynolds, for operations in Italy, awarded April 1944.

Reverend Captain J P Hart, for actions throughout his commission.

Captain D C Davies, RAOC, for operations in Italy, awarded April 1944.

Captain E H Dromey, Quartermaster, for operations in Italy, awarded April 1944.

Captain F D Hall, Regimental Technical Adjutant, for operations in Italy, awarded

April 1944.
Squadron Sergeant-Major H G Price, Headquarter Squadron, for operations in Italy 1943/1944.

## MILITARY CROSS
Captain John C Bishop, Royal Army Medical Corps, for 23 October to 4 November 1942, Battle of Alamein. London Gazette 29 December 1942.
Lieutenant U E Bond, One Troop A Squadron, for 20/21 March 1943, Battle of Mareth. London Gazette 18 May 1943.
Lieutenant E H Grieve, B Squadron, for 29 November 1943, Mozzagrogna, Italy.
Captain E T W Jenkin, for 14-21 March 1943, Mareth operations. London Gazette 18 May 1943. Awarded Bar August 1945 for operations in Greece.
Lieutenant G Keohane, Eight Troop B Squadron, for 12/13 December 1943, Italy.
Captain B Lush, Royal Army Medical Corps, recommended for 30 November 1943, Romagnoli, Italy (Not Approved)
Lieutenant (acting Captain) G B Moss, for 12 July 1943, Palazzolo Sicily. London Gazette 19 October 1943.
Lieutenant C B G Nixon, Eight Troop B Squadron, for Akarit-Sfax, April 1943. London Gazette 20 July 1943.
Captain V J Senior, for operations in Tunisia March to April 1943, Ten Troop C Squadron and second in command of C Squadron, awarded Bar August 1945 for operations in Greece.
Major W S Styles, commanding A Squadron, recommended for 20-23 March 1943, Battle of Mareth (Not Approved)
Major D P Venn, commanding C Squadron for operations Akarit-Sfax, April 1943. London Gazette 20 July 1943.
Lieutenant M O Waddell, Headquarter Squadron, for 19 July 1943, Gerbini, Sicily. London Gazette 19 October 1943.
Major L F Williams, commanding C Squadron, for 23 October - 4 November 1942, Battle of Alamein. London Gazette 12 January 1943.
Lieutenant R L Willson, recommended for 30 November 1943, Fossacesia Italy (Not Approved)

## DISTINGUISHED CONDUCT MEDAL
Sergeant P A H Lewis, for 22-23 March 1943, Battle of Mareth. Original recommendation was for Military Medal. London Gazette 18 May 1943.

## MILITARY MEDAL
Trooper A A Baker, for actions in Greece December 1944 - January 1945. London Gazette 15 March 1945.
Sergeant E R Broad, recommended for 20-23 March 1943, Battle of Mareth (Not Approved)
Sergeant E Butcher, Eight Troop B Squadron, recommended for 19 December 1943, Ortona-Orsogna, Italy (Not Approved)
Lance Corporal C Connah, for 14 May 1944, Orsogna Italy. Original

recommendation was for the Distinquished Conduct Medal. London Gazette 21 September 1944.

Trooper E W Edwards, for actions in Greece 31st Dec 1944. London Gazette 10 May 1945.

Corporal L J Finch, A Squadron, for 19 July 1943, Gerbini, Sicily. London Gazette 19 October 1943.

Corporal J Flaherty, Regimental Headquarters, for 22 March 1943, Battle of Mareth. London Gazette 28 May 1943.

Trooper R Greenfield, Headquarter Squadron, recommended for 19 July 1943, Gerbini, Sicily (Not Approved)

Sergeant T Hunter, for 14 May 1944, Orsogna Italy. London Gazette 21 September 1944.

Corporal (acting sergeant) Victor Law, Royal Corps of Signals, For operations in the Western Desert, July 1942 - May 1943. London Gazette 12 December 1943.

Corporal D R Lewis, Headquarter Squadron, for 23/24 October 1942, Battle of Alamein. London Gazette 29 December 1942.

Corporal F Maplesden, C Squadron, for 13/14 July 1943, Francofonte, Sicily. London Gazette 19 October 1943.

Trooper S W J Midwinter, driver for RMO, for 23 October - 4 November 1942, Battle of Alamein. London Gazette 29 December 1942.

Sergeant S B Nash, Ten Troop C Squadron, for 21/23 March 1943, Battle of Mareth. London Gazette 28 May 1943.

Corporal G E Prett, One Troop A Squadron, for 20/21 March 1943, Battle of Mareth. London Gazette 28 May 1943.

Squadron Sergeant Major L T Stanton, Echelon, for 29 November 1943, River Sangro, Italy. London Gazette 6 April 1944.

Sergeant E G Taylor, A Squadron, for 30 November 1943, Romagnoli, Italy. London Gazette 6 April 1944.

Trooper K Watkin, driver for RMO, for 20/23 March 1943, Battle of Mareth. London Gazette 28 May 1943.

Trooper T M Wilson, Nine Troop C Squadron, for 23 December 1943, Villa Grande Italy. London Gazette 6 April 1944.

Sergeant W Woodcock, recommended for 23 December 1943, Italy (Not Approved) awarded for outstanding leadership October 1944 - Febuary 1945, Greece.

## BRITISH EMPIRE MEDAL

Trooper Donaldson, for operations in Greece Dec 1944 - Jan 1945.
SQMS J Murray, for operations in Greece Dec 1944 - Jan 1945.
Sergeant W D Neal, for operations in Greece Dec 1944 - Jan 1945.
Trooper K V Sheppard, A Squadron, for 29 November 1943, Italy, granted April 1944.

## MENTIONED IN DESPATCHES

Major W D Bazley, for Alamein October-November 1942.

Corporal F Boosey, for actions in Greece, 20 December 1945.
Trooper A Bowen, for 22 January 1944, Villa Grande Italy.
Lieutenant M Brooke, for 4 January 1945, Athens.
Sergeant E Butcher, for 19 December 1943, Ortona-Orsogna, Italy.
Corporal E R Burtenshaw, for actions in Italy, awarded 1 May 1944.
Trooper S Campbell, for 20-23 March 1943, Mareth (Not Approved)
Major G Chapman, Adjutant, recommended for Alamein (Not Approved), awarded for actions in Italy, 1 May 1944.
Quartermaster Sergeant R Corran, for actions in Greece, awarded December 1945.
Captain D C Davies RAOC, recommended for Alamein October-November 1942 (Not Approved)
Trooper Donnison, for 16 September 1943, near Paterno Sicily. (Not Approved)
Trooper D Ford, for actions in Italy, 1943-44.
Lieutenant Gardner, information unavailable.
Captain F D Hall, recommended for Alamein October/November 1942 (Not Approved)
Sergeant J W Hall, for actions in Greece, awarded 20 December 1945.
Reverend Captain J P Hart, for actions in the Western Desert 1942-43.
Corporal J E Hedley, C Squadron Medical Orderly, for actions in Greece 1944-45.
Corporal J Henly, A Echelon, awarded July 1943.
Lieutenant T J W Howard, for Alamein October-November 1942 and 20-23 March 1943, Mareth (both Not Approved)
Major A P Hughes, commanding B Squadron, recommended for 4 Sept 1942, Alam Halfa (Not Approved)
Lieutenant E T W Jenkin, recommended for Alamein October/November 1942 (Not Approved)
Trooper G L Lewis, Regimental Headquarters, recommended for 22 March 1943, Mareth (Not Approved)
Major J D Masters, Adjutant, for actions in Greece, awarded 20 December 1945.
Sergeant W L Mitchell, for actions in Italy, 1943/44.
Sergeant S B Nash, Ten Troop C Squadron, recommended for 23 October - 4 November 1942, Alamein. (Not Approved)
Lieutenant C B Nixon, for actions in Sicily July 1943.
Major H B O'Sullivan, for actions in Salamis, Greece 1944-45.
Lieutenant K J Pillar (posthumous) for 30 November 1943, Romagnoli Italy. Original recommendation was for the Victoria Cross.
SSM H G Price, recommended for Alamein October-November 1942 (Not Approved)
RQMS E Pyemont, information unavailable.
Lieutenant V J Senior, Ten Troop C Squadron, recommended for March 1943, Mareth. (Not Approved)
MQMS C J H Smith, for actions in Italy, awarded April 1944.
SSM L T Stanton, for actions in Italy, awarded 1 May 1944.
RQMS T Vaughen (Royal Army Ordnance Corps)

Major D P Venn, recommended for 20-23 March 1943, Mareth (Not Approved)
Lance Corporal G S Walker, for actions in Greece, awarded 20 December 1945.
SSM S Williams, for actions in Greece, awarded 20 December 1945.

## FOREIGN DECORATIONS

| | |
|---|---|
| Lieutenant Colonel J D Carlton | Greek Order of George I with Swords for services to Greece. |
| Major H B O'Sullivan | Greek Distinguished Service Medal. for actions on Salamis Island 1944-45 |

## BATTLE HONOURS

Of the Battle honours awarded to the Royal Tank Regiment in World War Two; 50 RTR took part in the following.

**DEFENCE OF THE ALAMEIN LINE** – Overall Honour for the period of the July 1942 fighting.

**ALAM EL HALFA** – Awarded to eight armoured, five Yeomanry and six infantry British Regiments. Two Australian and sixteen New Zealand Regiments.

**EL ALAMEIN** – Awarded to thirteen British armoured regiments and to sixty-one other British and Commonwealth regiments.

**MARETH** – Awarded to the Royal Tank Regiment, eleven British infantry regiments and one Gurka regiment.

**AKARIT** – Awarded to three British armoured, two Yeomanry and eleven infantry regiments, and six Indian regiments.

**NORTH AFRICA 1940-43** – Awarded to all regiments serving in the campaign.

**GERBINI** – Awarded to the Royal Tank Regiment and two infantry regiments.

**ADRANO** – Awarded to the Royal Tank Regiment and eleven British infantry regiments, two Canadian armoured and eight infantry regiments.

**SICILY 1943** – Campaign Honour.

**THE SANGRO** – Awarded to one British armoured regiment and to forty-five other British and Commonwealth regiments.

**ITALY 1943-45** – Campaign Honour.

# Annex C
# OFFICERS OF 50 RTR

All the following officers served with 50 RTR. The dates and ranks on joining or leaving the regiment are as recorded in the War Diary. As a number of officers were already serving with the regiment at the outbreak of war, their date of joining is not recorded, so the date 1 Sep 1939 is given. It is unfortunate that not all dates of joining or leaving the regiment are recorded. However, some officers a calculated estimate of arrival can be given. For sake of clarity these have been marked with an *.

(SA) denotes seconded from the South African Armoured Corps. All names have been supplied by the Royal Tank Regiment and members of 50 RTR.

| Name | From | To |
|---|---|---|
| Altheer A, Captain | | |
| Anderson, Captain RAMC | 1 Nov 1942 | Jan 1943 |
| Apted R, Second Lieutenant | 1 Sep 1939 | – |
| Arm V E, Lieutenant | 4 Jan 1940 | 23 Sep 1942 |
| Atkinson A G, Second Lieutenant | 23 Jan 1941 | Jan 1944 |
| | | |
| Bacon, Lieutenant | | |
| Ballantine J H D, Lieutenant | 11 Dec 1939 | – |
| Bartrum D L, Lieutenant | 16 Jan 1946 | Apr 1946 |
| Bayley A J, Second Lieutenant | 4 Jul 1940 | – |
| Bazley W D, Captain | 1 Sep 1939 | 15 Jun 1945 |
| Beaumont C B, Second Lieutenant | 5 Feb 1941 | – |
| Bell W W, Captain Padre | | |
| Beno H E, Second Lieutenant | | |
| Berthoud, Lieutenant | | |
| Bishop J C, Lieutenant RAMC | 1 Sep 1939 | 1 Nov 1942 |
| Bluett A P Q, Second Lieutenant | 6 Nov 1939 | 13 May 1940 |
| Bond U E, Lieutenant | Apr 1942 | 19 Jan 1946 |
| Bouverie-Brine J I, Captain | Mar 1943 | |
| Bowden J, Captain | | |
| Briggs G G, Second Lieutenant | 29 Nov 1939 | 20 Oct 1940 |
| reposted | 6 Apr 1941 | – |
| Brooke M, Lieutenant | | Apr 1946 |
| Brown H M, Lieutenant-Colonel C.O. | Sep 1939 | Nov 1940 |
| Brown I, Lieutenant | 1 Sep 1939 | Aug 1942 |
| Brown J A, Lieutenant | 13 Feb 1946 | 30 Apr 1946 |

| | | |
|---|---|---|
| Bumpass C H, Lieutenant  QM | 10 Sep 1942 | – |
| Burd K J, Lieutenant | 1 Sep 1939 | – |
| Burton D C, Lieutenant | 13 Feb 1946 | – 21 Apr 1946 |
| | | |
| Cairnes J E, Lieutenant-Colonel C.O. | Apr 1942 | - Mar 1943 |
| Carlton J K, Second Lieutenant | 7 Jul 1941 | – |
| Carlton J R D, Lieutenant-Colonel C.O. | Aug 1944 | - Feb 1946 |
| Carmicheal S G, Lieutenant | 5 Feb 1941 | – |
| Carr N, Second Lieutenant | 19 Aug 1940 | – 15 Jun 1941 |
| Carter P A, Second Lieutenant | 10 Feb 1940 | – 22 Mar 1943 |
| Champion S A, Captain | | |
| Chapman C H, Lieutenant | 13 Sep 1942 | – |
| Chapman G, Second Lieutenant | 23 Jan 1941 | – 11 Aug 1943 |
| Chapman J A, Second Lieutenant | * 7 Mar 1941 | – 1942 |
| Chidell R B, Lieutenant | 14 Sep 1943 | – Apr 1946 |
| Chilver N J, Second Lieutenant | 7 Mar 1941 | – 17 May 1941 |
| Collins J O, Major (later Lt-Col) C.O. | * 23 June 1943 | – 1945 |
| Conlin P F, Captain | * Aug 1944 | – Apr 1946 |
| Coombe R, Captain | | |
| Corns E N, Second Lieutenant | 19 Aug 1940 | – |
| Coulter P J, Second Lieutenant | 19 Aug 1940 | – |
| Crook P J, Second Lieutenant | 12 Sep 1942 | – 1 Apr 1943 |
| Curtoys C H D, Second Lieutenant | 13 Sep 1939 | – |
| Curtoys O F, Major | 1 Sep 1939 | – 23 Apr 1942 |
| | | |
| Davies D C, Lieutenant RAOC | 17 Oct 1941 | – |
| Davies R G, MC Captain | 1 Sep 1939 | – 1 Oct 1940 |
| Deane E F, Second Lieutenant | 23 Jan 1940 | – Aug 1942 |
| Dening P O G, Second Lieutenant | 14 Dec 1939 | – 2 Dec 1940 |
| Ditchfield E, Second Lieutenant | Aug 1942 | – |
| Dollar G P, Major | 19 Aug 1940 | – 1941 |
| Dromey E H, Lieutenant | | – 1945 |
| Duncan H E, Lieutenant-Colonel C.O. | Apr 1942 | - Apr 1942 |
| Dupont A H, Lieutenant | 12 Sep 1942 | – |
| Durnford P, Lieutenant | | |
| | | |
| Eley J L, Lieutenant | | |
| Ellis A R P, Captain RAMC | Jan 1943 | – 2 Sep 1943 |
| Egerton A P H, Lieutenant RAMC | 14 Jan 1940 | – Mar 1940 |
| Evans H S, Second Lieutenant | 1 Sep 1939 | – |
| | | |
| Fanning W G, Captain | 22 Oct 1939 | – Mar 1942 |
| Fanshaw, Major | | – Feb 1942 |
| Feinmann L, Captain  RAMC | Dec 1943 | – Dec 1945 |

| | | |
|---|---|---|
| Furness J H, Lieutenant | 18 Sep 1942 | – 1945 |
| | | |
| Gardiner A D L, Second Lieutenant | 5 Feb 1941 | – 1945 |
| Garrett R, Captain | | – Jan 1944 |
| Gibaud F C, Major | 1 Sep 1939 | – 25 Apr 1940 |
| Giles J F, Lieutenant | 1 Sep 1939 | – 1940 |
| Glashen I R, Lieutenant (SA) | | – 23 Sep 1945 |
| Godfrey-Thomas C S G, Captain  Padre | 7 Dec 1939 | – |
| Godwin H P, Second Lieutenant | 29 Nov 1939 | – Mar 1943 |
| Gordon R C J, Second Lieutenant | 1 Sep 1939 | – 23 May 1941 |
| Greive E H, Lieutenant | Sep 1942 | – 1946 |
| Grimble, Lieutenant | 16 Jan 1946 | – |
| | | |
| Hall F D, Second Lieutenant | 19 Aug 1940 | – 1945 |
| Hall J C, Lieutenant | | |
| Hallard M, Lieutenant | | |
| Hallowes K D, Lieutenant             * | Jun 1943 | – 1946 |
| Halse A J K, Second Lieutenant | 4 Jul 1940 | – 4 Sep 1942 |
| Hanley J, Second Lieutenant | 6 May 1941 | – 22 Jul 1942 |
| Hardy K, Lieutenant | | |
| Hart J P, Captain  Padre | 5 Apr 1941 | – Jan 1944 |
| Hayward H A, Lieutenant | | – 30 Apr 1946 |
| Hayward S D, Lieutenant-Colonel C.O. | Nov 1940 | - Apr 1942 |
| Hazzeledene R, Major | 1 Sep 1939 | – |
| Hearn, Second Lieutenant | 24 May 1941 | – |
| Hibbert E V, Second Lieutenant | 25 Sep 1942 | – |
| Hobbs G L, Second Lieutenant | 5 Feb 1940 | – 22 Jul 1942 |
| Holloway R D, Lieutenant    RAMC | 11 Dec 1939 | – 19 Dec 1939 |
| Hogarth J N, Second Lieutenant | 8 Feb 1941 | – 15 Jun 1941 |
| Hopkins, Lieutenant | | |
| Hopkinson G R, Major | Apr 1943 | – 9 May 1943 |
| Howard T J W, Second Lieutenant | 25 Sep 1942 | – Jan 1944 |
| Howe, Captain   REME | | |
| Hughes A P, Major | 25 Apr 1940 | – 4 Sep 1942 |
| Hunter A G, Lieutenant | | – Apr 1946 |
| Huth S M,  Lieutenant  from Sgt | May 1943 | – 1 Aug 1943 |
| Hynes L G, Lieutenant-Colonel C.O. | Mar 1946 | - Apr 1946 |
| | | |
| Inch C B R, Lieutenant | Mar 1943 | – 6 Apr 1943 |
| Ingham W, Captain | May 1943 | – |
| Inkson G C, Second Lieutenant | 5 Feb 1940 | – 17 May 1941 |
| Iossifoglu C H, Second Lieutenant | | |
| | | |
| Jackson C I A, Major | 16 May 1943 | – |

| | | |
|---|---|---|
| Jackson D C, Lieutenant | 24 Aug 1943 | – 12 Nov 1943 |
| James F W E, Lieutenant | 12 Sep 1942 | – |
| Jayne, Major | 27 Mar 1942 | – Apr 1942 |
| Jefferies J P, Captain  Padre | | |
| Jenkin E T W, Lieutenant | 5 Sep 1942 | – 1945 |
| Jenkin E T W, Major | Oct 1945 | - Dec 1945 |
| Jennings J, Captain | | – 4 Sep 1942 |
| Jolley H, Second Lieutenant | 5 Feb 1940 | – Dec 1940 |
| reposted: | 27 Apr 1941 | – Mar 1943 |
| Jones G G H, Second Lieutenant | 17 Sep 1941 | – |
| | | |
| Keane D M, Captain | May 1943 | – 24 Jan 1946 |
| Kennedy J A, Second Lieutenant | 6 May 1941 | – |
| Kenyon, Lieutenant  RAOC | 11 Oct 1940 | – |
| Keohane G, Lieutenant | Oct 1943 | – 19 Dec 1943 |
| Kepple F H G, Lieutenant | May 1943 | – 1945 |
| King L C, Second Lieutenant | 5 Feb 1940 | – |
| Kirby E R B, Second Lieutenant | 1 Sep 1939 | – 23 Mar 1940 |
| Knaggs W P R, Lieutenant | | – 23 Sep 1945 |
| Knight C H, Captain | 7 Sep 1939 | – 17 May 1940 |
| | | |
| Lamond L, Lieutenant | 1 Feb 1946 | – 30 Apr 1946 |
| Lascelles H A, Lieutenant-Colonel C.O. | Jan 1944 | - Apr 1944 |
| Lee J P, Second Lieutenant | 6 May 1941 | – 19 Sep 1942 |
| Lee Captain | * Oct 1944 | – 1946 |
| Leigh J B, Second Lieutenant | 7 Feb 1941 | – |
| Lewis D R, Lieutenant from Cpl | 1943 | – |
| Lewis, Lieutenant | May 1942 | – 25 Apr 1946 |
| Lindley G, Lieutenant | | – 14 May 1944 |
| Lowson, Lieutenant | 28 Jan 1946 | – |
| Lush B S, Lieutenant   RAMC | 2 Sep 1943 | – 9 Dec 1943 |
| | | |
| Macgregor I, Lieutenant | 14 Sep 1943 | – |
| Macgregor I C, Lieutenant | 14 Sep 1943 | – |
| Macgregor L, Lieutenant (SA) | | – 18 Dec 1943 |
| MacLaren G R A, Major | 19 Mar 1943 | – 24 Mar 1943 |
| Marks A D, Lieutenant | 13 Feb 1946 | – 30 Apr 1946 |
| Mason D J, Second Lieutenant | 25 Sep 1942 | – Oct 1942 |
| Masters J D, Lieutenant | * Jun 1943 | – 31 Jan 1946 |
| Mathers A G F, Captain | 1 Sep 1939 | – 17 Jul 1941 |
| Mellor P B J, Lieutenant | May 1943 | – 19 Jul 1943 |
| Mills J W, Second Lieutenant | 1 Sep 1939 | – 10 Aug 1940 |
| Mitchell E S, Lieutenant | | |
| Morrison M M, Lieutenant | | |

| | | |
|---|---|---|
| Moss G B, Second Lieutenant | May 1942 | – 25 Apr 1946 |
| Moyens I C, Major | 24 Jan 1946 | – Apr 1946 |
| Murray I A, Lieutenant | | – 12 Dec 1945 |
| | | |
| Nash S B, Lieutenant  from Sgt | Jul 1943 | – Apr 1946 |
| Neethling J H, Captain (SA) * | Aug 1944 | – 1946 |
| Newman H, Second Lieutenant | 1 Sep 1939 | – |
| Nixon C B G, Second Lieutenant | | – 17 July 1943 |
| | | |
| Oates J B, Lieutenant | | |
| Orbach J L, Second Lieutenant | 7 Feb 1941 | – Mar 1943 |
| O'Sullivan H B, Captain | Jan 1944 | – |
| | | |
| Parrot R E, Lieutenant | 13 Feb 1946 | – 21 Apr 1946 |
| Paton W A, Major | Mar 1943 | – 21 Apr 1943 |
| Penneck, Lieutenant | | |
| Pickard, Lieutenant | 28 Jan 1946 | – |
| Pillar K J, Lieutenant | | – 30 Nov 1943 |
| Pitt-Rivers, Second Lieutenant | 16 Aug 1941 | – |
| Price G E, Second Lieutenant | 5 Feb 1941 | – Jan 1944 |
| Pritchett K N, Second Lieutenant | | – 9 Dec 1943 |
| Pulline W V, Second Lieutenant | 29 Nov 1939 | – 19 Jun 1940 |
| | | |
| Reeves, Captain | | |
| Reed F N, Lieutenant | May 1943 | – 19 Jul 1943 |
| Reynolds, Lieutenant   QM | | |
| Richards B B, Captain | | |
| Robertson D, Lieutenant   QM | 8 Dec 1939 | – 13 Sep 1942 |
| Rothwell H, Captain   REME | | – Apr 1946 |
| Rooke H, Captain   Padre | | |
| Rushbrooke J, Second Lieutenant | 1941 | – Aug 1942 |
| Russell G E, Major | 23 Apr 1942 | – 15 Mar 1943 |
| reposted as Lieutenant-Colonel: | 24 Mar 1943 | – 29 Nov 1943 |
| | | |
| Sawrey-Cookson, Second Lieutenant | 16 Aug 1941 | – |
| Senior V J, Second Lieutenant | Sept 1942 | – Nov 1943 |
| reposted: | May 1944 | – 11 Jan 1946 |
| Sexton J G, Lieutenant | | |
| Scofield E W, Second Lieutenant | Aug 1942 | – |
| Scott E J, Major | | – 23 Aug 1945 |
| Sheppard H H, Lieutenant from Sgt | | |
| Simpkins L S, Captain | | |
| Sleeman J C, Major (later Lt-Col) C.O. | 12 Aug 1943 | - Jan 1944 |
| Smith L C, Second Lieutenant | 10 Mar 1941 | – 18 Aug 1942 |

| | | |
|---|---|---|
| Smith G H, Second Lieutenant | 24 May 1941 | – 27 Jul 1942 |
| Spence C J, Lieutenant | May 1943 | – 23 Dec 1943 |
| Stanton L T, Lieutenant | May 1943 | – |
| Stevens B, Captain | | |
| Stewart M, Second Lieutenant | 10 Aug 1941 | – |
| Strang, Lieutenant | Mar 1943 | – |
| Styles W S, Second Lieutenant | 5 Jul 1940 | – 3 May 1943 |
| Sutherland, Major | Jan 1944 | – |
| | | |
| Thomas E M, Lieutenant | | – 2 Jan 1945 |
| Thompson I C M, Second Lieutenant | 6 May 1941 | – 27 Jul 1942 |
| Thompson M S D, Second Lieutenant | 13 Jun 1941 | – |
| Thurgood H C C, Major | 1 Sep 1939 | – 27 Oct 1940 |
| Towner F A, Lieutenant | | |
| Troward T J, Second Lieutenant | 6 Nov 1939 | – 14 Feb 1940 |
| Tuft, Lieutenant | 18 Jan 1946 | – 24 Jan 1946 |
| Turpin H F, Second Lieutenant | 5 Feb 1941 | – |
| Tyler A D, Lieutenant from Sgt | Sep 1939 | – |
| | | |
| Van der Linde, Lieutenant (SA) | | |
| Venn D P, Second Lieutenant | 23 Jan 1941 | – 16 Jan 1944 |
| Vincent F G R, Captain | | – 21 Mar 1944 |
| | | |
| Waddell M O, Lieutenant | May 1943 | – 30 Apr 1946 |
| Walters C E, Second Lieutenant | 29 Nov 1939 | – |
| Ward E, Second Lieutenant | 1 Sep 1939 | – |
| Watson A R, Lieutenant | | |
| Weston E C K, Major | 1 Sep 1939 | – |
| Wilcox E W, Lieutenant | 24 Aug 1943 | – |
| Wilkinson, Lieutenant | 18 Jan 1946 | – |
| Williams L F, Second Lieutenant | 6 May 1941 | – |
| Willis A, Lieutenant | Oct 1944 | |
| Wills D D, Major | Jan 1944 | – |
| Willson R L, Lieutenant | May 1943 | – 11 Dec 1944 |
| Winton de R P, Major | 1 Sep 1939 | – 30 Jun 1941 |
| Wood G W, Lieutenant | | – 26 Oct 1942 |
| Wykes C, Second Lieutenant | 12 Sep 1942 | – 6 Apr 1943 |

# Annex D
# WOUNDED IN ACTION

All the following personnel were recorded as wounded in action, while serving with 50 RTR.

| | | |
|---|---|---|
| Armstrong | Trooper | 6 Aug 1943 |
| Atkinson A G | Lieutenant | 10/21 Jul 1943 |
| August F | Corporal | 19 Dec 1944 |
| Bailey H | Trooper | 10/21 Jul 1943 |
| Bagwell P | Trooper | 10/21 Jul 1943 |
| Bennett J | Trooper | 10/21 Jul 1943 |
| Bishop J C | RAMC Captain | 23 Oct/1 Nov 1942 |
| Bouverie-Brine J I | Captain | 21/23 Mar 1943 |
| Bond U E | Captain | 10/21 Jul 1943 |
| | again | 14 Apr 1944 |
| | again | 11 Dec 1944 |
| Bray | Sergeant | 22 Jul 1942 |
| Broad | Sergeant | 21 Apr 1943 |
| Brown I | Lieutenant | Aug 1942 |
| Carter P A | Major | 22 Mar 1943 |
| Campbell S | Trooper | 22 Mar 1943 |
| Chidell B | Lieutenant | 3 Nov 1943 |
| Cliff L | Sergeant | 23 Oct/1 Nov 1942 |
| Cockayne J | Squad Sgt Major | 22 Jul 1942 |
| Cole J W | Corporal | 13 Jul 1943 |
| | again | 3 Nov 1943 |
| Cook T | Trooper | 10/21 Jul 1943 |
| Coombe R | Corporal | 21/23 Mar 1943 |
| Cooper T | Trooper | 23 Oct/1 Nov 1942 |
| Edwards J T | Sergeant | 10/21 Jul 1943 |
| Ellis A R P | RAMC Captain | 22 Mar 1943 |
| Essex R W | Sergeant | 22 Jul 1942 |
| Evans D C | Trooper | 22 Jul 1942 |
| Dance L | Trooper | 10/21 Jul 1943 |
| Daniell R | Trooper | 21/23 Mar 1943 |
| Davies R | Trooper | 10/21 Jul 1943 |
| Donnison | Trooper | 16 Sep 1943 |

| | | |
|---|---|---|
| Dunsmore J S | Trooper | 23 Oct/1 Nov 1942 |
| Finch | Sergeant | 16 Sep 1943 |
| Flaherty J | Corporal | 22 Mar 1943 |
| Ford W | Trooper | 23 Oct/1 Nov 1942 |
| Frost F | Trooper | 23 Oct/1 Nov 1942 |
| Furnival A T | Trooper | 22 Mar 1943 |
| Gabe-Jones A R | Sergeant | 21/23 Mar 1943 |
| | again | 10/21 Jul 1943 |
| Gardiner A D L | Lieutenant | 23 Oct/1 Nov 1942 |
| Garratt R | Captain | 10/21 Jul 1943 |
| Glen G | Trooper | Oct 1942 |
| | again | 10 Dec 1943 |
| Godwin P | Lieutenant | 22 Mar 1943 |
| Gould A | Trooper | 12 Nov 1943 |
| Greatbanks L | Trooper | 22 Jul 1942 |
| Greenham D | Trooper | 22 Jul 1942 |
| Grieve E H | Lieutenant | 1 Aug 1943 |
| Griffin H G | Corporal | 21/23 Mar 1943 |
| Hartley W | Sergeant | 23 Oct/1 Nov 1942 |
| Hallowes K B | Lieutenant | 19 Dec 1944 |
| Henderson J | Trooper | 21/23 Mar 1943 |
| Hewitt S | Trooper | 21/23 Mar 1943 |
| Horn E I | Trooper | 10/21 Jul 1943 |
| Howard T J W | Lieutenant | 6 Apr 1943 |
| Howells | Trooper | 10/21 Jul 1943 |
| Hurn J | Trooper | 19 Dec 1943 |
| Jolley H | Captain | 22 Mar 1943 |
| Jordon F C | Trooper | 27 Feb 1943 |
| Kearse R | Trooper | 10/21 Jul 1943 |
| Keohane G | Lieutenant | 13 Dec 1943 |
| | again | 19 Dec 1943 |
| Kepple F | Lieutenant | 8 Aug 1943 |
| Killoran D | Trooper | 6 Apr 1943 |
| Laird R H | Trooper | 23 Oct/1 Nov 1942 |
| Leggett E | Trooper | 21/23 Mar 1943 |
| Leigh J | Trooper | 21/23 Mar 1943 |
| Lewis J | Corporal | 10/21 Jul 1943 |
| Lister J | Trooper | 10/21 Jul 1943 |
| Lowe J | Trooper | 19 Dec 1944 |
| Lush B | RAMC Captain | 9 Dec 1943 |
| Lyons | Trooper | 6 Aug 1943 |
| McGough | Corporal | 13 Jul 1943 |
| Mason D | Second Lieutenant | 23 Oct/1 Nov 1942 |
| Merriman | Corporal | 21 Apr 1943 |

| Name | Rank | Date |
|---|---|---|
| Midwinter S J | Trooper | 23 Oct/1 Nov 1942 |
| Milsom | Trooper | Aug 1942 |
| Mitchell F | Trooper | 22 Jul 1942 |
| Moms J | Trooper | 19 Dec 1943 |
| Morris G | Trooper | 21/23 Mar 1943 |
| Morrison M M | Lieutenant | 22 Mar 1943 |
| Neeve H | Trooper | 10/21 Jul 1943 |
| O'Leary T | Trooper | 23 Oct/1 Nov 1942 |
| Paton W A | Major | 21 Apr 1943 |
| Perrin A | Trooper | 21/23 Mar 1943 |
| Prett G E | Corporal | 21 Mar 1943 |
| Price G E | Captain | 15 Jul 1943 |
| Pritchard M | Trooper | 23 Oct/1 Nov 1942 |
| again | | 21/23 Mar 1943 |
| Roberts T | Trooper | 10/21 Jul 1943 |
| Russell G E | Lieutenant Colonel | 23 Oct 1942 |
| again | | 4 Nov 1943 |
| Scott E J | Major | 14 Apr 1944 |
| Schofield E W | Lieutenant | 22 Mar 1943 |
| Shreeve D | Sergeant | 17 Aug 1942 |
| Slack W | Trooper | 23 Oct/1 Nov 1942 |
| Smale J | Corporal | 21 Dec 1943 |
| Smith A | Lance Corporal | 22 Jul 1942 |
| again | | 23 Oct/1 Nov 1942 |
| Souter A G | Trooper | 21/23 Mar 1943 |
| Spence C J | Lieutenant | 22 Dec 1943 |
| Stacey C | Trooper | 10/21 Jul 1943 |
| Staines J | Trooper | 21/23 Mar 1943 |
| Steinman | RAMC Captain | 27 Dec 1944 |
| Strang E | Lieutenant | 6 Apr 1943 |
| again | | 20 Apr 1943 |
| Taylor S | Trooper | 21/23 Mar 1943 |
| Thomas E M | Lieutenant | 2 Jan 1945 |
| Thomas J | Sergeant | 21/23 Mar 1943 |
| Thompson | Trooper | 10/21 Jul 1943 |
| Tite H | Trooper | 22 Mar 1943 |
| Vaughen W | Trooper | 23 Oct/1 Nov 1942 |
| Venn D P | Major | 21 Jul 1943 |
| Walters C E | Captain | 22 Jul 1942 |
| again | | 6 Apr 1943 |
| Ward D G | Lance Corporal | 22 Jul 1942 |
| Watkin K E | Trooper | 22 Mar 1943 |
| Watson K | Corporal | 10/21 Jul 1943 |
| Wilcox | Lieutenant | 4 Nov 1943 |

| | | |
|---|---|---|
| Williams E R | Trooper | 20 Mar 1943 |
| Wills R | Trooper | 10/21 Jul 1943 |
| Wood G W | Lieutenant | 23 Oct/1 Nov 1942 |
| Worsfold R | Trooper | 22 Mar 1943 |

It is to be regretted that not all the wounded were recorded by name. During the later operations in Italy and Greece very few names of those wounded (51 and 62 respectively) were actually recorded. However the following figures and dates were:

| | |
|---|---|
| 2 injured 20 Jul 1942 | |
| 1 wounded 4 Sept 1942 | B Squadron |
| 1 wounded 6 Apr 1943 | C Squadron |
| 5 wounded 14 Jul 1943 | |
| 3 wounded 17 Jul 1943 | |
| 6 wounded 19 Jul 1943 | A Squadron |
| 4 wounded 1 Aug 1943 | |
| 2 wounded 4 Nov 1943 | |
| 1 wounded 29 Nov 1943 | A Squadron |
| 2 wounded 30 Nov 1943 | A Squadron |
| Several wounded 9 Dec 1943 | |
| Several wounded 14 Dec 1943 | |
| 4 wounded 19/20 Dec 1943 | |
| Several wounded 26 Dec 1943 | |
| 7 wounded 20 Apr 1944 | |
| Several wounded 6 Dec 1944 | |
| 2 wounded 9 Dec 1944 | |
| 3 wounded 15 Dec 1944 | |
| 11 wounded 19 Dec 1944 | B Squadron |
| 2 wounded 27 Dec 1944 | |
| 5 wounded 31 Dec 1944 | |
| 13 wounded 2 Jan 1945 | |
| 5 wounded 3 Jan 1945 | |

# Annex E
# MISSING IN ACTION

The following personnel were all reported missing in action while serving with 50 RTR. Only subsequent events and research revealed their fate.
(pow – prisoner of war; dpow – died while prisoner of war; kia – killed in action; rtu – returned to unit)

| NAME | SQUADRON (as recorded) | RANK | DATE OF ACTION | |
|---|---|---|---|---|
| Ayton C M | A | Sergeant | 27 Jul 1942 | pow |
| Beynon R | | Corporal | 27 Jul 1942 | pow |
| Bowery W E W | | Trooper | 27 Jul 1942 | |
| Bray H | B | Sergeant | 4 Sep 1942 | pow |
| Britton R D | A | Sergeant | 22 Jul 1942 | pow |
| Brown A | Recce | Trooper | 13 Jul 1943 | kia |
| Bryant L | | Trooper | 22 Jul 1942 | |
| Bull G S | B | Trooper | 22 Jul 1942 | pow |
| Bull R E | B | Corporal | 27 Jul 1942 | pow |
| Caola E V | | Trooper | 27 Jul 1942 | kia |
| Cockayne J | B | Squadron Sergeant-Major | 22 Jul 1942 | pow |
| Champlin T | B | Sergeant | 4 Sep 1942 | pow |
| Cheese J I | B | Sergeant | 4 Sep 1942 | kia |
| Choate F | | Trooper | 10/21 Jul 1942 | pow |
| Cresswell G | | Lance-Corporal | 27 Jul 1942 | kia |
| Criddle J W | | Corporal | 22 Jul 1942 | pow |
| Crowther G | Recce | Trooper | 13 Jul 1943 | kia |
| Dempster J | A | Corporal | 22 Jul 1942 | kia |
| Duckworth E R | | Trooper | 22 Jul 1942 | |
| Duffield G | B | Trooper | 22 Mar 1943 | pow |
| Dunkerley W | | Sergeant | 21/23 Mar 1943 | |
| Dunkley J | | Corporal | 22 Jul 1942 | dpow |
| Evans F | | Corporal | 22 Jul 1942 | pow |
| Evans F C | | Trooper | 22 Jul 1942 | pow |
| Gaskell | B | Trooper | 4 Sep 1942 | pow |

| | | | | |
|---|---|---|---|---|
| Gibbons | | Trooper | 27 Jul 1942 | |
| Godson | B | Corporal | 4 Sep 1942 | |
| Greatbanks L | B | Trooper | 4 Sep 1942 | pow |
| Greatbanks W | | Trooper | 22 Jul 1942 | pow |
| Greenham D | | Trooper | 22 Jul 1942 | pow |
| Guy E | | Corporal | 10/21 Jul 1942 | pow |
| Harding F V | B | Corporal | 4 Sep 1942 | kia |
| Harding T | B | Trooper | 4 Sep 1942 | pow |
| Hargreaves E | A | Trooper | 19 Jul 1943 | kia |
| Hodge C F | | Trooper | 27 Jul 1942 | pow |
| Hollingsworth E | | Trooper | 27 Jul 1942 | |
| Hore K | | Trooper | 27 Jul 1942 | pow |
| House A | | Lance-Sergeant | 22 Jul 1942 | pow |
| Hughes G | B | Trooper | 4 Sep 1942 | |
| Ingall C | | Trooper | 10/21 Jul 1943 | pow |
| Jackson | B | Trooper | 4 Sep 1942 | |
| James G | B | Lance-Corporal | 4 Sep 1942 | kia |
| Jennings J | B | Captain | 4 Sep 1942 | kia |
| Johnson F L | | Corporal | 27 Jul 1942 | kia |
| Johnson W | | Lance-Corporal | 22 Jul 1942 | pow |
| Kettlety I | | Trooper | 27 Jul 1942 | pow |
| Lineker A V | B | Trooper | 4 Sep 1942 | pow |
| McCullough B | A | Trooper | 19 Jul 1943 | kia |
| McGee | | Sergeant | 28 Dec 1944 | pow/rtu |
| Mellor P B R | A | Lieutenant | 19 Jul 1943 | kia |
| Murphy A D | A | Lance-Corporal | 22 Jul 1942 | dpow |
| Naish L H | B | Sergeant | 4 Sep 1942 | pow |
| Patefield N B | | Trooper | 22 Jul 1942 | dpow |
| Pickthall L | | Trooper | 27 Jul 1942 | dpow |
| Pugh E | | Lance-Corporal | 4 Sep 1942 | kia |
| Pye | B | Trooper | 4 Sep 1942 | pow |
| Riley J E | | Sergeant | 27 Jul 1942 | dpow |
| Sherratt W | | Trooper | 22 Jul 1942 | dpow |
| Shreeve D A | | Sergeant | 22 Jul 1942 | pow |
| Smith A Q | | Lance-Corporal | 27 Jul 1942 | dpow |
| Smith G F | | Second Lieutenant | 27 Jul 1942 | pow |
| Smith R | A | Trooper | 19 Jul 1943 | kia |
| Spencer M | | Trooper | 27 Jul 1942 | pow |
| Stabbins F R | B | Trooper | 4 Sep 1942 | kia |
| Stansfield L J | A | Sergeant | 19 Jul 1943 | kia |
| Stokoe G S | | Trooper | 10/21 Jul 1943 | pow |
| Stone W | | Trooper | 22 Jul 1942 | dpow |
| Summerfield | B | Lance-Corporal | 4 Sep 1942 | |

| | | | |
|---|---|---|---|
| Summers A | Sergeant | 27 Jul 1942 | rtu/dow |
| Thomas J | Trooper | 27 Jul 1942 | kia |
| Thompson I C M | Second Lieutenant | 27 Jul 1942 | kia |
| Thompson N | Trooper | 22 Jul 1942 | dpow |
| Ward J | Trooper | 21/23 Mar 1943 | pow |
| Williams G | Trooper | 22 Jul 1942 | pow |
| Williams W | Corporal | 10/21 Jul 1943 | pow |
| Wimpory | Trooper | 27 Jul 1942 | |
| Wynn G | Trooper | 22 Mar 1943 | pow |
| Youldon T | Trooper | 28 Dec 1944 | pow/rtu |

# Annex F
# THOSE WHO SERVED

During the research for this annex, it very soon became apparent that no full list, of those who served with 50 RTR exists. To obtain the list below I have had to rely on the following sources: War Diary; *TANK*; journal of the Royal Tank Regiment ex-members of 50 RTR; Regimental Museum Bovington; next of kin of former members of the regiment; and, of course, the men themselves. The men's employment, squadron (temporary attachment not included) and rank are as finally recorded in the War Diary and Official papers.

Despite intensive research on this annex, it seems unlikely that it will ever be completed, because the information simply does not exist. At the time of writing, I believe this list to be as accurate as it can be.

Abbess A H – Fitter Armoured Fighting Vehicle (AFV) – A Squadron
Abbott L W – Tank crew – C Squadron
Ablett F
Abraham G E
Abraham R C
Adams A W
Adams C C
Adams E – Tank crew – C Squadron
Adams J
Adams J – Tank crew – C Squadron – Sergeant
Adams S G – Tank crew – C Squadron – Sergeant
Addicott J
Adolph J – Tank crew – B Squadron
Ainsworth N – Tank crew – B Squadron
Akitt J H
Alcock
Alford E G – Tank crew – C Squadron – L/Corporal
Allan A F – Tank crew – Trooper
Allmond J
Ambrose H F – Tank crew – C Squadron – L/Corporal
Anderson B
Andrews E C
Annette W E – Tank crew
Anstey J
Anthony D – C Squadron
Armstrong J – C Squadron
Armstrong R – C Squadron
Armstrong W
Ashwell F – Tank crew – C Squadron – Trooper
Astle F – Fitter AFV – Headquarter (HQ) Squadron – Trooper
Atkinson J – Regimental Technical Adjutant (RTA)
Atkinson K
Atkinson W
Atthews E E
August F W – Tank crew – B Squadron – Sergeant

Axford H W – B Squadron
Ayton C M – Tank crew – B Squadron – Sergeant

Bagwell C – Tank crew – Regimental Headquarters (RHQ)
Bagwell P – C Squadron
Bailey C
Bailey H H – Tank crew – A Squadron – Trooper
Bailey F – B Squadron
Bairs M F – B Squadron
Baker A E – Tank crew – A Squadron – Trooper
Baker A A
Baker F S – C Squadron
Baker L
Baker R – Tank crew – RHQ – Trooper
Ballam A – C Squadron
Ballem E
Ballard J – C Squadron
Ballard L
Banks J
Banks L – Royal Corps of Signals – Signalman
Bannister C
Barrker T – C Squadron
Barker C
Barker W
Barlow A L
Barlow J – C Squadron
Barlow J – B Squadron
Barlow L – B Squadron
Barlow T
Barnes J
Barnes K
Barratt T – C Squadron
Barrett L – Tank crew – B Squadron
Barrow R
Bartlett T
Barton F H – B Squadron
Barton R F – RHQ
Batch J
Batt H A

Bayley R
Beale S
Beard S
Beardmore T
Beaumont A J – B Squadron
Beavan
Beck W – C Squadron
Beckett P J
Begleman J W – C Squadron
Begsby T
Bell A
Bell A H
Bennett A
Bennett E C B
Bennett I – B Squadron
Bennett J – C Squadron
Bennett W
Beresford F
Berry L
Berry F R – A & B Squadron
Bessell S R
Betson H – C Squadron
Bettison F
Bevan H – Despatch Rider – HQ Squadron – Trooper
Beynon R W
Billson F J – B Squadron
Binns D A – Tank crew – A Squadron – Trooper
Bircher K
Birks H N – B Squadron
Birnie J
Birrell
Bishop J – C Squadron
Blackburn R W – B Squadron
Blackshaw A – C Squadron
Blackshaw A J
Blagrove P – Tank crew – B Squadron – Sergeant
Blake N J
Blastland F
Blayne W C
Blundell R J – C Squadron
Board A J – 23 Armoured Brigade HQ

Bolton L – C Squadron
Boor G – Tank crew – C Squadron – Sergeant
Boosey F
Bott C
Bossons A
Bottle L – C Squadron
Bottomley J – C Squadron
Bourn R W – Tank crew – C Squadron – Sergeant
Bouverie R H
Bovey F G – Tank crew – A Squadron – L/Sergeant
Bowen A – C Squadron
Bowen G
Bowker W H – Trooper
Bown – 8th Armoured Division H Q
Bown A
Bowery W E W
Bowyer W – C Squadron
Boyd J G – C Squadron
Boyt J E – Tank crew – C Squadron – Corporal
Bradbury H
Bradford G
Bradford W
Bradley – Tank crew
Brannan J – C Squadron
Bray H T – B Squadron
Brealey V – C Squadron
Brennan S
Bridge T H
Brierley F
Brimley A A
Britton R D – Tank crew – B Squadron
Broad E
Brock J
Brookes J – C Squadron
Brookes W A H
Brookes W J
Brown A – Recce Troop – Corporal
Brown A E
Brown E
Brown F – C Squadron

Brown G – Echelon
Brown L – C Squadron
Brown L R
Brown S
Brown W P
Brumpton W M
Bryant C
Bryant J
Bryant L
Bryant R – 8th A D HQ
Bryant R W – B Squadron
Bryden F
Buckley F – C Squadron
Buckneal H
Budd M – B Echelon
Buddle A
Buffery R W – Administration (Admin) – B Echelon
Bull G S – Tank crew – B Squadron
Bull K – Tank crew – A Echelon & A Squadron – L/Sergeant
Bull R E – Tank crew – B Squadron
Burlison A
Burnell R W R
Burtenshaw E R – B Squadron
Burton J – C Squadron
Burton R
Butcher E – Tank crew – B Squadron – Sergeant
Butchers G – C Squadron
Butler A H
Butler F N
Butler L J – Tank crew – C Squadron – Trooper
Button C

Caie L A
Campbell S – Tank crew – RHQ
Cannard M – Trooper
Caola E V – Tank crew – Trooper
Caplan – Trooper
Carr J L
Casey K
Cassidy E – Tank crew – A Squadron –

Corporal
Casson K
Casson W
Caswell – Corporal
Catford G J – Trooper
Cawthorne S A – Tank crew – Squadron Sergeant Major (SSM)
Chamberlain A – C Squadron – Trooper
Chamberlain E
Chambers J
Champion T L – Sergeant
Chapman G – Sergeant
Chappel I – L/Corporal
Chappell L
Chard W – Fitter AFV – A Echelon – Corporal
Charity C C – C Squadron – Trooper
Charlton C – Recce Troop – Trooper
Cheese J I – Tank crew – B Squadron – Sergeant
Cheney W H – Corporal
Chick N – C Squadron – Sergeant
Chiddy J – SSM
Childs S G – Trooper
Christie J – C Squadron – L/Corporal
Clapp A J – Tank crew – B Squadron – Corporal
Clapp S G – C Squadron – Trooper
Clare J – Corporal
Claridge A E – B Squadron – Trooper
Clark L – Storeman – RTA – Trooper
Clark R – C Squadron – Trooper
Clarke W T – SSM
Clayton J – Tank crew – B Squadron – L/Corporal
Cleary W H
Clements W G
Cliff L – Recce Troop – Sergeant
Clifford P – Tank Crew – A & C Squadron – L/Corporal
Clifton – Tank crew – B Squadron – Trooper
Clinch M L
Clegg J – Tank Crew – A Squadron

Clough L – C Squadron – Trooper
Coady D J – Trooper
Coady E J
Cobley L – L/Corporal
Cockayne J – Tank crew – B Squadron – SSM
Cohen M – Royal Corps of Signals – Signalman
Cohen S
Coke K
Cole F W
Cole J W – C Squadron – Sergeant
Cole R
Cole T – Sergeant
Coles K
Collard J
Collie A – RHQ & C Squadron – Trooper
Collins – Corporal
Collins C R – B Squadron – Corporal
Connah C – L/Corporal
Connings E E
Connor J – B Squadron
Cook E G
Cook L B – A Squadron – L/Corporal
Cook R
Cook T E – Tank crew – C Squadron – Trooper
Cooke N H
Coombe J – Corporal
Coombe R
Cooper G
Cooper T C – Tank crew – RHQ & B Squadron – L/Corporal
Cornes D H
Corran R – Quartermaster – HQ Squadron & RTA
Cossens L H
Cotgrove T H – B Squadron – Sergeant
Cottle E D
Cottrill P R
Couch D J
Coupe J – C Squadron & RTA – Trooper
Coutts J K – Royal Electrical & Mechanical Engineers (REME) –

S/Sgt
Cowap W T – L/Corporal
Cowe J – Regimental Sergeant Major (RSM)
Cowell E – Tank Crew – C Squadron – Trooper
Cowen R – Warrant Officer Class II (WOII) – B Echelon
Cox G – C Squadron – Trooper
Cox J S
Cox L G
Cox R
Cox R G
Coyle R D
Crane G S – B Squadron
Creasey E C – Tank crew – Sergeant
Cresswell G E – Tank crew – L/Corporal
Crew C A – C Squadron – Trooper
Criddle J – Tank Crew – B Squadron – Corporal
Cridland E – C Squadron – Trooper
Crisp J – Tank crew – B Squadron – Trooper
Crompton – SSM
Cromwell J
Crone R
Cronshaw H – Royal Army Ordnance Corps (RAOC) – Private
Crowther G – Recce Troop – Trooper
Cuell H C
Culling C – C Squadron – Trooper
Cunniff P – B Squadron
Curtis W – Echelon – Trooper
Cutting J

Dale R
Daley P – B Squadron
Dalton R
Dance L – C Squadron – Trooper
Daniel R
Darby – RTA – Trooper
Davenport R L – B Squadron
Davies F G
Davies K W – L/Corporal

Davies S E
Davis C J – A Squadrons A Echelon – Trooper
Davis E R W – C Squadron – Trooper
Davis R – B Squadron
Daw L G – Driver A Squadron Fitters
Deacon R D – C Squadron – Trooper
Deane F – C Squadron
Deane R N – Trooper
De Marco A J – RTA – Corporal
Dempster J J – A Squadron – Corporal
Dennis W – Sergeant
Derrick – Trooper
Dickenson H
Dicks R
Diment W – Corporal
Dinsdale S – B Squadron
Dix A L – C Squadron – Trooper
Dix F C – C Squadron – Trooper
Dix R E – C Squadron – Trooper
Dobb C
Donaldson – Trooper
Donnison S – Trooper
Doran V – C Squadron – Trooper
Dorras H – Tank crew – C Squadron – Trooper
Dougan J
Douglas B F – Corporal
Douglas J
Douglas T M – B Squadron – Sergeant
Dowie J H – C Squadron – Trooper
Drew C – Driver – Echelon – Trooper
Drew H – Tank crew – C Squadron – Trooper
Drywood G
Duckworth E R – Tank crew – B Squadron – Trooper
Duffield G – Tank crew – A Squadron – Trooper
Duffield R H
Duncan G
Dunkerly – Tank crew – Sergeant
Dunkley J W – Tank crew – Corporal
Dunn A

Dunn A N – L/Corporal
Dunsmore J S – Tank crew – Trooper
Dunstan W – C Squadron – Trooper
Durnford R

Edge A
Edge G – B Squadron – SSM
Edgely E H – Corporal
Edwards E W – Tank crew – C Squadron – L/Sergeant
Edwards G J – Tank crew – B Squadron – L/Corporal
Edwards I T – Sergeant
Ellery F O – Tank crew – A Squadron – Sergeant
Elliot J – C Squadron – Trooper
Elliot J C
Ellis E – L/Corporal
Emblen A T – L/Corporal
Emms H – RAOC – Private
Enfield J – Corporal
England G A – B Squadron – Corporal
Epstein C M – Tank crew – C Squadron – Trooper
Essex R W – Tank crew – B Squadron – Sergeant
Evans C
Evans D C – Trooper
Evans F – Echelon – Trooper
Evans F C – Trooper
Evans G L – C Squadron – Sergeant
Evans H – Sergeant
Evans J – Tank crew – C Squadron – L/Corporal
Evans L W – Corporal
Evans S – C Squadron – Trooper
Evans W H

Fardon W C
Farrell M F – Corporal
Farrelly C
Farrimond A E – Corporal
Faulkner F – Corporal
Faulkner W G – B Squadron

Ferris F A – Royal Army Catering Corps (RACC) – Private
Field E – C Squadron – Trooper
Fielden H – Trooper
Fildes
Finch L J – Tank crew – Sergeant
Fisher L A – Corporal
Fisher R
Flaherty J – Tank crew – RHQ – Sergeant
Fleming R – C Squadron
Fletcher J E
Fletcher J S
Ford D J – B Squadron
Ford W G L – Trooper
Francis J R – B Squadron
Frederick N T
Freer W H – A Squadron – Trooper
French A J – Sergeant
French J – Tank crew – B Squadron – Sergeant
Fricker C T R – L/Corporal
Frost F L – Trooper
Fuller H – Sergeant
Fuller P I – C Squadron – Trooper
Furnival A T – Tank crew – RHQ – Corporal
Furnival J – L/Corporal

Gabe-Jones A R – Tank crew – A Squadron – Sergeant
Gapper D C – C Squadron – Trooper
Garde – Sergeant
Gardiner A – C Squadron
Gardner H – B Squadron – Trooper
Gardner J – C Squadron – L/Corporal
Garland L W – Echelon – Corporal
Gartshore J
Garvie R
Gaskell G – B Squadron – Trooper
Gaskell J F
Gaunt J J – B Squadron – Corporal
Gauntlett L – C Squadron – Trooper
Gavin E R – Tank crew – RHQ – Trooper
Gazzard G

Gee E E B – Tank crew – C Squadron – Trooper
Gentry A G – B Squadron – Sergeant
George J J
Gibberd J P – Tank crew – B & C Squadron – Trooper
Gibbons F – L/Corporal
Gibbons K
Gibson L
Gilbert T
Gill A W
Gill C L – Recce Troop – Trooper
Gill I
Gillespie R
Gillmore D W
Glancey S – B Squadron
Glen G – C Squadron – Trooper
Goddard S F – L/Corporal
Godfrey H G – L/Corporal
Gold J
Goodall D
Goodall H F
Gooder C
Goodman J
Goodyer J – RCS – Signalman
Gorman L G
Gosden – B Squadron
Gough C
Gould A P – Recce Troop – Trooper
Gowan G W – Sergeant
Graham R – Fitter – A Echelon – Trooper
Grant J B
Gray Donald
Grayley J R – Echelon
Greatbanks L – Tank crew – B Squadron – Trooper
Greatbanks W – Tank crew – B Squadron – Trooper
Greaves J – A and HQ Squadron
Green J W – Echelon
Greenaway W A – Sergeant
Greenfield R – Recce Troop – Trooper
Greenham D A – Tank crew – B Squadron
Greenham
Greenhough D – L/Corporal
Greenwood H
Greenwood J – C Squadron – Trooper
Greet N – C Squadron – Corporal
Gregory R W
Gregson H
Greyhouse A
Griffin H G – Corporal
Griffiths A H
Griggs R P – B Squadron – Corporal
Grimes – Sergeant
Grimley – L/Corporal
Groombridge
Guy E

Haddrell W E – SQMS

Hadley E – C Squadron – L/Sergeant
Haft H – Tank crew – C Squadron – Trooper
Haggar A
Hague C – Echelon – Sergeant
Haigh F – RCS – Signalman
Hall A
Hall F – RCS – Signalman
Hall J W – Sergeant
Hall W
Hallmark H J – Tank crew – A Squadron – Trooper
Halsey F – C Squadron – Trooper
Hamblin D A – Tank crew – B Squadron – Sergeant
Hames R
Hammersley J – Corporal
Hammond A
Hammond A G
Hammond T H
Hampson E G
Hancock G J – Corporal
Hancock H – REME – Private
Hancox S
Handley P
Hannaford E – C Squadron – Trooper

Hannon G J – Tank crew – C Squadron – Trooper
Hardacre K H – B Squadron
Harding F
Harding F V – Tank crew – B Squadron – Corporal
Harding K L
Harding R – B Squadron – L/Corporal
Harding R
Harding T R – B Squadron – Trooper
Hardman V
Hargreaves E – Tank crew – A Squadron – Trooper
Hargreaves J – C Squadron
Hargreaves J C
Harris A W G – C Squadron – Trooper
Harrison H – B Squadron – Corporal
Harrison N
Hart E R M – Quartermaster – RTA
Hart J – Intelligence Sergeant
Hartland E T
Hartley W – Tank crew – Sergeant
Harvey F E – A Squadron – Trooper
Harwood M – Corporal
Hatherall I J
Haugh F J – B Squadron
Hawkins F H
Hayes A
Head R A
Hebington P
Hedley J E – Medic – C Squadron – L/Corporal
Heesom S – Tank crew – C Squadron – Trooper
Helliwell C A
Henderson J
Hendy S
Henley J H T – A Squadron A Echelon – Sergeant
Heppell J H – C Squadron
Hergest J H
Hewins R E – Recce Troop – Sergeant
Hewins N H
Hewitt S

Hexton W
Heywood A L – Corporal
Heywood G
Hicks W J – L/Corporal
Higgs S
Higham A
Hill D C – RCS – Signalman
Hill R – Tank crew – RHQ
Hillier N M – Tank crew – RHQ – Corporal
Hillyer L
Hindmarsh E
Hird L W – C Squadron – Trooper
Hoare – B Squadron – Sergeant
Hobbs R – Trooper
Hodder E – C Squadron – Trooper
Hodder L W
Hodge A G – B Squadron – Trooper
Hodge J
Hodgeson H – RHQ
Holder A J – Tank crew – B Squadron – Trooper
Holland A L – Clerk – B Squadron Echelon – Corporal
Hollands F – RCS – Signalman
Holliday
Hollings F C
Hollingsworth E – Trooper
Holman T – C Squadron – Corporal
Holman T J – Corporal
Holme R
Holmes W
Hookway S L – Tank crew – A Squadron & RTA – SQMS
Hooton P R – Tank crew – C Squadron – Trooper
Hopkins E R
Hore K – Trooper
Horn E E
Horn J
Horn J H – B Squadron – Corporal
Horsby C W
Horsmann – Trooper
Horton F J

Horton G – B Squadron
Hoskins J – C Squadron – Trooper
Hough W F – Recce Troop – Trooper
Houseman A J
Houseman H G
Houseman J
Howarth H – Trooper
Howarth P – Trooper
Howden L
Howe F – Corporal
Howell W G – C Squadron – Trooper
Howells R – C Squadron – L/Corporal
Howes C
Howes W J – B Squadron
Hoyland R W
Hudson W G – C Squadron – Trooper
Hughes E
Hughes G – B Squadron – Trooper
Hughes T – C Squadron – Trooper
Hughes T P
Hughes W E
Hughes W L
Hum A
Humphrey J E – Staff Sergeant
Humphries J
Hunt A – L/Corporal
Hunter F – Trooper
Hunter T – Tank crew – SSM
Hurn J – Tank crew – B Squadron
Hyde A E – B Squadron – L/Corporal

Isam H M – C Squadron – Trooper

Jackson B R
Jackson H – L/Sergeant
Jackson H
Jackson I M – C Squadron – L/Corporal
Jackson J P –Tank crew – C Squadron – Trooper
Jackson T
Jackson T H
Jackson W G – C Squadron – Trooper
James D W
James G H – B Squadron – L/Corporal

James S
Jamison J – A Squadron – Trooper
Jefferies C A – Trooper
Jefferies K – Trooper
Jenkins C R
Jenkins N
Jenkins P T
Jenner H – C Squadron – Corporal
Jenner R – C Squadron & RTA
Jennings H G – B Squadron
Jewell – Trooper
John G – C Squadron – Trooper
Johnson F L – HQ Squadron – Corporal
Johnson K L – L/Corporal
Johnson L – Trooper
Johnson W
Johnson W – L/Corporal
Johnstone A – C Squadron – Trooper
Johnstone J – RCS – Private
Jolley A K
Jones A R – L/Corporal
Jones C E – Trooper
Jones C G – REME – Private
Jones C R – A Squadron – L/Corporal
Jones D – RAOC – C Squadron – Private
Jones D – Corporal
Jones D J – L/Corporal
Jones E T S –Tank crew – B Squadron – Sergeant
Jones F A B – C Squadron – L/Corporal
Jones G F
Jones H H – Trooper
Jones J G – REME – Private
Jones J K – C Squadron – Corporal
Jones S – SSM
Jones T E
Jordan F C – Sergeant
Joyce F R – Tank crew – C Squadron – Sergeant

Kane P – Sergeant
Kearns R
Kearse R
Kearsley R K – B Squadron – Trooper

Keepin – Driver – Echelon – Trooper
Keily E W – L/Sergeant
Kennedy G E – B Squadron
Kenny T
Kent R D – B Squadron
Kerr A
Kerr G – C Squadron – Corporal
Kettlety I – Trooper
Kew H S – C Squadron – Sergeant
Killoran D M – C Squadron – Corporal
King W – A Squadron
King W J – HQ & C Squadron – L/Sergeant
Kingscott F W – C Squadron – Trooper
Kingscott R
Kirkwood D – C Squadron – Trooper
Knight G – Trooper
Knowles E – C Squadron – Trooper
Knowles R
Knowles R
Knox W – Medical Orderly – B Squadron – Sergeant

Laird R H – L/Corporal
Lambert H W – Tank crew – B Squadron – Trooper
Lambourne W
Lane A – REME – Private
Lane D – Trooper
Laney G A – B Squadron
Lansdown F T – C Squadron – Trooper
Langford G H
Langley – Trooper
Larkin J – Sergeant
Larvin J
Larway K – B Squadron – Trooper
Lavin E
Law V – RCS – Sergeant
Lawrence G G – B Squadron – L/Sergeant
Lawton A C
Layton J E – L/Corporal
Lea T H
Leah G – Corporal

Leaman S C C
Leaworthy S D
Lee H J – Corporal
Lee P E
Lee S
Leech H
Leeks C
Leggett J K F – Corporal
Leight – L/Corporal
Lemon F
Lever T
Levett E – Trooper
Levy L – REME – Private
Levy G
Lewing B – Corporal
Lewis A C
Lewis A C – C Squadron – Trooper
Lewis H H – RTA – Corporal
Lewis J E P – Tank crew – C Squadron – Corporal
Lewis G E – Sergeant
Lewis P A H – SSM
Lewis R N – Trooper
Lidgely D B – A Squadron – Corporal
Linaker A – Tank crew – B Squadron – Trooper
Lincoln G
Lister J – C Squadron – Trooper
Litten M R – Tank crew – RHQ – Trooper
Littlewood D – Echelon – Trooper
Lloyd D C
Lloyd J – B Squadron
Loaper – Trooper
Long H
Lovall J
Lovall P – Sergeant
Lowe J – Tank crew – B Squadron L/Corporal
Lucas K E – Corporal
Ludlam G – B Squadron
Ludlow E F – HQ Squadron
Luther C M

McArthur R – Trooper

McBlane J
McLoud L
McCullough B – Tank crew – A Squadron – Trooper
McDermott E N
McDonald A
McDonald W – A Squadron – Trooper
McDougall J – RTA – Trooper
McEwan J
McGough
McGuinness R
McKee J A
McLaren J C
McManus E N
McNaught E V – Tank crew – Sergeant
Mackintosh J G – Tank crew – A Squadron – Trooper
Mackman A F – L/Corporal
Madelin
Maggo – Echelon – Trooper
Maggs R – RHQ – Trooper
Malkin A E
Malley W J – C Squadron – Trooper
Maloney T – Sergeant
Manders J I – A Squadron – Trooper
Mansfield B
Manwaring–White E R – Tank crew – B Squadron – Trooper
Maplesden F – Tank crew – C Squadron – Sergeant
Markham G
Marquand F D – Fitter – C Squadron – Corporal
Marsh H – C Squadron – L/Corporal
Marshall J R N – C Squadron – Trooper
Marsland J
Martin A D
Martin H – RAOC – Private
Martin J
Maslen H J – C Squadron – Trooper
Mason F G
Massey J D – B Squadron
Matthews C T
Matthews G – C Squadron – Trooper

Mattock H W C – Recce Troop – Corporal
Mayers E A
Mayhew J – Tank Crew – A Squadron
Mee H A
Meers F F
Mendoza A
Menzies G B – RSM
Meredith G D
Merriman G – B Squadron – Corporal
Midwinter S W J – MO driver – Trooper
Milkins – Sergeant
Millard R J – SSM
Miller A C
Miller A D
Millington W – A Echelon – SSM
Mills B – C Squadron – Trooper
Mills H – Corporal
Milsom G – Tank crew – Trooper
Minett J M – C Squadron – Trooper
Mitchell F E – B Squadron & RTA
Mitchell W L – C Squadron – Sergeant
Moakes R
Moms G – Tank crew – B Squadron – Trooper
Moon J R H – HQ Squadron – Corporal
Moore J G – L/Corporal
Moran J A F
Moran P A
Moreton A L – C Squadron & B Echelon – Trooper
Morgan A E
Morgan R H
Morley J T – A Squadron
Morris E H J
Morris F M
Morris G – B Squadron
Morris N T – RTA – Trooper
Morrison – SQMS
Morse R – RAOC/C Squadron – Private
Moseley C – L/Corporal
Moseley W – C Squadron – Sergeant
Moss F W
Moss W – C Squadron – Trooper

Mossman A
Moyse G – RAOC – Private
Mullen P
Mulroy T W
Murphy A D – Tank crew – B Squadron – L/Corporal
Murray J – Echelon – SQMS
Murray P – C Squadron – Trooper
Murray P
Murray
Myatt P

Naish L H – B Squadron – Sergeant
Neal W D – C Squadron & RTA – Sergeant
Neall K W – Corporal
Neeve H – Trooper
Negri P – L/Corporal
Newbury F – C Squadron – Trooper
Newman E J – Sergeant
Newman C S – Tank crew – RHQ – Corporal
Newns N K – Tank crew – C Squadron – L/Corporal
Nicholas W J – Tank crew – B Squadron – Trooper
Nicholls S
Nicholson J – C Squadron – Trooper
Nicholson – RCS – Signalman
Norrish K
Northover J P – Sergeant
Northrop J
Norton F – L/Corporal
Norton J – Tank crew – C Squadron – Trooper

Oakes H – Tank crew – B Squadron – Sergeant
O'Brian A
O'Hara – Sergeant
O'Keefe
O'Leary T J – B Squadron
Oliver M J – RAOC – Private
Openshaw M – C Squadron – Trooper

Oram A P – A Squadron – Trooper
Ormrod H L
Osborne R D – B & C Squadron – Trooper
Osbourne S – C Squadron – Trooper
Owen A – C Squadron – Trooper
Owens A – Corporal

Page P N
Paige L
Palmer L C – Fitter – A Squadron
Palmer R A – L/Corporal
Parker B W
Parker J
Parker P A
Parkhurst E L
Parkin T
Parkins – L/Corporal
Parkinson A
Parkinson P – C Squadron – L/Corporal
Parry – REME – Private
Parslow E N
Pascoe T
Patefield N B – Tank crew – Trooper
Patrick J – L/Corporal
Patterson W H
Patton H B – L/Corporal
Paull H – B Squadron – Trooper
Pawson J W
Payne R E
Pearce H W – C Squadron – Trooper
Pearce J – B Squadron – Sergeant
Pearce R C
Pearce T V – Trooper
Pearson J
Pengelly – Tank crew – Trooper
Penney F G – A Squadron
Penton R
Pepworth J
Percival E V – Tank crew – C Squadron – Trooper
Perigrene G H – Corporal
Perkins E V – Sergeant
Perkins J – Corporal

Perrin A
Perry A – Sergeant
Perry D H
Perry S N – RTA – Trooper
Phillips A – Fitter – Trooper
Phillips A J
Phillpott – Corporal
Pickersgill S – C Squadron – Trooper
Pickthall L – Trooper
Pike J H
Pillinger H – B Squadron – Sergeant
Pimm F R – Tank crew – C Squadron – Trooper
Pine S – L/Corporal
Pinnegar R W
Pitt T A
Pitwell A – L/Corporal
Plant B – C Squadron – Trooper
Plant C – C Squadron – L/Corporal
Poole G
Pople E W – Trooper
Porter A G – C Squadron – Trooper
Porter R
Portingale R – RQMS
Potkins A W
Poulter E
Poultney V – RAOC/C Squadron – Private
Poustie A
Powell H – Corporal
Powell J
Powell R D
Powell W G
Pratt E – Corporal
Pratt H
Preston G – C Squadron – Trooper
Prett G E – Tank crew – A Squadron – Corporal
Price H C – RQMS
Price L C – RACC – Sergeant
Pritchard M N – B & C Squadron – Trooper
Proctor D
Proctor D Y

Prodger J E – B Squadron
Prosser – Sgt
Proud N
Puddick F E – L/Sergeant
Pugh E – Tank crew – B Squadron – L/Corporal
Pugh J
Pulling J
Pye W E J
Pyemont E – QMS – Echelon
Pymer – Corporal

Quarmley P
Quirk T – C Squadron – Corporal

Rabson W H – RSM
Randell J
Randell S – Echelon – SQMS
Rawlins E A
Raybould H
Raynor R E
Raynes C – C Squadron – Trooper
Rea – Trooper
Reed A
Rees D – C Squadron – Sergeant
Rees R – C Squadron – Trooper
Reid J – L/Corporal
Rendell – Echelon – Trooper
Reynolds W – RTA & A Echelon – Trooper
Richards B B
Richards D S – Corporal
Ricketts S – B & C Squadrons – Corporal
Ridge H
Riley J E – B Squadron – Sergeant
Rimmer A W – B Squadron
Rimmer J – RTA – Corporal
Rippen S – Trooper
Risdale H F – Trooper
Roache J
Roberts A
Roberts B – Corporal
Roberts B
Roberts G W

Roberts O B
Roberts T
Roberts T
Roberts T H – B Squadron – Trooper
Robertshaw A
Robins K I – Tank crew – RHQ – Trooper
Robinson A – C Squadron – Trooper
Robinson A
Robinson G
Robinson G W – A Squadron – Corporal
Robinson H – C Squadron – Trooper
Robinson P F
Robinson W F
Rochford H
Rodger J – Tank crew – B Squadron – Trooper
Rogers L
Ronson G J
Roper B
Rosekilly G H – C Squadron – Trooper
Rosen A G
Rosen S
Ross N L
Rossiter W J – L/Corporal
Rowe S – Trooper
Rowe T – RTA – QMS
Rowland C – C Squadron – Trooper
Rowlands H T
Rowlance E I
Rudd A – B Squadron
Rudd N R – Trooper
Rudman S J – B Squadron – SQMS
Ruffle A R – B Squadron – Trooper
Russell V A – Tank crew – RHQ – Corporal
Rugman R
Ryan S E – Corporal
Ryan F G
Ryan G
Ryan J
Ryhmes L J – L/Corporal

Salmon – Trooper
Sambells E I – Barber – B Echelon – Trooper
Sandell J H
Sandy C
Sandy F P – C Squadron – Trooper
Sanigar D
Sarginson R M – Tank crew – B Squadron – L/Corporal
Sarsfield T P – Sergeant
Saulters H
Saunders A T – A Squadron – Corporal
Sawyer A L
Sawyer S – Batman to Col Cairnes – Trooper
Scantelebury B – L/Sergeant
Scarland D R
Schafer C J – Corporal
Schofield G – B Squadron – L/Corporal
Scholfield H – RCS – Signalman
Scotcher G A – C & HQ Squadron
Scotchford L – L/Corporal
Scott J
Scourfield C – A Squadron – Trooper
Scully P
Seaborn R V – B Squadron
Selby G
Sellars G – C Squadron – Trooper
Settle – Trooper
Sewell W – C Squadron – Sergeant
Saxton – Sergeant
Shackwell H – Sergeant
Shapcott A E C – B Squadron – Sergeant
Sharkey C – Sergeant
Shaw – Echelon – SQMS
Shaw G A – B Squadron
Shaw J – RTA – Trooper
Shaw P A
Shepherd J H – C Squadron – Corporal
Shepherd R – RACC – Private
Sheppard K V – C Squadron – Trooper
Sheppard T – A Squadron – Sergeant
Sherrett W – Trooper
Shillcross G W – Tank crew – C Squadron – Trooper
Shopland E G

Shorten H
Shreeve D – Tank crew – B Squadron – Sergeant
Simmonds C – Trooper
Simons F L
Sims G
Sinclair D – C Squadron – Trooper
Skidmore E – C Squadron – Corporal
Skillcorn W K – Tank crew – C Squadron – Trooper
Skinner F
Slach R – Tank crew – B Squadron – Trooper
Slade A – C Squadron – Corporal
Slade W E
Slaney – Corporal
Slater P W
Slee G – Sergeant
Smale W J – Tank crew – B & C Squadron – Corporal
Smalley H – C Squadron – Trooper
Smalley J – C Squadron – Trooper
Smallman E R – Tank crew – B Squadron – Corporal
Smith A – RSM
Smith A – B Squadron
Smith A
Smith A – L/Corporal
Smith A
Smith A J – C Squadron – L/Corporal
Smith C J H – Echelon – QMS
Smith D
Smith E B – L/Corporal
Smith F J
Smith F L – Sergeant
Smith G – Corporal
Smith H
Smith H
Smith H E
Smith J E
Smith J C
Smith L
Smith R
Smith R – C Squadron – Corporal
Smith R – A Squadron – Trooper
Smith R
Smith R D – Corporal
Snape J – Clerk – B Echelon – Corporal
Snape V – C Squadron – SSM
Snow D – Trooper
Soper J
Souter A
Southern T
Southernland A
Southwood C – L/Corporal
Sparrow W
Spellman J E – B Squadron
Spiers D – Tank crew – B Squadron
Spiers F
Spiller E C – C Squadron – L/Corporal
Spowart D
Sprackland G H W – Trooper
Spruse K J
Squire H J – C Squadron – Trooper
Stabbins F R – Tank crew – B Squadron – Trooper
Stacey C W – L/Corporal
Stafford B
Staines – L/Corporal
Stallard W
Stamp – Trooper
Stanbrook T C – A Squadron – L/Corporal
Stanley C N
Stansfield L J – A Squadron – Sergeant
Stark J – C Squadron – Trooper
Statham L G – Despatch Rider – HQ Squadron – Trooper
Stein A – Tank crew – A Squadron – Trooper
Stephens P G – C Squadron – Sergeant
Stephenson E
Stevens A – Trooper
Stevens F – HQ Squadron – Trooper
Stevens H B – Sergeant
Steward L – C Squadron – Trooper
Stimpson F
Stinchcombe F C

Stobbs E
Stockall D E – C Squadron – Trooper
Stockdale F – B Squadron – Trooper
Stockton A
Stone C
Stone W – Trooper
Stone W
Strange G – RAOC/ C Squadron – Private
Strange R A G – Corporal
Stubbs W
Stump H J – Tank crew – C Squadron – Sergeant
Styzaker E
Sullivan B M
Summerfield J
Summerhayes J
Summerhill W F
Summers G – C Squadron – Trooper
Summers H A J – Corporal
Summers H F
Sumner J
Sutcliffe A
Sutcliffe J
Sutcliffe J E – Sergeant
Swain J
Swann E C – C Squadron – Trooper
Swanton H
Swindells D – L/Corporal
Sykes A – Corporal
Syme T – C Squadron – L/Corporal
Symmons J K – Trooper

Tamlyn – Sergeant
Tanner
Target R
Tarr G
Tarrant W A
Tatchell W J – Tank crew – B Squadron – Trooper
Taylor A L
Taylor E G – Tank crew – A Squadron – Sergeant
Taylor G – C Squadron – Corporal
Taylor G M – L/Corporal
Taylor H G
Taylor J G – B Squadron
Taylor J – Echelon – Trooper
Taylor J – C Squadron – Trooper
Taylor J J
Taylor R – Trooper
Taylor S
Taylor V G – C Squadron – Corporal
Tebbett G D – HQ Squadron – Sergeant
Templeman S G
Terry E G – B Squadron & Echelon – SQMS
Thomas A L – L/Corporal
Thomas G E – Tank crew – C Squadron – Trooper
Thomas J
Thomas J – Tank crew – A Squadron – Sergeant
Thomas J H – Trooper
Thomas N G – B Squadron
Thomas R L – L/Corporal
Thomas T
Thomas W – C Squadron – L/Corporal
Thompson C
Thompson F D
Thompson I B – Corporal
Thompson N J – Trooper
Thompson W
Thorne W J
Thornton T
Thurlow J W – C Squadron – Trooper
Timm J R – Tank crew – A Squadron – Trooper
Tite H – Tank crew – C Squadron – Trooper
Tomkins – A Squadron – L/Corporal
Tomlin N I
Tomlinson L
Torr G – Corporal
Tovey G – Sergeant
Travers H J – C Squadron – Trooper
Trebble K – C Squadron – Trooper
Tremlett D

Tressider H
Tressider W J – B Squadron
Tritton E – B Echelon – Staff Sergeant
Trowbridge S W
Tubb R W C – L/Corporal
Tuck D N R
Tucker S – B Echelon – Staff Sergeant
Turnbull T
Turnbull W A
Turner A B – Tank crew – RHQ
Turner A S A – C Squadron – Sergeant
Turner H – C Squadron – Trooper
Turner H J – L/Corporal
Turner H R
Turvey H – Tank crew – A Squadron – Sergeant
Tweedie R K
Twigg H
Tye W J J – Tank crew – C Squadron – Trooper
Tiley E J – Sergeant

Underwood N – Sergeant
Unsworth W B – C Squadron – L/Corporal
Unwin A – B Squadron
Ure J C
Urwin D – C Squadron – Trooper

Vaesen H
Varley C P – A Squadron – Sergeant
Vaughen A – REME/A Squadron – Sergeant
Vaughen T – MQMS
Veale V – Trooper
Venney D P
Vincent E
Vizard P

Wadey P – Tank crew – C Squadron – L/Corporal
Wadsworth T K
Wareing E R
Walker C G – B Squadron – Trooper

Walker E G
Walker G S – C Squadron – L/Corporal
Walker K – Corporal
Walker R A – Echelon – Trooper
Walker T V – Corporal
Walters T G
Warburton F
Ward D G – Tank crew – A Squadron – Sergeant
Ward F J
Ward H S – Corporal
Ward J
Ward W
Warr C – Sergeant
Warren C
Warren F – RAOC – Private
Wassell J
Waterhouse R
Watkin K E – Driver fo MO – Corporal
Watkins A – A Squadron – Trooper
Watson F E E
Watson K – C Squadron – L/Sergeant
Watson W H T – Corporal
Watt W – RCS – L/Corporal
Watts A J
Watts W
Weaver J
Webb D J
Webb E
Webb J
Webb W F
Webley A A – C Squadron – SQMS
Webster H
Weeks C P
Welsby T – A Squadron – Trooper
Welstead – Sergeant
Wenlock W – SQMS
Werrett R N – L/Corporal
Westlake R
Whelan J – Sergeant
Whiston A
Whitall I Q – Sergeant
Whitcomb T
Whitcoombe J – B Squadron – L/

Corporal
White F S
Whitebread W – RAOC/C Squadron – Private
Whitelegg P G – C Squadron – Sergeant
Whitfield C
Whitley J C
Whittaker N W – B Squadron – Corporal
Wiggins J – C Squadron – Trooper
Wilcox A – SSM
Wild J
Wilding R A – B Squadron – L/Corporal
Wilkinson – B Squadron – Trooper
Williams A L
Williams C
Williams E – RTA – Corporal
Williams E R – A Squadron
Williams G V R
Williams G – Tank crew – B Squadron – Trooper
Williams G
Williams G
Williams K E
Williams R – C Squadron – Trooper
Williams R L – A Squadron – L/Corporal
Williams R T
Williams S G – Sergeant
Wills E – Tank crew – C Squadron – Trooper
Wills W E
Wilmott R – Sergeant
Wilson G A – Corporal
Wilson T M – Tank crew – C Squadron – L/Corporal
Wiltshire G – Corporal
Wimport F

Wimport F
Wingrove W M
Winkworth G J – RAOC – Private
Winn A
Wood M L
Wood R C – Corporal
Woodcock C
Woodcock W – C Squadron – Sergeant
Woodhouse C B
Woods S
Woodward J
Wooley H C – C Squadron – Trooper
Woolrich F
Wolstenholme K
Wolstenholme N
Worsfold R H – Tank crew – C Squadron – Sergeant
Wrankmore A – B Squadron – Trooper
Wren D
Wright J – RTA – Corporal
Wright L F
Wroe A
Wyatt – Fitter – Trooper
Wynn G E – Tank crew – A Squadron – Trooper
Wynne J A

Yanez L – Trooper
Yates H – C Squadron Echelon – Trooper
Yates W R
Yeeles W
Yeomans E G – Trooper
Youdell W – Fitter – A Squadron – Sergeant
Youldon T G – C & HQ Squadron – Trooper

Zannetos P – C Squadron – Trooper
Zellinger

# Annex G
# A VERY SHORT HISTORY OF C SQUADRON'S MEN'S MESS

Despite extensive research, it appears that only C Squadron formed their own 'Men's Mess', which was separate from the Officers' Mess, Sergeants' Mess, Regimental Canteen and the NAAFI. This short history highlights just some of the characters that made up the squadron, and some of their activities while away from the front line; 'mess' seems to be the appropriate word.

The 'Men's Mess', formed by the men themselves, had its humble beginnings in June 1943, while the regiment was still at Sfax in Tunisia. There was a tent, a table with a few magazines and newspapers, a wireless and a gramophone. However, it was at Centuripe in Sicily the following month that the Mess really took off.

Corporal Fred Marquand, a fitter, became its first president and is always remembered for his fruity rendition of 'Tiger Rag', which always followed his fifth glass of wine. Trooper Bob Dix was elected as Treasurer and Trooper Cyril Epstein as chief Buyer. It was 'Eppie's' (as he was more commonly known) job to obtain all the odds and ends in the way of extras.

The men had taken to the wines of Sicily as a duck takes to water and at that time drinking Vermouth by the pint was not considered exceptional. So barrels and bottles of wine made their way into the Mess, and looking after it became a full time job. Entertainment varied from whist drives to community singing, with guest nights for NCOs and members of other squadrons. 'Dutch' Holland rigged up a temperamental 'Heath Robinson' microphone, which usually fell to pieces when Corporal Marquand started his 'Tiger Rag'.

It was one of the rules of the Mess that if anybody, member or guest, was called upon to do a 'turn' he had to do one: excuses were not accepted. It did not matter what he did sing – tell a joke or stand on his head – and in that way many a good impromptu concert was held. It also proved to be a good way of discovering new talent. It was here that such stalwarts shot to fame as Jock Syme and the Jones Family (Ginger, Ken and Dai), Sid Adams and his accordion, 'Ticker' Hudson, Jimmy Smalley and Jim Taylor, Clough and Christie (two very low comedians from Lancashire) and Jock Dowie (an even lower comedian from Scotland).

The Men's Mess war diary records: 'This rule of doing a turn provided some hilarious entertainment on guest nights, and it will be remembered was the cause of Major Senior giving us that pathetic ditty about the baby that vanished down the 'plug ole.'

It was soon evident that one tent was not enough to meet the demands of the ever growing needs and membership of the Mess. In an amazing effort a number of sheets were rigged between lorries, with the result that the revamped Mess resembled a cross between a 'beer tent at an agricultural show and a Bedouin encampment.'

When the regiment went to Italy, the frequent moving resulted in the Mess being suspended for a short time. It was not until they reached Teano that the Mess came into its own again. Here it was split into two parts, one for the tank crews up front with Ginger Jones in charge, and one for the Echelon and the remainder of the squadron leaguered near Teano. This was successfully run by Eppie and Syd Clapp, and those who knew it will never forget it it was best described as 'What a dive!'

The Mess itself was in a room in a farmhouse, partly occupied by the squadron. It was a large room, but not large enough. As the evening wore on the air became so thick that you had difficulty recognising your friend on the other side of the room. It soon became known as 'Eephards Hell'.

The variety of strong liquor sold in the 'Hell' soon exceeded anything in the history of the Mess. Eppie's expeditions in search of wine resulted in the appearance of some strange and potent brews. On one occasion a certain signalman was entrusted with the wine buying; the stuff he brought back was so rough it 'well nigh rasped the roof of your mouth away.' The drinking of 'rot gut' by the pint had to stop, so correct glasses made their first appearance in the Mess. Yes, you are correct in your assumption; it didn't make a difference, the men just doubled up to the bar twice as often.

As the tank crews at this time were up at the front, any extras that came by were quite rightly sent to them, Eppie making midnight excursions on Jim Taylor's jeep or Bob Walker's truck.

At the end of March 1944 when the regiment moved back to the Eighth Army side and the tanks had crossed the River Moro, the Mess was opened up within a few thousand yards of the enemy. It must have been the most forward Mess in the British Army and occasionally came under fire.

At Caldari the men discovered a cellar which was just the job, and typical of a C Squadron dive. It was 'blacked-out' and lighting set up, and a wireless was appropriated for the much sought after news. Despite the close proximity of the enemy the lads continued to enjoy their nightly tipple. Two months later the regiment left Italy and returned to Egypt. However the Mess did not function successfully until it reached Amirya, when at this most unlikely spot in the desert, the most successful concert in the history of the Mess took place. Guests included members of HQ, A and B Squadrons, and the newly formed D Squadron (46 RTR).

The bar on this occasion was run by 'Moonstone and Co.' (Eppie and Jock Begleman) who saw to it that no-one got a drink without paying for it. A sergeant from the 46th gave the best turn of the evening with a snake charming act. There was also a very strange duet by the Medical Officer and Syd Adams on the accordion; not content with this performance, the MO proceeded to dive off the bar. Lieutenant Thomas recited the epic 'Eskimo Nell' and Jock Dowie (who was working in the Sergeants' Mess) got in some wicked cracks about his favourite

NCOs, while Ken Jones brought the house down with stories about the Welsh. The War Diary records: 'There were some rather seedy specimens on parade the next morning and a great demand for health salts and aspirins.' Colonel Carlton who was in attendance, was heard to remark that "C Squadron certainly know how to put on a lively evenings entertainment." History does not record whether alcohol influenced his statement.

After the move to Athens in October 1944 the Mess was suspended for a short time, which was only to be expected in view of all the counter-attractions in the city. The Mess was eventually set up in Sina Street and soon got into its stride. Retsina was obtained in an unlimited supply. At one concert Brian Chidell introduced the squadron to the songs 'Where the ELAS can't get at me' and 'The Hole in the Wall'; these subsequently became C Squadron drinking songs and were heard in taverns in many parts of Greece. Mr Chidell must accept full responsibility for his actions.

In the New Year the Squadron moved to Corinth and was housed in billets that had been previously occupied by Greeks, prisoners of war, Italians, ELAS and goats. After moving to more comfortable billets in the town, the Mess was set up in a room under the Squadron Office, where an attempt was made to set up a stove – result: the shutters were set on fire and the room filled with smoke.

The next move was to Mindologli, a few miles beyond Patras, where for the first time in Greece, egg and chip suppers were served at 1/6d (7½p) per head. Now at Patras things moved up a gear, and three large dances were held, the first at the Café Splendide in Patras, though pessimists declared it could never succeed.

Of course, for a dance you needed GIRLS, the one commodity the Army did not supply. The Committee had three main worries:

1: There would not be any girls at all.
2: If any decent girls turned up, they would walk out.
3: The only girls who would turn up, would be the lowest of the ladies of easy virtue, who thrived strongly in Patras.

So in a combined operation, C Squadron Men's Mess Committee set out to prove the pessimists wrong.

On the night of the dance things started very quietly, and for half an hour, it seemed the pessimists would be proved right. However, everyone had overlooked the Greek idea of time. When the girls did turn up, the dance proved to be a success: so successful that a further two were held, this time, in a large empty house in Mindologli.

Then came the announcement of VE Day: 'That was some party, the party of all parties, where all the drink was given out 'buckshee', about £30 worth of it and every cask and bottle was drained to the last drop.'

This sadly was the last 'fling' for C Squadron's Mens Mess, for on 15 May 1945 the squadron moved to Loutraki and joined Headquarters, where the Regimental canteen was in operation and so the Mess was suspended. Itwas never officially opened again.

In June 1945 the Men's Mess released its 'Memoirs', a small booklet for posterity. One wonders how much was actually censored!

# BIBLIOGRAPHY

Baker, A., *Battle Honours of the British Army*, Ian Allan, 1986.
Blumenson, M.,*Sicily,* Pan Ballantine
Gibson and Ward, *Courage Remembered,* HMSO, 1989.
Halstead, E., *Freyberg's Men*, Heinemann Reed, 1985.
Hart, L., *The Tanks*, Cassell, 1959.
Horrocks, B., *A Full Life* , Leo Cooper
Howarth, P.,*My God, Soldiers*, Hutchinson
Keegan J. and Holmes R.,*Soldiers*, Sphere
Lewin, R., *Montgomery as Military Commander*, B T Batsford
Macksey, K.,*Afrika Korps,* Pan Ballantine
Masters, D., *With Pennants Flying,* Eyre & Spottiswoode
Maule, H., *Scobie, Hero of Greece*, Arthur Baker Ltd
Messenger, C., *Tunisian Campaign*, Ian Allen
Montgomery, Vicount & others *Alamein and the Desert War,* Sphere, 1967.
Moorehead, A., *African Trilogy,* Hamish Hamilton
Peniakoff, V.,*Popski's Private Army*, Pan
Perrett , .,*Through Mud and Blood*, Robert Hale
Perrett, B., *Valentine in North Africa*, Ian Allen
Phillips, *Alamein,* White Lion
Playfair, I. S. O.,*History of the Second World War,* HMSO
Rosignoli, G., *The Allied Forces in Italy*, David and Charles, 1989.
Smith, E. D,. *Even the Brave Falter,* Robert Hale
Smith E. D., *Victory of a Sort*, Robert Hale
*British Tanks 1939 to 1945*, Tank Museum
*The Rommel Papers,* Collins

War Diaries for the 50th, 46th and 40th Royal Tank Regiments
*A Short History of 50 RTR 1939–1944* by Major Walter Bazley
*A History of 23rd Amoured Brigade* by Capt A A Ash
*Tank,* Regimental Journal of the Royal Tank Regiment

# INDEX
# British and Commonwealth Military Unit Index

## INFANTRY

2nd Airborne/Para Brigade, 208, 209, 217, 228
7th Batt Argyll and Sutherland Highlanders ,60, 62, 66, 67
8th Batt Argyll and Sutherland Highlanders, 168
2/28th Bn Australian, 30, 32, 39
2/43rd Bn Australian, 39
3/10th Baluch Regt, 73
1st Black Watch, 118
5th Black Watch, 116; in Sicily, 138, 139
7th Batt Black Watch, 66, 67, 112, 118
5th Batt Cameron Highlanders, 70; in Sicily, 154
1st Batt Dorset Regt, 138
6th Batt Durham Light Inf, 88, 91- 92, 100
8th Batt Durham Light Inf, 88, 91, 93
9th Batt Durham Light Inf, 88, 91, 93, 100
5th East Yorkshire Regt, 92
1/5th Batt Essex Regt, 168, 191, 193
1/12th Batt Frontier Force Regt, 178, 190, 202
6/13th Batt Frontier Force Rifles, 188
6th Batalllion Gloucestershire Regiment, 13
1st Batt Gordon Highlanders, 55, 59-60, 81
5/7th Batt Gordon Highlanders, 60 in Sicily, 139
7th Batt Green Howards, 88
2/7th Batt Gurhka Rifles, 231
2nd Batt Highland Light Inf, 2218, 228
11th Batt Kings Royal Rifle Corps, 134; in Greece, 208, 217
2/5th Batt Leicestershire Regt, 231
2nd Batt London Irish Rifles, 158
1/5th Batt Mahratta Light Inf, 179, 185, 195
1/7th Batt Middlesex Regt, 112; in Sicily, 145
5th Batt Northamptonshire Regt, 166
3/15th Batt Punjab Regt, 182, 185
5th Batt Royal East Kents, 157
5th Batt Royal West Kents, 166, 179

6th Batt Royal West Kents, 157
2nd Batt Seaforth Highlanders, 70, 72-74,120; in Sicily, 143, 144
5th Batt Seaforth Highlanders, 70
Special Boat Service, 226
1st Batt Sussex Regt, 130

## INFANTRY BRIGADES

11th, 157
28th , 2 29
36th, 157, 158; in Italy, 167, 172
69th, 92
139th, 229
151st, 91, 100, 106
24th Australian, 29, 30
3rd Greek Mountain, 211
201st Guards Motor, 114, 131
152nd Highland, 56, 70, 71, 87, 114-119; in Sicily 140, 153
153rd Highland, 60, 67; in Sicily, 140, 148
11th Indian, 230. 231
5th Indian, 56, 72, 75, 128, 130
7th Indian, 128
17th Indian, 164-167, 170, 175-179, 182, 187
19th Indian, 165, 168, 176
21st Indian, 165, 170, 175-179, 182-185
38th Irish, 158
231st Malta, 138, 143
5th New Zealand, 47, 53
6th New Zealand, 47
131st Queens, 85
1st and 2nd South African, 26

## INFANTRY DIVISIONS

4th, 226, 229
5th, 199

1st Canadian, 183, 184
51st Highland, 53, 55-58, 60, 80, 86, 90, 114, 119; in Sicily, 136, 152
4th Indian, 70, 72, 73, 90, 111, 114, 127-128, 201; in Greece; 230, 238
8th Indian, 164, 170, 176, 184, 200, 201
56th Indian, 205
56th London, 131
2nd New Zealand, 56, 90
46th North Midland, 199, 200; in Greece, 232
50th Northumbrian, 78, 79, 88, 90, 91, 100, 108, 111, 114
1st South African, 53
88th US Infantry, 199, 200

## ROYAL TANK REGIMENTS

2nd RTR, 203, 205
5th RTR, 14, 108, 109
8th RTR, 14, 35, 41
40th RTR, 18, 21, 27-29, 38, 45-47, 53,79-82, 88, 110, 112, 121, 124, 128, 134, 160; in Italy, 199-201; in Greece, 208, 214, 218
41st RTR, 21, 94
44th Bn Royal Tank Corps (later 44th RTR), 12, 13, 35; in Italy, 178, 183, 185, 188, 193, 196
45th RTR,21
46th RTR, 18, 21, 27, 28, 38, 53, 53, 72, 77, 78, 81, 134; in Sicily,136, 140, 142, 146, 152, 154, 158, 160; in Italy, 153, 155-158, 198; in Egypt, 206; in Greece,212, 214, 226, 229, 234, 235, 236, 241
47th RTR, 21
14th Canadian Tank Regt,182, 184, 196

## ROYAL ARMOURED CORPS

Kings Dragoon Guards, 225
Staffordshire Yeomanry, 54
Queens Bays, 54
12th Lancers, 82, 86
17/21st Lancers, 231
11th Hussars, 83
4th Recce Regt, 239
56th Recce Regt, 158
3rd County of London Yeomanry, 182, 183, 188

## ARMOURED BRIGADES

1st Armoured, 27, 38
4th Light Armoured (later 4th Armoured), 85; in Sicily, 159, 160; in Italy, 163, 164, 170, 172, 181, 183, 184, 188, 195, 197
7th Armoured, 202
22nd Armoured, 26, 46, 53, 79, 82, 108, 121
23rd Tank Brigade (later 23rd Armoured), 18, 21, 22, 24-28, 30, 38, 41, 46, 52, 53, 57, 70, 86, 87, 90, 109, 127-128, 131; in Sicily, 150, 152, 160, 170; in Italy, 197, 200; in Egypt, 206; in Greece, 216, 226, 233
24th Armoured, 21, 24
26th Armoured, 231
1st Canadian, 200

## ARMOURED DIVISIONS

1st Armoured, 26
7th Armoured, 44, 58, 85, 87, 88
8th Armoured, 21, 22, 24, 25, 57

## ARTILLERY

5th Regt Royal Horse Artillery, 30
11th Regt Royal Horse Artillery, 138
12th Field Regt RA, 70
61st Anti-Tank Regt, 112
73rd Anti-Tank Regt RA, 30
149th Anti-Tank Regt, 128
296th Anti-Tank Battery, 115, 117
37th Light Anti-Aircraft Battery RA, 30

## ROYAL ENGINEERS

275th Field Co, 115
295th Field Co, 72
9th Field Squadron, 92, 112
626 Field Squadron, 176

## GERMAN AND ITALIAN

Ramcke Parachute Regt, 91
Young Fascist Div, 91
8th Panzer Regt, 91
15th Panzer Div, 44, 90, 91, 99, 100
16th Panzer Div, 165
21st Panzer Div, 44
26th Panzer Div, 129, 183
26th Panzer Regt, 190
90th Light Division, 26, 44, 46, 47, 91, 131
1st Fallschirm Parachute Div, 141; in Italy, 191
1st Parachute Regt, 145
3rd Parachute Rifle Regt, 157

29th Panzer Grenadier Div, 141
90th Panzer Granadier Div, 183
41st Infantry Div, 208
334th Infantry Div, 183
54th Napoli Div, 141
412th Ost Bn, 201
11th Luftwaffe Div, 208

# GENERAL INDEX

Acropolis: the, 214
Agheila, 77-79
Alamein: first battle of, 14-29
Alamein: second battle of, 54,55
Alam el Baoshaza, 45, 53
Alam el Dakar, 45
Alam Halfa, 44-46
Alexandria, 30, 53, 77, 207
Adrano, 156, 157
Arielli river, 193
Atessa, 172
Athens, 208, 209, 212, 235
Aurora: HMS, 207
Ben Gardane, 85, 86
BERTRAM: Operation, 59
Biferno river, 164
BIGOT HUSKY: Operation, 133
Blockforce, 229, 280
Bronte, 157
Buerat, 80, 81, 84
Caldari, 187
Capetown, 23, 24
Casalbordino, 167, 168, 197
Cassino, 200
Castelforte, 199
Castelfrentano, 201
Catania, 146, 156, 159, 163
Centruipe, 153, 158
Colorado Ridge, 138, 139
Consalve, 191
Corinth, 231, 233, 236, 237
Crowborough, 18-22
Dittaino river, 149
Djebel Garci, 127-130
El Adem, 77-80
ELAS, 208, 211, 212, 215, 234
Enfidaville, 127-131
Fossacesia, 170
Francofonte, 143, 144

Gabes, 112, 113
Garigliano river, 199
Gerbini, 148
Gornalunga river, 145
Hill 26 (Egypt), 28, 38
Impossible Bridge, 185, 202
Italy, 163
Kasserine, 88
Kidney Ridge, 73
Lanciano, 182, 185, 201, 202
LIGHTFOOT: Operation, 58, 59
Loutraki, 236, 237, 238
Loutraki Carnival, 238
MANNA: Operation, 208
Manna barracks, 214
Mareth Line, 86-90
Medenine, 86, 88
Mersa Matruh, 77, 78
Miteiriya Ridge (aka Ruin Ridge), 26, 29-32, 39
Mooltan: HMT, 22-24
Moro river, 184, 185, 188, 201
Mount Etna, 156, 157
Mount Macerone, 158
Mount Rivoglia, 157, 158
Mozzagrogna, 174, 175, 176, 177, 178, 179
Munnassib Depression, 53
Nino Bixio, 41
Noto, 140
Omonoias Square, 214, 217, 228
Orsogna,187, 188, 200, 202
Ortona, 183, 187, 188
Osento river, 171
Pachino, 138, 139
Paglieta, 171, 172, 174, 175
Palestine, 160, 205, 206
Paterno, 160, 161
Patras, 229, 230, 231, 232, 233, 236
Pescara, 183
Phaleron, 225, 240
Piraeus, 207, 208, 211, 229
Poggiofiorito, 202
Port Said, 205
Port Tewfik, 24
Possacesia, 178
Qattara Depression, 26, 54, 58
Qattara track, 30-34. 59, 60
Ramacca, 146, 153
Randazzo, 159

Rhaman track, 73
Romagnoli, 179
Roumana, 101-107
Ruweisat Ridge, 26, 28, 38, 45, 58, 70
Salamis: island of, 211, 214, 233
Salonika, 238
Sangro river, 168, 169, 171, 172, 174, 182, 183
San Salvo, 165, 166
Scerni, 170, 171
Scordia, 144, 145, 155
Sfax, 121-127, 131, 122
Sferro, 147, 148, 152, 153
Sicily, 134-162
Simeto river, 157
Sinello river, 168
Sparta, 241
Spearforce, 121
Stimpata, 150, 152
Stimpeto, 147, 138
SUPERCHARGE: Operation, 70, 73, 75
Takrouna, 128
Taranto, 164
Teano, 197, 199, 200
Tel el Aqqaqir, 73
Tel el Eisa, 35, 69
Tel el Makh Khad, 39
Thebes, 234
Trigno river, 164, 168
Tripoli, 81, 82-84
Vasto, 165, 167, 168
Vickers-Armstrong Ltd, 17
Villa Grande, 191, 193, 195
Vizzini, 141, 142, 144
Wadi Akarit, 91, 113, 114, 121, 171
Wadi el Chebir, 81, 84
Wadi Zessar, 86, 87
Wadi Zeus, 86
Wadi Zigzaou, 88, 90, 92, 112
Zuara, 84, 85